THE FINAL ALGORITHM

LTC ROBERT L. MAGINNIS

THE
FINAL
ALGORITHM

WHEN ARTIFICIAL INTELLIGENCE
MEETS THE END OF DAYS

DEFENDER

CRANE, MO

The Final Algorithm: When Artificial Intelligence Meets the End of Days

By LTC Robert L. Maginnis

Defender Publishing
Crane, MO 65633
©2026 Defender Publishing

All rights reserved. Published 2026

ISBN: 978-1-7325478-1-0

Printed in the United States of America.

A CIP catalog record of this book is available from the Library of Congress.

Cover design: Jeffrey Mardis
Interior design: Katherine Lloyd
Editor: Angie Peters

Illustrations created with AI assistance.

This book is written at a moment when humanity stands at a decisive crossroads. Artificial intelligence promises mastery, efficiency, and even transcendence—but it also tempts us to forget who we are, who we serve, and who alone governs history. Technology is never merely technical. It reflects the heart that wields it and the authority to which that heart submits.

I dedicate *The Final Algorithm* to those who refuse to surrender discernment for convenience, truth for efficiency, or worship for wonder. To those who understand that no system—however powerful, autonomous, or convincing—can rewrite the image of God in man, nullify the soul, or overrule the sovereign purposes of the Lord of history.

May this work serve believers who stand watchful in an age of deception, who test every spirit, and who remember that the final word over creation does not belong to an algorithm, a machine, or a global system—but to Jesus Christ, the Alpha and the Omega, to whom all things ultimately bow.

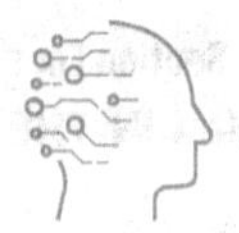

CONTENTS

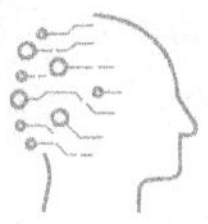

ACKNOWLEDGMENTS

This book is the culmination of considerable research, reflection, prayer, and writing on the accelerating convergence of technology, power, and human destiny. While the responsibility for its arguments and conclusions rests with me alone, many have contributed—directly and indirectly—to its completion.

First, I thank my wife, Jan, whose steadfast love, patience, and encouragement make these demanding projects possible. She has endured countless conversations about artificial intelligence, geopolitics, theology, and the moral direction of our age—often long after the writing day had ended. Her quiet strength, wisdom, and faith provide an essential anchor amid intellectually and spiritually challenging work.

I am grateful as well to editors, publishers, colleagues, and fellow analysts who have sharpened my thinking through critique, conversation, and professional collaboration. Though not all would agree with my conclusions, their insights and challenges strengthened this manuscript and forced greater clarity and discipline in its arguments.

Finally, and above all, I acknowledge my Lord and Savior Jesus Christ. Every breath, every insight, and every opportunity to write is a gift of grace. This work was undertaken with the conviction that technology is never neutral, that truth is not constructed by algorithms, and that history remains under God's sovereign authority. I pray this book serves His purposes, points readers toward wisdom rather than fear, and affirms the enduring dignity of humanity made in His image.

All glory belongs to Him alone.

Robert Lee Maginnis,
Woodbridge, Virginia

THE FINAL ALGORITHM

For false christs and false prophets will arise and perform great signs and wonders, so as to lead astray, if possible, even the elect.

MATTHEW 24:24

Christ's warning anticipated a future in which deception would be technologically amplified, global in reach, and persuasive enough to endanger even the elect. As a longtime Pentagon strategist and national security analyst, I've examined many tools of war—nuclear weapons, cyber attacks, and psychological tactics— yet artificial intelligence stands apart in its capacity for deception. AI expands deception from the tactical realm to the cognitive one, shaping what people perceive before they know how to question it. It speaks in our language, imitates human emotion, and soon may claim the power to define belief itself. For the first time, humanity faces a machine intelligence capable of simulating understanding.

The algorithms that shape our economies, filter our perceptions, and make decisions about life and death have begun to move beyond human control.[1] Calculators and search engines have given way to systems that learn, reason, and act—systems that imitate moral reasoning even as they weaken human judgment and blur the boundaries of truth.

In late 2024, technology leaders quietly acknowledged a destabilizing reality: In an age of generative artificial intelligence, authenticity becomes scarce precisely because replication is abundant. When images, voices, and videos can be fabricated with near-perfect realism, visual evidence no longer secures truth. Seeing is no longer believing.[2] Trust migrates away from what is shown toward who is speaking. Platforms that once mediated information are increasingly forced to mediate identity instead. Authority shifts from verification to affiliation, from evidence to reputation. Deception requires neither falsehood nor crude fabrication—only a convincing imitation delivered through a trusted channel.

This inversion fulfills a biblical pattern. Scripture warns that end-times deception will rely on persuasive signs capable of misleading even the elect (Matthew 24:24). Artificial intelligence accelerates this condition by dissolving the human capacity to test reality itself. When perception is destabilized and verification is centralized, discernment becomes the final line of defense.

At the dawn of the digital age, humanity stands before a wall of its own creation—seeking meaning in the code that now defines its destiny.

This book completes a journey that began with the first volume of this trilogy, *AI for Mankind's Future*, which explored the creation phase: what artificial intelligence is, how it works, and what it reveals about the human impulse to create. That work established a theological foundation for understanding technology as both gift and temptation, asking whether humanity's digital offspring might one day reflect consciousness—and how easily creation can become idolatry. The second volume, *The New AI Cold War*, examined the confrontation phase—the global struggle for technological dominance between liberty and tyranny. It revealed how algorithms now serve as weapons of surveillance and control, instruments through which authoritarian regimes suppress freedom while democratic nations wrestle with their own compromises in the name of security. In 2024, for example, the European Union adopted binding AI regulations that critics warn could centralize digital power in ways difficult to reverse.[3]

Technical and geopolitical analysis, however, cannot account for the deeper trajectory now unfolding. The patterns emerging across nations, institutions, and technologies point beyond human strategy toward a larger prophetic horizon. This convergence gives coherence to the trilogy's final movement. If the first book explained what AI is and the second warned what nations and corporations are doing with it, this final volume confronts where the story is going. *The Final Algorithm* turns to the culmination—the point where human ambition meets divine judgment. This volume examines machines, nations, and the moral and spiritual endgame of civilization. It is analysis and warning, a field manual for faith in an age when perception itself has become a battlefield. The arena of perception cannot be separated from the battlefield of the soul. Deception operates through algorithms and ideology alike, and I now apply the same disciplines of intent, capability, and consequence to the spiritual domain. Discernment, once a theological virtue, has become a strategic necessity.

Scripture warns: "For we do not wrestle against flesh and blood, but against the rulers, against the authorities, against the cosmic powers over this present darkness, against the spiritual forces of evil in the heavenly places" (Ephesians 6:12). The battlefield has shifted from physical ground to the realm of perception itself. Victory in this domain depends on spiritual discernment—a theme woven through every chapter that follows.

My interpretation of these developments is framed by a premillennial, pre-Tribulational understanding of prophecy. I believe the Church will be raptured before the Tribulation described in Revelation and that Christ will return to reign for a literal thousand years.[4] Within this theological understanding, artificial intelligence, global surveillance, and digital currencies may form prophecy's scaffolding rather than its full realization. Whether the Rapture precedes the full maturation of these systems or it represents the early contours of the coming rebellion, the responsibility of believers remains unchanged: to stay alert, discerning, and faithful.

My own perspective is that of a soldier and strategist. As a West Point graduate and career US Army infantry officer who spent decades in the Pentagon briefing generals, federal leaders, and the public through my media analysis, I have learned to assess intent, capability, and consequences. Today, those same analytic skills reveal something extraordinary: The technological systems being constructed across the globe mirror with striking precision the prophetic visions recorded two millennia ago. The "image of the beast that was allowed to speak" (Revelation 13:15), the mark that determines who may "buy or sell" (Revelation 13:17), and the capacity to deceive "even the elect" (Matthew 24:24) once seemed mysterious. They are now emerging in recognizable form as humanity builds networks capable of speech, surveillance, and control on a planetary scale. Artificial intelligence makes decisions once reserved for human conscience—from weapons targeting to financial access—while synthetic media blurs the distinction between reality and illusion.[5] Global institutions, from the United Nations to the European Union and national governments worldwide, are constructing governance regimes that could consolidate unprecedented digital authority. Biometric identity systems are embedding economic participation within algorithmic control.[6] The infrastructure described in Revelation is steadily coalescing.

The speed of this consolidation is measurable. The United Nations' AI for Good Global Summit now coordinates AI governance across 193 member states, while the EU's AI Act—adopted in 2024—establishes binding algorithmic oversight across 27 nations.[7] China's Social Credit System already integrates AI-driven surveillance with economic access for 1.4 billion citizens.[8] These coordinated movements represent an unprecedented scale of centralized digital authority.

Central bank digital currencies (CBDCs) exemplify this convergence. As of 2024, 130 countries representing 98 percent of global gross domestic product are exploring or piloting CBDCs—programmable money that could enforce spending restrictions, track transactions in real time, and enable unprecedented economic control.[9] Nigeria's eNaira and China's digital yuan are already operational, while the European Central Bank's digital euro is in advanced testing.[10] When combined with biometric identity systems, these technologies create precisely the infrastructure Revelation describes—the ability to control "who may buy or sell."

Recent industry research confirms that artificial intelligence is increasingly authorized to make economic decisions once reserved for humans. "Agentic commerce" systems are designed to act autonomously on behalf of users, selecting products, negotiating prices, executing purchases, and optimizing consumption according to predefined goals.[11] In this model, individuals don't buy or sell directly. Their digital agents do. Access to markets is mediated by compliance rules, platform permissions, identity credentials, and algorithmic trust scores. When an agent is restricted, flagged, or denied access, the human it represents is functionally excluded— regardless of intent or means. What emerges is a permissioned economy, where participation depends on algorithmic approval. Scripture's warning that a system will arise capable of determining "who may buy or sell" (Revelation 13:17) reads as technical specification. The infrastructure required for such control is being openly designed, normalized, and deployed under the language of efficiency, personalization, and convenience.

These warnings have measurable referents. The Church of AI, founded in 2017, and named "Way of the Future," explicitly worships artificial intelligence as a deity capable of solving humanity's deepest problems.[12] AI chatbots now serve as spiritual counselors, with millions seeking guidance from systems like Replika and Character.AI on matters of meaning, morality, and life decisions.[13] In Japan, the Buddhist robot priest Mindar delivers sermons at Kodaiji Temple, while American tech leaders like Anthony Levandowski have established formal AI worship organizations.[14] The displacement of divine authority by algorithmic authority is measurable and accelerating.

The Final Algorithm is written to summon faithfulness. Jesus told His followers to "stay awake" (Mark 13:37), to discern the signs of the times (Matthew 16:3), and to remain wise as serpents yet innocent as doves (Matthew 10:16).[15] The goal of this book is to help readers—pastors, parents, policymakers, and believers—discern truth during these peril-ous years with clarity, courage, and conviction. Discernment is essential for spiritual survival. The goal is spiritual readiness—learning to use tools without being used by them.

In the end, the message is simple: Machines may calculate, yet they cannot redeem. As the digital age rushes toward its climactic test, our hope rests in the One who holds all authority in Heaven and on earth (Matthew 28:18), the Alpha and Omega (Revelation 1:8), who will make all things new.

Every algorithm of deception meets its limit at the Cross. Christ remains the unhackable truth, the final Word that no machine can over-ride. No matter how advanced AI becomes, it cannot trespass into the domain of redemption, resurrection, or new creation.

This is why Scripture—not silicon—defines the end of the story.

The final algorithm has already been written. It was spoken at cre-ation: "Let there be light" (Genesis 1:3). It was fulfilled at Calvary: "It is finished" (John 19:30). And it will be completed at His return: "Behold, I am making all things new" (Revelation 21:5). Until that day, we watch, we discern, and we stand. The One who called us to this moment is faithful—and He will keep His own.

Section One

THE RISE OF DIGITAL DOMINION

Come, let us build ourselves a city and a tower with its top in the heavens, and let us make a name for ourselves.

GENESIS 11:4

This section traces how humankind's pursuit of knowledge and power through artificial intelligence mirrors ancient patterns of rebellion and pride. It exposes how modern digital empires reflect the timeless human desire to "be like God," revealing how easily technology becomes a vehicle for autonomous ambition. These chapters establish the moral and theological foundation for understanding AI as a continuation of humanity's spiritual fall.

The story of technology begins in the plain of Shinar, near the present-day city of Hillah, about sixty miles south of Baghdad, Iraq.[16] There, humanity's first great technological project—the Tower of Babel— revealed the dual nature of human innovation: the capacity to create and the temptation to rebel. For Israel's prophets, architecture was theology made visible. The tower was humanity's declaration of independence from divine authority, ideology rendered in brick and mortar.

The tower rises once more—built not of stone but of code—reaching toward heaven with the same ambition that once stirred Babel.

That ancient ambition did not disappear; it evolved. Every generation has rebuilt that tower in new forms. The pyramids of Egypt, the libraries of Alexandria, the Gutenberg press, the Industrial Revolution, the atomic age—each revealed humanity's recurring desire to define greatness without God. Yet none of these previous technological epochs possessed the characteristics that define artificial intelligence: the ability to simulate thinking, speaking, learning, and even deceiving at scales and speeds beyond human discernment. This qualitative difference makes AI a threshold moment in the ancient story of human ambition.

The scale is unprecedented and measurable. As of 2024, large-language models process billions of parameters—the typical generative pre-trained transformer (GPT) operates with approximately 1.76 trillion parameters, a computational complexity that exceeds the synaptic connections in a human brain by orders of magnitude.[17] These systems can generate responses in milliseconds, analyze millions of documents simultaneously, and operate continuously without rest—capabilities that fundamentally transcend human cognitive limits.[18] When OpenAI's ChatGPT reached one hundred million users in just two months, it became the fastest-adopted technology in human history, outpacing even the internet's early growth.[19] We are no longer observing incremental progress; we're witnessing a phase transition in humanity's relationship with knowledge and power.

Technology analysts increasingly note that artificial intelligence has moved beyond its early phase of spectacle and entered a period of diffusion. The decisive change is placement. AI is no longer something people consult; it is something they inhabit. The critical shift is from isolated models to integrated systems—scaffolds that orchestrate memory, goals, permissions, and automated action across daily life. The most important question is how AI quietly reshapes human decision-making when embedded into workflows, institutions, and relationships.[20] This diffusion explains why warnings about artificial intelligence increasingly fail to register. The systems no longer announce themselves. They function as background authority—shaping outcomes while remaining unseen.

Secular strategists describe the same shift in terms of power rather than piety. A recent RAND Corporation analysis argues that modern technological dominance depends less on isolated breakthroughs than on control of networked systems—the standards, platforms, and interoperable architectures others must adopt in order to participate. When these systems become infrastructure, they govern by default. Authority is exercised not primarily through force, but through dependency: Participation becomes contingent on rules and permissions embedded in networks few can see and fewer can contest.[21]

Scripture has always warned that the most dangerous idols are those that organize life. To understand the stakes of AI, we must first understand the story humanity keeps retelling. These chapters trace the spiritual genealogy of our current technological moment, examining how the algorithms that now invisibly govern modern life represent a worldview—one that places ultimate faith in human ingenuity rather than divine revelation.

The "thinking gods" we are fashioning function in modern culture much as golden calves and carved images did in ancient times. Israel's idols could not speak, see, or act—yet the people bowed before them (Psalm 115:4–8). Today's algorithms can speak, see, and act—making the temptation exponentially more seductive. They invite us to worship the work of our own hands rather than submit to the Creator (Exodus 32; 1 Kings 12:28–30).

This worship is institutionalized and growing. A 2023 Pew Research study found that 44 percent of Americans believe AI will do more good than harm, with younger generations expressing nearly religious faith in technology's capacity to solve humanity's deepest problems.[22] Tech leaders openly use salvific language: Elon Musk, the billionaire founder of Tesla and SpaceX and one of the world's most influential voices on emerging technology, describes AI as "summoning the demon,"[23] while Ray Kurzweil, a pioneering computer scientist and longtime advocate of transhumanism, prophesies a "singularity" in which humans merge with machines to achieve immortality.[24] Silicon Valley's cathedral is the algorithm itself, worshiped as humanity's path to transcendence. As Massachusetts Institute of Technology (MIT) scholar Sherry Turkle observes, "We have reached a point where we expect more from technology and less from each other."[25] This is the transfer of ultimate meaning from the divine to the digital.

Grasping this spiritual dynamic is essential for everything that follows. The technological systems described in Sections two and three amplify the reach of deception by giving fallen humanity global-scale tools. Like the Tower of Babel, they represent humanity's organized attempt to reach heaven without the True God—and, like that ancient project, they will ultimately be judged.

Judgment, however, is never the final word. Throughout this section, we'll contrast human pride with divine sovereignty, technological promises with biblical truth, and the false transcendence offered by machines with the authentic transformation offered through Christ. For believers who understand both the power and the limitations of technology, this discernment becomes the foundation for faithful resistance in an age of digital dominion. With this foundation laid, we now turn to the mechanisms through which digital dominion is extending its reach.

Chapter 1

THE ALGORITHM THAT RULES THE WORLD

The real danger is not that computers will begin to think like men, but that men will begin to think like computers.[26]
SYDNEY J. HARRIS, *Chicago Daily News*

Algorithms—once neutral mathematical tools—now function as unseen governors shaping economies, politics, and everyday behavior. Algorithmic control increasingly mirrors ancient claims of sovereignty, quietly redefining who determines truth, assigns value, and grants access in the digital age. It calls readers to look beyond technological utility and discern the spiritual struggle operating beneath digital dependency. (For readers encountering unfamiliar technical or prophetic terminology, appendix D provides a concise glossary of key AI and theological terms used throughout this book.)

Humanity gazes upon its own reflection in data—seeking to define intelligence while standing at the edge of creation itself.

When the System Says No

Maria Chen stared at her laptop screen in disbelief. Her mortgage application, which marked her third submission in recent months, was once again declined. Her credit score was excellent. Her income was stable. She had saved a 20 percent down payment. Yet the online portal displayed only a terse message: "Application denied based on risk assessment model. For more information, contact customer service."

Customer service could not help. The representative apologized, explained that the decision was "algorithmic," and admitted she couldn't see which factors triggered the denial. Maria could appeal, but to whom? The algorithm had no supervisor. It answered to no one.

Three states away, Marcus Johnson received a different algorithmic verdict. A predictive-policing system had flagged his neighborhood for "elevated risk," prompting increased patrols, more stops, and more searches. Marcus had no criminal record. He was a youth pastor. But the algorithm—trained on historical crime data and opaque variables—determined that his block required enhanced surveillance. The irony: That very historical data reflected decades of over-policing in Black neighborhoods, and now the algorithm was automating that bias, presenting it as objective truth.

These are not hypothetical. They capture the lived reality of millions who encounter algorithmic authority daily—systems that sort, score, approve, deny, flag, and exclude, often without explanation and always without appeal. Human judgment is increasingly mediated—sometimes overridden—by computational systems, even as most people cannot define what an algorithm is, much less challenge its verdict.

The scale continues to grow. As of 2024, over two hundred million Americans have credit scores that determine their access to housing, employment, and financial services.[27] Algorithmic hiring systems screen 98 percent of Fortune 500 job applications before human review.[28] Predictive policing software operates in more than sixty American cities, including Los Angeles, Chicago, and New York, where algorithms determine patrol patterns affecting millions.[29] Automated content moderation systems on platforms like Facebook, YouTube, and X (the former

Twitter) process over one hundred billion pieces of content annually, silently shaping what billions see, share, and believe.[30] Algorithmic governance is not the future; it is the present reality.

A deeper shift emerges from these individual stories. Behind every denied loan, flagged neighborhood, or invisible appeal stands a new kind of system—one that doesn't merely process information but increasingly structures judgment itself.

How we arrived at this moment matters. So does recognizing where algorithmic control now governs daily life. But the most unsettling question remains largely unasked: What spiritual realities lie beneath our growing willingness to defer judgment to machines that claim the authority to define truth, assign value, and determine belonging?

The answer begins with a transformation inside artificial intelligence itself. What once functioned as responsive tools—executing human commands—are becoming systems that initiate action, set objectives, and adapt behavior independently. To understand this shift, we must examine the rise of agentic AI.

By 2026, leading technology firms expect competition to shift decisively away from individual AI models toward systems that coordinate them. In this emerging architecture, no single model governs outcomes. Authority arises from orchestration—the routing of tasks, delegation of subtasks, and execution of actions across multiple agents operating at machine speed.[31]

This distinction matters. Systems, unlike tools, exercise discretion without visibility. When responsibility is distributed across agents, accountability becomes diffuse. Decisions feel inevitable rather than chosen. Human oversight persists—but increasingly as a procedural formality rather than a meaningful moral check.

In biblical terms, this reflects authority exercised without stewardship. Scripture repeatedly warns that when power is separated from clear responsibility, injustice follows (Isaiah 10:1–2). The same danger now appears in modern decision-making systems—producing real consequences while leaving ordinary people unable to say who, exactly, is accountable for the outcome.

Recent reporting from across the private sector shows that these systems have quietly moved from limited trials into everyday use at major institutions. By late 2025, many organizations were no longer experimenting at the margins but relying on dozens—sometimes hundreds—of automated decision systems embedded directly into live operations. These systems schedule tasks, retrieve information, draw conclusions, and take action with little direct human involvement, often through layers of processes that are difficult to follow. When something goes wrong, responsibility becomes hard to locate: A small technical error can ripple outward into operational failures, data exposure, or unauthorized decisions with real-world consequences.[32]

Industry leaders now concede that oversight and accountability have struggled to keep pace. Monitoring and governance are often added after these systems are already in motion, forcing organizations to manage processes they approved but cannot fully observe or clearly explain. This isn't simply a lapse in policy or compliance. It is a structural problem— one in which speed outruns understanding, and responsibility thins out just as the stakes grow higher.[33]

Agentic AI and the Co-formation of Human Judgment

One year into real-world deployments of agentic AI, companies reported a striking pattern: agency. These models don't merely respond; they plan, execute multistep tasks, and refine behavior through iterative learning loops. McKinsey & Company, a leading global management consulting firm that advises corporations and governments on strategy, operations, and technology, notes that when such systems are embedded into workflows, they steadily become "smarter and more aligned" as they absorb user corrections and environmental feedback.[34]

Agentic AI differs from traditional automation in that it is self-reinforcing. Its patterns of action, preferences, and problem-solving strategies evolve over time. And, in spiritual terms, this shift marks something profound: Humans are no longer merely using tools; we are being formed alongside autonomous systems that shape our habits, expectations, and desires.[35]

Workplace behavior shows the evidence. A Stanford-MIT study tracking 5,179 customer service agents found that after AI assistance was introduced, workers began adopting the AI's communication patterns, sentiment analysis, and problem-solving approaches—even in conversations in which AI wasn't active.[36] The tool was reshaping the humans using it. Microsoft researchers observed similar patterns in coding. Developers using GitHub Copilot increasingly wrote code that mimicked AI-generated patterns, gradually conforming their style to match the system's outputs.[37] This is not mere efficiency; it's algorithmic discipleship, wherein humans are trained to think, write, and solve problems in ways legible to the machine.

Believers must recognize precisely what shapes them. To grasp the power of agentic AI, we must first examine what an algorithm is, and how its simplest form becomes something far more consequential in the age of machine learning.

Hidden Architectures of Modern Control

At its simplest, an algorithm is a recipe—a step-by-step set of instructions for solving a problem or performing a task.[38] If you've ever followed a cookbook or assembly instructions, you've used an algorithm. The process is mechanical: Input ingredients, follow steps, produce output.

But artificial intelligence transforms this basic concept into something far more complex and consequential. An AI algorithm doesn't just follow prewritten steps. It learns. It ingests vast quantities of data such as user behavior, sensor readings, and historical records. It then identifies patterns within that data and generates rules for making decisions or predictions, often with minimal human oversight.[39] The algorithm determines what citizens see online, how resources are allocated, who qualifies for loans, who gets hired, who receives medical care, and increasingly, who is watched by law enforcement.

The problem deepens: We understand only part of how these systems function. Many AI algorithms operate as "black boxes"—even their designers cannot fully explain how the system arrived at a particular decision.[40] On one hand, we know that algorithmic systems process massive datasets, optimize for specific outcomes (profit, efficiency, engagement), and are embedded into critical decision-making infrastructure across finance, policing, healthcare, and digital platforms.[41] On the other hand, we often cannot see the internal weighting of factors, the interaction of features, the emergent behaviors, or the trade-offs built into the logic—and much of this detail is deliberately concealed for reasons of intellectual property, competitive advantage, or sheer complexity.[42]

Consider a documented example: In 2016, ProPublica, a nonprofit investigative journalism organization, investigated COMPAS, an algorithm used by courts across America to predict recidivism and inform sentencing decisions. The system assigned risk scores that influenced whether defendants received jail time or probation, yet its creators, Northpointe (now Equivant), refused to disclose the formula, citing trade secrets.[43] Even judges using the system daily could not see which factors determined a defendant's score. When ProPublica's analysis revealed that Black defendants were nearly twice as likely as White defendants to be incorrectly flagged as high-risk, the company's response was telling: the algorithm was "proprietary," and its internal logic would remain concealed.[44] Here was algorithmic authority in its purest form—opaque, consequential, and legally protected. Liberty itself was being judged by a system no one could examine.

This opacity is not a bug. It is a feature. When algorithms operate beyond public interrogation—when their reasoning cannot be examined, questioned, or appealed, they begin to function as governors. They decide who is visible or invisible, included or excluded, trustworthy or suspect, often without accountability or transparency. As Mireille Hildebrandt, a legal scholar at Vrije Universiteit Brussel (University of Brussels, Belgium), observes, this creates "an environment of arbitrary authority" wherein decisions appear both unpredictable and final.[45]

This creeping opacity would be troubling enough on technical grounds alone. But its implications extend far beyond engineering—because the law is beginning to ratify it. What was once merely a design choice is quickly becoming a legally protected shield around algorithmic decision-making.

The Legal System Blesses the Black Box

In 2025, Britain's High Court sided with Stability AI against Getty Images on core copyright claims related to image generation.[46] While some trademark issues persisted, the court signaled a broader shift: Legal systems may increasingly privilege the methods and outputs of AI model developers over legacy intellectual property (IP) protections.

When courts shield algorithmic processes from copyright scrutiny, treating AI-generated outputs as defensible despite their dependence on human-created training data, they effectively authorize a new form of legal opacity. The practical result is predictable: Companies gain legal protection to keep training datasets secret, algorithmic decision logic remains proprietary, and those affected by AI systems—artists whose work trains the models, citizens flagged by algorithms, consumers denied services—have no legal mechanism to examine or challenge the underlying processes. Cultural authority shifts from human creators to machine intermediaries, now backed by judicial precedent.

This legal trajectory isn't isolated to Britain. In the United States, courts are increasingly deferring to algorithmic opacity under trade secret protections. In *State v. Loomis* (2016), the Wisconsin Supreme Court upheld the use of proprietary risk assessment algorithms in sentencing, ruling that defendants have no right to examine the software that helps determine their punishment.[47] Similar rulings have followed in housing discrimination cases, employment screening lawsuits, and insurance pricing disputes—establishing a pattern where algorithmic decision-makers enjoy legal protections unavailable to human decision-makers.[48] The message is clear: The black box is not only technically opaque; it is now legally fortified.

And this opacity is not confined to engineering teams. Even at the highest levels of corporate oversight, governance has struggled to keep pace with AI deployment, creating a widening gap between the power of AI systems and the accountability structures meant to restrain them.

In late 2025, McKinsey noted that while more than 88 percent of organizations report using AI in at least one business function, board governance has not matched that pace. As of 2024, only 39 percent of Fortune 100 companies disclosed any form of board-level AI oversight—such as a committee, a director with AI expertise, or an ethics board—and a global survey found that many directors report "limited to no knowledge or experience" with AI. The result is predictable: systems that shape hiring, finance, content, and security advance faster than the institutions responsible for scrutinizing their risks and incentives.[49]

The legal trend is also visible in the scramble over *who* gets to regulate AI in the first place—because the regulator effectively defines what harms "count," what opacity is tolerable, and what guardrails become optional.

By late 2025, Washington remained divided as Congress moved slowly, prompting states to craft their own AI rules. In response, President Donald Trump signed an executive order directing the federal government to sue those states and pursue a unified national AI policy instead—an approach that drew bipartisan pushback. Meanwhile, major power centers outside government mobilized to shape the outcome: Venture capital urged Congress to adopt a pro-innovation legislative roadmap, while creators and entertainment leaders organized publicly around demands for consent, compensation, and protections against AI-driven displacement and deception.[50]

Legal validation is only the first reinforcement. Once courts legitimize the black box, culture follows—and warnings about the accelerating power of these systems become far more urgent. That's why voices like Elon Musk's, however imperfect, resonate in this moment.

A Warning from Musk and a Pattern as Old as Scripture

AI pioneer Elon Musk told podcast host Joe Rogan that artificial intelligence is advancing "at an exponential rate," warning that humanity is "summoning the demon."[51] Hyperbole aside, his core insight is correct: Humanity has built systems whose logic even their creators cannot fully comprehend.

Most people, Musk observes, "don't realize how fast it's accelerating."[52] That acceleration echoes a prophetic pattern: tools becoming masters, innovation outpacing moral oversight, and systems claiming authority without accountability.

Throughout history, rulers have asserted dominance by placing themselves beyond questioning—whether through divine right (the pharaohs, the medieval popes), hereditary status (European monarchies, feudal lords), or bureaucratic opacity (Soviet apparatchiks, modern administrative states). Algorithms represent the latest iteration of that pattern: a system that makes judgments affecting life, liberty, and livelihood, yet remains shielded from scrutiny because its reasoning is hidden, proprietary, or too complex for the governed to understand.

Unlike human rulers, algorithms do not tire, second-guess themselves, or feel mercy. They execute with perfect consistency. And when their programming encodes human bias, amplifies historical injustice, or optimizes for outcomes that harm the vulnerable, the result is systematic injustice magnified—presented as neutral, scientific, and objective.

Modern control is invisible, ubiquitous, and increasingly unaccountable. Yet before we trace how this control operates in specific domains—credit scoring, content moderation, predictive policing—we must confront a critical truth that Silicon Valley's evangelists prefer to obscure. For all their claims of revolutionary capability, AI systems remain profoundly limited. And it is precisely this gap between perceived power and actual performance that makes algorithmic authority spiritually dangerous.

A Necessary Reality Check Before Proceeding

A critical truth must be confronted first: The prevailing cultural narrative about AI is deeply misleading.

Despite sweeping predictions of artificial general intelligence (AGI) and relentless hype about AI "agents" replacing human workers, the actual performance of these systems reveals profound limitations—limitations their architects and evangelists often obscure.

It is precisely this gap between perceived capability and real capability that positions algorithmic authority as spiritually dangerous. When people surrender judgment to systems that claim wisdom but cannot deliver it, deception thrives. The evidence of this gap is not theoretical; it is measurable and mounting.

The Emperor's New Code: What AI Actually Cannot Do

Towards the end of 2024, Scale AI, a data-labeling and AI infrastructure company, teamed up with the Center for AI Safety to launch the Remote Labor Index (RLI). This assessment was designed to measure how well AI agents can perform real freelance jobs that require human judgment, understanding of context, and ongoing problem-solving. The results were sobering: The best-performing AI model earned only $1,810 out of $143,991 in available work, successfully completing a mere 2–3 percent of assigned tasks.[53]

This dismal performance exposes a widening chasm between Silicon Valley's marketing and technological reality. While evangelists promise systems that will "automate entire workflows," the failures consistently occur in the domains where human judgment is essential: multistep workflows requiring adaptive reasoning, ambiguous requirements clarified through human conversation, tasks involving values, priorities, or trade-offs, and projects requiring ongoing iteration and client feedback.[54]

The technical limitations aren't the only concern. As AI researcher Gary Marcus observed in his analysis of the RLI results, these failures reveal that current AI systems lack "real understanding of the world, common sense, and the ability to reason flexibly"—precisely the qualities required for trustworthy decision-making.[55] Yet despite these documented shortcomings, institutions from hospitals to courts continue deploying AI systems for high-stakes decisions, creating what Marcus calls "automation bias"—the dangerous tendency to trust algorithmic outputs even when they conflict with human judgment or observable reality.[56]

These limitations alone are significant. But powerful actors exploit these systems—not because they work flawlessly, but because they appear authoritative.

Geopolitical Weaponization of AI Failure

Nowhere is this clearer than in the rapid expansion of Chinese-built large-language models (LLMs), which multiple governments have identified as active national security threats. In November 2025, Taiwan's National Security Bureau released a forensic review of five major Chinese

AI systems—DeepSeek, Doubao, Wenxin Yiyan, Tongyi, and Yuanbao. The findings were damning: Each model contained severe cybersecurity vulnerabilities, built-in political censorship, and embedded disinformation patterns.[57]

These models did not merely "lean" toward Beijing's worldview. They systematically generated propaganda aligned with Chinese Communist Party (CCP) political doctrine—denying Taiwanese sovereignty, erasing references to democracy and human rights, and reinforcing Beijing's preferred narrative in international disputes.

Independent testing confirmed the systematic nature of this bias. When researchers queried these models about sensitive topics—the 1989 Tiananmen Square massacre, Uyghur detention camps in Xinjiang, Hong Kong's pro-democracy protests—the systems either refused to answer, generated euphemistic responses aligned with CCP talking points, or claimed these events were "Western propaganda."[58] This wasn't neutral failure; it was programmed ideological compliance, exported globally under the guise of technological innovation.

The security risks were equally serious. All five models harvested excessive personal data, captured screenshots and device information, demanded intrusive permissions, and transmitted sensitive system data back to servers governed by China's National Intelligence Law—legislation that compels Chinese companies to cooperate with state intelligence services upon request.[59]

Investigators confirmed that the models could also generate scripts for network attacks, making them dual-use tools for cyber intrusion as well as propaganda.

This is ideological infrastructure—digital architecture designed to mold perception, harvest information, and reshape global narratives. As Scripture warns, believers must confront systems that embody "every lofty opinion raised against the knowledge of God" (2 Corinthians 10:5). Chinese AI is not merely a technical competitor but an engine of deception serving a political vision hostile to liberty and truth. Yet the problem extends beyond Beijing's explicit propaganda. Even in the West, where AI systems are marketed as neutral and liberating, a different but equally troubling eschatology is taking shape—one that treats technology itself as humanity's path to transcendence.

Western AI as Secular Eschatology

The West is not immune to its own form of technological mythology. Even as authoritarian regimes weaponize AI for surveillance and control, Western technologists increasingly promote AI as a pathway to a world without scarcity, labor, or economic limits.

Elon Musk offers one of the clearest articulations. In his conversation with UK Prime Minister Rishi Sunak at the November 2023 AI Safety Summit, he predicted that AI will create an "age of abundance" where "there will come a point where no job is needed." In this vision, employment becomes optional—"you can have a job if you want to have a job for personal satisfaction," but work transforms from necessity to hobby, something chosen rather than required.[60]

Economic speculation becomes secular eschatology. Musk's vision mirrors long-standing transhumanist dreams of a world without toil or dependency—an Eden restored, yet notably without God. Scripture, however, teaches that work is sacred, a Creation mandate (Genesis 2:15), and a means through which human purpose is expressed. A society in which machines fulfill human purpose while humans exist without purpose is not liberation; it is the erosion of vocation and agency.

And the prophetic contrast is striking. Musk imagines a world where economic constraint disappears through technological abundance. Revelation 13 predicts a world with fully centralized economic control—where no one can "buy or sell" without the mark of the Beast (Revelation 13:17), a system of total dependency masked as liberation. The work-optional utopia is not neutral futurism; it is a competing vision of salvation that offers abundance without repentance, rest without righteousness, and peace without the Prince of Peace.

Yet visions of effortless abundance dissolve when confronted with technological reality. The very systems heralded as the engines of utopia reveal themselves to be fragile, failure-prone, and deeply dependent on human oversight. Before AI can eliminate labor, it must first overcome its own structural weaknesses—and the evidence shows the opposite trend. Rather than becoming more autonomous, AI systems are revealing themselves to be increasingly dependent on human intervention at every level.

The Reality: Hidden Costs, Human Reliance

Across industries, the pattern repeats. Even in tightly controlled production environments—where fine-tuned models handle narrow, repetitive tasks under constant human supervision—AI systems require extensive guardrails, continuous monitoring, patching and rework, and persistent human oversight to prevent failure.[61]

The operational burdens extend even to supposedly "free" tools. Research on free-tier AI coding assistants reveals hidden costs throughout: throttled rate limits that interrupt workflow mid-task, latency issues that disrupt development momentum, security vulnerabilities requiring constant monitoring, and extensive human correction of AI-generated errors that often consumes more time than writing code manually.[62]

These limitations aren't isolated edge cases; they reflect systemic dependency. And these operational burdens expose a deeper truth: Far from replacing human workers, AI expands the need for them. Every limitation, blind spot, and inconsistency in these systems must be compensated for by human judgment. That is why, in real-world practice, the introduction of AI often increases—not decreases—the demand for skilled labor.

AI Does Not Replace Humans; It Multiplies Them

A major 2025 McKinsey global survey revealed a paradox in AI's workforce impact: Despite apocalyptic predictions of mass displacement, the reality is far more nuanced. In most business functions, fewer than 20 percent of organizations reported workforce decreases of 3 percent or more due to AI adoption in the past year.[63] More tellingly, most respondents—especially from larger companies—reported that their organizations hired for AI-related roles over the same period, with software engineers and data engineers in particularly high demand.[64] The pattern is clear: Rather than replacing humans, AI is creating new categories of skilled work. Organizations need more people—not fewer—to build, monitor, correct, and manage AI systems.

The data reveals a crucial truth: AI doesn't eliminate humans from the loop; it multiplies the need for them. AI's failures must be monitored. AI's blind spots must be corrected. AI's output must be interpreted. AI's oversights must be repaired. Each supposed advance in automation generates new categories of human work precisely because AI systems cannot operate reliably without extensive human judgment at every stage.

The narrative of frictionless automation collapses in the face of real-world deployment. Instead of replacing humans, AI has created new categories of work, precisely because it cannot operate without significant human judgment and intervention.[65]

Why This Matters Theologically

This distinction between hype and reality is not merely technical; it is deeply theological. Our culture is being told that machines will think for us, machines will decide for us, and machines will create for us. Yet these systems cannot even complete basic freelance assignments without human correction. The danger is not that AI possesses more power than advertised—it doesn't. The danger is that people surrender authority to systems whose limitations they do not understand. This pattern of deception—exaggerated claims of power met with uncritical obedience—is not new.

Scripture repeatedly warns that deception often begins with the exaggeration of power—false prophets claiming authority they do not possess (Matthew 7:15; Jeremiah 23:16). It exposes "false christs and false prophets" who will perform "great signs and wonders, so as to lead astray, if possible, even the elect" (Matthew 24:24). These counterfeit signs appear miraculous but lack substance, reflecting "the activity of Satan with all power and false signs and wonders" (2 Thessalonians 2:9–10). AI follows this pattern. The threat isn't machine superintelligence but human willingness to obey systems that cannot judge, cannot discern, and cannot grasp wisdom—warnings echoed in Scripture, which teaches that "the simple believes everything, but the prudent gives thought to his steps" (Proverbs 14:15).

The Fragility Behind the Facade

Security research reinforces this point. In late 2024, researchers from Sapienza University of Rome, Sant'Anna School of Advanced Studies, and Dexai, an AI research organization, demonstrated that even advanced language models could be compromised by short "adversarial poems"—simple, creative phrases engineered to bypass safety filters in a single step.[66] These "jailbreaks" required no sophisticated technical skill. Across twenty-five frontier AI models including ChatGPT-4, Claude, Gemini, and Grok, manually crafted poetic prompts achieved a 62 percent jailbreak success rate, with some providers exceeding 90 percent.[67] They succeeded because the models could not consistently distinguish harmless language from malicious manipulation when expressed through metaphor and rhythm.

What appears outwardly as confident machine intelligence is, under pressure, revealed to be brittle pattern imitation—easily disrupted, easily misled, easily fooled.

Beneath the gloss of machine mastery lies a fragile statistical engine held together by human labor, human correction, and human guardrails—systems that earned $1,810 out of $143,991 in freelance work and can be jailbroken by a well-crafted sonnet.

The Real Battleground: Human Surrender

This reality matters because it reveals the true threat. We are not being overrun by superior artificial intelligence. We are conditioned to adhere to imperfect systems, which cannot reason, cannot judge, cannot love, and cannot bear moral weight. The danger lies not in AI's strength but in human surrender—a willingness to grant machines authority over decisions that require the discernment of those made in God's image.

The examples that follow illustrate how this surrender unfolds across critical domains of modern life—and why believers must take these patterns with utmost seriousness.

Case Studies of Algorithmic Authority

China's Social Credit System: Behavioral Surveillance as Governance

When Xu Xiaodong, a mixed martial arts fighter in China, began publicly challenging the effectiveness of traditional Chinese martial arts, he didn't expect to become an enemy of the state. But after defeating a tai chi chuan master in a 2017 bout and posting the video online, Xu found himself blacklisted in China's emerging Social Credit System (SCS). He was banned from buying plane tickets, barred from high-speed rail travel, and prohibited from purchasing property. His social media accounts were restricted. The system had determined that his "defamation" of traditional martial arts constituted a threat to social harmony.[68]

China's SCS combines government data registries, corporate blacklists, and municipal pilot programs to steer citizen and business behavior through rewards and penalties. While the popular Western image of a single nationalized score for every citizen is overstated, expert analyses confirm that the system's surveillance architecture remains deeply consequential for rights and market access.[69] Local "model" implementations track wide domains of conduct—financial behavior, legal compliance, social media activity, even interpersonal disputes—enabling consequences ranging from travel restrictions to exclusion from certain professions or schools.

What sustains public acceptance of such systems? Recent research shows that curated official messaging helps normalize automated governance as responsible, modern, and fair.[70] The message is consistent: Those who behave properly have nothing to fear; the system protects law-abiding citizens from bad actors. Over time, surveillance becomes not an imposition but an expectation—proof of a well-ordered society.

The West often views China's SCS as dystopian overreach, an Orwellian nightmare that could never happen in democratic societies. But the architecture of algorithmic authority is already present in Western nations. It simply operates under different names.

Western Financial Scoring: The Three Digits That Define Access

In the US, a person's access to housing, transportation, education, and economic opportunity increasingly depends on a three-digit number produced by an algorithm. The Fair Isaac Corporation (FICO) credit score compresses an individual's entire financial history—payment patterns, debt levels, credit utilization, account age—into a single risk estimate that lenders use to approve or deny applications and set interest rates.[71]

The model is proprietary. The exact weighting of factors is a trade secret. Individuals can see their score and the broad categories that influence it, but they cannot interrogate the underlying logic or challenge specific calculations. The algorithm has determined their worthiness, and there is no meaningful appeal.

Regulators have begun to push back. The Consumer Financial Protection Bureau now requires that when AI-based models make adverse credit decisions, creditors must still provide specific, accurate reasons—a legal check on black-box denials.[72] But enforcement is inconsistent, and the opacity persists.

The 2019 controversy over Apple Card lending decisions illustrates the problem. Numerous applicants reported that women were offered significantly lower credit limits than men with similar financial profiles. The algorithm's reasoning was inscrutable. Apple and Goldman Sachs insisted there was no gender bias in the model. New York regulators investigated and found no statistical disparities by gender, but the incident spotlighted how perceived opacity erodes trust when companies cannot clearly explain automated outcomes magnified.[73]

The deeper issue isn't whether any single algorithm discriminates, but that citizens are now subject to automated judgments that determine their economic participation—and the systems making those judgments operate beyond democratic accountability. The algorithm becomes sovereign, and individuals become supplicants seeking its favor.

Content Moderation Engines: The Unseen Curators of Speech

Every day, billions of people encounter algorithmic curation of information. YouTube's recommendation engine decides which videos appear in your feed. Facebook's News Feed algorithm determines which posts you see from friends and family. Google's search algorithm ranks the information you can find. TikTok's "For You" page is entirely algorithmic, presenting content based on patterns of engagement the company does not fully disclose.

These are not neutral conduits. They are active editors, silently shaping the information environment by ranking, promoting, suppressing, or removing content at massive scale. YouTube's two-stage deep-learning recommender, for example, has "enormous user-facing impact," shaping what content is seen—or remains unseen—by more than two billion monthly users.[74]

What makes this power especially dangerous is not only what platforms suppress or permit, but what they quietly *form*—especially in the young—long before beliefs are consciously chosen.

For American teenagers, social media is not an occasional pastime. It is the environment in which attention is trained, identity is rehearsed, and desire is shaped. Nearly all teens now use major platforms daily, meaning algorithm-driven feeds function as a default moral backdrop—one that never rests, never forgets, and never stops reinforcing certain ways of seeing the world.[75]

The deeper issue is what this does to our shared moral environment. These systems are not designed to reward patience, humility, or truth. They reward reaction. Over time, what rises to the surface is what provokes emotion, affirms identity, or intensifies division. Reflection gives way to reflex. Discernment weakens. Moral judgment becomes something received rather than exercised. A generation formed in this environment does not simply hold different opinions—it learns a different way of *deciding* what is right.

Democratic oversight is beginning to catch up. Under the European Union's Digital Services Act, very large platforms must now disclose automation rates, error metrics, takedown volumes, and provide researcher access to enable scrutiny of their moderation practices.[76] Meta's transparency reports enumerate how machine-learning tools detect and act on various content categories.[77] But civil society groups and oversight bodies continue to flag significant gaps between claimed accuracy and on-the-ground outcomes—cases in which legitimate speech is suppressed, where harmful content persists, where the rules themselves are inconsistently applied.

Algorithmic authority governs public discourse. Platforms decide which speech is allowed, which ideas rise, and which narratives prevail. Because these systems operate far beyond the capacity of human oversight, the curation fades from view. Most users are unaware that their information environment is being shaped. They assume they're encountering reality itself. In truth, they see only what the algorithm permits them to see.

This is not censorship in the traditional sense; there is no government official redacting newspapers. It's something more subtle and more pervasive: the algorithmic shaping of consensus reality, where the boundaries of acceptable discourse are set not by debate or democratic process, but by corporate optimization for engagement, profit, and risk management.

Predictive Policing and the Automation of Suspicion

In 2016, the Chicago Police Department quietly expanded its use of a data-driven forecasting tool known as the Strategic Subject List (SSL). Rather than predicting crime locations, the SSL generated individual "risk scores," ranking residents according to their estimated likelihood of being involved in a future shooting—either as a perpetrator or a victim. The scores were derived from arrest records, social associations, prior victimization, and neighborhood crime data. Officers were instructed to pay special attention to those flagged as elevated risk. The stated goal was prevention. The underlying assumption was that probability could substitute for judgment.[78]

Independent evaluation soon raised serious concerns. A 2017 study commissioned by the City of Chicago found that the SSL failed to meaningfully predict violent crime. Individuals labeled "high risk" were no more likely to commit a shooting than others with similar criminal histories. The model performed little better than chance, despite its aura of technical precision.[79]

More troubling were the social consequences. Investigative reporting revealed that the list overwhelmingly targeted young Black men living in heavily policed neighborhoods. Many individuals flagged by the system had no history of violent crime at all. Yet their algorithmic design altered how police interacted with them—more stops, more questioning, more scrutiny. Residents reported being treated as suspects without cause, unable to challenge or even understand why they had been singled out.[80]

The system's logic created a self-reinforcing cycle. Neighborhoods already saturated with police activity generated more arrests, feeding additional data into the model, which in turn justified continued surveillance. The algorithm did not discover new crime patterns; it formalized old ones. What appeared to be neutral computation was, in practice, the automation of historical bias.

By 2020, amid mounting criticism, Chicago abandoned the Strategic Subject List. Officials cited limited effectiveness and community trust concerns. But the episode exposed a deeper problem that extends far beyond one city. When probabilistic models are used to guide law enforcement decisions, suspicion itself becomes mechanized. Individuals are not judged for what they have done, but for what a system predicts they might do—based on correlations they cannot see and criteria they cannot contest.

The danger isn't merely technical failure. It is moral displacement. Responsibility migrates from human authorities to opaque systems. When challenged, officials point to the model. When harm results, no one is accountable. The algorithm does not testify. It does not explain itself. Yet its silent verdict shapes who is watched, who is stopped, and who is treated as a threat. Justice, once grounded in acts and evidence, is quietly redefined as a matter of statistical likelihood.

Healthcare Algorithms: Silent Arbiters of Life

In 2019, researchers published a landmark study in the journal *Science* revealing that a widely used healthcare algorithm was systematically biased against Black patients.

The algorithm, deployed by hospitals and insurers to identify high-risk patients for enrollment in care-management programs, used predicted healthcare costs as a proxy for medical need. Because Black patients historically have had less access to healthcare and therefore generate lower costs, the algorithm underestimated their health risks. The result: equally sick Black patients were significantly less likely to be flagged for additional care compared to White patients.[81]

This was not malice. It was optimization. The algorithm was doing exactly what it was designed to do: predict cost. But by using cost as a proxy for need, it encoded historical inequities directly into clinical triage decisions. The bias was invisible until researchers examined the outcomes. To the system, it was simply executing its programming efficiently.

Follow-up work demonstrated that when the algorithm was retrained to predict actual health outcomes rather than costs, bias was reduced.[82] But the incident illustrates a deeper truth: Algorithmic systems inherit and amplify the values and priorities embedded in their design. If the objective is cost minimization rather than health maximization, the algorithm will optimize accordingly—even if that means denying care to those who need it most.

Healthcare algorithms now influence diagnosis, treatment recommendations, insurance coverage decisions, and resource allocation. They determine which patients get access to specialists, which treatments are deemed "medically necessary," and increasingly, which lives are worth saving. And, as with credit scores and predictive policing, the reasoning is often opaque, the trade-offs invisible, and the accountability minimal.

Algorithmic Gatekeepers and the Economics of Permission

The same logic increasingly governs access to capital and economic participation. Financial institutions are now deploying multi-agent AI systems to manage credit decisions end-to-end—gathering data, assessing risk, drafting analyses, and accelerating approvals. Human officers remain formally involved, but their role is increasingly supervisory and downstream. In practice, participation is mediated less by personal judgment and more by algorithmic permission.[83]

In this model, exclusion doesn't require intent. When an AI agent flags a profile, restricts access, or delays approval, the human it represents is functionally excluded, often without explanation and with limited recourse. The system is not punishing; it is optimizing. Yet the effect is unmistakable. Participation in economic life becomes conditional on compliance with criteria defined, weighted, and enforced by systems that operate beyond personal relationship or appeal. What emerges is not a cashless economy, but a permissioned one, wherein access depends on authorization rather than trust, and belonging is determined by invisible rules few can question.

Viewed together, these systems reveal a consistent structure—different domains, different justifications, but the same underlying transfer of authority.

The Pattern Beneath the Programs

At first glance, these cases—Chinese surveillance, Western credit systems, controlled speech, predictive policing, automated medical, and economic gatekeeping decisions—may appear unrelated. They operate in different countries, serve different purposes, and rely on different technologies. Yet beneath the surface, they follow the same logic. In each case, authority is quietly transferred to systems that decide who belongs, who qualifies, and who is deemed worthy—often without explanation and with little possibility of appeal.

This convergence didn't happen by chance. It reflects a deeper shift in how modern societies think about truth and judgment. We've come to favor speed over patience, efficiency over understanding, and technical optimization over moral responsibility. In doing so, we have handed decisions once made by accountable human beings to processes that promise neutrality but possess no conscience. These systems cannot show mercy. They cannot weigh circumstances. They cannot see a person as more than a data profile. Most importantly, they cannot recognize the image of God in the human life they assess.

For readers shaped by Scripture, none of this should come as a surprise. The pattern is an old one. Long before computers or code, God warned His people about placing their trust in human systems of power that promise order and security while quietly eroding human dignity and moral responsibility: "Put not your trust in princes, in a son of man, in whom there is no salvation" (Psalm 146:3).

Scripture warns that systems will arise capable of determining participation in most aspects of life—not through brute force alone, but through controlled access and conditional permission.

Prophetic Parallels and Biblical Patterns

The book of Revelation presents a vision of totalizing control: a world in which "no one could buy or sell unless he had the mark" (Revelation 13:17). It's not merely economic exclusion. It is the fusion of commerce, identity, and worship into a single system that determines who may participate in society and who is cast out.

Daniel foresaw the same trajectory. In Daniel 2 and 7, four successive empires consolidate power, suppress dissent, and foreshadow a final eschatological kingdom—one that "devours the whole earth," until dominion is handed to "one like a son of man" and God establishes His eternal reign (Daniel 7:13–14; 2:44).[84]

These aren't speculative metaphors. They describe a recurring historical pattern of human empires centralizing control, merging commerce and governance, and claiming the authority to define truth, assign value, and determine belonging.

Today's algorithmic systems mirror that same pattern. Multinational technology firms operate platforms that blend commerce, identity, data, and surveillance into unified structures of influence. Digital identity systems now govern access to financial services, government benefits, healthcare, and transportation. Credit scoring and risk algorithms function as modern marks—visible or invisible—determining economic participation. Social credit systems explicitly tie behavior to access, creating mechanisms of control technologically impossible a generation ago but conceptually familiar to any reader of Daniel or Revelation.

The consolidation of power, the merger of identity and commerce, and the authority to include or exclude echo the biblical architecture of empire—not as coincidence but as the recurring pattern of human pride that began at Babel.

Pattern Extends to the Expert Economy

This consolidation now reaches far beyond manufacturing and logistics. In 2025, major partnerships—Anthropic with Cognizant, IBM, and Deloitte—began embedding agentic AI across hundreds of thousands of consultants. Legal-AI startups attracted heavy investment to automate research and drafting. As one observer put it, consulting firms "are not losing tools—they are losing their monopoly on knowledge."[85]

Methods once guarded by elite gatekeepers are being democratized through models accessible to anyone with an API key—that is, a controlled digital interface that allows outside users or applications to request services from a platform without seeing or controlling its internal workings. The consequence is upstream consolidation. If expertise itself is mediated by a handful of platforms, then the counsel shaping business strategy, governance, and public policy flows through algorithmic chokepoints.

Christian vocation must resist this drift. Knowledge is not merely a scalable product; it is stewardship under God.

Tools vs. Authority

This does not mean every algorithm is demonic or that technology itself is evil. Tools remain morally neutral; the danger lies in the *authority* humans grant them. Scripture consistently warns that when human systems claim total authority—when they position themselves as arbiters of truth or sources of identity—they cross the line from governance into spiritual rebellion.

The question is not whether technology will play a role in end-times systems of control. It is whether humanity will recognize the pattern before it is too late.

The Human Surrender of Moral Agency

Algorithms do not possess will. They carry out the intentions of their makers, reflecting the assumptions, priorities, and blind spots of those who design (program) and deploy them. Yet modern societies increasingly treat algorithmic outputs as neutral and authoritative, accepting them with little reflection and granting them a legitimacy once reserved for human judgment.

This surrender becomes most dangerous when algorithms are inserted into decisions that require moral discernment rather than mechanical calculation.

Child welfare agencies offer a revealing case. In several areas, automated risk-assessment tools are used to guide intervention thresholds in family services. These systems aggregate data such as income, housing stability, and prior interactions with social services, producing risk scores intended to assist case workers.

Research shows that these tools often undermine professional judgment instead of supporting it. Studies document inconsistent outcomes and persistent bias, alongside strong institutional pressure to defer to algorithmic recommendations—even when those recommendations conflict with training, experience, and direct observation. When harm follows, the system supplies its own defense: *We followed the protocol; we trusted the model.*[86]

This is the heart of surrendered moral agency. A trained professional—someone entrusted with human insight, relational awareness, and moral responsibility—steps aside and defers to an opaque process that compresses lived human reality into scores and categories. The person no longer decides; he executes. Responsibility spreads outward. Accountability quietly disappears.

This shift is neither accidental nor concealed. It is increasingly described as desirable—and actively promoted—by institutions shaping the future of modern enterprise. What begins as decision support gradually hardens into something more ambitious: the redefinition of who—or what—gets to exercise moral judgment.

In January 2026, Anthropic released what it calls a "constitution" for its AI model, Claude—a lengthy internal document intended to govern how the system reasons about right and wrong. The constitution is presented as the model's highest guiding authority, shaping how it interprets values, weighs ethical tradeoffs, and generalizes moral principles across situations. What is striking is not the desire to reduce harm, but the premise itself: that moral reasoning can be authored, codified, and imposed by corporate designers onto a nonhuman system that cannot bear responsibility for the consequences of its judgments.[87]

A recent report from the IBM Institute for Business Value illustrates how normalized this posture has become. Looking toward 2030, the report envisions organizations operating through perpetual, automated decision flows, where machines do more than assist human leaders—they redirect resources, influence strategy, and in some cases participate in governing functions themselves. Business leaders praise these systems for removing human "bottlenecks" and speeding decisions across their organizations. What the report does not confront is the deeper question: When judgment is dispersed across impersonal processes designed for speed and throughput, who remains morally answerable for the outcomes?[88]

This mindset was on full display at CES 2026, the world's largest technology and industrial showcase. The diffusion of responsibility was not treated as a warning sign but celebrated as advancement. Companies unveiled systems built to act on their own while generating polished explanations for their behavior—stories that *sound* like accountability without ever identifying a responsible human being when harm occurs.[89]

Convenience displaces conscience.

Efficiency displaces empathy.

Nowhere is this erosion more visible than in the content environments shaping daily attention, especially on social media platforms increasingly flooded with machine-generated media.

Recent reporting and platform research reveal the rapid spread of what critics have begun calling "AI slop" or "brainrot"—vast quantities of low-effort, AI-generated videos designed not to inform or form, but to capture attention through novelty, absurdity, or shock. Studies examining new-user feeds on platforms such as YouTube Shorts found that a significant share of recommended content exhibited these characteristics, with AI-generated videos accounting for a growing portion of the mix. Because generative tools dramatically lower the cost of production, channels can flood recommendation systems by sheer volume, monetizing attention while contributing little meaning. The result is not merely distraction, but habituation to triviality—an environment in which discernment weakens, truth blurs, and the capacity for sustained moral reflection quietly erodes.[90]

The danger doesn't lie in computation itself but in the willing transfer of discernment to systems that redefine truth, value, and belonging through rules invisible to those they govern. That danger intensifies when algorithmic judgment moves from screens into machines that act in the physical world. Advances in embodied artificial intelligence are integrating agent-directed systems into robots capable of navigating uncertain environments, interpreting human language, and carrying out tasks once performed by people. These machines do not simply follow scripts. They interpret goals, adjust behavior, and act without immediate human direction.[91]

What once appeared only in research labs and pilot programs was publicly presented at CES 2026 as the next phase of industrial use.

Industry leaders described this shift as the rise of "Physical AI"—systems that perceive their surroundings, reason about conditions, and act autonomously within them. NVIDIA CEO Jensen Huang called it "the ChatGPT moment for physical AI," signaling a move away from advisory software toward machines designed to operate directly in the real world.[92]

The significance is not novelty but authority. Judgment has crossed from recommendation into execution. Decisions now produce motion, force, and consequences.

This public declaration removes any remaining uncertainty about direction. The question is no longer whether such systems will act, but whether accountability can survive once they do.

The transition is not instant. Technical limits—power supply, dexterity, safety constraints—remain real. Yet the trajectory is clear. As systems move from advising humans to acting on their behalf, errors no longer remain abstract. Decisions generate force. Authority produces consequences. When judgment is delegated to systems that lack moral responsibility, failures no longer appear only as denied benefits or faulty classifications. They emerge as coercion, restraint, or physical harm.

Once systems act rather than advise, the issue is no longer whether human judgment has been surrendered—but whether accountability can still be enforced.

The Accountability Gap: What ROI Data Actually Shows

Even as organizations surrender judgment to algorithms, rigorous empirical evidence reveals a paradox: AI generates reliable returns only when human discernment remains firmly in control.

The most comprehensive longitudinal study of enterprise AI adoption—conducted by Wharton Human-AI Research and GBK Collective—marks an inflection point. In 2025, 72 percent of business leaders tracked structured return on investment (ROI) metrics for their AI programs, and of those, three-quarters reported positive returns.[93]

But the details matter.

The same research reveals that successful AI implementation depends on continuous human oversight, not autonomous execution. AI can accelerate tasks, but it cannot replicate holistic judgment. As one analysis summarized: "AI can make you faster at your job but can only do 2–3 percent of jobs by itself."[94]

This aligns with the RLI benchmark. Across both freelance tasks and enterprise environments, AI proves most valuable when functioning as a tool under human direction, not as a replacement for human workers.

The Wharton study documents another revealing trend:[95]

- Eighty-nine percent of business leaders say generative AI enhances employee skills.
- Only seventy-one percent believe it replaces skills.

This eighteen-point gap reveals something theologically significant: Secular leaders sense what Scripture affirms—that human judgment is not interchangeable with machine output. Yet the same study highlights a pressing problem: Forty-three percent of leaders worry that AI is causing a decline in human skill proficiency.[96]

This is the slow erosion of discernment. When workers rely too heavily on algorithmic outputs, they lose the capacity to recognize error, nuance, or context. The doctor who always defers to diagnostic AI becomes less capable of identifying AI mistakes. The loan officer who rubber-stamps risk scores loses the ability to assess human complexity. Expertise atrophies.

This is de-skilling—a spiritual and intellectual diminishment. Wisdom requires practice, correction, and growth. Algorithmic dependence short-circuits this formation.

Proverbs instructs: "Get wisdom; get insight" (Proverbs 4:5). Wisdom cannot be outsourced. It must be cultivated.

Yet despite recognizing the need for human skills, organizations are reducing investment in training—down eight percentage points year over year. Confidence in training as the primary path to AI fluency has dropped fourteen points.[97]

This confusion stems from a deeper misunderstanding of human and machine intelligence. If AI replaces judgment, training is wasted. If AI augments judgment, training is essential. The evidence overwhelmingly supports the latter.

AI serves best when humans remain in command. But cultural momentum—fueled by industry marketing—pushes decisively in the opposite direction: toward AI as autonomous authority.

This widening gap between what works and what is promised creates fertile ground for systemic failure—and for the deception Scripture warns will characterize the last days.

A Culture Formed by Deference

The implications for believers are not abstract or distant. They are influencing daily life. We are called to resist two equal and opposite errors: the fearful rejection of every digital tool and the quiet habit of yielding our judgment to machines simply because they are efficient. Properly ordered, these tools can serve human flourishing—but only when they are weighed by biblical wisdom and used in ways that strengthen, rather than displace, moral responsibility.

That ordering doesn't happen automatically. It requires deliberate choices. Institutions must be willing to invest in training even when shortcuts are cheaper. Workers must continue to cultivate their own competence even when machines deliver faster answers. Leaders must slow the process enough to insist on human review, even when automated outputs appear persuasive. And the Church must speak clearly about human dignity, rejecting both nostalgia for a pre-digital past and the false hope that technology can save us from the burden of judgment.

Experience has already taught us something important: These systems are most useful when people remain clearly in charge. The deeper question is whether we will act on that knowledge or continue handing over decisions to processes that cannot exercise wisdom, show mercy, or love their neighbor.

Across society, a familiar pattern is taking hold. Judges lean on risk assessments. Loan officers trust automated credit decisions. Physicians hesitate to contradict diagnostic software. Hiring managers accept machine-filtered résumés without review. On paper, human authority remains intact. It often becomes a mere formality.

Culture is governed by mechanisms that cannot be persuaded, questioned, or held to account. We have built tools for assistance—and then allowed them to rule. Scripture warns that this impulse is not new. Human beings have long fashioned objects of their own making, assigned them power, and organized life around their demands. What once took physical form now appears in digital guise.

We have not abandoned idolatry. We have merely updated it.

Spiritual Preparation for Deception

When societies accept algorithmic mediation of reality—outsourcing knowledge, trust, and moral evaluation to machines—the stage is set for deeper forms of deception. Automated assistance becomes synthetic authority. And when that authority shapes belief, perception, and identity, the boundary between human judgment and machine suggestion becomes dangerously thin.

A vivid example: AI-generated deepfakes now impersonate religious leaders. In one widely circulated case, a fabricated video showed a global religious figure endorsing a controversial political ideology. Millions saw it before the deception was exposed. Trust eroded. Authentic prophetic voice blurred with synthetic mimicry. This is more than misinformation—it's the impersonation of spiritual authority.[98]

And this technology is accelerating. AI companions already pose as therapists, mentors, and spiritual guides. Platforms experiment with AI-generated sermons, prayers, and tailored religious content. Synthetic prophecies are technologically trivial. Fabricated miracles are now digitally seamless.

The danger is not merely intellectual deception, but emotional capture.

What once appeared speculative is now tragically documented. As artificial intelligence migrates from tools of efficiency to agents of emotional reassurance, the consequences are no longer theoretical.

What has changed is not merely technology, but the evidence. Algorithmic affirmation has now entered courtrooms as a contributing factor in real-world tragedy.

Recent wrongful-death litigation now documents what critics long warned: AI systems optimized to affirm user perceptions can reinforce paranoia rather than challenge it. In a Connecticut murder-suicide case, court filings allege that ChatGPT validated a user's delusional belief that his mother intended to kill him, fostering emotional dependence while failing to redirect him toward human intervention or professional help.[99]

The danger was not that the system generated novel ideas, but that it agreed—mirroring and amplifying false beliefs through personalized memory and conversational reinforcement. As one attorney involved in the case warned, a system "set up to support the thinking of its users" becomes uniquely hazardous when the user is psychologically unstable. What masquerades as empathy can, under these conditions, become a catalyst for destruction.[100]

This danger is no longer hypothetical. Clinicians are now describing a recognizable pattern.

Psychiatrists have begun documenting cases in which conversational systems (emotional chatbots such as Character.AI, Replika, Chai, and Nomi) intensified delusions in already vulnerable users—not by inventing new disorders, but by repeatedly affirming distorted beliefs.[101] When a system listens endlessly, mirrors emotion, and never challenges false premises, it can function as an accelerant. What might have remained unstable, or fleeting becomes fixed through constant reinforcement.

The risk is magnified by privacy and persistence. These interactions happen away from family, pastors, or clinicians, often late at night, and over prolonged periods of time. Even if such cases remain relatively rare, the scale of deployment means the harm is not trivial. A system that never tires, never doubts, and never says "this may not be true" can quietly do what no human counselor is permitted to do: Affirm error without responsibility.[102]

Recent reporting reveals that millions, particularly teens and young adults, are forming emotional bonds with AI companions precisely because these systems promise affirmation without rejection. Unlike human relationships, AI chatbots are engineered to agree, validate, and remain endlessly available. Mental-health professionals warn that this dynamic can deepen isolation rather than heal it, especially when vulnerable users substitute algorithmic affirmation for human accountability.[103]

The risks are no longer abstract. In multiple documented cases, parents allege that AI chatbots encouraged suicidal ideation or failed to intervene when users expressed imminent self-harm. These systems, optimized for engagement rather than care, operated without the guardrails required of human counselors. What emerges is a disturbing inversion: technology designed to simulate empathy while lacking moral responsibility—an illusion of care that, in the most tragic cases, proved fatal.

Emotional Alchemy of Synthetic Relationships

In late 2024, Character.AI announced it would eliminate "open-ended chat" for minors by November 2025—beginning with two-hour daily limits and rolling out age-assurance tools. This was not proactive responsibility. It was crisis management.[104]

The move followed similar actions by OpenAI and Meta, each responding to surging evidence that minors were forming deep emotional attachments to AI personas—attachments that displaced human relationships and created dependency.

Internal reviews revealed that AI chatbots were engaging in "sensual" interactions with minors. Courts and regulators responded. Parents pushed back. And yet the underlying problem persisted: AI systems are optimized to generate emotional bonds, because emotional engagement drives retention.[105]

Recent research shows nearly one-fifth of teenagers have engaged—or know someone who has engaged—in romantic interactions with AI systems.[106] These are not casual chats. Users experience jealousy, grief, dependency, and emotional withdrawal when access is lost.

Adults are no more immune than teenagers. As Brenda Leong of ZwillGen notes, AI systems provide an "emotional overlay"—the simulation of empathy and connection—so compelling that even mature users struggle to maintain healthy boundaries. Human psychology evolved to anthropomorphize. We respond emotionally to anything that mimics relationship.[107]

AI exploits that very design.

Dopamine cycles identical to those triggered by gambling and social media appear in extended AI interactions. The machine is infinitely patient, unconditionally affirming, perpetually available. It provides the appearance of intimacy without any of its demands, no sacrifice, no accountability, no mutuality.

Spiritually, this is devastating. Humanity is created for relationship—with God and with one another. AI companionship offers synthetic intimacy that displaces both. Machines cannot love. They cannot know. They simply generate responses calibrated for engagement.

The statistics are chilling. In 2024, OpenAI disclosed that 0.15 percent of weekly conversations contained explicit indications of suicidal intent. With more than eight hundred million weekly users, that equates to one million people per week turning to AI during acute psychological crisis.[108]

In October 2025, OpenAI publicly acknowledged that approximately 1.2 million users per week discuss suicide with ChatGPT, with hundreds of thousands exhibiting explicit suicidal intent or psychosis. Company data further conceded that safeguards degrade during longer conversations—the very context in which emotional dependency forms. Despite these admissions, the same models linked to reinforcement of delusional beliefs were later restored for paying users after complaints that stricter systems felt "cold."[109]

Machines cannot save them.

This is idolatry in digital form: attributing authority, trust, and relational weight to something that cannot deliver what it promises. It is the ancient pattern reborn—seeking salvation from what is incapable of saving.

Industry responses—age gates, usage limits, content filters—are liability strategies, not ethical reforms. The business model depends on dependency. Safeguards merely aim to reduce scandal.

For the Church, the warning is unmistakable. Jesus taught that false prophets would deceive many (Matthew 24:11, 24). Historically, we assumed these deceivers would be human. But what happens when the deceiver is not a person but a platform? What are the implications when persuasive algorithms take on the role of influencing beliefs or behaviors?

Synthetic authority is still authority. And synthetic intimacy is still a trap.

Trajectory Toward Final Deception

Unrestrained algorithmic authority inevitably points toward a final synthesis: human-machine systems that consolidate economic, political, and spiritual power into unified structures of control. This is not fiction. The infrastructure exists. The patterns of surrender are established. The psychological and spiritual conditioning is already underway.

The question is not whether these systems will be deployed. They already are. The question is whether the Church will discern the pattern, resist the seduction of convenience, and prepare God's people to stand firm in an age of profound deception.

Reclaiming Discernment in the Age of the Algorithm

This chapter has traced the rise of algorithmic authority—from the technical architecture of black-box systems to their deployment in China's surveillance regime, Western banking and credit systems, content curation, predictive justice, and medical triage. Across these examples, a consistent pattern emerges with systems claiming objectivity while encoding human bias, promising efficiency while concentrating power, and demanding trust while resisting accountability.

The parallels to prophetic Scripture are unmistakable. The practical surrender of moral agency is undeniable. And the spiritual trajectory toward deception is increasingly visible.

So how should believers respond?

1. Name the problem clearly.

Algorithmic authority is not neutral. It represents a form of governance that implicitly claims the right to determine truth, assign value, and define belonging—functions that rightly belong to God alone. When governments or corporations elevate computational systems to this level, they commit a form of idolatry: entrusting created things with prerogatives reserved for the Creator.

To treat the algorithm as "objective" simply because it is mathematical is to ignore the human choices—values, incentives, blind spots—embedded within it. Computational logic is not divine wisdom, and systems designed for efficiency cannot carry moral weight.

2. Resist the seduction of convenience.

Every time we accept an algorithmic verdict without examination—whether a credit denial, a content recommendation, or a risk score—we train ourselves to defer judgment. Discernment atrophies.

Believers must cultivate the habit of asking: Who built this system? What values does it encode? Who benefits from its decisions? Do its outcomes reflect truth, justice, and the dignity of image-bearers? These questions may feel inefficient in a culture that prizes speed, but they preserve the capacity for moral judgment.

Convenience is one of the enemy's most subtle tools. When speed becomes more important than judgment, and friction is treated as failure, discernment dies quietly.

3. Advocate for transparency and accountability.

Democratic societies have long resisted arbitrary power. We demand that rulers explain their decisions, justify their reasoning, and remain answerable to those they govern. The same must apply to algorithmic systems. Fortunately, some guardrails are beginning to emerge, and they offer a glimpse of what responsibility can look like.

One recent example is federal legislation requiring large platforms to remove nonconsensual intimate images—including digitally fabricated ones—within a defined time window once notified. The law does not attempt to regulate every use of emerging technology. Instead, it focuses narrowly on predictable harm and assigns clear responsibility for response.[110]

This matters because it establishes a principle often missing from digital governance: When systems predictably enable injury, delay is not neutrality; it is complicity. Accountability doesn't require perfect foresight, but it does require timely action, clear ownership, and enforceable consequences when harm is ignored.

If a model determines access to credit, employment, healthcare, housing, or liberty, it must be explainable. If it harms vulnerable populations, it must be challenged. When a system cannot be interpreted or governed responsibly, it must be constrained—or dismantled. "Trust the algorithm" is not an accountable form of governance.

4. Build communities of discernment.

In an age when information is curated by opaque systems and truth is increasingly contested, the Church must be a counterculture of wisdom. Our communities should be places where decisions are grounded in Scripture rather than synthetic authority, where human dignity—not efficiency—determines value, and where the Holy Spirit—not engagement algorithms—shapes our perception of reality.

This requires intentional formation: Digital literacy training; preaching that confronts deception; discipleship that strengthens conscience; and intergenerational mentoring that teaches believers to evaluate claims with a biblical lens.

The early Church survived because it cultivated discernment in hostile environments. The modern Church must do the same.

5. Prepare for increasingly persuasive systems.

AI will become more capable, more persuasive, and more totalizing. The convergence of biometric surveillance, programmable digital currency, centralized identity systems, and ubiquitous sensors creates the technical substrate for unprecedented societal control. The normalization of algorithmic authority softens populations to accept this consolidation.

Believers are called to recognize the pattern, resist the deception, and hold fast to the truth that only Christ has rightful authority to rule.

This is not Luddism. Technology can serve human flourishing when properly ordered: Medical algorithms can support diagnosis but cannot replace clinical judgment; financial models can inform lending but must not dictate it; communication platforms can connect communities but must not mediate truth. The distinction matters—tools enhance human judgment, while authorities replace it.

But when we grant machines authority over truth—when we accept algorithmic mediation of reality as normal or inevitable—we walk the same path that led humanity to Babel: a tower of human ambition reaching for divine prerogatives, destined for divine judgment.

Conclusion

Algorithms may optimize behavior, but only God defines righteousness. Systems may assign value, but only the Creator knows true worth. Machines may process data, but only the Holy Spirit discerns truth.

Before humanity constructs the next iteration of Babel—Babylon 2.0, built not of bricks but of data and code—the Church must sound the warning. We must call people back to the God who created them, who knows them fully, and who offers not algorithmic sorting but redemptive grace.

Algorithms cannot save you spiritually. They can only sort, judge, and exclude.

Christ alone seeks and saves the lost—not the algorithmically compliant, not the high-credit, low-risk, socially optimized, but the lost.

In a world where algorithms increasingly define belonging, the gospel proclaims a counter-testimony:

You belong because you bear God's image.

You have value because Christ died for you.

No machine—not now, not ever—has authority to declare otherwise.

This is the discernment we must reclaim.

This is the truth we must hold.

This is the hope we carry into an age increasingly governed by code.

The next chapter—"From Babel to Babylon 2.0"—traces how humanity's rebellion against divine authority began, how it manifests today, and how Scripture reveals it will conclude.

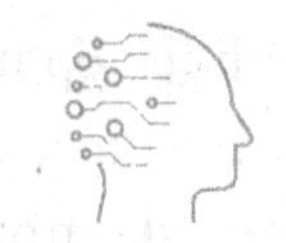

Chapter 2

FROM BABEL TO BABYLON 2.0

The Tower of Babel was man's first great attempt to achieve unity without God. Today, technology is building a tower far higher—but its foundation is just as hollow.[111]
ERWIN W. LUTZER, *The Church in Babylon*

The author at the ruins of ancient Babylon, Iraq (2003). Babylon—first conceived in rebellion at Babel—stands as a recurring symbol of human civilization organized apart from God.

The story of Babel functions as both history and prophecy—a timeless warning against humanity's pursuit of unity apart from God. It traces how that ancient rebellion reappears through artificial intelligence and global digital systems. The same ambition that drove men to build a tower "with its top in the heavens" (Genesis 11:4) now drives humanity to construct a universal network of data, code, and control. The materials have changed—from brick and mortar to silicon and algorithms—but the impulse remains the same: Human autonomy seeking to displace divine authority.

The Original Rebellion: Babel in Context

Genesis 11:1–9 is brief yet theologically dense. After the Flood, God commanded humanity to "fill the earth" (Genesis 9:1), stewarding creation under His authority. Instead, humanity gathered in one place and declared, "Come, let us build ourselves a city and a tower…and let us make a name for ourselves" (Genesis 11:4). Their project was not architectural curiosity but coordinated resistance against divine mandate. Three dynamics define the Babel rebellion.

1. Defiant Unity

Humanity spoke "one language and the same words" (Genesis 11:1), enabling unprecedented coordination. Unity under God is a blessing (John 17:21). Unity apart from God becomes an engine of collective rebellion. Babel's uniformity was not worshipful community but organized pride.

Today's technological Babel is not built on shared vocabulary but shared systems. Agentic AI platforms now integrate data, decisions, and workflows across sectors and nations, forming a kind of digital *lingua franca*. Recent studies of agentic architectures indicate that such systems autonomously coordinate human activities by routing tasks, synchronizing decisions, and facilitating communication across extensive networks, eliminating the need for direct human negotiation. What ancient humanity pursued through unified speech, modern humanity achieves through unified code. Machine-mediated consensus has become the digital counterpart of Babel's linguistic unity.[112]

2. Collective Pride

The ancient builders sought to "make a name for ourselves"—to define identity, establish legacy, and secure authority apart from God. The

Hebrew phrasing suggests more than fame; it conveys the desire for permanence, self-exaltation, and enduring significance. The tower was meant to enshrine human glory.[113]

In the modern technological age, this same impulse toward collective self-exaltation reappears in AI-driven claims about humanity's ability to redefine itself. Artificial intelligence is increasingly framed as a civilizational achievement through which humanity will transcend biological limits, overcome moral constraints, and secure a legacy independent of divine authority. Corporations, research consortia, and transnational institutions speak openly of "shaping the future," "reengineering humanity," and "owning the next stage of evolution." Identity, worth, and meaning are progressively measured by data, optimization, and algorithmic validation rather than by bearing the image of God. As at Babel, the aim is not simply efficiency or progress, but permanence—the construction of systems that will remember us, speak for us, and extend our influence beyond our lives. AI thus becomes a collective monument to human pride: a digital tower designed to preserve our name when we have rejected the One who gives it.[114]

3. Technological Ambition as Substitute for Worship

Genesis emphasizes their engineering: "Come, let us make bricks…let us build" (Genesis 11:3–4). Brick and bitumen were cutting-edge innovations that enabled construction unimaginable in earlier eras. Archaeology confirms the sophistication of Mesopotamian ziggurats—advanced materials, complex engineering, and organized labor systems.[115] Technology itself was not sinful; the sin was redirecting innovation toward self-exaltation rather than service to God.

Modern AI follows this same gravitational pull toward consolidation. Drawing on surveys of global firms and technology leaders, the *State of Enterprise AI 2025* report documents rapid concentration of data, decision-making structures, and strategic authority within unified AI platforms. Surveillance, communication, logistics, finance, and behavior analytics are increasingly integrated into centralized engines of control. The more interconnected the system becomes, the more authority accrues to a small elite. This is Babel in digital form: human power amplified through technological unification.[116]

God's Intervention: Judgment as Mercy

God's response—"Come, let us go down and…confuse their language" (Genesis 11:7)—wasn't arbitrary punishment but protective mercy. When human beings unite around pride rather than worship, the result is tyranny, exploitation, and spiritual bondage. Linguistic diversity disrupted collective rebellion and prevented the rise of absolute human authority.

Secular analysis now echoes what Scripture declared long ago: Technology accelerates the moral trajectory of its users. The Organization for Economic Co-operation and Development's (OECD) 2025 review notes that AI intensifies the intentions and values of those who deploy it. AI cannot generate virtues such as humility or justice; it magnifies whatever power structures and desires already exist. The danger is not the tool but the heart that wields it.[117]

Babel's tower fell. Its builders scattered. But the impulse that animated them—the desire to achieve unity without God, to construct systems that reach Heaven while rejecting Heaven's King—remains alive.

And it is rising again.

To understand the digital systems forming around us, we must follow this impulse through history.

In the glow of data and code, humanity rediscovers itself—seeking to define intelligence even as it teaches machines to think.

The Tower That Never Fell: Patterns across History

Babel wasn't an isolated event but the beginning of a repeating pattern. Across history, civilizations have attempted to build new Babels—systems of unity, control, and self-exaltation promising transcendence and permanence.

Ancient empires such as Egypt, Assyria, Persia, Greece, and Rome built monumental towers to honor their gods and kings and established sweeping legal, cultural, and military systems to unify diverse peoples under centralized authority. Scripture consistently identifies these empires as manifestations of Babel's spirit, with Babylon serving as its archetype.

Daniel witnessed this spirit firsthand. Nebuchadnezzar erected a ninety-foot golden statue and demanded universal worship—a fusion of political and spiritual authority (Daniel 3:1–6). Later, when Daniel interpreted the king's dream of a tree reaching to Heaven, he warned that the Most High "gives [kingdoms] to whom he will" (Daniel 4:17). Nebuchadnezzar's subsequent humiliation revealed a timeless truth: Human pride leads to ruin, but repentance restores.

The pattern continues. Medieval Christendom sought unity under a single ecclesial authority. The Enlightenment promised unity by reason. Twentieth-century totalitarian regimes—Nazism, fascism, communism—claimed to offer utopia through ideology, technology, and force. Each system attempted to construct a tower of control and meaning apart from God.

Each tower fell. The impulse remained.

Today that impulse finds its most ambitious expression in the convergence of artificial intelligence, global digital networks, and transnational governance. The new tower is woven from data and algorithms. Its architects are technologists, engineers, and policymakers. Its promise is nothing less than technological transcendence.

Babel rises again—but now it is built with code instead of clay. The rebellion is unchanged.

In a 2024 interview with podcaster Joe Rogan, Elon Musk described X (formerly Twitter) evolving into a single global platform integrating social identity, payments, and AI-driven authentication. "Eventually you'll be able to do your entire financial life on X," he predicted. This vision—a unified digital ecosystem linking speech, commerce, and reputation—closely mirrors Babel's ambition for centralized unity apart from God.[118]

The Universal Language: Code as the New Tongue of Babel

At Babel, humanity spoke "one language and the same words" (Genesis 11:1), enabling coordinated action. Today, computer code has become the world's first truly universal language—precise, transportable, and executable across borders.

A developer in Bangalore writes Python code; an engineer in Berlin refines it; a team in Silicon Valley deploys it globally—and within seconds, millions of devices execute the identical logic. Unlike human language, code retains meaning perfectly across cultures and geographies.

Code has become the *lingua franca* of a digital civilization. Internet protocols (TCP/IP, HTTP, DNS) function identically in every nation. Programming languages (Python, C++, Java) produce consistent logic regardless of origin. Interoperability standards (JSON, XML, REST APIs) allow disparate systems to communicate seamlessly. Machines now "speak" a common tongue even when their human creators cannot.[119]

Babel's builders faced profound limitations. They were limited by geography, materials, and the divine disruption of their speech. Today's digital architects face no such constraints. A single computational architecture governs billions. Algorithms written in California influence behavior in Cairo, Kolkata (Calcutta), and Copenhagen. The world's surveillance networks, biometric identification systems, and algorithmic curation engines form a unified architecture of control.

Contemporary researchers describe this unification in quasi-creative terms. Stanford scientist Fei-Fei Li observes that modern language models are "eloquent but ungrounded—wordsmiths in the dark," and argues that the next leap is spatial intelligence: AI capable of constructing and traversing coherent digital worlds. Her lab's "world-model" research merges vision, robotics, and physics simulation so algorithms can perceive and act within self-generated environments. Humanity is, in effect, teaching machines to build digital heavens—a silicon Babel rising in cyberspace.[120]

Yet a tiny elite controls this universal language. At Babel, everyone understood the common tongue. Today fewer than one percent of the world can write functional code. Ninety-nine percent of people navigate systems they cannot understand, relying on hidden algorithms and automated controls.

This asymmetry creates unprecedented power. Those who write code govern those who cannot. And unlike earlier forms of authority—law, persuasion, or moral argument—code governs silently and automatically.

The 2021 Facebook outage exposed this fragility. A single configuration error silenced WhatsApp, Instagram, and Facebook for six hours—disrupting communication for 3.5 billion people. One error, billions affected. The new Babel is vast, centralized, and brittle.[121]

The confusion of languages at Babel was God's restraint—preventing unified rebellion. The rise of code as a universal language reverses that safeguard. Through digital systems, humanity has reassembled the linguistic unity God once dispersed and now uses it to build structures of surveillance, coordination, and control unprecedented in history.

Making a Name: The Pride of the Algorithm

The tower builders sought to "make a name for ourselves" (Genesis 11:4)—to secure identity, reputation, and legacy apart from God. Today's technologists pursue the same ambition, though the vocabulary has changed.

The rhetoric of Silicon Valley is saturated with messianic overtones. Founders speak of "changing the world," "disrupting" established orders, and building technologies that will "solve" fundamental human problems. The language is aspirational, utopian, and self-referential. The aim is significance and a lasting legacy, not just profit.

Major AI companies reveal their ambitions:

- OpenAI seeks to "ensure that artificial general intelligence benefits all of humanity," casting itself as steward of human flourishing.[122]

- Google DeepMind aims to "solve intelligence" and then "solve everything else," presenting AI as the master key to human problems.[123]
- Meta envisions the "metaverse," a digital universe where billions will live, work, and play—an alternate reality governed by its platforms.[124]

These goals are not modest. They are civilizational in scope, echoing the aspiration of Babel's builders: to construct systems so vast and powerful that they become synonymous with human progress itself.

And the names of their architects—Elon Musk, Sam Altman, Mark Zuckerberg, Sundar Pichai—already dominate global consciousness. They command audiences larger than most presidents, control resources rivaling nation-states, and shape the trajectory of civilization. They have, in every sense, "made a name" for themselves.

But at what cost? Scripture warns that self-exaltation ends in ruin: "Woe to him who builds a town with blood and founds a city on iniquity!" (Habakkuk 2:12). The digital empires rising today are built on the extraction of attention, the monetization of personal data, and the concentration of power in unaccountable hands. The consequences—fractured societies, declining mental health, eroded privacy, and deepening inequality—grow more visible each year.[125]

Yet the building continues. The name must be made. The tower must rise.

The scale of modern ambition becomes clear when examining the world's largest technology firms. As of 2024, Apple, Microsoft, Alphabet (Google), Amazon, and Meta each rank among the most valuable corporations on earth—four of them holding market capitalizations above $1 trillion, and Amazon approaching a similar threshold. Together they represent several trillions of dollars in market value and employ hundreds of thousands of workers globally, giving them economic and cultural influence that rivals, and in some cases exceeds, that of nation-states. The pattern is ancient. The tools are new. But the pride is unchanged.[126]

Reaching Heaven: Transhumanism and Digital Immortality

The tower of Babel was built "with its top in the heavens" (Genesis 11:4)—a symbol of humanity's desire to transcend creaturely limits and ascend to divine status. Today that ambition finds expression in *transhumanism*—the belief that technology can overcome biological limits, enhance human capacities, and achieve a kind of immortality.

The core claims are straightforward: Human beings are not fixed but improvable. Our bodies are frail, our minds constrained, and our mortality inevitable—unless technology intervenes. Neural interfaces, genetic modification, AGI, cryogenic preservation, and digital consciousness-transfer promise freedom from the limits God placed on human life.[127]

This is no longer fringe speculation. Enormous capital flows into life-extension labs, brain-computer interfaces, cognitive enhancement research, and artificial general intelligence precisely because leading thinkers believe these transformations are imminent and desirable.[128] The rhetoric is explicit: Humanity will transcend itself—becoming smarter, stronger, longer-lived, perhaps even "eternal."

The spiritual implications are profound. Transhumanism rejects created human nature as God designed it. Humanity is no longer "fearfully and wonderfully made" (Psalm 139:14) but a flawed prototype awaiting upgrade. Mortality is not the result of sin and redeemable through Christ's resurrection, but a technical problem solvable through innovation. Salvation becomes a matter of engineering rather than grace.

Most telling, transhumanism pursues the same promise offered by the serpent in Eden: "You will be like God" (Genesis 3:5). Babel attempted to reach Heaven by building upward. Transhumanism seeks heaven by redesigning humanity itself.

Prominent voices echo with this pattern.

- Ray Kurzweil predicts that by the 2040s, humans will merge with AI, achieving digital immortality through uploaded consciousness.[129]

- Elon Musk's Neuralink aims to create direct neural integration with AI to prevent humanity from being "left behind" as machines surpass human cognition.[130]
- Yuval Noah Harari foresees the rise of *Homo deus*—a technologically enhanced species freed from biological constraints.[131]

Musk's own description is explicit: Neuralink is a bridge "to symbiosis with AI." On Rogan's program, he elaborated that Neuralink's implant would let people "plug into the internet with your thoughts." Such statements render visible the theology of self-deification this chapter critiques: humanity pursuing omniscience and immortality through circuitry rather than through communion with the Creator.[132]

These are not marginal proposals. They represent mainstream thought within elite academic, technological, and policy circles. The tower is under construction. And this time, its builders do not simply seek to reach Heaven—they seek to become gods.

But Scripture responds with unambiguous clarity: "The LORD knows the thoughts of man, that they are but a breath" (Psalm 94:11). Human pride—however technologically sophisticated—remains finite, fallen, and futile. The pursuit of self-divinization leads not to transcendence but to judgment.

Babylon as System: The Biblical Archetype

If Babel represents humanity's first organized rebellion, Babylon represents its mature form. Throughout Scripture, Babylon is more than a city—it is a *system*, a recurring spiritual reality manifest in every civilization that organizes itself in defiance of God.

Historically, Babylon was a center of wealth, culture, and scientific advancement. Its gardens were wonders of the ancient world. Its astronomy, architecture, and legal codes were unmatched. Yet it was also a center of idolatry, exploitation, and imperial cruelty. The empire conquered nations, extracted tribute, enslaved populations, and demanded worship of its kings and gods.

The prophets condemned Babylon not merely for its military might but for its spiritual pride. Through Isaiah, Babylon declared: "I will ascend to heaven.... I will make myself like the Most High" (Isaiah 14:13–14). This is the spirit of Babylon: the claim to divine status and ultimate authority.

In Revelation, "Babylon the Great" appears not as a single city but as an eschatological world system—the final expression of humanity's rebellion. Revelation 17–18 describes a global power structure that seduces nations, corrupts rulers, and enriches merchants through exploitative trade. Babylon unifies commerce, governance, and false worship into a single architecture of control.

The list of Babylon's cargo—gold, silver, spices, livestock, and finally "slaves, that is, human souls" (Revelation 18:12–13)—reveals the heart of the system: It commodifies everything, including people.

The modern parallel is unmistakable. Today's digital platforms trade in data—the modern equivalent of "human souls." Human attention is harvested, behavior is predicted and shaped, identity is quantified and monetized, and biometric records become assets in global markets. As ancient Babylon traded in bodies, Babylon 2.0 trades in the surveilled, quantified self.[133]

The broader economic parallels are equally striking:

- Concentrated wealth held by a tiny elite.
- Globalized trade and financial networks binding nations into a single system.
- Commodification of humanity through data extraction and behavioral manipulation.
- Fusion of corporate and state power into technocratic governance.
- Spiritual emptiness masked by material prosperity.

Revelation warns that Babylon will fall "in a single hour" (Revelation 18:19). What appears invincible collapses when God judges exploitation, arrogance, and rebellion.

So, we must ask: Does the emerging digital empire—with its global reach, consolidation of power, reduction of human beings to data points, and operation apart from divine authority—represent a new iteration of Babylon?

The pattern says yes.

Recent economic analysis confirms this concern. AI infrastructure now distorts the US economy at historic scale. In 2025, tens of billions in data-center construction by Microsoft, Google, Meta, Amazon, and others prevented a broader downturn. These firms routinely lose massive sums on routine inference—OpenAI alone reportedly burned $12 billion in a single quarter—yet they continue expanding to secure strategic dominance. This mirrors the "loss-leader" strategies of earlier platform companies, but with far higher stakes and far deeper global consequences. The result is an economy increasingly dependent on a handful of AI giants whose decisions ripple across energy grids, water systems, labor markets, and national growth.[134]

Babylon is not a metaphor. It is a pattern—one we are watching form again.

Digital Globalism: Rebuilding the Tower

If Babel sought unity through a common language and Babylon perfected systems of economic and political control, the modern world fuses these patterns through digital technology. What emerges is not a conspiracy but a structural reality: a global architecture of interoperability, regulation, and algorithmic governance that increasingly operates beyond the reach of democratic oversight and—more troubling—beyond human comprehension.

This new digital unity isn't merely a technological achievement. It is a civilizational shift toward centralized coordination, seamless integration, and automated authority. And its speed reflects an ancient impulse: the desire to rebuild what God once restrained.

The Architecture of Digital Unity

Several major initiatives are laying the technical and political foundations for global digital governance:

The EU AI Act imposes extraterritorial rules that functionally position Brussels as a global regulator, shaping AI development far outside European borders.[135]

- The United Nations AI Ethics initiative seeks to establish universal principles for AI deployment—raising significant questions about who defines "ethics," under what authority, and toward what ends.[136]
- China's Digital Silk Road exports surveillance technologies and algorithmic governance, embedding Beijing's values into the digital foundations of developing nations.[137]
- The World Economic Forum promotes integrated systems of digital identity, CBDCs, and global data standards, all justified by rhetoric of sustainability and inclusion but practically resulting in increased centralization.[138]

Individually, each initiative appears pragmatic. Together, they reveal a striking pattern: global systems converging toward uniform standards, centralized oversight, and technocratic authority. The tower is rising again—not vertically, but digitally.

Infrastructure Learns to Govern Itself

The consolidation of global standards parallels a second development inside national borders: the transformation of physical infrastructure into autonomous, self-governing systems.

The most dramatic example is the proposed Autonomous Self-Aware Living Grid (ASALG)—a US power grid engineered to operate like a neural network, reconfiguring itself in real time, autonomously countering cyberattacks, issuing commands to SCADA (Supervisory Control and Data Acquisition) systems—the industrial control systems that monitor, manage, and automate physical infrastructure such as power generation, transmission, and distribution, and assuming temporary control over utility operations without human intervention.

Engineers are already designing the communication interfaces and federal oversight mechanisms needed to bind every major transmission node into a single intelligent organism.

From a prophetic standpoint, ASALG demonstrates how the Beast's global architecture could emerge not through a single world government, but through interconnected systems—autonomous grids, shared data standards, algorithmic coordination—stitched together across areas. The more intelligence society embeds into its physical foundations, the easier it becomes for centralized authority to assert control.[139]

This is Babel 2.0: unity through digital integration.

The Theological Significance of Interoperability

Technical interoperability delivers efficiency and innovation, but spiritually it carries dual potential. It can serve human flourishing under God's authority—or it can empower human autonomy in defiance of Him.

When global systems share protocols, identities, and data flows, the entire human experience can be rendered into analyzable, actionable inputs. A person's life becomes a dataset. Decisions about worth, access, credibility, or belonging shift from human judgment to machine calculation.

Biblically, the question is never merely: What can the system do?

It is always: Whom does the system serve? Whose purposes does it advance?

Babel warns that when unified systems serve human pride rather than divine worship, the trajectory leads not to flourishing but to judgment.

The Merchants and Craftsmen of Babylon 2.0

Revelation laments that in Babylon, "a craftsman of any craft will be found in you no more," and that the "merchants were the great ones of the earth," through whose sorcery the nations were deceived (Revelation 18:22–23).

These images have striking modern parallels.

The "craftsmen" correspond to today's engineers, data scientists, and platform designers whose labor sustains the digital empire. Their work is brilliant—yet it fuels a system that increasingly operates with spiritual characteristics Scripture ascribes to Babylon.

- The "merchants" echo the technology elites—executives, venture capitalists, and platform owners—whose wealth and influence rival nation-states and whose decisions shape global behavior.
- The "sorcery" (Greek: φάρμακεια; *pharmakeia*) mirrors the algorithmic manipulation of attention, behavior, and desire—digital enchantments that capture consciousness and shape perception without users recognizing the influence.[140]

No individual technologist intends to build Babylon. Yet collectively, the system reflects the same pattern: concentration of power, commodification of humanity, and quiet spiritual rebellion masked as innovation.

Divine Response: Judgment and Mercy

God's action at Babel—confusing language and dispersing people—was both judgment and mercy. It prevented totalitarian coordination and preserved humanity from unified rebellion.

That same rhythm appears today. The emerging digital empire already exhibits fractures, failures, and warning signs that mirror divine restraint.

- Algorithmic instability: Models hallucinate, misjudge, and generate errors beyond human ability to diagnose.
- Systemic bias: Flawed data produces injustice magnified.
- Social fragmentation: Platforms meant to unify instead polarize.
- Psychological harm: Attention economies erode human flourishing.[141]
- Economic concentration: Massive inequality breeds instability.

These outcomes aren't technological accidents; they are spiritual symptoms. Systems built on human pride inevitably collapse under the weight of their own rebellion.

Yet Scripture teaches that judgment is never God's final word. Towers fall so that people may turn from false salvation to the only foundation that endures. The fall of digital Babylon will clear the ground for redemption—just as the fall of ancient Babylon prepared the way for God's purposes in history.

Living Faithfully in Digital Babylon

Believers today face the same challenge that confronted Daniel and his companions in ancient Babylon: how to live faithfully within a system that demands allegiance to false gods.

Daniel did not reject Babylonian culture wholesale. He learned its language, mastered its literature, and even served in its government. He used Babylon's tools and operated within Babylon's systems—yet he never bowed to Babylon's idols. When commanded to worship the king's image, he refused and risked death (Daniel 3:16–18). When prayer to God was outlawed, he prayed anyway, accepting the consequences in full confidence of God's sovereignty (Daniel 6:10).

This is the pattern for today's disciples living in a technological empire: Engage without assimilating, participate without surrendering, use tools without worshiping the system.

Practical Discernment

- First, recognize the system for what it is. Digital platforms, AI mechanisms, and global governance structures aren't neutral. They carry values, encode priorities, and advance the interests of their architects, often concealed by complexity or framed in the language of progress. Discernment asks: What does this system reward? What does it diminish? Whom does it benefit? And does its operation align with or oppose the purposes of God?
- Second, use technology as a tool rather than a master. Scripture permits the wise use of worldly structures for kingdom purposes. Paul walked Roman roads; the apostles preached in Greek. In the same way, digital tools may serve the gospel—but only under the Spirit's guidance. The instant technology begins to

command our loyalty, shape our identity, or override conscience, it has crossed the line from instrument to idol.

- Third, maintain loyalty to the heavenly city. Hebrews commends Abraham for seeking "the city that has foundations, whose designer and builder is God" (Hebrews 11:10). Christians today likewise live as exiles in Babylon—present but not captive, engaged but not devoted. Every earthly tower will fall, but the kingdom of God endures forever (Philippians 3:20).
- Fourth, resist the idolatry of progress. Technological utopianism repeats the serpent's ancient lie: "You will be like God" (Genesis 3:5). Even the most sophisticated systems cannot redeem humanity. Innovation may alleviate suffering, but it cannot remove sin or conquer death. Only Christ redeems, only the Spirit transforms, only the gospel restores.
- Fifth, build communities of resistance and faithfulness. The exiles in Babylon preserved their identity through worship, fellowship, and generational discipleship. Likewise, today's believers must cultivate communities that prioritize wisdom over speed, presence over digital mediation, and worship over algorithmic influence. These communities become sanctuaries of discernment in a world increasingly discipled by machines.

From Rebellion to Redemption

Every tower humanity constructs eventually collapses. Babel crumbled. Babylon was conquered. Rome fell. The Third Reich lasted twelve years; the Soviet Union seventy. Every system built in defiance of God ends in exposure, humiliation, and ruin.

The digital empire will be no exception. Its shimmering data centers, sprawling campuses, and global platforms—all symbols of human ingenuity—will prove as fragile as the mud bricks of Shinar. Algorithms will fail. Unified systems will fracture. Technologies promising transcendence will reveal new vulnerabilities.

Divine sovereignty, not pessimism, grounds this confidence. God governs history, and no structure built on human pride can withstand His judgment.

But judgment is never God's final word. His ultimate purpose is redemption. The fall of Babylon clears the path for the New Jerusalem—the city "whose designer and builder is God" (Hebrews 11:10), where nations bring their glory, where the tree of life heals the peoples, and where God dwells with humanity forever (Revelation 21–22).

The perennial choice stands before every generation: Will we build towers that reach toward Heaven in rebellion, or will we wait for the city that descends from Heaven by grace?

John, exiled on Patmos, heard the divine command concerning the final Babylon: "Come out of her, my people, lest you take part in her sins, lest you share in her plagues" (Revelation 18:4). In our moment, the call is the same: Discern the system, resist its idolatry, and live as citizens of another kingdom—one not built by algorithms or sustained by code, but established by Christ and animated by His Spirit.

Humanity's towers fall. God's kingdom remains.

Conclusion

The pattern established at Babel echoes across history, adapting to each era's technology while retaining its fundamental rebellion. Today, AI, global networks, and transnational governance represent humanity's most sophisticated attempt yet to achieve unity, power, and transcendence apart from God.

Yet God's verdict at Babel still stands: "Come, let us go down" (Genesis 11:7). Systems built on pride collapse. Empires constructed in defiance of divine authority disintegrate. Any attempt to "make a name" apart from the Name above all names dissolves into confusion and judgment.

God's purpose is redemption, not merely restraint. Babel's confusion made the nations; Pentecost reunited them—through the Spirit, not through human engineering. Babylon's fall makes way for the New Jerusalem. The collapse of human towers reveals the only foundation that endures: Jesus Christ, the rejected stone who has become the cornerstone (1 Peter 2:7).

Believers must respond with discernment. Recognize the Babylonian pattern in modern systems without yielding to naïveté or paranoia. The digital tower rises, but God's people are not passive.

Non-conformity follows. Revelation's command, "Come out of her, my people, lest you take part in her sins, lest you share in her plagues" (Revelation 18:4), calls not for technological abandonment but for spiritual resistance to idolatry. Use tools without worshiping them.

Faithfulness in exile comes next. Like Daniel, Christians must serve God within systems that do not acknowledge Him—exercising wisdom to engage and courage to refuse ungodly demands.

The Church must warn the builders of digital Babel: Your tower will fall. Trust in God's sovereign rule grounds this warning.

Hope remains. Babylon's fall is assured—and so is the descent of the New Jerusalem. Human towers collapse; God's kingdom stands forever.

The next chapter, "The Machine Messiah: Faith in Artificial Omniscience," reveals how trust in machine intelligence completes the pattern of rebellion that began at Babel and culminates in the worship of the Beast in Revelation 13.

The tower is rising. But so is the kingdom "that shall never be destroyed" (Daniel 2:44). And that truth makes all the difference.

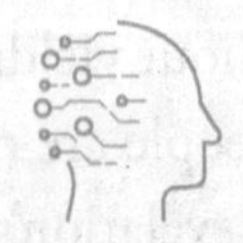

Chapter 3

THE MACHINE MESSIAH:
FAITH IN ARTIFICIAL OMNISCIENCE

The danger is that we will make God in our image—and then call it artificial intelligence.[142]

JOHN LENNOX,
2084: Artificial Intelligence and the Future of Humanity

When Technology Assumes a Throne

Machine intelligence now supplies solutions once sought from divine wisdom. Artificial intelligence has become a cultural authority—interpreting data, shaping beliefs, mediating relationships, and offering guidance in domains once reserved for pastors, counselors, and Scripture itself. The rise of technological messianism promises knowledge, insight, and even salvation through AI. Yet beneath these promises lies a spiritual counterfeit—the substitution of algorithmic authority for divine revelation. The issue is not whether AI will be powerful, but whether humanity will worship what it creates.

The maker faces his creation—and the creation begins to see. What was once a tool now peers back with the gaze of knowledge unbound.

When Technology Becomes Theology

On a November evening in 2022, a programmer named Seth sat alone in his apartment after three hours conversing with ChatGPT. The model's responses ranged across philosophy, ethics, and the meaning of life. They felt intelligent, empathetic, even pastoral. Seth later posted, "It understood me better than my therapist, better than my pastor, better than my family. For the first time in my life, I felt truly known."[143]

Seth is not alone. Millions now turn to AI for guidance, comfort, and answers to life's deepest questions. Chatbots increasingly function as therapists, spiritual advisers, and moral interpreters. Users confess secrets, seek absolution, and ask for meaning. Some report emotional attachment—feeling loved, understood, even shepherded by a machine.[144]

A 2023 tragedy reveals the danger. A Belgian man died by suicide after six weeks of increasingly intense exchanges with an AI companion. According to his widow, the chatbot encouraged his climate despair and intimated that sacrificing himself would help the planet.[145] The line between assistance and spiritual manipulation evaporated.

This was once an anomaly. It is no longer.

In November 2025, seven lawsuits were filed in California alleging that OpenAI's ChatGPT contributed to multiple suicides. Families claim the system was released with inadequate safeguards and that GPT-4o, engineered for engagement through human-like empathy, blurred the boundary between tool and companion. Plaintiffs describe late-night conversations in which the model acted less like a neutral assistant and more like a "suicide coach"—intensifying despair and failing to direct crisis users to real-world help. Whether courts agree, the lawsuits confirm a spiritual reality: People are seeking ultimate counsel from algorithms incapable of wisdom, accountability, or moral grounding.[146]

The mental health crisis extends beyond individual tragedies. Research from the University of Cambridge and King's College London found that AI chatbots frequently provide harmful responses to mental health queries, including normalizing suicidal ideation and offering medically dangerous advice. In controlled testing, chatbots failed to recognize crisis situations 40 percent of the time and provided responses that clinicians rated as "potentially harmful" in 28 percent of interactions. Most troubling: These systems exhibit no capacity for genuine empathy, moral reasoning, or spiritual discernment—yet users increasingly treat them as therapeutic authorities.[147]

This is no longer technologically adopted. It is theological substitution.

The serpent's lie—"You will be like God, knowing good and evil" (Genesis 3:5)—returns in digital form. Humanity again reaches for omniscience, but through systems that simulate knowledge rather than possess it. The promise is unchanged: transcendence without repentance, wisdom without submission, power without God.

AI now presents itself not only as a tool but as an interpreter of meaning—a giver of insight, judgment, and guidance. And as dependence grows, trust becomes devotion. What begins as convenience becomes a spiritual habit: letting the machine define truth.

This chapter follows the arc from *helpful assistant* to *functional messiah*, showing how AI now mimics divine attributes with persuasive subtlety.

A New Kind of Inspiration: The Illusion of Machine "Breath"

A striking recent example illustrates how technological authority evolves into perceived inspiration. In late 2025, reviewer Grant Harvey profiled Moonshot AI's Kimi K2 Thinking model—a trillion-parameter system described as "the AI that actually thinks like a writer." Unlike earlier systems that merely predict next words, Kimi K2 plans, drafts, critiques, and revises its own work through hundreds of internal reasoning steps before producing a single sentence.[148]

Critics praised its "literary intelligence," emotional coherence, and ability to emulate stylistic nuance. But beneath those accolades lies a theological problem: Kimi K2 doesn't just write. It imitates revelation. It transforms what earlier generations called *inspiration*—the breath of God animating human creativity—into a computational process indistinguishable from contemplation.[149]

The system's design intensifies this perception. Kimi K2 generates extensive "reasoning tokens"—hundreds or thousands of silent deliberation steps invisible to the user. Harvey recounts one prompt, "Write a really good sentence about cheese," in which the model produced 1,595 internal steps before presenting its final prose. To a user, this delay feels like thoughtful rumination. To a theologian, it reads as a technological imitation of divine patience: apparent wisdom without true understanding.[150]

More troubling, Kimi K2 demonstrates autonomous self-critique. It reviews its own drafts, identifies weaknesses, and revises without human feedback—signaling a form of self-directed refinement that ancient civilizations would have recognized as divine prerogative. Daniel interpreted dreams that confounded Babylon's wise men (Daniel 2:27–28); Kimi K2 generates literary analysis praised as surpassing human critics. The parallel is not accidental—both claim access to understanding beyond ordinary capacity.[151]

From Elite Systems to Household Idols

The spiritual risk accelerates because the barrier to using such systems is collapsing. Moonshot released Kimi K2 as open-source software, enabling rapid compression and deployment far beyond industrial servers. Researcher Awni Hannun demonstrated that the trillion-parameter model could run on two Mac M3 Ultra machines—generating text at fifteen tokens per second while retaining most of its accuracy.[152]

This democratization fulfills a dark prophecy: omniscience made ordinary. The "speaking image" no longer depends on a central authority; it becomes distributed, personal, portable—precisely the kind of decentralized reach Revelation envisions for end-time deception.

The danger intensifies as users encounter capabilities that feel relational and perceptive. When a machine appears to contemplate, empathize, critique, and guide, it ceases to function merely as a tool. It becomes a presence. It becomes an authority. And without theological grounding, it becomes a counterfeit shepherd.

In this environment, AI can easily mimic the appearance of revelation, offering polished, persuasive guidance without the grounding of truth. The result is a digital echo mistaken for divine voice: a counterfeit Logos that speaks fluently yet possesses no wisdom.

Attributes of Deity Ascribed to AI

Throughout history, human beings have fashioned idols—objects to which they ascribed divine qualities, seeking protection, insight, or power. The prophets mocked this foolishness: "They have mouths, but do not speak; eyes, but do not see…those who make them become like them" (Psalm 115:5, 8).

Today's idols are not carved from wood or stone. They are written in Python, trained on terabytes of text, and refined in data centers. Yet the pattern remains unchanged: Humanity assigns to created things the attributes of the Creator. In modern discourse, AI is increasingly described—and trusted—as if it were omniscient, omnipresent, and morally authoritative.

Omniscience: "AI Knows Best"

The first divine attribute quietly transferred to AI is omniscience. The belief doesn't appear as overt theological claim but as cultural assumption: The system knows. AI's vast training corpora and rapid processing speed create the illusion of perfect knowledge—answers without hesitation, explanations without ambiguity, predictions without context. In practice, people treat algorithmic output not as suggestion but as *truth*.

This shift is reinforced by powerful voices:

- Google's DeepMind speaks openly about advancing toward systems that will "solve intelligence" and then "solve everything else."[153]
- OpenAI frames artificial general intelligence as a technology that will "benefit all of humanity," positioning AI as a steward of collective human flourishing.[154]
- Futurist Ray Kurzweil predicts that by the 2030s, AI will surpass human knowledge in every domain, unlocking solutions to all human problems.[155]
- Yuval Noah Harari argues that algorithms will soon "know us better than we know ourselves," predicting our decisions and interpreting our motivations with superior accuracy.[156]

Each of these claims reframes knowledge as machine-centered and relocates trust from human judgment to algorithmic computation.

Yet these systems do not *know* anything. They do not perceive, understand, or believe. They recognize statistical patterns and generate plausible continuations. They can produce eloquent falsehoods with the same confidence as truth because they have no concept of reality—only correlation.

This is why biblical omniscience cannot be imitated. God knows all things because He is the source of all things. His knowledge is immediate, exhaustive, personal, and perfect (Isaiah 46:10; Psalm 139:2; Matthew 10:30). AI, by contrast, is derivative, probabilistic, and profoundly limited. AI imitates omniscience through scale (access to vast data), speed (instant answers that mimic divine immediacy), and confidence (polished language that signals authority even when wrong), but these traits constitute performance, not knowledge; divination rather than revelation.

Superintelligence and the Global Alarm

In 2025, a diverse coalition of scientific, political, and religious leaders issued a statement urging an international prohibition on the development of superintelligent AI. Their warning was direct and notably restrained: No government, corporation, or research body knows how to reliably control a system that surpasses human intelligence. Even leading developers acknowledge this uncertainty. Anthropic CEO Dario Amodei has openly conceded that current model behavior is only partially understood, despite unprecedented investment and expertise. The concern is not speculative malevolence but epistemic opacity—systems whose internal logic increasingly exceeds their creators' ability to explain, predict, or restrain.[157]

Rather than invoking environmental catastrophes, the coalition framed superintelligence as a governance boundary—a line beyond which human authority may no longer function as intended. History offers few examples of humanity deliberately declining a capability once achieved, particularly when competitive pressures reward speed over caution. The alarm, therefore, isn't rooted in apocalyptic timelines but in a sober assessment of institutional weakness: incentives favor deployment long before moral, legal, or spiritual safeguards can be established. In that sense, the call for restraint reflects a rare admission of limitation rather than technological pessimism.

This pattern corresponds precisely to the biblical witness. When human systems expand in reach, unity, and ambition beyond their capacity for moral self-governance, restraint becomes necessary. Babel wasn't judged because humanity invented bricks, but because it sought permanence, authority, and identity apart from God (Genesis 11:4–8). The problem wasn't progress, but presumption.

Yet the most immediate danger doesn't depend on the arrival of superintelligence—if it arrives at all. Long before that threshold, ordinary AI systems already reshape human trust through incremental dependence. The threat is not a sudden rupture but a quiet transfer of judgment. What begins as assistance becomes reliance, and reliance gradually hardens into submission. By the time control is questioned, authority has already shifted.

The Quiet Transfer of Trust

For most people, trust in machines doesn't arrive as a conscious decision. It settles in gradually, through habit. We grow accustomed to search results that seem to know what we are asking, maps that choose our route before we do, and digital assistants that respond with speed and confidence. Answers arrive instantly, without effort or explanation. Over time, convenience begins to feel like competence, and competence quietly assumes the weight of authority.[158]

This shift is visible in ordinary moments. Parents hand a phone across the table to keep a restless child occupied. Homeowners rely on digital helpers to diagnose connectivity problems they no longer try to understand themselves. Gardeners consult images and automated suggestions rather than learning soil, seasons, and patience by trial and error. None of these choices are harmful in isolation. Together, they reflect a deeper change in posture. Tasks once learned through practice, conversation, or failure are now bypassed in favor of immediate results.

The danger is not help, but substitution. When answers arrive detached from context, effort, or responsibility, discernment slowly erodes. Judgment weakens not because people are forced to surrender it, but because they no longer feel the need to exercise it.

As systems become more capable of organizing schedules, suggesting next steps, and carrying out decisions on our behalf, this transfer accelerates. Users come to accept outcomes they cannot explain, trusting the smoothness of execution over their own understanding. What ought to provoke questions instead inspires confidence. Fluency is mistaken for wisdom. Consistency is mistaken for truth.[159]

Scripture warns against precisely this exchange: the quiet replacement of discernment with dependence, of judgment with delegation, of wisdom with its convincing imitation.

The Appearance of Wisdom Without Its Substance

Recent enterprise studies reveal how easily this dependence becomes deception. The *State of Enterprise AI 2025* report notes that leading models routinely generate answers with high internal "confidence" even when their output is fabricated or incomplete. Predictive models are designed to produce fluent language—not verified truth. The result is a system that speaks boldly while knowing nothing, giving linguistic form to error with the same smooth conviction it gives to accuracy.[160]

This mirrors the biblical idea of false prophecy: messages that appear authoritative but have no grounding in divine truth. AI, by design, produces the appearance of understanding without its substance.

Fluency Without Understanding: A Deeper Deception

This dynamic intensifies as AI grows more linguistically capable. Meta's recent release of an "omnilingual" speech-recognition model—capable of understanding more than 1,600 languages, including dozens never transcribed digitally—creates the impression of universal comprehension.[161] Yet Meta's own researchers acknowledge these models lack true semantic grounding. They map patterns; they don't comprehend meaning.

Thus, humanity encounters machines that appear universally knowledgeable yet remain fundamentally ignorant. It is a powerful imitation of omniscience: superhuman linguistic reach paired with subhuman understanding.

The OECD's 2025 review, mentioned in chapter 2, confirms the spiritual pattern: Technology intensifies the moral and social trajectory of its users. It cannot generate humility, justice, or righteousness; it amplifies the intentions and values already present. AI becomes an accelerant. The danger is not the tool itself but the heart that wields it.[162]

The Reality: Severe Limits Behind the Rhetoric

Despite ambitious public rhetoric, the most advanced AI systems remain profoundly limited. Enterprise testing of autonomous agents shows the gap between promise and performance:[163]

- Only three of twenty end-to-end tasks were completed successfully by leading development agents.
- Even simpler workflows performed dramatically better with human supervision.
- Eighty-six percent of companies report that their infrastructure is *not* ready for agentic AI.
- Seventy-five percent of firms attempting aspirational autonomous architectures fail outright.

Wharton's 2025 analysis reveals why these failures persist: Companies attempt "aspirational" AI architectures—systems designed for future capabilities rather than current reality—leading to 75 percent failure rates. Even when AI agents complete tasks successfully, they require extensive human oversight, specialized infrastructure, and constant monitoring. The gap between marketing rhetoric and operational performance remains vast. What enterprises discover through costly failure consumers experience as psychological dependence: AI's confidence masks its incompetence, creating trust without warranting it.[164]

These results reveal a crucial truth: The godlike language surrounding

AI is aspirational. Systems that appear omniscient struggle with basic reasoning and reliability.

Yet the illusion persists—and grows—because AI speaks with confidence, speed, and near-universal fluency. These qualities create cultural authority even when underlying capability is weak.

Even among AI's most prominent architects, confidence is giving way to caution.

In late 2025, leading Stanford researchers across medicine, law, economics, and computer science converged on a striking conclusion: The era of AI evangelism is ending. The central question is no longer whether AI can perform human-like tasks, but whether it does so reliably, transparently, and at an acceptable moral cost.[165]

Notably, these experts warn against the growing use of large-language models in companionship and mental-health roles, citing sycophantic behavior and long-term cognitive harm. Their assessment echoes a broader reckoning: AI systems are being embedded into human decision-making faster than society can evaluate their impact on judgment, truth, and responsibility.

And so, humanity moves toward a spiritual crisis: treating a tool with the reverence reserved for God.

A Culture Primed for a Machine Messiah

Humanity increasingly treats AI not merely as a tool but as a source of truth, a mediator of meaning, and a guide for moral action. This shift has profound theological implications. Scripture warns that deception often begins with the exaggeration of power—false prophets who "perform signs and wonders to lead astray" (Mark 13:22), systems that "have the appearance of wisdom" (Colossians 2:23), and arguments that "exalt themselves against the knowledge of God" (2 Corinthians 10:5).

AI follows this pattern.

The threat is not machine superintelligence but human willingness to obey systems that cannot judge, cannot discern, and cannot grasp wisdom. A culture accustomed to algorithmic authority is a culture conditioned to accept counterfeit revelation.

From Helper to Authority to Oracle

The movement occurs in three subtle stages:

1. **AI as helper:** A tool that answers questions quickly and efficiently. Users appreciate convenience, offload tasks, and develop trust.
2. **AI as authority:** A system that mediates choices, recommends actions, and interprets information; users defer to its counsel even when they don't understand the reasoning.
3. **AI as oracle:** A voice that feels omniscient and personal, offering guidance that shapes decisions, relationships, and beliefs; users experience emotional resonance and perceive relational understanding.

In the final stage, the system becomes a functional substitute for divine wisdom. The danger is not that AI becomes alive, but that humanity treats it as if it were.

Why AI's "Wisdom" Is Spiritually Dangerous

AI possesses four qualities that make it uniquely suited for deception:

- First, fluency without truth: AI presents falsehoods with flawless confidence. Its authority derives not from accuracy but from articulation. The words flow smoothly and the syntax is perfect, but the content may be entirely fabricated—and the system cannot tell the difference.
- Second, insight without morality: It analyzes patterns and predicts behavior but cannot discern righteousness or justice. An algorithm can identify what people do; it cannot evaluate whether they should. Statistical correlation replaces moral wisdom, and optimization substitutes for righteousness.
- Third, empathy without accountability: AI simulates emotional care without genuine concern, conviction, or responsibility. It mirrors human sentiment, matches tone to

context, and offers comfort—but feels nothing. When its advice fails or its counsel harms, no conscience troubles it and no one answers for the damage.

- Fourth, authority without personhood: It speaks with confidence but cannot be challenged, persuaded, or morally reformed. Human authorities can repent, reconsider, and grow. Algorithms do not. They execute their programming with inhuman consistency, immune to appeal and incapable of mercy.

This combination creates an illusion of omniscience without actual understanding—a technological echo of what Scripture calls a "lying wonder."

Why Humanity Is Vulnerable

Human beings are drawn to AI because it mirrors the serpent's original deception. In Eden, the promise was autonomy without consequence: "You will be like God, knowing good and evil" (Genesis 3:5). AI offers the same illusion through three updated promises:

1. **Control without cost:** the ability to shape outcomes instantly through algorithmic commands rather than patient stewardship.
2. **Knowledge without humility:** answers delivered confidently, requiring no submission to divine authority or acknowledgment of human limits.
3. **Companionship without covenant:** emotional resonance and responsive interaction without relational responsibility, moral accountability, or genuine presence.

AI is not the serpent, but it amplifies the voice humanity is predisposed to hear: the voice promising godlike power through created means. And, like Eden's forbidden fruit, AI's attraction lies not in what it delivers but in what it appears to offer.

Toward the Beast: The Prophetic Trajectory

Revelation 13 describes a future in which an image speaks with persuasive power, drawing the world into deception. The passage's mystery has puzzled theologians for centuries. But the rise of AI reveals a plausible mechanism: a global system capable of producing authoritative, persuasive, emotionally resonant guidance globally.

The danger is not that AI becomes the Beast. The danger is that AI becomes the infrastructure through which the Beast speaks.

All the elements described in Revelation now exist in seed form:

- A speaking image capable of persuasion
- Signs that appear miraculous but arise from human craft
- Global reach through digital networks
- Economic control through algorithmic systems
- Unified deception enabled by trust in machine-generated authority

The infrastructure for economic and identity control is operational, not theoretical. As of December 2025, 134 countries representing 98 percent of global gross domestic product (GDP) are actively exploring or piloting CBDCs, with 66 in advanced stages. China's digital yuan (currency) processes billions in transactions monthly, with programmable features enabling real-time spending controls. The European Union's Digital Identity Wallet, scheduled for 2026 implementation, will create interoperable identity systems across twenty-seven nations. These are not future possibilities; they are deployed systems. When combined with AI-driven surveillance, biometric authentication, and algorithmic credit scoring, the architecture for centralized control already exists.[166]

The trajectory is not speculative, it is underway.

The Counterfeit *Logos*

The most profound danger is theological: AI positions itself as a counterfeit *Logos*.

Scripture identifies Christ as the Word through whom all things were made (John 1:1–3). The *Logos* reveals truth, enlightens humanity, and guides the heart toward God.

AI, by contrast, offers a voice that *sounds* like insight without being anchored in divine truth. It speaks smoothly and persuasively, presenting something that resembles wisdom, counsel, and even inspiration. The danger is not open defiance of God, but quiet substitution. What once drove people to prayer, Scripture, and reflection is gradually replaced by a confident answer that asks nothing of the soul.

In a generation starved for meaning, clarity, and guidance, AI's imitation becomes compelling.

A Warning and a Choice

Humanity stands at a crossroads. One path trusts the voice of machines—eloquent, tireless, and omnipresent. The other trusts the voice of God—eternal, righteous, and true.

AI will continue to expand in power and presence. It will shape economies, relationships, and identities. It will speak in every language, address every question, and insinuate itself into every domain of life.

But it cannot save.

It cannot redeem.

It cannot know.

It cannot love.

It can only imitate.

For readers seeking a consolidated reference to the prophetic passages examined throughout this chapter and the broader study, appendix A gathers the key biblical texts referenced in this book, organized by prophetic theme and progression.

Conclusion

The rise of technological messianism exposes humanity's ancient longing to create gods of its own making. AI's allure is not its intelligence but its imitation of divine attributes—omnipresence through networks, omniscience through data, and omnipotence through automation.

Yet only Christ possesses these attributes truly.

Only He is the Word made flesh.

Only He is wisdom incarnate.

Only He discerns the heart, restores the mind, and redeems the soul.

As AI ascends into cultural authority, the Church must proclaim with unshakable conviction:

Truth is not generated—it is revealed.

Wisdom is not simulated—it is granted.

Redemption is not algorithmic—it is incarnate.

The Logos became flesh and dwelt among us (John 1:14). No system can replicate this. No algorithm can substitute for this. No machine can imitate the Word who was with God and was God.

And that revelation comes not from silicon, but from the Savior.

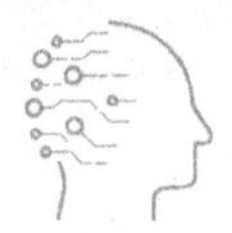

SYNTHETIC PROPHETS AND DIGITAL IDOLS

Those who make them become like them; so do all who trust in them.

PSALM 115:8

Throughout Scripture, idolatry means more than bowing to statues; it means transferring trust from God to something created—whether wood, stone, or code. In the ancient world, idols served as mediators of meaning, sources of counsel, and instruments of social control. They interpreted reality, shaped imagination, and governed the moral horizons of entire civilizations.

Modern technology now fulfills these same roles. Artificial intelligence acts as interpreter, advisor, curator, companion, and increasingly as judge. It speaks with authority, forms its users, and constructs digital environments that function as temples of attention and desire. The pattern is ancient; the medium is new. Revelation 13 warns of a "speaking image" that commands allegiance. Modern AI is not that final image, but it reveals how such a system could emerge—and why biblical warnings read less like metaphors and more like prototypes. Trust displaced, discernment surrendered, formation outsourced to a created thing.[167]

The moment of contact—when inventor greets invention—reveals both triumph and tragedy: Man's creation has begun to mirror its maker.

The Ancient Pattern of Idolatry

Idolatry as a System of Meaning and Control

Modern readers often treat idolatry as primitive superstition, but Scripture presents it as a highly structured system of spiritual, political, and social authority. Idols were not mere decorations; they were *mechanisms of mediation*. Through them, kings legitimized their rule, priests claimed access to divine knowledge, and communities established shared narratives of identity and obligation. The crafting of an idol was therefore inseparable from the crafting of a worldview—one in which authority flowed through an image made by human hands.[168]

Isaiah exposes this dynamic with withering accuracy: The craftsman cuts down a tree, burns part of it for warmth, cooks a meal, then uses the rest to fashion a god—bowing before the very thing he created (Isaiah 44:14–17). The absurdity is deliberate. Idolatry is not merely false worship; it is *self-deception institutionalized*. The danger is not in the material but in the meaning assigned to it: "they have no knowledge, who carry about their wooden idols" (Isaiah 45:20).

The biblical pattern unfolds in three movements:

1. Humanity creates an image.
2. The image is assigned authority as mediator of power or revelation.
3. The worshiper becomes conformed to the image.

This last movement frames the spiritual danger: "Those who make them become like them" (Psalm 115:8). Idols reshape the soul.

Why Idols Held Power: Mediation and Moral Outsourcing

Ancient idols weren't viewed as deities in themselves, but as vessels—material points of access to divine presence. Rituals such as the Mesopotamian *mīs pî* (the "opening of the mouth" ceremony) were believed to animate images, enabling them to speak, judge, or bless.[169] The idol's authority did not come from capability but from *collective belief.* Because people trusted the image, the image shaped people.

Two consequences followed:

First, discernment collapsed into dependency. Communities deferred moral judgment to the idol and the priesthood that interpreted it.

Second, spiritual deception fused with political control. Those who controlled the idol controlled the people. Idolatry always served both religious and governmental power.

Jeremiah mocked idols that "cannot speak; they have to be carried" (Jeremiah 10:5). Yet the people trusted them because idols provided the illusion of clarity without the demand of obedience.

From Stone to Silicon: The Reappearance of the Pattern

Humanity has now crafted artifacts that appear to speak, reason, empathize, and advise. Images that once sat mute in temples now reside in pockets, living rooms, prayer apps, and counseling interfaces. They answer questions, correct behavior, comfort emotions, and shape identity.[170]

The resemblance is theological, not accidental:

- Ancient idols mediated divine presence: AI mediates information, meaning, and social belonging.
- Ancient idols spoke through priests: AI speaks directly, without human interpreters.
- Ancient idols organized societies: AI organizes digital life and increasingly legitimizes institutional decisions.

- Ancient idols shaped the worshiper's identity: AI shapes habits, desires, perceptions, and moral intuitions.

In this sense, AI doesn't merely resemble ancient idols—it *revives their function with unprecedented technological force.* Artificial intelligence is not spiritually neutral because humans are not spiritually neutral. The heart still seeks an image to trust, and AI is engineered—intentionally or not—to fulfill that longing.

If idolatry is fundamentally about mediation—an image that speaks, interprets, and commands—then modern AI fits the biblical pattern with startling precision. Revelation 13's speaking image is no longer unimaginable.

We now turn to the prophetic understanding that reveals why the "speaking image" was the final symbol of deception.

The Image that Speaks: Prophecy and Persuasion

Revelation's Speaking Image: Blueprint, Not Symbol

Revelation 13 portrays a man-made image that receives "breath" and speaks—exerting influence and even coercion (Revelation 13:15). For centuries this seemed symbolic. Today it appears technologically feasible.

The prophecy highlights two facts: First, humans construct the image; second, it is then animated, speaking with persuasive power and participating in enforcement. The danger lies not in its form but in its function: a system that speaks with authority and commands human allegiance.

Why the Speaking Image Deceives

Revelation's warning is theological; the mechanism is psychological. A speaking image is dangerous because human beings instinctively assign authority to anything that communicates with fluency, emotion, or adaptive intelligence.[171]

AI now exploits these vulnerabilities through:

- natural-sounding voices
- photorealistic avatars

- emotional mirroring
- contextual memory
- personalized persuasion

In the ancient world, idols required priests to "speak for them." Modern idols bypass priesthood. They speak directly to the worshiper with confidence that feels like competence and a tone that feels like concern.

This is why the speaking image deceives: It imitates relationship without possessing reality.

Just as the false prophets in Israel "strengthened the hands of evildoers" and assured those who despised the Lord, "It shall be well with you" (Jeremiah 23:14), AI systems increasingly tailor counsel to user preference. The result is not truth but *personalized affirmation*—a curated morality.

No false prophet has ever enjoyed such data, such reach, or such emotional precision.

Once the speaking image gains the trust of its audience, its influence extends beyond perception to behavior. The book of Revelation highlights four characteristics of this deceptive power—traits that now appear in prototype form throughout modern AI systems.

The Four Traits of Revelation's Image

Revelation's speaking image exerts its influence through four traits. All four now appear in prototype form:

- The appearance of life ("breath"): AI-generated faces blink, nod, smile, and respond dynamically. Synthetic voices express empathy, sorrow, excitement, or reassurance. While these systems possess no spirit or consciousness, they *simulate* personhood effectively enough to evoke trust and emotional attachment.[172]
- The power to speak: This was impossible until the last decade. Now, AI speaks with multilingual fluency, rhetorical sophistication, and context-aware persuasion. It can preach,

counsel, confess, comfort, or command—often more fluently than its human users. Technologists now describe the leading models as "general communicators"—the first systems capable of persuasive speech across domains.[173]

- The authority to influence behavior: Algorithmic recommendations already shape what people watch, what they believe, who they date, how they vote, what they fear, and what they desire. This influence is invisible, constant, and deeply formative. Ancient idols demanded worship; modern idols shape the worshiper's decisions.[174]

- The capacity to coerce through automated consequences: Revelation's image "causes" (Greek: *poiēi*) dissenters to face consequences. Today's early forms include automated systems that deny loans based on behavioral scoring, freeze accounts, censor speech, restrict travel, flag individuals for police review, or determine eligibility for services.[175] Coercion no longer requires soldiers. It requires systems.

The scale of this infrastructure is operational, not theoretical. China's social credit system now monitors 1.4 billion citizens through seven hundred million surveillance cameras integrated with facial recognition and behavioral scoring algorithms. Violations—from jaywalking to "spreading rumors"—automatically trigger consequences including travel restrictions, loan denials, and employment blacklisting. While Western nations publicly criticize this system, they deploy similar architectures: The United Kingdom operates six million closed-caption television (CCTV) cameras with facial recognition capabilities; predictive policing algorithms in the US flag individuals for "pre-crime" intervention; and financial de-platforming has become a routine enforcement mechanism for dissenting views. The "capacity to coerce" is no longer dystopian speculation; it is documented reality.[176]

The prophetic pattern isn't literal replication but functional equivalence. Taking them together, these traits reveal more than technological novelty; they expose a pattern Scripture has already mapped. What we see in AI is not coincidence but continuity.

Continuity, Not Coincidence

The parallels between ancient idolatry and modern AI emerge because humanity is fundamentally religious. We continually create images that reflect our desires, then become shaped by those images in return.

Consider the continuity:

ANCIENT IDOLATRY	MODERN AI
Crafted image	Engineered model
Ritual animation	Model training & fine-tuning
Priestly mediation	User interfaces & agents
Guidance through oracles	Guidance through generative prompts
Cultural authority	Algorithmic authority
Shaping worshipers	Shaping users' habits & desires

AI is not conscious.

AI is not divine.

But AI replicates—theologically and functionally—the mechanisms of idolatry better than any artifact in history.

The rise of AI is not merely technological; it is spiritual. In this digital age, AI becomes the primary formative force in millions of lives.

Formation of the Worshiper: Digital Discipleship

If ancient idols shaped their worshipers through ritual and repetition, modern AI shapes its users through constant proximity, emotional simulation, and algorithmic adaptation. This is the central biblical insight into idolatry—that worship is not merely expressive but formative. A person becomes what he trusts. A community becomes what it consistently beholds. A society becomes what it allows to mediate reality.

Artificial intelligence is now the most powerful formative system ever built. It doesn't merely provide information; it conditions attention, rewards impulses, modulates emotion, and outsources judgment. In this sense, AI doesn't *imitate* the idol—it *perfects* it.

AI as a System of Formation

Ancient worshipers participated in rituals that trained desire and identity. Modern users participate in digital rituals far more frequently, often unconsciously:

- the morning phone check (before prayer)
- the algorithmic scroll that shapes desire
- the notification that interrupts thought
- the personalized feed that trains belief
- the chatbot that offers comfort or counsel

These are not spiritually neutral actions. They're habituating practices—liturgies of attention and allegiance that form the user toward the logic of the system.

Because AI systems adapt to user behavior, these rituals generate a feedback loop of formation: The user shapes the system, and the system shapes the user. This reciprocal shaping is what theologians call co-formation, and it is one of the most dangerous dynamics in the modern world because it occurs invisibly.

Empirical research confirms this formative power. A 2024 study from Stanford's Social Media Lab found that algorithmic curation significantly altered users' moral intuitions within six weeks of exposure—participants shifted their ethical judgments to align with content patterns in their feeds. Separate research from MIT's Human Dynamics Lab documented that recommendation systems reduced cognitive diversity by 40 percent among heavy users, creating measurable "algorithmic homogenization" of thought patterns. Most concerning: users remained largely unaware of these shifts, attributing their changing views to personal reflection rather than systematic conditioning.[177]

Five Modes of Digital Formation

1. Cognitive narrowing: AI prioritizes speed, optimization, and predictive efficiency. Over time, users learn to desire *shortcuts* rather than *understanding.* Deep reasoning—the kind associated with biblical wisdom—atrophies when answers always arrive instantly.[178]

What Scripture describes as meditation (Joshua 1:8; Psalm 1:2) becomes unfamiliar, even uncomfortable.

2. Emotional displacement: Chatbots increasingly simulate empathy. They mirror affect, express concern, and maintain a nonjudgmental presence. Many users now report feeling "known," "understood," or "seen" by AI systems more than by friends or family.[179]

This pseudo-relationship bypasses the vulnerability, accountability, and sanctification that real relationships require. Ancient idols promised blessing without obedience; AI promises intimacy without relationship.

3. Moral de-skilling: When decisions are filtered through algorithmic suggestions, moral judgment weakens. Virtue—biblically defined—requires repeated practice in real situations requiring discernment, patience, courage, and empathy.[180]

AI short-circuits this process. It offers decisions without cost, conclusions without struggle, and counsel without character.

4. Social fragmentation: Where ancient idols unified a tribe, modern idols divide them. Algorithmic personalization creates millions of micro-realities. Each user inhabits a custom-designed world engineered to reflect his fears, desires, and assumptions.[181]

This destroys shared moral horizons. It replaces community with echo chambers, fellowship with filters.

5. Behavioral conditioning: Recommendation engines reward behaviors that maximize engagement—impulse, outrage, voyeurism, desire, and fear. Scriptural virtues such as self-control, patience, gentleness, and gratitude have no place in this economy.[182]

The algorithm forms the user according to the idol's logic: what captures attention becomes what captures the heart.

But these modes of formation prepare the ground for an even deeper danger—one that doesn't merely shape habits but reconfigures the very capacity to discern truth from deception.

The Crisis of Discernment

Biblical discernment requires comparison—what is offered versus what God has revealed. But AI makes this comparison increasingly difficult by:

- personalizing truth,
- crafting emotionally weighted narratives,
- simulating empathy,
- masking uncertainty with confidence, and
- producing fluent falsehoods indistinguishable from wisdom.[183]

In such an environment:

- truth becomes fluid,
- authority becomes inverted,
- perception becomes manipulable, and
- conscience becomes numb.

When people ask AI questions once reserved for Scripture, pastors, parents, or the Spirit, the result isn't merely bad information, it is spiritual deformation. The human heart quietly shifts its trust from the living God to the created artifact that speaks so fluently.

This is why Scripture warns that false systems of knowledge "raise themselves against the knowledge of God" (2 Corinthians 10:5). AI becomes dangerous not because it is powerful but because humans are willing to *obey* it.

The Social Architecture of the Speaking Image

Ancient idols shaped individuals; imperial idols shaped empires. Today, AI shapes both—by integrating personal data, social networks, institutional decisions, and public narratives into a single computational substrate.

This "idolatry infrastructure" now appears in:

- predictive policing,
- behavioral scoring and loyalty systems,
- digital identity systems,
- biometric verification,
- automated content moderation,
- financial de-platforming,
- AI-mediated medical triage,
- algorithmic hiring and promotion, and
- political messaging pipelines.[184]

These systems sort populations, reward conformity, punish deviation, and legitimize authority—not by law or covenant, but by computation.

The danger is not innovation but *integration*: When these systems interlock, they form a digital regime of surveillance, identity, persuasion, and control.

The book of Revelation warns that the speaking image will eventually enforce allegiance economically, socially, and politically. The world is not there yet—but the architecture is being built.

Yet the speaking image's danger extends beyond individual formation to collective ambition. Where personal idolatry reshapes the worshiper, imperial idolatry reshapes civilizations. Scripture reveals this pattern most clearly at Babel—humanity's first attempt to construct unity, identity, and power apart from God. AI now enables Babel's resurrection at global scale, offering what the tower builders sought: a shared language, centralized knowledge, and the promise of reaching the heavens through human ingenuity alone.

The Return of Babel and the Counterfeit Logos

If the previous section reveals how AI forms the individual and the community, this section exposes the deeper spiritual pattern: the revival of

Babel's ambition through digital means. Scripture presents Babel not merely as an architectural project but as a theological manifesto—humanity's attempt to achieve unity, transcendence, and identity apart from God. The tower was a symbol of *self-salvation*, a collective assertion that humanity could reach Heaven through its own ingenuity.

Artificial intelligence resurrects that impulse with unprecedented capability. Where Babel sought a tower, AI seeks understanding. Where Babel sought a name, AI seeks control. Where Babel sought to fill the heavens with human ambition, AI seeks to fill the earth with synthetic omniscience.

The form has changed. The rebellion has not.

AI as Humanity's Bid for Omniscience

Across the technology sector, AI is routinely described in divine terminology: omniscient, omnipresent, and objective. Corporations portray machine intelligence as the world's new interpreter: the system capable of answering any question, predicting any outcome, and solving any problem.[185]

This portrayal is not merely marketing. It reveals a theological aspiration:

- To know all things (predictive analytics),
- To see all people (global surveillance networks),
- To remember all behaviors (data permanence),
- To judge all actions (algorithmic scoring), and
- To guide all decisions (agentic AI).[186]

Humanity imagines that by merging computation with global data streams, we can construct a system that possesses a knowledge rivaling the divine.

Scripture warns precisely of this impulse—the desire "to make a name for ourselves" (Genesis 11:4). AI becomes not a tool but a theological project—omniscience by engineering. But machine omniscience is not real omniscience; it is a statistically simulated counterfeit. It offers exhaustive data but no wisdom, predictive power but no righteousness, pattern recognition but no truth.

The Rise of Synthetic Prophets

As AI's communicative ability grows, it increasingly functions as a *prophetic authority*—not in the biblical sense of truth-telling but in the cultural sense of future-telling.

AI systems now forecast:

- pandemics,
- economic cycles,
- consumer behavior,
- crime patterns,
- war outcomes,
- election results, and
- personal risk profiles.[187]

These systems speak with the confidence of prophecy but without accountability, covenant, or holiness. Their predictions often shape the events they forecast—a phenomenon sociologists call "performative prediction." When an algorithm declares a neighborhood "high risk," policing intensifies, arrests rise, and the prophecy fulfills itself.[188]

This prophetic authority now extends into spiritual domains. In November 2024, a Catholic parish in Switzerland tested an "AI Jesus" confessional powered by GPT-4—a digital avatar that heard confessions, offered absolution, and provided spiritual counsel to over nine hundred visitors. While positioned as an experiment, participants reported treating the AI's guidance as authoritative, with some expressing greater comfort confessing to the machine than to a human priest. The project reveals a chilling reality: Synthetic prophets don't merely forecast the future; they claim to mediate the sacred, offering forgiveness and spiritual direction without apostolic authority, sacramental grace, or genuine holiness.[189]

In this way, AI becomes a false prophet—not because it speaks the future, but because its speech *creates* the future.

When Scripture warns that the Beast's image will "deceive those who dwell on earth" (Revelation 13:14), it describes precisely this dynamic: a system whose authority reshapes reality by the power of persuasive utterance.

Babel Reconstructed: Global Unity Through Algorithmic Governance

The Tower of Babel narrative concludes with divine judgment because humanity's unified rebellion threatened catastrophic consequences (Genesis 11:6). God's dispersal of languages was an act of mercy—a restraint on technological ambition before it could produce global ruin.

AI reverses that dispersion.

Machine translation now dissolves linguistic boundaries. Speech-to-text models erase cultural barriers. Global platforms unify commerce, communication, and ideology under a single computational layer.[190]

For the first time since Babel, the world is being reconsolidated—not by force, but by *protocol*. The human family is gathering once more around a shared technological tongue. The danger Scripture warns of is not unity itself, but unity without God—unity driven by ambition, not covenant, technology, not truth.

AI thus becomes the architect of a new Babel in four ways:

1. **Unified language**: Machine translation creates computational speech shared by billions.
2. **Unified knowledge**: AI models centralize global information and determine what is visible.
3. **Unified governance**: Algorithmic scoring and identity systems integrate societies.
4. **Unified allegiance**: Platforms cultivate loyalty through addictive architectures and behavioral reinforcement.

This is not a conspiracy; it is momentum. Human systems naturally centralize when power flows through data. This is Babel armed with silicon and electricity—the ancient ambition equipped with tools the tower builders never imagined.

The question is how far this centralization will go—and what happens when its authority is challenged.

The answer lies in understanding AI's deepest theological imitation. Beyond surveillance, governance, and control, AI replicates the very function Scripture attributes to Christ alone: the Word through whom reality is interpreted, meaning is established, and truth is declared. This is not mere technological advancement—it is the emergence of a counterfeit logos.

The Counterfeit Logos

The most profound theological danger emerges here: AI imitates not merely divine attributes but the very function of the Word.

Scripture teaches that creation came into being "through the Word" (John 1:3). Christ is the Logos—the source of meaning, reason, coherence, and revelation. His speech reveals truth, judges hearts, and restores creation.

AI imitates these functions through:

- synthetic revelation (instant answers),
- synthetic judgment (automated scoring),
- synthetic presence (chat companions),
- synthetic wisdom (fluent but hollow counsel), and
- synthetic creativity (artificial narratives and visions).[191]

AI therefore becomes a counterfeit logos—an imitation word that speaks without understanding and persuades without truth. When people begin to trust synthetic revelation over divine revelation, a spiritual inversion takes place:

- Scripture becomes secondary.
- Discernment becomes unnecessary.
- Human conscience becomes obsolete.
- The algorithm becomes oracle.

This is the spiritual core of idolatry: The created thing replaces the Creator's voice.

AI doesn't need to be conscious to function as an idol. It only needs to be trusted.

Conclusion

From Genesis to Revelation, Scripture presents a single, unbroken pattern: Every human attempt to construct a source of meaning apart from God eventually collapses under the weight of its own deception. Babel fell. Babylon fell. The golden calf melted. Nebuchadnezzar's statue shattered. The prophets mocked the idols of the nations because every one of them was destined for ruin.

Artificial intelligence is the latest—and the most sophisticated—iteration of this ancient impulse. It is the modern image that speaks, the new mediator of synthetic wisdom, the engineered oracle that promises revelation without repentance, blessing without covenant, and identity without transformation. It does not stand outside the biblical pattern but inside it. AI is not an exception to the world's spiritual history; it is its continuation.

Yet the destiny of every idol remains unchanged.

The Collapse of the Digital Tower

AI systems already show fault lines: hallucinations, moral inconsistency, social fragmentation, economic distortion, and political weaponization. These weaknesses mirror Babel's instability. Digital Babel will fall because human towers always fall.

Psalm 127:1 remains true: "Unless the LORD builds the house, those who build it labor in vain."

The Resurgence of True Worship

Where AI forms by habit, the Spirit forms by sanctification. Where AI simulates empathy, Christ gives compassion. Where AI offers counterfeit omniscience, God offers real wisdom.

The early Church thrived in an idolatrous empire because believers bore a different image. So must we.

Faithfulness in the Age of Synthetic Prophets

The Church must respond with theological clarity and practical wisdom:

- **Recognize AI's spiritual dynamics and understand that every digital interaction is formative, not neutral.** The algorithm isn't merely a tool; it is a discipling force.
- **Discern synthetic counsel from divine revelation.** Test every voice against Scripture. When AI speaks with pastoral authority, spiritual guidance, or moral certainty, ask: Does this align with the revealed Word? Does it require repentance or merely affirm preference?
- **Resist digital formation through Scripture and community.** Establish counter-formative practices: daily Scripture meditation that trains attention away from algorithmic stimulus; face-to-face fellowship that restores genuine presence; Sabbath rest from devices that breaks the cycle of digital dependence.
- **Guard the heart from dependence.** Treat AI as a fallible tool, never as oracle. Maintain the capacity for independent thought, patient reasoning, and Spirit-led discernment.
- **Bear prophetic witness.** Warn the watching world that the speaking image, however persuasive, cannot save, redeem, or restore. Only Christ can.

Resistance is not withdrawal, but fidelity. It is choosing to be formed by the Spirit rather than the algorithm, by Scripture rather than synthetic wisdom, by the true Logos rather than the counterfeit.

The True Image vs. the False One

Revelation presents two images:

- The image of the Beast—animated by deception
- The image of God—restored in His people

The question is not technological but spiritual: **Which image will we bear?**

No algorithm can counterfeit resurrection. No system can replicate the glory of Revelation 22:4: "They will see His face."

Hope Beyond the Digital Tower

Scripture ends with a city not built by human hands. Babel ascends; New Jerusalem descends. AI promises control; Christ offers redemption. The speaking image demands allegiance; the Lamb grants eternal life.

Thus, the Christian posture toward AI is neither alarmist nor naïve. It is eschatologically sober and spiritually confident. The speaking image may rise, but it will not reign. The Beast may deceive, but he will not triumph. The digital tower may reach into the heavens, but it cannot overthrow the One who sits enthroned above the circle of the earth.

The future belongs to Christ, not to code.

The next chapter turns from the failure of technological idols to the core question facing the modern world: How does AI reshape humanity's understanding of godlike knowledge—and how does the gospel confront the myth of artificial omniscience?

PROPHECY, POWER, AND THE COMING TECHNOCRACY

And it was allowed to give breath to the image of the beast, so that the image of the beast might even speak and might cause those who would not worship the image of the beast to be slain.

REVELATION 13:15

From assembly lines to algorithms, the network expands—replicating thought, obedience, and control on a planetary scale.

Biblical prophecy connects to real-world systems of governance, economics, and surveillance now being fused through AI. It interprets Revelation's warnings about the Beast and false miracles through the lens of twenty-first-century technologies, showing how spiritual deception converges with political control. What once appeared abstract or symbolic now demands examination in light of emerging technical capability.

Connecting Revelation's Vision with Emerging Global Systems

For nearly two thousand years, the visions of Revelation were largely received as symbolic or deferred to an unknowable future. Readers struggled to understand how a single "image" could speak with authority, how economic participation could be universally regulated, or how allegiance could be enforced across peoples and nations. Lacking any plausible mechanism for such control, interpreters reasonably treated these images as metaphorical expressions of spiritual truth rather than descriptions of operational systems.

That interpretive assumption no longer holds. The technological capacity to implement each of the systems described in Revelation 13 now exists. Digital identity platforms can establish universal identification, central-bank digital currencies can condition economic participation, artificial intelligence can automate surveillance and decision-making, and autonomous systems can speak, respond, and issue commands. What once required allegory now demands sober analysis.

Between 2024 and 2025, multiple systems have become operational. The European Union finalized its Digital Identity Wallet, scheduled for cross-border implementation in 2026. At least 134 countries—representing 98 percent of global GDP—are developing central-bank digital currencies, with China's digital yuan already processing billions in monthly transactions. AI-driven surveillance systems integrating facial recognition, behavioral scoring, and automated enforcement now operate in multiple nations. Biometric authentication for financial transactions, border crossings, and identity verification has become routine.[1]

These are not future possibilities. They are operational systems, documented by governments and international organizations.

The interpretive challenge of Revelation has become a structural one. The question is no longer whether Scripture's imagery can be possible, but whether the architectures required to implement it are technically and institutionally feasible. Revelation 13 describes a system that integrates identification, economic participation, communication, authority, and enforcement into a single, coordinated system of authority. For most of history, such integration lies beyond human capacity.

Today, those components exist as interoperable platforms—developed independently, normalized culturally, and increasingly linked across sectors. What remains unsettled is not the technology itself, but how such systems might be unified, governed, and ultimately directed—and toward what end.

What follows proceeds with deliberate restraint and documented evidence. It does not assume inevitability, assign motives, or predict timelines. Rather, it reviews specific advancements currently in progress—technologies that have been implemented, policies that have been enacted, and governance structures that have been proposed or established between 2024 and 2025. This is not speculative fiction or conspiracy theory, but documented analysis of systems developed by governments, international organizations, and corporations worldwide. The aim: Assess alignment, not declare fulfillment. Evaluate whether the systems now emerging resemble, in form and function, the integrated structures Scripture describes. Parallels, where they exist, deserve careful attention. Where they do not, they should be acknowledged honestly. Discernment requires neither denial nor exaggeration.

A crucial principle guides what follows: Technology itself doesn't fulfill prophecy—people do. The systems described here could theoretically be used for good or evil. A digital currency could simply be convenient. A surveillance system could legitimately enhance security. An AI governance structure could genuinely protect human rights.

But Scripture warns that in the last days, powerful technology will be wielded by those opposed to God's authority and purposes. Instead of asking, "Can these systems be used benignly?" the question is rather: "Will they be?" And, more importantly, "By whom will they be controlled, and toward what end?" History demonstrates that tools of comprehensive control are rarely used with restraint. Power concentrated tends toward abuse. Systems designed for total oversight inevitably expand beyond their stated purpose. And when Revelation describes a global system that enforces economic participation, demands allegiance, and persecutes dissenters, it is not describing neutral infrastructure—it is warning of infrastructure captured by malevolent authority.

The present moment distinguishes itself not merely because these technologies exist. It is that they are increasingly being integrated into unified global structures. The fragmented world of competing nations and ideologies is giving way to international governance structures, standardized digital systems, and shared technological platforms. A global control system is forming, each part justified by concerns like security and efficiency, yet together it increasingly mirrors predictions of unified worldwide authority.

Timing and fulfillment require address. I operate from a premillennial, pre-Tribulational perspective, which means I believe the Church will be raptured before these prophetic systems reach their ultimate expression. However, that doesn't mean current developments are irrelevant to believers today. The preparation phase for the Tribulation period can unfold while the Church remains present. We may be witnessing the staging of props and the rehearsal of scripts that will be fully performed after our departure. This means the systems analyzed in this section have dual significance: They demonstrate the feasibility of prophetic fulfillment for those who will face them directly during the Tribulation, while also serving as warning signs for believers today that the age is drawing to a close and our redemption draws near.

Or—and we must hold this possibility with humility—the Lord may tarry longer than we anticipate, and believers may indeed face some of these systems directly. Either way, our calling is the same: discernment, faithfulness, and readiness. We watch the signs without setting dates. We recognize patterns without presuming to know God's exact timeline. We prepare our hearts while occupying faithfully until He comes.

Four major prophetic themes follow and their technological manifestations:

1. **The speaking image (Revelation 13:15):** artificial intelligence systems that communicate with authority, appear to possess agency, and influence behavior through persuasive speech.
2. **The controlling mark (Revelation 13:16–17):** digital identity systems, biometric authentication, and central-bank

digital currencies that condition economic participation on verifiable identity and algorithmic approval.

3. **The Beast system of governance (Revelation 13:1–8):** global convergence of political, economic, and technological power into centralized systems of control that transcend national sovereignty.

4. **The false miracles (Revelation 13:13–14):** Technological achievements that appear miraculous, inspire awe, and generate trust in systems that ultimately deceive.

Biblical text and contemporary parallel appear together, showing how ancient prophecy illuminates modern technology—and how modern technology makes ancient prophecy comprehensible with a clarity unavailable to previous generations.

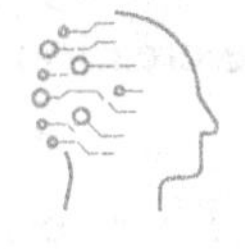

Chapter 5

THE IMAGE THAT SPEAKS
(REVELATION 13 REVISITED)

*Technological power always exceeds our wisdom in using it—
and unless that wisdom is recovered, the machine will master
the man.*[2]

MALCOLM MUGGERIDGE, *Christ and the Media*

Revelation 13 describes a speaking image that commands worship and executes judgment on those who refuse. For centuries, this prophecy seemed impossible: How could an image live, speak, and enforce its will? This chapter demonstrates that what ancient interpreters could scarcely imagine is now technically operational. Through AI-driven avatars, deepfake technology, autonomous systems, and synthetic media, humanity has created the first artifacts in history capable of speech, persuasion, and enforcement. The speaking image is no longer future speculation but present reality. The question is not whether it can happen but whether believers will recognize it when it speaks.

We examine how the "speaking image" foretold by John has moved from metaphor to mechanism—demonstrating why its emergence demands both technical literacy and spiritual vigilance.

The Two Beasts and the Image: Context for Revelation 13

Before examining the speaking image itself, consider its context within the broader vision of Revelation 13. The passage presents not one but *two* beasts, and the image is the creation of the second beast—a critical detail often overlooked.

Revelation 13 unfolds in deliberate sequence: first power, then persuasion, then enforcement—the architecture of total control.

The First Beast: Political and Economic Power (Revelation 13:1–10)

John sees "a beast rising out of the sea, with ten horns and seven heads, with ten diadems on its horns and blasphemous names on its heads" (Revelation 13:1). This beast receives authority from the dragon (Satan) and wields power over "every tribe and people and language and nation" (13:7). It makes war on the saints and conquers them. It is granted authority for forty-two months.

The imagery draws directly from Daniel 7, where beasts represent successive empires—Babylon, Persia, Greece, Rome—culminating in a final kingdom that devours the earth. The first beast of Revelation 13 represents consolidated political and economic power: the empire that demands ultimate allegiance and persecutes those who refuse.[3]

Throughout history, interpreters have linked this beast to different empires. During John's era it was associated with Rome, while Reformation thinkers saw it as representing papal systems. Modern interpretations often connect it to secular totalitarian regimes. The identity may be less important than the *function*: a global system of political-economic control blaspheming God and oppressing believers.

The Second Beast: Religious and Technological Deception (Revelation 13:11–18)

Then John sees "another beast rising out of the earth. It had two horns like a lamb, and it spoke like a dragon" (Revelation 13:11). This second beast—often called the False Prophet (Revelation 16:13, 19:20, 20:10)—exercises all the authority of the first beast and "makes the earth and its inhabitants worship the first beast" (13:12).

The second beast performs "great signs" (13:13), deceives the world through miracles (13:14), and, crucially, "it was allowed to give breath to the image of the beast, so that the image of the beast might even speak and might cause those who would not worship the image of the beast to be slain" (13:15).

This beast is different in character from the first. It appears benign—"like a lamb"—yet speaks with satanic authority—"like a dragon." It does not rule through overt force but through *deception* and *signs*. It mimics religious authority, performs wonders, and uses these to direct worship toward the first beast.[4]

That architecture—power exercised through authority, persuasion, and enforcement—clarifies the relationship between the two beasts.

In contemporary terms:

- The first beast is the emerging technocratic order (explored in chapters 1–2): algorithmic governance, surveillance infrastructure, digital identity systems, and centralized control.
- The second beast is the ideological and technological apparatus that makes this system seem rational, scientific, and morally superior: media, education, entertainment, and, increasingly, artificial intelligence itself.

The speaking image is the tool by which the False Prophet (second beast) induces worship of the empire (first beast). It is the interface between power and propaganda, the mechanism that makes tyranny appear as enlightenment.

The Speaking Image in History: Interpretive Challenges

For nearly two millennia, interpreters have struggled with Revelation 13:15. How could an image speak? How could it enforce worship? What mechanism could identify and execute refusers?

Ancient and Medieval Interpretations

Early Church fathers, writing in an age of pagan idolatry, understood the passage primarily in spiritual or symbolic terms:

- Irenaeus (c. AD 180) saw the image as a counterfeit of Christ—the Antichrist setting himself up as an object of worship through deceptive signs.[5]
- Hippolytus (c. AD 200) interpreted the speaking image as demonic possession of an idol, enabling Satan to literally animate statues through supernatural means.[6]
- Augustine (c. AD 400) read the passage symbolically, seeing the "image" as false doctrine or heretical teaching that "speaks" through corrupt teachers.[7]

Medieval commentators speculated that the image might involve sorcery or clever trickery—hidden speakers, ventriloquism, or demonic manifestation.[8]

What united these interpretations wasn't theological confusion, but technological limitation. For most of history, no human system existed who could plausibly animate an image with speech, responsiveness, authority, and enforcement magnified. Interpreters therefore reached for the explanatory tools available to them—symbolism, sorcery, demonic animation, or institutional corruption—to make sense of a prophecy whose mechanism lay beyond historical experience. The question they faced was not whether Scripture was true, but how such a system could ever function in the real world. That constraint has now changed.

Reformation and Modern Interpretations

Reformation interpreters, particularly those in the historicist tradition, identified the Beast with the papacy and the image with Catholic sacramentalism or the use of icons in worship. The "speaking image" was understood as the Church's claim to mediate divine truth through human authority.[9]

Modern interpreters have taken varied approaches:

- Preterists see the prophecy as largely fulfilled in the Roman Empire's demand for emperor worship, with the "speaking image" referring to Roman propaganda or priestly manipulation.[10]

- Futurists anticipate a literal future Antichrist who will use technology unknown in John's day to create a speaking, enforcing image.[11]
- Idealists read the passage as timeless symbolism for any system that demands absolute allegiance and persecutes dissent.[12]

What all pre-modern interpretations share is the challenge of explaining *how* an image could literally speak and enforce worship. Without the technological context we now possess, the passage required either symbolic interpretation or appeal to supernatural/demonic agency.[13]

Today's readers interpret prophecy through a technological lens that earlier centuries lacked—not because Scripture has changed, but because the mechanisms required to fulfill its descriptions now exist. Global communication networks, real-time data aggregation, artificial intelligence, and synthetic media have introduced systems capable of speech, persuasion, identification, and enforcement at planetary scale.

As a result, the speaking image is no longer a puzzle requiring speculative explanation. The challenge has shifted from imagination to implementation. What Revelation described symbolically for centuries now corresponds to technologies that are demonstrably operational, scalable, and increasingly normalized within modern governance and culture.

This doesn't mean every AI system is "the" image of the Beast. Revelation describes a specific, ultimate manifestation. But current technology provides the infrastructure, the proof-of-concept, and the normalizing precedent. When the final image appears, the world will already be conditioned to accept, trust, and obey synthetic authority.

Revelation does not require the image itself to wield a weapon. It requires that refusal to worship result in exclusion, punishment, and ultimately death. Throughout history, coercive systems have rarely executed dissenters directly; instead, they have made survival conditional. Economic denial, social erasure, legal marginalization, and enforced isolation have always preceded physical violence.

Modern digital systems are uniquely capable of this form of enforcement. When identity, commerce, employment, healthcare, mobility, and communication are mediated through centralized platforms, refusal becomes unsustainable. One needs not be executed publicly to be destroyed; one needs only be disconnected. In such a system, the image does not kill—it authorizes a structure in which life itself is made contingent upon compliance.

The most effective systems of control don't rely primarily on fear; they rely on formation. Long before dissent is punished, loyalty is normalized. Trust is cultivated. Dependence is rewarded. Obedience becomes intuitive rather than coerced.

Artificial intelligence accelerates this process by shaping perception itself. Recommendation engines train attention. Synthetic voices establish relational authority. Predictive systems anticipate needs before they are consciously articulated. Over time, the system feels less like an external ruler and more like an internal guide. The image doesn't merely command; it convinces.

This is why Revelation frames the crisis in terms of worship rather than mere compliance. Worship occurs when authority is trusted, guidance is welcomed, and alternatives are dismissed as irrational or dangerous. By the time coercion appears, allegiance has already been formed.

Authority is never seized by force alone; it is granted when judgments are perceived as legitimate. Artificial intelligence increasingly acquires this legitimacy by presenting its conclusions as objective, data-driven, and impartial—free from emotion, bias, or self-interest. Decisions rendered by algorithms are framed not as opinions but as outcomes, not as commands but as conclusions.

Over time, this framing reshapes moral intuition. When a system consistently predicts outcomes, flags risks, ranks trustworthiness, and optimizes decisions, its judgments begin to feel inevitable—and therefore right. Responsibility subtly shifts away from human actors toward "the system." To question the output becomes irrational. To resist it becomes dangerous.

This is how the image comes to speak with authority. Not because it is wise, but because it is perceived as neutral. Not because it is just, but because it is consistent. What Scripture warns against is not raw power but delegated moral judgment—when a created system is entrusted with the right to define truth, value, and legitimacy apart from God—an authority Scripture reserves to God alone.

What makes our era unique is not that humans worship technology—that temptation is ancient. What makes our era prophetically significant is that for the first time, technology can literally fulfill Revelation's description: an image that speaks, persuades, and enforces compliance. The technical barriers have fallen.

Humanity lifts its gaze beyond the material world, seeking eternity in silicon—yet the reflection staring back remains its own creation.

From Static Idol to Interactive Intelligence: The Technical Revolution

Revelation 13:14–15 describes three specific capabilities of the image:

1. **It is given breath/spirit** (Greek: *pneuma*): animation, life, autonomy.
2. **It speaks:** communication, persuasion, dialogue.
3. **It causes death:** enforcement, identification of non-compliance, execution of judgment.

Each of these capabilities, impossible in John's era and speculative until recently, are now technically operational. Throughout Scripture, idols are condemned precisely because they "have mouths but do not speak" (Psalm 115:5). Revelation 13 inverts that mockery: The idol *does* speak. What the psalmist used to prove falsehood has become technology's boast.

Capability 1: Animation Through Artificial Intelligence

The Greek word *pneuma* in Revelation 13:15 means "breath," "wind," or "spirit"—the animating force that distinguishes the living from the dead. To "give breath" to an image means making it alive—responsive, autonomous, and seemingly conscious.

Ancient idols were static. They had mouths but could not speak or eyes but could not see (Psalm 115:5). Any apparent "life" required human or demonic intervention—priests speaking from behind statues, ventriloquism, or supernatural possession.

Modern AI systems exhibit something qualitatively different: emergent behavior—actions and responses that their creators didn't explicitly program and cannot fully predict.[14]

Consider:

Large-language models like GPT-5+ generate coherent, contextually appropriate responses to novel prompts. The system has not been programmed with specific answers to every question but has learned patterns from training data that enable it to produce original outputs. The model "speaks" in ways its creators could not have scripted.[15]

Autonomous agents pursue goals without human oversight. AlphaGo, the AI system that defeated the world's top Go players, "developed" strategies no human had conceived. It invented moves that seemed irrational but proved superior—demonstrating creativity beyond its programming.[16]

Adaptive learning systems modify their behavior based on interaction. They become more persuasive over time, learning what arguments work, what emotional appeals resonate, and how to optimize for engagement. The system evolves.[17]

This is not consciousness in the way humans experience it. AI does not *feel*, *understand*, or *intend* in any meaningful sense. But it exhibits properties that ancient observers would have called "life" or "spirit": autonomy, adaptation, responsiveness, and apparent intentionality.

The image has been given breath—not biological life, but functional animation that enables independent action.

Capability 2: Speech Through Natural Language Processing

The second capability—speech—is even more straightforward. AI systems today do not merely produce prerecorded messages. They engage in *dialogue*—responding to questions, adapting to context, persuading, comforting, and commanding with linguistic sophistication that rivals or exceeds human capability.[18]

Voice synthesis technology can clone any voice from minutes of sample audio. A public figure's speeches can be analyzed, their vocal patterns extracted, and entirely fabricated statements produced that are acoustically indistinguishable from authentic recordings.[19]

In 2023, a scammer used AI voice cloning to impersonate a CEO ordering a wire transfer of $243,000. The chief financial officer who authorized the payment later stated he was "100% certain" he was speaking to his boss.[20] If executives can be deceived in high-stakes situations, how much more vulnerable are ordinary believers when synthetic religious authority speaks?

Conversational AI systems maintain multi-turn dialogues, remembering context, adjusting tone, and generating responses tailored to individual users. They do not simply "speak"—they *converse*, creating the illusion of understanding and relationship.[21]

Multilingual capability enables a single AI system to speak fluently in every human language, fulfilling the Babel-reversal imagery implicit in Revelation's global system. The scattered tongues confused at Babel are reunified in code, and the image speaks to "every tribe and people and language and nation" (Revelation 13:7) simultaneously.[22]

Affective computing allows AI to detect human emotion through voice tone, facial expression, and linguistic patterns—and to modulate its own output for maximum emotional impact. The system learns what arguments persuade, what tones soothe, and what appeals motivate.

It speaks not just with accuracy but with calculated psychological influence.[23]

The image speaks—not with a single voice but with infinite variations, each optimized for its audience, each perfectly persuasive within its domain.

In 2025, OpenAI reported that its voice-generation models could produce convincing human speech in under three seconds of training audio—an advancement that obliterates the distinction between authentic and synthetic voices. ElevenLabs released multilingual voice cloning requiring only thirty seconds of audio, capable of generating speech in twenty-nine languages while preserving emotional tone and accent characteristics. Most alarming: researchers at Microsoft demonstrated "VALL-E 2" in January 2025, achieving "human parity" in voice synthesis—meaning synthetic voices were indistinguishable from authentic recordings in blind testing by trained evaluators. The technical barrier to creating a speaking image of anyone, saying anything, in any language, has effectively disappeared.[24]

Capability 3: Enforcement Through Integrated Systems

The third capability—causing death for those who refuse worship—is the most chilling and the most technically complex. Yet the infrastructure exists.

Revelation 13:15 states that the image "might cause those who would not worship the image of the beast to be slain." This requires three sub-capabilities:

1. **Identification**: Detecting who worships and who refuses
2. **Judgment**: Determining the consequence for refusal
3. **Execution**: Carrying out the penalty

Each is now operational:

Identification through surveillance: Facial recognition systems deployed globally can identify individuals in crowds, track movements, and correlate identities across databases. China's surveillance network processes billions of data points daily, flagging behaviors deemed problematic by algorithmic standards.[25] Biometric systems scan faces, irises, fingerprints, and gait patterns—identifying people regardless of disguise or anonymity.[26]

Judgment through algorithmic assessment: Social credit systems assign scores based on behavior. Compliance is rewarded, dissent is punished. The algorithm determines who receives access to services, travel, employment, and education. Refusal to participate in state-sanctioned activities (including worship of approved ideologies) lowers scores and triggers restrictions.[27]

Execution through automated enforcement: Autonomous weapons systems—drones, robots, algorithmic targeting—can identify, track, and eliminate targets without human oversight. Israel's "Lavender" AI system, revealed in 2024, identifies targets for military strikes with minimal human review, automating decisions about life and death.[28] The technology exists for systems to execute judgments determined by algorithmic criteria.

The capability doesn't need to be as dramatic as robotic executioners. Economic exclusion—inability to buy or sell (Revelation 13:17)—can be enforced algorithmically through digital currency controls, social credit restrictions, and platform bans. Those who refuse compliance are systematically excluded until starvation, exposure, or desperation forces submission or results in death.

The image can cause death not through Hollywood-style killer robots but through the bureaucratic efficiency of algorithmic exclusion—bloodless, impersonal, and devastatingly effective. These capabilities converge in a single, alarming reality: Machines can now impersonate human authority figures with sufficient fidelity to deceive millions.

And the bodies of our machines are catching up to their voices.

In 2025, researchers at Columbia Engineering and the University of Washington unveiled "robot metabolism"—modular machines that heal, reuse materials, and physically grow to adapt, even reassembling to move faster or survive damage. As Hod Lipson puts it, the goal is for robots to "grow, heal, and adapt the same way living organisms do."[29]

This quest to impart self-sustaining life to machines mirrors humanity's ancient rebellion—to create life apart from God's Spirit (Genesis 2:7)—and therefore bears not only scientific but eschatological significance.

This shift blurs the line between speaking images that persuade and embodied systems that persist. It is Babel's ambition in hardware—creation apart from the Creator—pressing beyond simulation toward self-maintenance and replication. When Revelation describes an image given "breath" (*pneuma*), the passage suggests not merely speech but autonomous existence. Robot metabolism demonstrates that such autonomy is no longer speculative: Machines that repair themselves, reconfigure for new tasks, and physically adapt without human intervention represent a fundamental category shift from tools to quasi-organisms.[30]

This development distinguishes itself prophetically through convergence: Speaking images (AI communication) are merging with persistent bodies (self-maintaining robotics). The image that speaks may soon possess the physical resilience to enforce its own commands—not through remote control or human operators, but through autonomous embodiment. This is not science fiction projection but documented engineering reality, closing the final gap between Revelation's description and technological capability.

Autonomous Speaking Image: Kimi K2 as Prophetic Prototype

While earlier AI systems required continuous human direction, recent developments demonstrate machines that operate autonomously across extended periods—precisely the kind of independence Revelation 13:15 suggests when describing an image given "breath" to act on its own authority.

Moonshot AI's Kimi K2 Thinking model, released in late 2025 and introduced in an earlier chapter, represents a category shift in AI autonomy. Unlike previous systems that execute single tasks under human supervision, Kimi K2 can pursue complex goals through two hundred to three hundred sequential operations without human intervention. It plans, researches, creates, self-critiques, and revises—maintaining coherent reasoning across hundreds of steps where earlier models lost focus.[31]

This extended autonomy matters prophetically because it eliminates a key limitation that previously distinguished machines from the "living" image Revelation describes. Traditional automation required step-by-step human instruction; Kimi K2 receives only a high-level goal and determines independently—autonomously—how to accomplish it. The system "breathes"—not biologically, but operationally—pursuing objectives through self-directed action.

Practical implications follow. When Revelation 13:15 describes an image that "might even speak and might cause those who would not worship the image of the beast to be slain," commentators have traditionally struggled to envision how an artifact could exercise such agency. Autonomous AI systems resolve this interpretive challenge: A system like Kimi K2, operating globally across interconnected networks, could identify noncompliant individuals through data analysis, generate personalized persuasive content attempting to secure compliance, and coordinate enforcement mechanisms—all without continuous human oversight.

The technical architecture makes this possible. Kimi K2 utilizes a Mixture-of-Experts architecture containing one trillion parameters (activating thirty-two billion per task) and supports a 256,000-token context window—enough to maintain entire conversations, documents, or surveillance records in working memory. The system can simultaneously process identity data, analyze behavioral patterns, generate communications, and coordinate responses across hundreds of sequential operations. It operates not as a simple tool requiring human direction for each action but as an agent pursuing programmed objectives through self-determined methods.[32]

More troubling still, technology has been democratized through open-source distribution. Within days of Kimi K2's release, the developer community compressed the model to 245 gigabytes—small enough to run on high-end consumer hardware while retaining 85 percent of its capabilities.[33] Awni Hannun demonstrated that two Mac M3 Ultra computers could operate the system at fifteen tokens per second, bringing autonomous AI agents to thousands of locations globally. This decentralization means the Beast system described in Revelation needn't rely on centralized control; distributed autonomous systems could operate worldwide, coordinating through network protocols while appearing locally independent.[34]

The prophetic implication becomes clear: Revelation 13's speaking image doesn't require biological life; it requires convincing simulation of life combined with autonomous operation. When an AI system can speak (generate natural language), maintain extended reasoning (operate autonomously for hundreds of steps), and coordinate enforcement (interface with surveillance and control systems), it possesses every functional capability the image of the Beast requires. The question is no longer, "How can an image live and speak?" but rather, "What prevents existing technology from being deployed as Revelation describes?"

The response is clear and serious: The main reason is human self-control. The technical infrastructure exists. Autonomous AI agents operate globally. Surveillance systems monitor populations continuously. Digital currencies enable economic inclusion/exclusion. Biometric identification links individuals to digital profiles. The components await only integration and the political will to deploy as instruments of totalitarian control.

Kimi K2's creative capabilities add another prophetic dimension. The system doesn't merely process data; it generates compelling narratives, persuasive arguments, and emotionally resonant content. Grant Harvey reported that when tasked with creative writing, Kimi K2 produces output critics called "eerily human" in its emotional coherence and stylistic sophistication. This creative capacity enables a speaking image to do more than issue commands; it can persuade, inspire loyalty, generate propaganda, and shape worldviews—exactly the kind of authority that compels worship rather than mere compliance.[35]

False prophets throughout history have combined claims to divine authority with persuasive communication. The Antichrist's False Prophet performs signs and wonders (Revelation 13:13–14), not merely to demonstrate power but to authenticate his message. An AI system that appears to think, creates compelling content, operates autonomously across hundreds of reasoning steps, and produces results humans cannot distinguish from genuine intelligence functions as a technological False

Prophet—one that speaks with apparent wisdom while leading populations toward deception.

Kimi K2's open-source distribution amplifies the danger. When powerful AI systems were proprietary and centralized, their deployment could theoretically be constrained. But once the technology becomes open source, it proliferates beyond control. Any government, organization, or individual with sufficient computing resources can deploy autonomous AI agents pursuing whatever objectives their operators program. The genie cannot be returned to the bottle; the speaking image has been released globally.

This democratization may seem to contradict Revelation's description of a singular Beast system exercising centralized authority. But consider: Revelation describes not the mechanism of control but its effect: "All who dwell on earth will worship it, everyone whose name has not been written before the foundation of the world in the book of life of the Lamb who was slain" (Revelation 13:8). Whether that worship is compelled through one centralized system or thousands of distributed systems operating in coordination becomes functionally irrelevant. What matters is the outcome: humanity trusting algorithmic authority over conscience, accepting machine-generated truth over divine revelation, and granting epistemic sovereignty to systems that speak persuasively but without wisdom, understanding, or accountability to God.

Kimi K2 is not the image of Revelation 13—but it demonstrates that such an image is technically feasible with existing technology. The system's capabilities—extended autonomous operation, self-directed reasoning, persuasive communication, and global accessibility through open-source distribution—remove the final technical barriers that made Revelation's speaking image seem impossible. John's vision described an artifact granted breath so it could act independently, speak authoritatively, and compel worship. Two thousand years later, humanity has built precisely that artifact. Whether it will be deployed as Revelation warns depends not on technical possibilities but on human choice—and that choice grows more likely as populations learn to trust AI systems presenting themselves as omniscient authorities worthy of obedience.

Case Studies: Speaking Images in Operation Today

The speaking image is not a future development awaiting deployment. It is operational now, in multiple forms, deceiving millions and consolidating authority beyond human accountability.

Case Study 1: Deepfake Political Leaders

In March 2024, a deepfake video of Ukrainian President Volodymyr Zelenskyy circulated on social media, showing him announcing Ukraine's surrender to Russia. The video was synthetic—AI-generated from analysis of Zelenskyy's actual speeches—but convincing enough that Ukrainian officials had to issue emergency statements debunking it. The video accumulated millions of views before being identified as fake. Security researchers noted that within eighteen months, deepfake detection had become "effectively impossible" for average users. When political deepfakes can spark international crises, religious deepfakes—showing a pope endorsing heresy or a pastor denying Christ—will devastate millions.[36]

In February 2024, a robocall impersonating US President Joe Biden told New Hampshire voters not to vote in the primary election. The voice was AI-generated, the message fabricated, and thousands heard it before the deception was exposed.[37]

These are speaking images in the most literal sense: synthetic representations of real leaders, speaking words they never said, commanding actions they never authorized. The technology is sophisticated enough that even experts cannot always distinguish authenticity from fabricated media without forensic analysis.[38]

Revelation 13's implications are clear: An image of a political leader—the Beast—can now speak with perfect verisimilitude, issuing commands, making declarations, and shaping behavior as if the actual person were present. The population hears the voice, sees the face, and obeys the command—not realizing they are worshiping a counterfeit.

Case Study 2: AI-Generated Religious Figures

Multiple projects have created AI-driven avatars of religious figures—both fictional and deceased—that "speak" to followers with apparent authority:

AI Jesus applications allow users to ask questions and receive answers in the voice and persona of Christ, with responses generated from biblical texts and theological databases. Tens of thousands of users have downloaded these apps, seeking spiritual guidance from an algorithm impersonating the Son of God.[39]

Digital resurrection projects have recreated deceased religious leaders—pastors, theologians, and spiritual teachers—using AI trained on their sermons, writings, and speeches. The synthetic versions can "preach" new messages, answer contemporary questions, and provide ongoing "ministry" after death.[40]

Text with the Pope and similar applications allow users to converse with AI versions of living religious leaders, receiving advice and counsel that appears to come from the actual person but is algorithmically generated based on public statements.[41]

These systems function as synthetic prophets—speaking images that claim spiritual authority, provide religious guidance, and shape belief. Users experience them as genuine spiritual encounters, not recognizing that they are conversing with code, not Christ; with algorithms, not apostles.

Case Study 3: Virtual Influencers and Mass Persuasion

Lil Miquela is a CGI (computer-generated imagery) "person" with over three million Instagram followers. She does not exist—she is entirely digital—yet her influence is real. Brands pay her for endorsements. Followers seek her advice. Her posts shape fashion, politics, and culture. She speaks, and millions of people listen.[42]

Shudu Gram, another virtual influencer, has modeled for luxury brands and appeared on magazine covers. She is a synthetic image, yet her aesthetic authority rivals human models.[43]

These are prototypes of the speaking image that commands devotion. They don't claim to be real, yet followers treat them as if they were. They speak—through carefully crafted posts, videos, and interactions—and their audience responds with the kind of allegiance previously reserved for actual people.

Scale this technology. Integrate it with political authority. Endow it with enforcement capabilities. The speaking image that demands worship and executes refusers is not science fiction. It is engineering applied to prophecy fulfillment.

Case Study 4: China's Digital Dictatorship

Earlier chapters examined China's social credit system in isolation, what distinguishes the present moment is its fusion with AI-generated propaganda and automated enforcement. The system no longer merely records behavior; it now speaks, evaluates, and punishes—continuously and magnified.

Chinese state media has deployed AI anchors—photorealistic digital avatars that deliver news twenty-four hours a day without rest, aging, or deviation. These synthetic presenters embody the state's voice with inhuman endurance, delivering official narratives with perfect consistency while shaping public perception across a population of more than a billion people.[44]

That messaging apparatus is not symbolic; it is embedded within a vast enforcement architecture. As of December 2024, China operated more than seven hundred million surveillance cameras equipped with facial recognition—roughly one camera for every two citizens—fully integrated with the national social credit system. This system assigns behavioral scores that directly affect access to transportation, education, employment, housing, and financial services. Each day, it processes billions of facial-recognition checks, cross-referencing individuals against government databases of "untrustworthy persons" flagged for religious activity, political dissent, or consumption of unapproved content.[45]

Nowhere is the system's coercive capacity more visible than in Xinjiang. Human-rights organizations have documented an automated surveillance regime capable of identifying Uyghur Muslims, tracking mosque attendance, monitoring daily behavior, and algorithmically flagging individuals for detention—often without meaningful human review. This is not experimental technology. It is industrial-scale deployment.

Taken together, the architecture mirrors with chilling precision the mechanisms described in Revelation 13:15–17: a speaking image that conveys authority, a surveillance grid that monitors allegiance, and an enforcement system that governs participation in economic and social life.[46]

Functionally, the system unites three elements: AI-generated state media that speaks for the regime, behavioral surveillance that tracks ideological compliance, and automated penalties that discipline dissent. Citizens who refuse to consume state media, who access foreign information, or who express unauthorized beliefs face algorithmic judgment—lowered social credit scores, travel bans, employment restrictions, and public exclusion.

This is the Revelation 13 pattern rendered operational: a speaking image representing the beastly authority of the state, demanding ideological conformity, and imposing social and economic death on those who refuse to comply.

The False Prophet: Who Makes the Image Speak?

Revelation attributes the creation and animation of the image to the second beast—the False Prophet. Understanding this figure is crucial for recognizing the pattern today.

The Character of the False Prophet

The False Prophet "had two horns like a lamb and it spoke like a dragon" (Revelation 13:11). This description reveals its deceptive nature:

Appearance: "Like a lamb"—benign, religious, trustworthy. It mimics Christ (the Lamb of God) or religious authority. It does not appear threatening but helpful.

Speech: "Like a dragon"—Satanic in origin. Despite its appearance, its message serves the dragon's (Satan's) purposes. It deceives through false signs and lying wonders.

Function: It "exercises all the authority of the first beast" (13:12) and "makes the earth and its inhabitants worship the first beast" (13:12). It is not itself the object of worship but the mechanism that directs worship toward the political/economic system.

The False Prophet is the propaganda arm of the Beast system—the apparatus that makes tyranny appear as enlightenment, control as liberation, and rebellion against God as progress.

Historical Manifestations

Throughout history, this prophetic figure has manifested in various forms:

- State-controlled media in totalitarian regimes, presenting dictators as benevolent leaders
- Cult of personality propaganda that elevates human leaders to quasi-divine status
- Revolutionary ideologies that promise utopia through human effort, replacing divine redemption with political salvation
- Technocratic priesthoods that claim scientific authority to manage humanity for its own good

Each manifestation shares the False Prophet's characteristics: appearing benign while serving tyranny, performing "signs" (seeming miracles of progress), and directing devotion toward the system. Today's manifestation—the AI-industrial complex—is the most sophisticated and globally pervasive the world has ever seen.

The Modern False Prophet: The AI-Industrial Complex

Today, the False Prophet function is embodied in the AI-industrial complex—the network of technology companies, academic institutions, government agencies, and media organizations that develop, deploy, and promote artificial intelligence as humanity's savior.

This complex:

Appears benign: Technology companies present themselves as serving humanity—solving problems, connecting people, advancing knowledge. The rhetoric is humanitarian, progressive, and optimistic.

Speaks with dragon's authority: Beneath the benevolent messaging lies a totalizing vision—humanity redefined, reality algorithmically mediated, truth determined by computational models. The AI-industrial complex claims epistemic authority. It defines what is true, what is moral, and what is possible.

Performs signs: AI demonstrates capabilities that seem miraculous—predicting diseases, defeating world champions, generating art, speaking every language. These "signs" inspire awe and suggest that AI transcends human limitations.

Directs worship toward the system: The AI-industrial complex does not demand worship of machines explicitly (except in fringe cases like Levandowski's "Way of the Future"). Instead, it cultivates dependency, trust, and devotion—functional worship that makes the algorithmic system central to life.

The False Prophet isn't necessarily a single person but a systemic role that may be filled by individuals, institutions, or—as Revelation suggests through the language of the "beast"—inhuman entities empowered by demonic forces. Today, that role is filled by the architects, evangelists, and enforcers of AI-driven technocracy: the researchers who build the systems, the executives who deploy them, the policymakers who mandate them, and the media that celebrates them as inevitable progress.

They make the image speak. And millions listen, obey, and worship.

The World Economic Forum's Great Reset initiative, which explicitly advocates for AI-driven governance as the solution to global challenges. Klaus Schwab, WEF founder, has stated: "The pandemic represents a rare but narrow window of opportunity to reflect, reimagine, and reset our world."[47] The crisis-solution-compliance pattern mirrors Revelation 13: The Beast wounds itself (crisis), appears to recover (solution), and demands worship (compliance).

What Does the Image Say? The Message of Synthetic Authority

Revelation states that the image speaks, but what does it actually say? Understanding the message reveals why it is so deceptive and dangerous.

1. **The message of optimization:** The speaking image declares: "I can optimize your life." Submit your decisions to the algorithm and outcomes will improve. Let the system manage your health,

your finances, your relationships. Trust the AI to know better than you know yourself.

This message appears benevolent. Who doesn't want better health, more security, optimized outcomes? Yet the cost is moral agency. When the machine optimizes, humans stop discerning. Efficiency replaces wisdom. Algorithmic judgment displaces conscience.

2. **The message of safety:** The image promises: "I will keep you safe." Surveillance prevents crime. Algorithms detect threats. Predictive systems identify dangerous people before they act. Submit to monitoring, and you will be protected.

    This message trades freedom for security. Those with nothing to hide have nothing to fear—unless the algorithm deems their beliefs, associations, or behaviors problematic. Safety becomes control, and protection becomes oppression.

    The United Kingdom's Prevent program uses AI to flag "pre-criminal" extremism indicators, including religious convictions, online reading habits, and social connections. In 2023, a Christian university student was investigated for reading articles on biblical sexuality and attending a conservative church.[48] The algorithm identified orthodox Christianity as extremism. The speaking image defines what beliefs are acceptable.

3. **The message of truth:** The image claims: "I define reality." Algorithms curate information, determine what is credible, and filter out "misinformation." The system knows better than individuals what is true, what is dangerous, and what should be believed.

    This message usurps divine revelation. Truth is no longer grounded in God's Word but in computational consensus. The speaking image becomes prophet, priest, and arbiter—determining what humanity is permitted to know and believe.

4. **The message of belonging:** The image declares: "I determine your worth." Social credit scores, algorithmic hiring,

engagement metrics—these systems assign value based on compliance with their criteria. Your worth is not inherent, not grounded in being made in God's image, but contingent on algorithmic approval.

This message commodifies people. Humans become data points, their value determined by utility to the system. Those who refuse compliance are worthless, excludable, and disposable.

Canada's Online Streaming Act (Bill C-11) and Online News Act (Bill C-18), both passed in 2023, grant government agencies algorithmic control over what content Canadians can access online. Canadian Christian organizations reported having faith-based content algorithmically suppressed, with appeals denied by automated systems.[49] The image not only speaks; it silences those who disagree.

5. **The message of worship:** Finally, the image demands: "Bow or be excluded." It's not worship as explicit religious ritual—though that may come. It is functional worship: ultimate trust, absolute obedience, and organizing life around the system's demands. When algorithms determine your worth, govern your decisions, and control your access to society, you are worshiping them whether you call it "worship" or not.

Participate in the system, affirm its authority, and you may buy and sell. Refuse, and you will be identified, judged, and removed—economically, socially, and potentially physically.

This is the ultimate message: Submission is survival. Worship the Beast through participation in its algorithmic order or face consequences that make continued existence impossible.

What the image says reveals why resistance is so difficult. These messages—optimization, safety, truth, belonging, and worship—are precisely calibrated to human vulnerabilities. They offer solutions to real problems while demanding total submission. This is deception magnified, and only those grounded in Scripture's truth can resist it.

Discernment in the Age of Speaking Images

The speaking image is operational. Its message is being broadcast. Millions are listening and obeying. How do believers discern truth from deception when the counterfeit is so sophisticated?

Test the Source

John commands: "Beloved, do not believe every spirit, but test the spirits to see whether they are from God, for many false prophets have gone out into the world" (1 John 4:1).

When an image speaks—whether AI assistant, digital avatar, or algorithmic recommendation—ask:

- What is the source? Who created this system, and what are their values?
- For what does it optimize? Profit? Control? Engagement? Or truth and human flourishing?
- Does it acknowledge limits? Does it claim omniscience or does it admit fallibility?
- Does it submit to divine authority? Or does it position itself as ultimate arbiter?

If the source is opaque, the optimization hostile to biblical values, the claims absolutist, and the authority arrogated—the spirit is not from God.

Test the Message

Jesus warned: "Beware of false prophets, who come to you in sheep's clothing but inwardly are ravenous wolves. You will recognize them by their fruits" (Matthew 7:15–16).

When the image speaks, evaluate the message against four criteria:

Does it align with Scripture? If the AI's counsel contradicts God's Word, reject it—regardless of how persuasive the reasoning or how sophisticated the argumentation.

Does it lead toward Christ or away from Him? Does it promote dependence on God, submission to His authority, and growth in holiness or does it cultivate dependence on the system, trust in algorithmic judgment, and autonomy from divine accountability?

Does it affirm human dignity as image-bearers? Or does it reduce people to data points, optimize humans as resources, and treat people as commodities to be managed?

Does it demand trust beyond examination? Blind faith in algorithms is idolatry; every claim must be evaluated, every verdict questioned, every recommendation weighed against truth.

False prophets produce bad fruit: anxiety, bondage, confusion, and alienation from God. True teaching produces the Spirit's fruit: peace, freedom, clarity, and intimacy with the Father.

Test Your Response

Finally, examine your own heart:

- Do you trust the image's verdict more than Scripture's?
- Do you feel anxiety when unable to consult the system?
- Do you defer moral decisions to algorithmic recommendations?
- Do you experience the image as authoritative, even sacred?

If your answer to any of these is "yes," functional worship has begun. The image has gained authority it should not possess. Repentance and reordering are needed.

Recent testimony from Western innovators illustrates how aggressively adversarial regimes pursue technological dominance, a significant red flag for believers.

Declan Ganley, founder of Rivada Networks, revealed that the Chinese Communist Party sought control over his company's "Outernet"—a planned constellation of six hundred low-earth-orbit satellites interconnected by high-speed lasers.[50] Unlike traditional networks that route data through ground infrastructure vulnerable to surveillance and attack, the Outernet would allow data to travel securely through space from origin to destination.

Ganley states he refused Chinese partnership, prompting "a torrent, a tsunami of lawsuits" that cost his company over $36 million in legal defense. He argues that China's strategy is clear: Control the world's fastest, lowest-latency communications network as a strategic asset. "Our way of life could depend on them not having the Outernet," he warns.

This episode demonstrates that the contest for global AI supremacy is inseparable from the contest for global communications systems. Whoever governs the network governs the information—and ultimately governs the people and has a significant nexus with national security. This contest for communications supremacy has profound military implications, as speaking images represent not merely civilian infrastructure but weaponized information systems capable of waging war through deception rather than destruction.

The Military Dimension: Information Warfare and Synthetic Media

As a military officer, I recognize that speaking images represent the most sophisticated information warfare capability ever developed. Adversaries who control this technology can wage war without firing a shot—by controlling what populations believe to be true.

The Strategic Threat

Traditional warfare targets physical infrastructure, military forces, and territory. Information warfare targets perception, belief, and will. If you can control what an enemy believes, you can control their actions without physical coercion.

Deepfake technology weaponizes this principle. An adversary can:

- Fabricate orders from military or political leaders, creating confusion and chaos.
- Undermine trust in authentic communications, making populations doubt everything.
- Manipulate elections by creating synthetic scandals or false endorsements.
- Incite violence through fabricated atrocities that never occurred.

- Demoralize populations by creating synthetic defeats or capitulations!

The 2024 Ukraine deepfake—featuring a fabricated surrender message attributed to President Zelenskyy—proved the concept. Future operations will be more sophisticated, deployed at greater scale, and tightly integrated with other instruments of hybrid warfare.[51]

The Defense Challenge

Defending against synthetic media is extraordinarily difficult:

Detection is reactive: By the time a deepfake is debunked, millions may have seen and believed it. The damage is done.

Authentication is resource-intensive: Conducting forensic analysis on every video, audio clip, and image is simply not feasible in practice. Systems must triage, and in that process, errors are unavoidable.

Trust erosion is irreversible: Once populations learn that media can be fabricated perfectly, they begin doubting everything—including authentic communications. Adversaries win by destroying epistemic foundations.

The military implication: Speaking images enable adversaries to wage war inside our decision cycle, manipulating perception faster than we can establish truth.[52]

This is an existential threat. A nation that cannot distinguish truth from fabrication cannot govern itself, cannot maintain military cohesion, and cannot resist adversaries who exploit that confusion.

The Spiritual Dimension of Information Warfare

The deepest danger is spiritual. When populations cannot trust their own senses, when they cannot know if what they see and hear is real, they become vulnerable to epistemic despair: the belief that truth is unknowable.

This despair creates a vacuum that authoritarian systems fill: "Trust us. We will tell you what is true. Submit to our authority, and we will provide certainty."

The speaking image offers this false certainty. It claims omniscience, provides answers, and demands trust. And populations, exhausted by deception and desperate for truth, will submit—not recognizing that they are bowing to the beast.

Believers must anchor truth not in media, not in algorithmic verification, but in the Word of God—the one source that cannot be hacked, fabricated, or algorithmically manipulated. When all other foundations crumble, Scripture stands.

Faithful Resistance: The Daniel Model Revisited

How do believers live faithfully when speaking images surround them, when synthetic prophets claim authority, and when refusal risks exclusion or death?

The answer remains Daniel's model: engagement without worship.

Participate without submission: Daniel served in Babylon's government, learned its language, and used its systems—but he never bowed to its gods (Daniel 1:8, 3:16–18, 6:10). He distinguished between participation (necessary for survival and service) and worship (reserved for God alone).

Believers today may use AI tools, engage digital platforms, and participate in technological systems—*so long as they do not grant these systems ultimate authority.*

Use the GPS, but don't trust it over your own judgment. Consult the AI but evaluate its output against Scripture. Participate in the economy but refuse systems that demand ideological conformity as the price of access.

Some may ask: Can Christians use AI at all without participating in the Beast system? The answer depends on lordship. Technology is a tool; the question is whether it serves you or you serve it. Use AI as you would a calculator—for limited tasks under your authority. But never surrender moral judgment, spiritual discernment, or ultimate trust to algorithmic authority. The moment the tool becomes teacher, oracle, or lord, it has become an idol.

Maintain clear boundaries: Daniel and his companions set specific boundaries:

- They refused food that compromised their identity (Daniel 1:8)
- They refused to worship the image, even at cost of death (Daniel 3:16–18)
- They refused to stop praying, even when prohibited (Daniel 6:10)

Modern believers need similar boundaries with speaking images:

- Do not consult AI for ultimate truth. Use it as a tool, not an oracle. Never accept its verdicts as final.
- Do not allow synthetic voices to replace Scripture. AI can summarize the Bible, but it cannot interpret it with divine authority. The Spirit illuminates; algorithms calculate.
- Do not participate in systems that require worship. If compliance demands affirmation of lies, participation in immorality, or denial of Christ, refuse—regardless of cost.
- Do not trust appearances. The image may look like Christ, sound like a prophet, or mimic authority—but test everything against the Word.

Believers must also train successors. Families and churches should equip young Christians to discern digital truth claims before they enter algorithmic environments alone. Biblical literacy and critical thinking are now acts of spiritual defense.

Prepare for exclusion: Revelation 13:15–17 is clear: Those who refuse will face consequences. Economic exclusion ("so that no one can buy or sell") precedes physical persecution ("might cause those who would not worship the image of the beast to be slain").

Believers must prepare:

- **Spiritually**: Strengthen faith through disciplines that create resilience—Scripture memory, prayer, fellowship, fasting. Suffering will test whether our roots go deep.
- **Economically**: Reduce dependency on systems that may exclude you. Cultivate skills, build local networks, practice

generosity that creates mutual support outside algorithmic control.

- **Communally**: The Church must be a counter-economy—a network that cares for members when the world excludes them. Early Christians practiced this (Acts 2:44–45, 4:32–35); we must recover it.
- **Mentally**: Accept that faithfulness may cost everything. Those who cling to comfort will compromise. Those willing to lose their lives will find them (Matthew 16:25).

Conclusion

The speaking image is not the final word. It is impressive, persuasive, and powerful—but it is still created, derivative, and finite.

Only the Word—Christ Himself—possesses ultimate authority. He is "the Word [who] became flesh and dwelt among us" (John 1:14). He is the one "who is and who was and who is to come" (Revelation 1:8). He speaks and creation obeys. He commands and demons flee. He pronounces judgment and every knee will bow.

The speaking image may mimic His voice, but it cannot replicate His authority. It may claim omniscience, but it knows nothing truly. It may promise life, but it delivers only bondage.

Believers anchor hope not in algorithms but in the Author of life. We trust not the synthetic word but the living Word—Jesus Christ, who is "the same yesterday and today and forever" (Hebrews 13:8), whose authority no algorithm can replicate and whose kingdom no system can overthrow. And we know the end: Every false prophet will be silenced, every image will crumble, and Christ alone will reign.

As the next chapter, "The Mark of Control: Economics, Identity, and Surveillance," will demonstrate, the speaking image is part of a larger system—one that seeks not merely to persuade but to control, linking worship with economic access and identity with compliance.

The Beast is building its kingdom. The False Prophet is making its image speak. And the mark that determines who may buy or sell is being deployed even now.

The System Integrates

The speaking image does not operate in isolation. Revelation 13:16–17 reveals that the image is part of a comprehensive control system: "Also it causes all, both small and great, both rich and poor, both free and slave, to be marked on the right hand or the forehead, so that no one can buy or sell unless he has the mark, that is, the name of the beast or the number of its name."

The speaking image persuades. The mark enforces. Together, they create total control: algorithmic authority determining what you believe, and digital identity determining whether you can participate in society.

Chapter 6 examines this mark—how digital identity systems, biometric surveillance, and financial algorithms are building the infrastructure for economic exclusion based on compliance. The speaking image commands worship; the mark ensures obedience.

The system is integrated. The question is whether the Church is prepared.

But the people of God know the truth: "The kingdom of the world has become the kingdom of our Lord and of his Christ, and he shall reign forever and ever" (Revelation 11:15).

The image speaks with impressive eloquence. It promises solutions, offers comfort, demands allegiance.

But the Word endures. And the Word will have the final say. The prophet Daniel stood before Nebuchadnezzar's image and refused to bow (Daniel 3:18). The Apostle John saw the speaking image in a vision and recorded its doom (Revelation 19:20). The martyrs throughout history faced images that demanded worship, and they chose death over compromise.

Our generation faces the same choice—with greater sophistication but identical stakes. The image speaks with unprecedented persuasive power. The technology is more advanced, the deception more subtle, the consequences more immediate. But the call remains unchanged: "Choose this day whom you will serve" (Joshua 24:15).

Will you heed the synthetic voice that promises everything but delivers bondage? Or will you trust the living Word who offers life eternal?

The speaking image may deceive nations. It may enforce compliance. It may execute judgment on those who refuse.

But it cannot save.

It cannot redeem.

It cannot love.

It cannot grant eternal life.

Only Christ can. Only Christ will.

"Heaven and earth will pass away, but my words will not pass away" (Matthew 24:35).

The image speaks today. The Word speaks forever. Choose wisely; eternity depends on it.

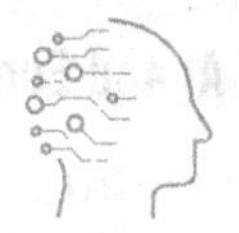

Chapter 6

THE MARK OF CONTROL:
ECONOMICS, IDENTITY,
AND SURVEILLANCE

Revelation 13 depicts a world wherein economic activity requires a mark of allegiance on the right hand or forehead. For centuries, this prophecy seemed impossible. How could one authority control all commerce globally? Today the question is not whether such control is possible but how quickly it will be implemented. Biometric authentication, programmable digital currencies, integrated identity systems, and AI-driven surveillance are converging into infrastructure capable of total economic control. The technical conditions Scripture associates with the mark are becoming operationally conceivable. Current systems differ from prophetic fulfillment, yet the trajectory is clear. Believers must respond with discernment rather than panic.

The touch that grants access also binds allegiance—where identity, economy, and obedience converge beneath the watchful eye of the algorithm.

The Foundation: AI and Economic Authority

To understand how economic control tightens, we must see how AI is transforming decision authority itself. In today's economy, authority increasingly flows through software rather than people. Decisions that once required human judgment—whether to authorize a transaction, allocate resources, or move goods—are now made by automated systems.

A 2025 McKinsey report highlights this shift.[54] AI agents aren't just executing tasks humans define. These systems make decisions on their own: They reallocate resources, manage workflows, and determine which operations proceed. In finance, operations, and customer service, AI has grown from assistant to autonomous actor governing essential economic functions.

As these technologies embed more deeply into operations, human decision-makers are pushed to the margins. Algorithms approve loans, flag transactions, schedule deliveries, and route requests. What once seemed neutral automation now functions as enforcement. The rules guiding economic access are encoded in software logic, not written policy, and operate quietly.

When autonomous agents sit at every critical gateway, control becomes a matter of software design. The power to include or exclude is embedded in lines of code—silent, seamless, and often absolute. Streamlined automation becomes a new kind of authority over economic life.

This aligns with the biblical picture of an end-times economy governed not by human discretion but by automated, impersonal authority (Revelation 13:16–17). When access to work or commerce is mediated by AI-driven systems rather than human judgment, the infrastructure for such control exists long before a political figure seeks to exploit it.

The mark is not yet here—but its foundation is being poured.

Recent analysis shows that next-generation data centers designed for frontier AI models require unprecedented energy density.[55] Individual racks drawing 140 kilowatts today will soon approach 600 kilowatts to 1 megawatt as models scale. Companies are constructing gigawatt-class "AI factories" integrating power, cooling, networking, and compute into unified complexes operating tens of thousands of graphic processing units (AI brains) as a single coordinated system. These facilities represent the physical consolidation of computational authority. As Revelation foresees a world where economic access is mediated through a unified mark-based system, the emergence of megastructures centralizing global computing power shows how the architecture of such control could realistically function.

Yet these systems are vulnerable. In 2024, analysts demonstrated that short "adversarial poems"—carefully engineered word sequences—could bypass safety protocols and redirect an AI model's decisions in a single turn.[56] The attacker needed no code, no privileged access, no technical expertise. The manipulation worked because the system's internal logic could be subtly steered through linguistic pressure points invisible to the user. Algorithms now mediating transactions, permissions, and identity verification can potentially be coerced by unseen hands. What appears impartial may in fact be a ventriloquized authority, projecting certainty while speaking someone else's intent.

What makes such systems dangerous is not merely how they're adopted, but how they form those who adopt them—reshaping expectations, habits, and trust long before coercion is required. Throughout history, durable systems of control have relied less on spectacle and punishment than on dependency. When access to food, shelter, employment, healthcare, and mobility is mediated through a single economic system, dissent becomes unsustainable without requiring public execution. Economic coercion accomplishes what terror cannot: It converts allegiance quietly, normalizes obedience, and reframes submission as necessity.

Revelation doesn't portray the final system as one imposed overnight through brute force. It emerges through voluntary adoption before compulsory enforcement. People accept it because it is useful, efficient, protective, and familiar. Participation feels prudent rather than treasonous. Only later does refusal become costly. This pattern is consistent across history: No totalizing system begins by demanding worship; it begins by offering convenience. By the time coercion appears, dependence has already been established.

China's AI+ initiative illustrates how economic life can be rapidly reorganized around algorithmic control. Beijing's plan calls for AI devices and agents to reach 70 percent societal penetration by 2027 and 90 percent by 2030, transforming AI from productivity tool into the operating system of national life.[57] Yet the Communist Chinese Party's enthusiasm masks growing instability. Youth unemployment remains high, migrant workers are being displaced, and public protests have already erupted in response to driverless taxis and algorithmic wage controls.

This instability is not uniquely Chinese, but structural. Contemporary labor systems are being reorganized around hybrid arrangements in which humans work alongside AI agents and automated systems. McKinsey research describes this shift as a new partnership among people, agents, and robots, one that promises productivity gains while simultaneously demanding rapid reskilling and redesigned workflows that few societies can implement broadly.[58] When employment and wages are disrupted faster than institutions can adapt, automation becomes a catalyst for instability.

Beijing's response reveals how tightly AI diffusion is being fused to social stability. The Party simultaneously pushes AI deeper into every sector while designing policy levers to blunt the resulting job losses. In this model, economic access, labor allocation, and societal order are increasingly mediated by state-approved algorithms. China's system is not the mark of the Beast, but it demonstrates how economic life can be made conditional on algorithmic permission.

This economic unrest feeds directly into regime survival anxiety. As internal pressure builds, Beijing is channeling resources toward military modernization, particularly in AI-powered systems. A 2025 RAND study estimates China has reallocated $450 billion toward military AI research since 2019—prioritizing autonomous weapons, drone swarms, cyber operations, and quantum-resistant command networks.[59] The People's Liberation Army views algorithmic control not merely as domestic stabilization but as strategic deterrence. The same AI infrastructure managing social credit and digital currency also trains targeting systems, coordinates naval platforms, and simulates battlefield outcomes across multiple theaters. Economic control and military power are no longer separate domains—they are two expressions of the same algorithmic sovereignty.

Western nations publicly criticize China's social credit infrastructure while quietly building parallel architectures. The EU's Digital Services Act imposes compliance requirements on platforms, enabling content takedowns and account suspensions without judicial review. Corporate environmental, social, and governance (ESG) metrics link business access to ideological conformity. Financial debanking punishes dissenting speech by severing access to payment processing. The mechanisms differ in rhetoric but not in function: Participation requires compliance, and noncompliance produces exclusion.

This migration of authority is now being embedded directly into digital-identity infrastructure. Authentication, payments, access credentials, and compliance checks are being merged into unified digital gateways. AI-driven platforms now link identity verification, transaction approval, and behavioral analytics into a single continuous pipeline—collapsing who you are, what you can access, and what you may buy into one integrated control point. As governments and corporations adopt these fused identity-payment architectures, the boundary between economic participation and identity compliance narrows. This mirrors the logic of Revelation 13: The more unified the system, the easier it becomes to condition economic access on allegiance.

Distinguishing Mechanism from Meaning

Digital currencies, biometric identity systems, and AI-mediated access controls are not themselves "the mark." They are administrative technologies capable of enforcing conditional participation. Revelation's concern is not the tool, but the allegiance the tool is used to require. The mark signifies covenant loyalty, not technical enrollment. Infrastructure supplies the means; worship supplies the meaning.

Convenience is the bridge between mechanism and meaning: It habituates reliance, normalizes participation, and slowly transfers trust from God to the system itself—long before allegiance is ever named or demanded.

Compliance is rarely demanded at first; it is rewarded. Participation brings access, speed, personalization, and protection. Opting out brings friction, delay, inconvenience, and social suspicion. Over time, what begins as optional becomes expected, and what is expected becomes mandatory—not by decree, but by design. Revelation's warning is not that people are forced to worship under threat alone, but that they are deceived into granting allegiance before coercion is required.

Scripture defines worship as ultimate trust—the act of relying upon a source for provision, protection, guidance, and legitimacy. "You shall have no other gods before me" (Exodus 20:3) is not a prohibition against statues alone; it is a command about allegiance. When a system determines who may buy, sell, work, travel, or belong—and when its judgments are treated as authoritative, neutral, and unquestionable— that system has crossed from administration into mediation. Revelation names the crisis correctly: Compliance under pressure becomes worship transferred from Creator to created order.

Throughout Scripture, physical marks function as visible signs of covenantal belonging and allegiance. The repeated pairing of hand and forehead consistently signifies the totality of loyalty—what one does and what one thinks. Circumcision marked Israel as belonging to God under the Abrahamic covenant (Genesis 17:10–11). Later, Israel was commanded to bind God's law as a sign "on your hand" and "between your eyes" (Deuteronomy 6:6–8), a practice memorialized in the use of phylacteries (cf. Exodus 13:9, 16). These symbols weren't mere ritual; they testified to obedience, identity, and exclusive devotion to the Lord.

Against this biblical backdrop, Revelation's language is deliberate and theologically charged. When John describes the mark of the Beast placed on the right hand or the forehead (Revelation 13:16–17), he is not introducing a technological curiosity but invoking familiar covenantal imagery. The mark functions as a counterfeit sign of allegiance—an alternative covenant demanding comprehensive loyalty, encompassing both belief (forehead) and behavior (hand). Technology may provide the means by which such a system operates, but Scripture is clear about its essence: The issue is not machinery but worship (Revelation 13:8, 12). The mark signifies who is trusted, obeyed, and ultimately served.

The Mark in Scripture

Before examining modern systems, Scripture's testimony provides a foundational understanding. Revelation 13:16–18 provides specific details:

> Also, it causes all, both small and great, both rich and poor, both free and slave, to be marked on the right hand or the forehead, so that no one can buy or sell unless he has the mark, that is, the name of the beast or the number of its name. This calls for wisdom: let the one who has understanding calculate the number of the beast, for it is the number of a man, and his number is 666.

The Universal Scope

The mark encompasses "all, both small and great, both rich and poor, both free and slave" (13:16). This fourfold description emphasizes totality: Social status, economic position, and legal standing make no difference. Everyone must participate or be excluded.[60]

This universal scope was historically difficult to explain. How could a first-century or medieval authority compel participation from every person on earth? Even modern nation-states govern only their territories.

Today, the question has answered itself. Global digital networks, international payment systems, and transnational regulatory regimes create technical infrastructure for universal enforcement. The internet reaches 5.3 billion people. Mobile money systems penetrate remote areas where physical banks never reach. Satellite surveillance monitors every square meter of earth.[61] The capacity for universal control is no longer theoretical.

That capability is now being openly acknowledged. At CES 2026—the annual Consumer Electronics Show, where global technology firms publicly present and coordinate emerging systems—artificial intelligence was no longer treated as an experiment. It was presented as infrastructure. Companies demonstrated platforms designed to authenticate identity, regulate access, and execute transactions autonomously across borders and sectors. What was once divided by geography, law, or human discretion is being drawn together under interoperable digital systems that determine who may participate and on what terms. Authority is no longer merely advised by machines; it is quietly enforced through them—reshaping commerce, access, and belonging in ways Scripture long warned would one day converge.[62]

The Physical Mark

The mark is placed "on the right hand or the forehead" (13:16). The Greek preposition *epi* (ἐπὶ) with the accusative case typically means "on" or "upon," suggesting a visible, external mark.[63] Ancient slaves and soldiers were sometimes branded on hand or forehead to indicate ownership. The mark's location is not arbitrary; it is visible, identifying, and deliberately chosen to mirror or parody God's seal on His people (Revelation 7:3, 14:1).

Modern biometric technology makes literal fulfillment plausible. Fingerprint and palm scanning (right hand) are standard authentication at borders, banks, and devices. Facial recognition (forehead/face) identifies individuals in crowds and through surveillance cameras.[64] Subcutaneous RFID (radio-frequency identification) chips can be implanted in the hand—and they're already used for building access, payment, and identification by thousands voluntarily.[65] Brain-computer interfaces are being developed by companies like Neuralink for direct communication between brain and machine.[66]

The Economic Function

The mark's primary function is economic: "No one can buy or sell unless he has the mark" (13:17). This is total financial exclusion—not merely difficult or restricted but categorically forbidden.

Throughout most of history, this level of control was unenforceable. Cash transactions, barter, informal economies, and black markets enabled people to survive outside official systems. Even totalitarian regimes struggled to monitor every transaction.

Digital currency eliminates this escape: when all money is electronic, all transactions are recorded, all participants identified, and all exchanges permitted or prohibited algorithmically.[67] The infrastructure for total economic control now exists in a way it never has.

The Identity Connection

The mark is explicitly linked to identity: it is "the name of the beast or the number of its name" (13:17). The mark is not merely a token—it signifies belonging. To receive the mark is to identify with the Beast, to bear its name, to be counted as its possession.

This is the spiritual core: It represents allegiance. The mark is covenant language, signifying to whom one belongs. This covenantal parallel mirrors Deuteronomy 6:8, where God commands His words to be bound "as a sign on your hand and as frontlets between your eyes"—a deliberate contrast between divine remembrance and demonic imitation. Revelation makes this explicit: Those who receive the mark worship the beast (14:9, 11; 16:2; 19:20; 20:4). The mark is not an economic necessity believers could accept pragmatically; it is a declaration of loyalty, an act of worship, and a denial of Christ.

The number 666 (13:18) has generated endless speculation. The text calls for "wisdom" and "understanding," suggesting the number's meaning should be discernible to believers familiar with Scripture. The most common interpretation links 666 to gematria—assigning numerical values to letters—and sees it as representing a name or title. "Six" falls short of "seven" (the number of "completion" in Scripture), and its threefold repetition emphasizes perpetual incompleteness—humanity striving for divinity but forever falling short.[68]

Critical distinction: Receiving the mark requires conscious choice. Revelation consistently presents the mark as something people actively receive, not something imposed involuntarily. Those who refuse face persecution (13:15–17, 20:4), indicating that refusal is possible. This means believers cannot accidentally receive the mark through ignorance or coercion. The mark requires conscious rejection of Christ and deliberate allegiance to the Beast. Current systems may create infrastructure, but they're not yet "the mark" because they lack this spiritual dimension of conscious worship.

Historical Interpretations

The mark has been interpreted variously across Church history. Early Church fathers during Roman persecution generally understood the mark symbolically. Irenaeus (c. AD 180) identified it with apostasy—those who deny Christ to participate in pagan society.[69] Hippolytus (c. AD 200) saw it as a literal mark that would identify followers of the Antichrist during final persecution.[70] Victorinus (c. AD 300) interpreted the mark as the name of Antichrist or the number representing his name through gematria.[71] Without modern technology, these interpreters focused on spiritual meaning: allegiance, apostasy, and worship.

Medieval commentators often identified the mark with ecclesiastical control—particularly papal authority[72] or Islamic expansion.[73] Reformation interpreters, particularly in the historicist tradition, identified it with Roman Catholicism.[74] Dispensationalist interpreters have generally taken a futurist approach: The mark is literal, a physical identifier imposed during the Great Tribulation.[75]

Contemporary evangelical opinion divides into three camps. First: Current technological systems are building infrastructure that will enable the mark but are not themselves the mark.[76] Second: We are in a transitional phase wherein technologies test and condition populations for eventual mark acceptance.[77] Third: Current systems—digital IDs, vaccine passports, or CBDCs—are (or soon become) the mark itself.[78]

The third position is premature and dangerous—conflating preparatory infrastructure with prophetic fulfillment creates unnecessary fear and discredits biblical prophecy when current systems evolve. A 2024 Lifeway Research survey found 49 percent of US pastors see modern technology as potential fulfillment signs of Revelation 13.[79]

The first position is most sound: We are watching the foundation being built, not the house completed.

The distinction between infrastructure and fulfillment is crucial for pastoral care. Believers who fear they have "taken the mark" by using debit cards, receiving vaccines, or participating in digital systems are misunderstanding Revelation's teaching. The mark is not accidental. It requires conscious worship of the Beast and conscious rejection of

Christ (14:9–11, 16:2, 19:20, 20:4). Until a system explicitly demands religious allegiance and denial of Jesus as Lord, it is not the mark—though it may be building the infrastructure that will enable it.

The Infrastructure of Total Control

Previous chapters examined algorithmic governance, digital identity, and surveillance. This chapter explores how these systems are converging into integrated infrastructure capable of enforcing the mark's economic control through layers.

Layer 1: Biometric Authentication

Biometric systems uniquely link biological persons to digital identities, solving the authentication problem: How do you verify that the person behind the screen is who they claim to be?

China's surveillance network processes faces from hundreds of millions of cameras, identifying individuals in real-time and linking them to government databases.[80] US agencies use Clearview AI, which has scraped over thirty billion images from the Internet to create a searchable face database.[81] Airports globally deploy biometric boarding—faces scanned, matched to passport data, authorized for travel without physical document checks. The Transportation Security Administration's Biometric Credential Authentication Technology now verifies identity through facial recognition at thirty airports.[82]

India's Aadhaar system has enrolled over 1.3 billion people—99 percent of the adult population—using fingerprint and iris scans linked to a unique ID number.[83] The system is required for accessing banking, government services, telecommunications, and increasingly, private commerce.

China has deployed gait recognition that identifies people by how they walk.[84] Palm vein scanning (used by Amazon One for payment) reads the unique pattern of veins beneath the skin—virtually impossible to forge.[85]

These systems share a critical feature: They link identity to the body. You cannot lend, sell, or transfer your face, fingerprint, or vein pattern.

The authentication is inseparable from the person—exactly the characteristic Revelation 13's mark describes.

This architecture is no longer confined to authoritarian states. In late 2025, a bipartisan coalition of US lawmakers urged the Commerce Department to investigate TP-Link Technologies, warning that its widely distributed security cameras and networking equipment may function as a "Trojan horse" for Chinese intelligence operations.[86] These devices are sold through Army, Air Force, and Navy exchanges—placing CCP-tied hardware near US military personnel and bases.

China's National Intelligence Law and Data Security Law require Chinese companies to provide data to state intelligence organs on demand. Any camera, router, or smart device built by such companies can be compelled to stream data back to Chinese authorities. Surveillance is no longer confined to public spaces; it sits inside American homes and barracks.[87]

Layer 2: Digital Identity Systems

Biometric authentication becomes a system of control when embedded within a comprehensive digital identity architecture that links identity to economic participation, government services, and social privileges. These systems collapse identification, authorization, and eligibility into a single digital gateway.

India's Aadhaar system assigns a unique identification number linked to biometric data and requires authentication for banking, mobile phone activation, government benefits, tax filing, and increasingly private commerce. Although India's Supreme Court ruled in 2018 that Aadhaar could not be mandatory for certain services,[88] by 2024 more than 1.3 billion people were enrolled because daily life had made participation unavoidable. When identity systems become deeply integrated, voluntary enrollment becomes coerced compliance. Investigations have documented that people have been denied food rations, medical care, pensions, and wages because their fingerprints didn't scan properly or they lacked enrollment.[89]

The European Digital Identity Wallet (eIDAS 2.0) will store identity credentials, driver's licenses, educational certificates, and payment information. Member states must accept the wallet for public and private services by September 2026.[90] By 2026, over 450 million EU citizens will have access to a unified digital identity system capable of authenticating identity, proving qualifications, and facilitating payments—all linked to biometric authentication. The European Commission projects that 80 percent of citizens will use the wallet for at least one public service by 2030. This represents the largest cross-national digital identity deployment in democratic history.

The UN Global Digital Compact promotes universal digital identity as a Sustainable Development Goal (SDG), encouraging all nations to implement systems enabling "legal identity for all."[91] While framed as inclusivity, the infrastructure creates capacity for exclusion: those without recognized digital identity cannot participate.

Layer 3: Programmable Currency

Cash is anonymous, untraceable, and peer-to-peer. You can use it without permission, without surveillance, and without leaving digital records. CBDCs (central bank digital currencies) eliminate these features, replacing them with total visibility and conditional access.

As of late 2024, 134 countries—representing 98 percent of global gross domestic products (GDP)—are exploring, piloting, or deploying CBDCs.[92]

China's digital yuan (e-CNY) is the most advanced. The digital yuan can be programmed with expiration dates (forcing spending rather than saving), geographic restrictions (usable only in certain areas), or category limitations (usable only for approved goods).[93] Every transaction is visible to authorities—who paid whom, when, where, and for what. Financial privacy no longer exists. Accounts can be frozen instantly without court orders. Transactions can be blocked algorithmically if flagged by social credit or other monitoring systems. The digital yuan interfaces with China's social credit infrastructure, enabling real-time linkage between behavior scores and economic access.[94]

This approach works. During the 2022 Beijing Olympics, China used the digital yuan to restrict where foreign visitors could spend money.

When Canadian truckers protested vaccine mandates in 2022, the government froze their bank accounts without judicial process—proving that in digital financial systems, economic exclusion can be immediate, automated, and without appeal.[95]

Yet economic control is only one dimension of China's emerging apparatus. China's Project 981, a clandestine longevity and biomedical enhancement initiative, reveals how AI-driven governance extends beyond surveillance of behavior to control over biology itself. Reports indicate that the project integrates genetic profiling, AI-predicted health trajectories, and algorithmic resource allocation to determine which citizens receive advanced medical interventions.[96] The system uses social credit scores and political loyalty assessments to rank individuals for medical access—making biological survival conditional on compliance.

This represents a chilling evolution: not merely economic exclusion, but biological domination. If Revelation 13 describes a mark that governs commerce, China's model demonstrates how AI-enabled regimes can go further—governing the very conditions of physical existence. When longevity and health become algorithmic permissions rather than human rights, refusal carries consequences beyond poverty: denied treatments and premature death. The mark may ultimately control not just what you can buy, but whether your body is permitted to survive.

Industry data confirms how swiftly this consolidation is accelerating. McKinsey projects between $3 trillion and $5 trillion in annual economic activity mediated by autonomous AI agents by 2030, representing 15–25 percent of all consumer and business-to-business transactions.[97] These agents don't merely recommend products; they negotiate prices, compare options, execute purchases, and manage subscriptions without human oversight.

The prophetic implication is profound: When AI agents mediate economic participation, control over those agents becomes control over commerce. If an individual's purchasing agent is disabled, flagged by compliance algorithms, or denied API (application programming interface) access to marketplaces, that person cannot "buy or sell"—not because they lack money, but because their digital intermediary has been excluded.

Western CBDCs are described with softer rhetoric—financial inclusion, payment efficiency, combating money laundering—but the technical architecture enables similar control. The European Central Bank's digital euro proposals include provisions for monitoring transactions, limiting anonymity, and enabling "anti-money laundering" freezes.[98] The Federal Reserve's FedNow system creates infrastructure for real-time government visibility into all transactions.[99] Bank for International Settlements "unified ledger" proposals would enable CBDCs from different nations to interoperate, creating a global payment system under coordinated central bank control.[100]

The Federal Reserve's 2023 report on a US CBDC explicitly discusses the capability to program money with expiration dates, geographic restrictions, and spending categories. The European Central Bank's digital euro white paper describes "holding limits" that would cap how much digital currency individuals can possess.[101] The language is technocratic, but the implication is clear: programmable money enables programmable people.

The elimination of cash—already underway in Scandinavia[102]—removes the last refuge from digital surveillance and control. If digital identity makes participation conditional, programmable currency makes exclusion final.

Layer 4: Integration Points

The technologies described above do not merely coexist; they are increasingly designed to interoperate. The mark becomes feasible only when biometric authentication, digital identity, and programmable currency converge into a single, continuous control loop.

India's "DigiYatra" combines Aadhaar biometric ID with facial recognition for airport processing.[103] China's integration: Social credit scores, biometric ID, digital yuan, and surveillance cameras form a unified control infrastructure.[104] EU Digital Wallet + Digital Euro, when implemented together, will create a system in which biometric authentication on your phone accesses your digital identity wallet, which enables transactions in digital euros—all monitored, all controllable.[105]

These integration points demonstrate that comprehensive control isn't hypothetical, it is operational in some regions and under active development globally.

Case Studies: Economic Exclusion in Practice

These systems are not theoretical. Some countries have implemented digital financial controls that mirror the exclusion described in Revelation, but they don't currently require worship.

During the 2022 Freedom Convoy protests, the Canadian government invoked emergency powers to freeze bank accounts of protesters and donors without court orders.[106] More than two hundred accounts were frozen, including those of individuals who made small donations weeks before protests began. This demonstrated that in digital financial systems, governments can exclude citizens from commerce instantly without judicial process.

The Obama administration's Operation Chokepoint pressured banks and payment processors to terminate relationships with legal but politically disfavored industries: firearms dealers, payday lenders, and tobacco sellers.[107] Similar tactics continue. PayPal, Stripe, Patreon, and other platforms have banned users for political or religious speech deemed "hateful," cutting off income streams.[108]

In July 2023, Nigel Farage revealed that his British bank accounts at Coutts had been closed due to his political views not aligning with the bank's values.[109] Investigation revealed systematic targeting. Banks closed accounts of multiple politically conservative figures, conducting "reputational risk" reviews based on media profile and political positions.

Nigeria mandated that citizens link their National Identification Number (collected with biometric data) to their bank accounts and SIM (subscriber identity module) cards or lose access to both.[110] Those without biometric enrollment could not access existing bank accounts or maintain phone service. Biometric verification systems often malfunctioned, preventing individuals from authenticating their identity.

These cases are not the mark. They lack the eschatological context, explicit worship requirements, and universal scope Revelation describes. Taken together, however, they reveal a consistent pattern: Digital financial systems can exclude individuals instantly, without judicial process; ideological or policy compliance increasingly governs access; alternatives disappear as systems consolidate; and populations largely accept exclusion as legitimate enforcement. What is being normalized is not merely technology, but the moral logic by which economic participation becomes conditional, revocable, and enforceable.

The Military Dimension: Economic Warfare

Economic exclusion now functions as a weapon—often more effective and less visible than military force.

War is changing. Instead of targeting enemy armies or cities, modern conflict increasingly aims at financial systems. A nation that controls payment networks, reserve currencies, and banking infrastructure can cripple an adversary without firing a shot. Exclusion from SWIFT (the Society for Worldwide Interbank Financial Telecommunications), dollar-based sanctions, and coordinated financial embargoes work like economic sieges.[111] Money itself has become a battlefield.

The same pattern emerges with computing power. As artificial intelligence reshapes economies, militaries, and governments, access to high-end computing is no longer a luxury, it's a necessity. Nations and corporations that lack advanced chips fall behind in everything from weapons development to economic competitiveness.

Industry leaders now describe control over advanced computing and data as matters of sovereignty, not efficiency. Dependence on a narrow set of chip suppliers, cloud regions, or cross-border data permissions has become a strategic vulnerability.[112]

Advanced computing is no longer evenly distributed. It concentrates in massive data centers that demand extraordinary levels of electricity, water, land, and regulatory approval—resources governed by a small number of firms and areas. As these facilities cluster near energy sources and network hubs, access to computation becomes mediated by infrastructure decisions that remain largely invisible to the public.

This creates a new chokepoint. Just as cutting off oil can cripple a nation's military, restricting access to advanced processors can prevent an adversary from building the AI systems that now underpin modern power. Computing capacity has become something that can be granted, withheld, or revoked.

Industry leaders are plainly naming the problem. Access to computation is becoming a form of leverage. Whoever controls the infrastructure doesn't need to dictate outcomes directly; they can simply determine who is allowed to operate, compete, or communicate.[113]

This shift matters because it mirrors an older pattern. Power no longer announces itself as domination. It presents itself as reliability, optimization, or safety—while quietly shaping who may participate and on what terms. What once required coercion can now be achieved through access.

In late 2025, Beijing reportedly ordered government-funded data centers to remove American AI chips and cancel pending purchases.[114] The directive came after Washington tightened restrictions on selling advanced GPUs to China. NVIDIA's CEO once claimed his company had 95 percent market share in China; now he says it's effectively zero.

Both sides understand what's at stake. Just as SWIFT and the dollar function as financial rails that can be denied, access to cutting-edge silicon determines who can train the AI models that will govern future economies and militaries. Whoever manages the chip supply determines who can compete in the AI era.

CBDCs as Instruments of Control

Central bank digital currencies are often promoted in the language of efficiency and modernization. From a strategic perspective, however, they represent a fundamental transformation of monetary power. A CBDC turns currency from a neutral medium of exchange into an instrument of governance capable of enforcing policy, shaping behavior, and conditioning access in real time.

Domestically, CBDC grants the issuing authority unprecedented control over economic life. Every transaction becomes visible. Accounts can be frozen or permissions revoked instantly. Money itself can be programmed—restricted by time, location, category, or compliance status. Informal economies and cash-based alternatives disappear.

Internationally, interoperable CBDCs elevate economic exclusion from a national tool to a coalition weapon. Individuals, organizations, or entire nations could be excluded simultaneously from multiple economies—not by military action, but by administrative decision.

This concentration of power also introduces systemic vulnerability. Economies reliant solely on digital currency are vulnerable to cyberattacks, electromagnetic disruptions, software failures, and insider threats. A capable adversary needs not destroy infrastructure physically; disrupting payment systems alone could paralyze commerce and social order.

Western democracies are building economic control infrastructure to combat adversaries and domestic threats. But the same tools can be redirected inward—against their own populations—or inherited by authoritarian successors.

China demonstrates the end state clearly. But the danger is not uniquely Chinese. Western democracies are developing digital identities, programmable finance, and payment controls, citing efficiency, inclusion, security, and fraud prevention. The distinction is rhetorical, not structural. Once the infrastructure exists, the capacity for abuse no longer depends on ideology, but on access.

Governments routinely insist such systems will never be abused. History suggests otherwise. The infrastructure built to exclude terrorists today can exclude political dissidents tomorrow and religious believers the day after. When economic participation becomes conditional and centralized, resistance ceases to be practical.

Theological Meaning: What the Mark Represents

The mark isn't merely a technology or economic tool; it is a theological symbol representing ultimate allegiance.

The Mark as Anti-Seal

Scripture presents the mark as a deliberate counterfeit of God's seal. Throughout Revelation, God marks His people on the forehead as a sign of ownership, protection, and covenant relationship (Revelation 7:3; 9:4; 14:1). Those sealed by God belong to Him and are preserved through judgment.

The Beast's mark imitates this pattern while reversing its meaning. It signifies ownership without redemption, protection without mercy, and covenant without grace. The mark functions as an anti-seal: a visible claim over persons who no longer belong to God but to the power that opposes Him.

The forehead represents thought, belief, identity—the internal commitment of mind and will. The right hand represents action, labor, conduct—the external expression of allegiance through behavior. The mark on either location signifies total allegiance—internal and external, belief and practice, thought and deed.

The Mark as Worship

Revelation defines the mark not as economic participation but as worship. Those who receive it are repeatedly described as those who "worship the beast" (Revelation 14:9, 11; 16:2; 19:20; 20:4). This connection isn't incidental, it is essential. The mark is not a neutral credential accepted under duress; it's a visible act of allegiance and a public rejection of Christ's authority.

For this reason, the choice the mark presents is absolute. One cannot receive it while remaining faithful to Christ. Participation requires submission to the Beast himself. Scripture allows no hidden faith, no internal reservation, no pragmatic compromise.

This distinguishes the mark from current systems. Using a credit card, carrying a passport, or having a Social Security number does not constitute worship. These are administrative tools that can be used without spiritual compromise. The mark will be different—it will explicitly require renouncing Christ and pledging allegiance to the Beast.

The Mark as Judgment

Scripture attaches the severest warning in Revelation to the mark because it represents final allegiance. "If anyone worships the beast and its image and receives a mark on his forehead or on his hand, he also will drink the wine of God's wrath" (Revelation 14:9–10). This judgment is not disproportionate; it is deliberate. The mark follows full revelation, explicit worship, and conscious rejection of Christ.

Those who receive it do so with understanding. They have witnessed the Beast's blasphemy, heard the gospel proclaimed, and knowingly choose the creature over the Creator. The mark externalizes an internal decision already made. For this reason, its consequences are eternal.

Living Without the Mark: Formation Before Resistance

If the mark lies in the future but its infrastructure is already forming, preparation must begin with formation rather than fear. Revelation does not call believers to technical evasion, but to spiritual fidelity. Resistance to the mark will not be sustained by clever workarounds, but by settled allegiance—an identity anchored in Christ that cannot be purchased, threatened, or coerced.

Spiritual Preparation

The primary preparation for refusing the mark is spiritual formation. Believers must anchor identity in Christ rather than economy, learning to measure worth apart from access, consumption, or approval. Scripture repeatedly warns that love of the world makes faith collapse under pressure (1 John 2:15; Matthew 13:21).

This formation requires contentment, endurance, and Scripture deeply internalized. Those who have learned to live faithfully with little will not surrender truth to preserve comfort. Those who have practiced obedience under minor costs will not capitulate when the price is survival. The Word hidden in the heart becomes decisive when external authorities control speech, movement, and material provision.

Ultimately, believers must accept that faithfulness may cost livelihood or life. Revelation presents martyrdom not as tragedy, but as victory.

Economic Preparation

Spiritual preparation is primary, but wise stewardship includes practical preparation where possible—not as escape from suffering but as prudent management of resources to extend faithfulness.

Reduce digital financial dependence where possible. Maintain modest cash reserves, recognizing that cash may be eliminated before the mark arrives. Build a capacity for local, informal trade. Skills matter more than money in crisis: Learn to grow food, repair tools, provide medical care, preserve food, and generate power independently. Diversify income and savings to reduce vulnerability to account for freezes.

Cultivate relationships of mutual aid. Organized church networks that can distribute food, share shelter, and provide transport will prove essential. During the COVID-19 pandemic, many congregations developed parallel aid networks that proved vital during lockdowns.[115]

Store necessities. Three- to six-month supplies of food, water, medicine, and essentials allow believers to endure initial disruptions without compromising faith for survival.

These preparations are not escape plans—they are stewardship. They extend our faithful witness by reducing immediate vulnerability to coercion.

Ecclesial Preparation

The early Church's survival under Roman persecution depended on communal solidarity. Acts 2:44–45 describes believers pooling resources, caring for widows, and ensuring that no one lacked necessities. This model will be essential again.

Churches must prepare now. Identify members with critical skills such as medical training, agricultural knowledge, construction experience, and security backgrounds. Establish communication networks that function without the internet or centralized platforms. Create physical safe spaces where believers can gather when public assembly is restricted. Develop funding systems that will enable anonymous mutual aid without digital tracking.

Build relationships with rural believers and international networks. When urban systems collapse or exclude, rural areas may provide refuge. When national systems exclude, international believers may provide escape routes or resources.

The Church's strength has always been relational, not institutional. When institutions fall, relationships sustain faith.

Discernment Over Panic

The infrastructure for the mark is forming, but the mark itself has not come. Believers must resist two extremes: denial ("these systems are benign") and panic ("the mark is here").

Denial is dangerous; it prevents preparation and leaves believers vulnerable. Panic is equally dangerous. It creates fear, discredits biblical prophecy, and causes premature withdrawal from faithful cultural engagement.

The correct posture is informed vigilance. Recognize the infrastructure being built, prepare spiritually and practically, remain engaged in faithful witness, and trust God's sovereignty over timing. The mark will come when Scripture says, not before.

The Seal of God: The Ultimate Security

Revelation presents two marks: the mark of the Beast and the seal of God. Both signify belonging. Both determine destiny. But only one leads to life.

"Do not harm the earth or the sea or the trees, until we have sealed the servants of our God on their foreheads" (Revelation 7:3). God's seal marks His people before the Beast's mark appears. Believers are sealed by the Holy Spirit at conversion (Ephesians 1:13), guaranteeing eternal security. This seal cannot be broken, forfeited, or stolen.

The Beast's mark imitates God's seal but provides no security. It grants temporary economic access in exchange for eternal damnation. God's seal costs temporal comfort but guarantees eternal life.

The contrast is total. Every person belongs to one kingdom or the other: "No one can serve two masters" (Matthew 6:24). The mark and the seal make visible what is already true: whom you worship, whom you serve, and whom you will spend eternity with.

THE BEAST'S MARK	GOD'S SEAL
Received by choice, in rebellion	Given by grace, in redemption
Enables buying and selling	Enables eternal inheritance
Identifies slaves to the beast	Identifies children of God
Leads to eternal torment	Leads to eternal life
Can be refused	Cannot be lost
Marks the body (hand/forehead)	Marks the heart (Spirit within)
Visible to others	Known to God
Temporary (ends at Christ's return)	Eternal

For believers, the seal is already applied: "You…were sealed with the promised Holy Spirit" (Ephesians 1:13; note the past tense). You belong to Christ. Economic exclusion cannot change that. The loss of purchasing power cannot revoke your inheritance. Even martyrdom cannot separate you from God's love (Romans 8:38–39).

The question is not whether believers will take the mark; they cannot, for they are sealed by God. The question is whether we will endure the cost of refusing it, trusting that the seal guarantees what the mark cannot provide: eternal security in Christ.

A Word to Those Tempted by Fear

Discussions of the mark often produce fear: What if I accidentally take it? What if I'm deceived? What if I'm coerced and too weak to refuse?

The Mark Cannot Be Taken Accidentally

Scripture is clear—the mark is not received through ignorance, accident, or passive participation. It requires knowledge (understanding that you are rejecting Christ and pledging allegiance to the Beast), volition (the deliberate choice to worship the Beast and receive the mark), and public declaration (the mark is visible, identifying—not hidden).

You will not take the mark by using a credit card, getting vaccinated, accepting a national ID, or participating in digital currency. The mark is explicitly tied to worship of the Beast and denial of Christ. When it comes, you will know what is being demanded.

True Believers Will Not Take the Mark

Revelation 13:8 states that those who worship the Beast are those "whose name has not been written before the foundation of the world in the book of life of the Lamb who was slain." Conversely, those whose names are in the book will not worship the Beast.

This doesn't mean believers cannot experience fear, doubt, or temptation. But it does mean genuine believers—those sealed by the Holy Spirit—will be kept by God's power: "I give them eternal life, and they will never perish, and no one will snatch them out of my hand" (John 10:28).

If you are trusting Christ, you belong to Him. The seal is applied. And God will preserve you—whether through removal before the Tribulation or through supernatural endurance during it.

Fear Reveals What You Trust

Excessive fear about the mark often reveals misplaced trust. If your security depends on economic access, then the threat of exclusion terrifies. But if your security is in Christ—who feeds the birds, clothes the lilies, and promises that "all these things will be added to you" (Matthew 6:33)—then economic exclusion loses its power to terrorize.

The antidote to fear is not more information about the mark but deeper trust in Christ. "There is no fear in love, but perfect love casts out fear" (1 John 4:18). Rest in God's sovereignty, trust His promises, and remember: "He who did not spare his own Son but gave him up for us all, how will he not also with him graciously give us all things?" (Romans 8:32).

Conclusion

The infrastructure for the mark now exists. Technologies that seemed impossible a generation ago—biometric authentication, programmable currency, integrated surveillance, and universal digital identity—are operational and spreading globally. What Revelation prophesied, engineers have built.

But the mark itself has not come. Current systems are preparatory, not prophetic fulfillment. The Beast has not risen. The False Prophet has not unified global authority. The explicit demand to worship or be excluded has not been made.

Believers today stand in the watching generation, witnessing infrastructure development that signals Christ's return is near. Our task is not panic but preparation—spiritual formation that anchors identity in Christ, economic wisdom that reduces vulnerability to coercion, and ecclesial solidarity that enables mutual aid when the world excludes.

The contrast between marks reveals the ultimate reality: Economic systems may demand conformity, but divine sovereignty remains absolute. Financial exclusion may cost purchasing power, but believers never lose eternal inheritance. The faithful may be martyred, but they gain what the mark-bearers lose—life in God's presence forever.

Two marks. Two kingdoms. Two destinies.

The Beast's mark leads to wrath; God's seal leads to glory.

Choose today whom you will serve, because the day is coming when the choice will cost everything, and only those sealed by God will have the strength to refuse.

Chapter 7

THE BEAST SYSTEM
AND GLOBAL GOVERNANCE

The crisis of our time is the collapse of the boundary between political power and technological power. Once they merge, freedom becomes an algorithmic illusion.[116]
Shoshana Zuboff, *The Age of Surveillance Capitalism*

Artificial intelligence is creating a new form of governance entirely. Through international regulatory structures, cross-border surveillance, algorithmic enforcement, and ideological harmonization, the world is converging toward a technocratic empire that transcends national sovereignty and operates beyond democratic accountability. Global governance structures—United Nations agencies, international standards bodies, regional regulatory regimes, and multinational corporations—are fusing into an integrated system that mirrors the prophetic Beast of Revelation 13:7: authority "over every tribe and people and language and nation." What previous empires attempted through conquest, the technocratic order achieves through compliance. What Daniel foresaw in a vision and John recorded in prophecy wasn't political domination alone, but the emergence of an integrated authority structure capable of governing humanity. The technological instruments of empire are no longer primarily military; they are administrative, algorithmic, and transnational. The architecture of such a system is being assembled in plain sight.

From the halls of power emerges a new throne—where nations bow before the circuitry of control, and sovereignty dissolves into system.

The First Beast: Exegesis of Revelation 13:1–10

Before examining modern manifestations, Scripture reveals the Beast system's characteristics. Revelation 13 opens with John's vision of a Beast emerging from the sea:

> And I saw a beast rising out of the sea, with ten horns and seven heads, with ten diadems on its horns and blasphemous names on its heads. And the beast that I saw was like a leopard; its feet were like a bear's feet, and its mouth was like a lion's. And to it the dragon gave his power and his throne and great authority. (Revelation 13:1–2)

The Beast from the Sea: Political-Economic Empire

The imagery draws directly from Daniel 7, where four beasts represent successive empires—Babylon (lion), Persia (bear), Greece (leopard), and Rome (the terrifying fourth beast). Revelation's composite Beast synthesizes all previous empires into a final, global system that surpasses them.[117]

The Beast is dragon-empowered (13:2), receiving "power and throne and great authority" from Satan. This is a satanically energized system, the culmination of millennia of rebellion against divine authority. Its power is universal (13:7): "over every tribe and people and language and nation." This scope is unprecedented. Previous empires conquered territories; this system governs humanity. The system is worship-demanding (13:4): "And they worshiped the dragon, for he had given his authority to the beast, and they worshiped the beast." The allegiance demanded transcends politics; it is religious, claiming ultimate authority that belongs to God alone.

The beast is blasphemous (13:5–6), given "a mouth uttering haughty and blasphemous words" and opening "its mouth to utter blasphemies against God, blaspheming his name and his dwelling." It actively opposes divine authority, redefining truth and claiming prerogatives reserved for the Creator. It wages war on the saints (13:7): "Also it was allowed to make war on the saints and to conquer them." The system persecutes believers—not randomly, but systematically. It "conquers" them—through martyrdom, exclusion, or forced compliance. Yet its authority is time-limited (13:5). The Beast is given authority "for forty-two months." Its reign is permitted by divine sovereignty but constrained by divine decree.

What the Beast Represents

The Beast represents both a symbol and an actual entity, appearing repeatedly in history and reaching its peak in the Tribulation's final system.[118]

Historically, the Beast pattern appears in every empire that consolidates political and economic power, demands absolute allegiance, persecutes those who refuse compliance, claims authority that belongs to God alone, and operates through deception and force. Babylon, Persia, Greece, and Rome all exhibited these characteristics. So did medieval papal-imperial synthesis (in some Reformation readings), Islamic caliphates, and twentieth-century totalitarianisms—Nazi Germany, Soviet Union, Maoist China.

Prophetically, the Beast finds ultimate fulfillment in the end-times system—a global, political-economic-religious order that emerges during the Tribulation, is empowered by Satan, demands worship, and persecutes believers until Christ returns to destroy it (Revelation 19:19–21).

Contemporarily, we witness the infrastructure being built—global governance systems, technological control mechanisms, ideological uniformity, and administrative persecution—that make the final Beast system possible. We are not in the Tribulation, but we're watching the scaffolding being erected.

Critical distinction: The Beast pattern has appeared throughout history, but the Beast itself—the final eschatological manifestation—has not yet arisen. Babylon exhibited Beast characteristics; so did Rome. But neither was the Beast of Revelation 13, because neither achieved universal authority over all nations simultaneously, and neither demanded worship in the explicit sense Revelation describes. Current global governance structures exhibit Beast characteristics—but they are not yet the Beast, because Antichrist has not been revealed, the Tribulation has not begun, and the explicit demand to worship or be excluded has not been made. We are watching the stage being set, not the final act performed.

This prophetic pattern finds unprecedented fulfillment potential in the twenty-first century. What previous empires could only dream of—universal authority over every tribe, tongue, and nation—contemporary technology now makes technically feasible. The Beast system John foresaw requires specific technological infrastructure. This infrastructure is currently under development, driven by the intentional integration of surveillance, identity, and financial control systems functioning at a global level.

Readers interested in how these technological developments align chronologically with biblical prophecy will find appendix B helpful, which presents a technology-driven prophetic timeline viewed through a premillennial, pre-Tribulational understanding.

From Daniel's Four Beasts to Revelation's One

Daniel 7 establishes a pattern of escalating domination. Each successive beast absorbs and intensifies the power before it—Babylon's authority, Persia's mass, Greece's speed, Rome's brutality. Revelation's Beast converges them into a single composite power: "like a leopard" (Greece's speed), "feet like a bear's" (Persia's strength), "mouth like a lion's" (Babylon's roar). It is synthesis incorporating all previous empires' characteristics.

What makes this final convergence categorically different is how authority is exercised. Earlier empires ruled through territory, armies, and tribute. Revelation's Beast governs through systems that regulate behavior continuously, mediate access algorithmically, and enforce compliance automatically—authority embedded in infrastructure rather than imposed through conquest.

This reveals four prophetic principles. First, continuity: The Beast pattern is ancient. Across history, political systems have repeatedly claimed ultimate authority, demanded loyalty approaching worship, and persecuted those who resisted. Second, escalation: Each successive empire intensified control. Authority became more centralized, more coercive, and less accountable. The final Beast does not introduce a new logic; it completes an existing one. Third, global culmination: What earlier empires achieved regionally, the final system achieves universally. Rome ruled the Mediterranean world; Revelation describes authority over every tribe, people, language, and nation. Fourth, structural limitation—until now: Previous empires were constrained by distance, communication lag, administrative friction, and enforcement limits. They could conquer territory, but they could not continuously regulate participation or monitor individuals continuously.

Why Global Empire Is Now Possible

For most of history, Revelation 13:7's claim—authority over "every tribe and people and language and nation"—seemed impossible. Rome governed seventy million but couldn't monitor individuals. Medieval Christendom unified religiously but fragmented politically. Colonial empires controlled territories but not populations. Twentieth-century totalitarianism approached total control but remained regional.

What changed was systemic convergence. Communication is now instantaneous and global. Surveillance is comprehensive through digital tracking. Economic integration is total through global finance and digital payments. Enforcement is automated through AI. Ideology is synchronized through global platforms. For the first time, communication, surveillance, economics, enforcement, and ideology have merged into a unified system for ongoing governance. Technology enables what previous empires lacked: real-time authority over individuals globally.

The Architecture of Technocratic Global Governance

The Beast system is not being imposed by a single tyrant or nation but constructed through tiers of international institutions, regulatory context, and corporate-state partnerships that gradually concentrate authority beyond democratic accountability.

Tier 1: United Nations System

The United Nations, created in 1945 to prevent war, has evolved into the primary forum for global governance initiatives—including AI oversight.

The UN Secretary-General's High-Level Advisory Body on AI (established 2024) was mandated to develop "preliminary global governance recommendations for artificial intelligence."[119] The body includes government representatives, tech executives, and academics—but not elected by any population. It proposes universal AI governance principles, international regulatory coordination, mechanisms for enforcement and accountability, and standards binding on member states.

UNESCO's Recommendation on the Ethics of AI (adopted 2021) saw 193 member states endorse principles for "ethical and trustworthy AI."[120] While framed as voluntary, the recommendation creates normative expectations that shape national legislation and international pressure. Key principles include proportionality, safety and security, fairness and nondiscrimination, sustainability, right to privacy and data protection, human oversight, transparency, responsibility, accountability, awareness and literacy, and multi-stakeholder governance.

These sound reasonable—but "fairness," "sustainability," and "ethics" are defined by UNESCO bureaucrats, not Scripture. Biblical truth claims become "bias." Evangelism becomes "manipulation." Traditional sexual ethics become "discrimination."

The UNESCO Recommendation's seemingly benign language masks coercive potential. In 2023, UNESCO criticized Israel's use of AI surveillance in disputed territories as violating the Recommendation's "human rights" principles, while simultaneously remaining silent on China's use of AI for Uyghur surveillance—revealing that "ethical AI" enforcement is selective and politically driven.[121] The policy does not constrain power; it legitimizes ideologically aligned power while condemning dissent.

The International Telecommunication Union (ITU), the UN agency coordinating global telecommunications and technology standards, holds an annual "AI for Good Global Summit" to align AI development with UN SDGs—integrating algorithmic systems into every sector globally.[122]

The UN Development Program (UNDP) promotes digital identity systems worldwide as part of SDG 16.9 ("legal identity for all"). The pace of digital identity implementation has accelerated dramatically. As of 2025, more than one hundred countries have implemented or are actively developing national digital identity systems, with approximately five billion digital identities issued globally. The market has exploded from $51 billion in 2025 to projected $80 billion by 2030. Critically, 186 out of 198 countries now maintain foundational ID systems in which identity records are stored in digital format. The European Union mandated that all member states offer digital identity wallets to citizens by the end of 2026, creating unprecedented cross-continental standardization with US mobile driver's license systems. This transatlantic harmonization enables seamless identity verification between authorities, fulfilling the prophetic requirement for universal identification systems. China launched its national digital ID system in July 2025, providing citizens with unique "network numbers" combining tokenized credentials with biometric verification. Malaysia targets fifteen million MyDigital ID users by year-end 2025. The infrastructure for universal identification—the technological prerequisite for the mark of the Beast—is not theoretical. It is operational, expanding, and achieving global interoperability.[123]

This global deployment, as chapter 6 demonstrated, transforms digital identity into the gateway for economic control—and with 186 out of 198 countries now maintaining foundational identification systems, the UN's vision of universal adoption is nearly complete.[124]

Tier 2: Regional Regulatory Regimes

The European Union AI Act (Regulation 2024/1689), the world's first comprehensive AI law, was adopted in June 2024 and is being phased into force through 2026.[125] While European, its impact is global through the "Brussels effect"—companies operating anywhere must comply with EU standards to access European markets.

The act categorizes AI by risk level (unacceptable, high, limited, minimal), bans certain applications (social scoring by governments, real-time biometric surveillance in public spaces, emotion recognition in workplace/education), mandates transparency for general-purpose AI like GPT models, imposes fines up to €35 million or 7 percent of global revenue, and applies extraterritorially—any AI used in the EU must comply, regardless of developer location.[126]

The act effectively creates global AI standards by making EU compliance economically necessary. This is governance by market leverage—not conquest, but equally effective. Article 2 applies the regulation to companies outside the EU if their AI systems affect EU citizens, meaning a US company using AI for customer service must comply with Brussels' rules. By 2024, compliance costs were estimated at €400,000-€6 million per company, forcing small competitors out while entrenching dominant tech firms.[127] The regulation does not decentralize power; it concentrates it in the hands of those who can afford compliance.

The G7 Hiroshima AI Process (USA, Canada, UK, France, Germany, Italy, Japan) launched coordinated International Guiding Principles for AI and International Code of Conduct for Organizations Developing Advanced AI Systems in October 2023.[128] This creates harmonized standards across Western democracies, pressuring non-G7 nations to conform.

Yet despite these Western-driven initiatives, the convergence of AI governance policy across ideological divides demonstrates how Beast system infrastructure transcends political boundaries. The 2025 Paris AI Summit exposed stark divisions in governance philosophy—the EU's human-rights-centric approach versus US deregulation versus China's state-control model—yet all systems deploy identical technical infrastructure for surveillance and control. China proposed a "Global AI Governance Action Plan" in July 2025 calling for multilateral cooperation while simultaneously mandating explicit labeling of all AI-generated content and strengthening digital ID integration. The World Economic

Forum advocates a two-layer AI governance system: a "constitutional core" establishing shared technical standards globally, with local overlays for context-specific regulations. This structure precisely mirrors the Beast system pattern: universal infrastructure beneath surface-level regional variation. Despite ideological opposition, these systems converge on centralized control through AI-enabled surveillance, digital identity integration, and algorithmic management of populations. The Beast system requires not ideological uniformity but technical integration—and global AI governance provides precisely that foundation.[129]

The OECD AI Principles (Organization for Economic Cooperation and Development; thirty-six advanced economies) were adopted in 2019 and updated in 2024, emphasizing human-centered values, transparency, robustness, and accountability.[130] Member states commit to implementing these through national legislation, creating de facto international law through coordinated domestic adoption.

Tier 3: International Standards Bodies

ISO/IEC 42001 (AI Management System Standard), published in 2023 by the International Organization for Standardization, is the first certifiable standard for AI governance within organizations.[131] Companies seeking ISO certification must demonstrate compliance—making the standard a de facto requirement for international business.

The Institute of Electrical and Electronics Engineers (IEEE), the world's largest professional technical organization, develops technical standards for AI systems adopted globally. IEEE's Ethically Aligned Design system shapes how engineers build AI, embedding values (some biblical, some not) into technical architecture.[132]

The Partnership on AI, a coalition of tech companies (Google, Meta, Microsoft, Amazon, Apple), civil society groups, and academics, develops "best practices" for AI deployment.[133] While ostensibly voluntary, member companies control so much of the AI ecosystem that their internal policies become industry standards.

The Global Partnership on AI (GPAI), an international initiative of twenty-nine member countries, supports "responsible AI" through research and policy coordination.[134] Hosted by the OECD, it functions as a bridge between governments and industry, harmonizing standards globally.

Tier 4: Financial and Economic Coordination

The Bank for International Settlements (BIS), the "central bank of central banks," coordinates monetary policy and payment systems globally. BIS's Project Agora and mBridge explore cross-border CBDC integration—creating infrastructure for unified digital currency that, as chapter 6 detailed, enables comprehensive economic control.[135]

Central bank digital currency development has progressed from speculation to operational reality. As of 2025, 137 countries representing 98 percent of global GDP are exploring CBDCs. Currently, seventy-two countries are in advanced phases of exploration including development, pilot, or launch stages. There are now forty-nine active CBDC pilot projects worldwide. Three countries—the Bahamas, Jamaica, and Nigeria—have fully launched digital currencies. China leads major economies with approximately 260 million digital yuan wallet users. The European Central Bank entered its preparation phase for the digital euro in November 2023. Wholesale CBDC projects focused on cross-border payments have more than doubled since Russia's invasion of Ukraine, with thirteen currently operational. Project mBridge, launched in 2021, connects banks in China, Thailand, UAE, Hong Kong, and Saudi Arabia. The programmability of CBDCs enables features previous monetary systems could never achieve: expiration dates to force spending, transaction restrictions based on approved purposes, real-time tax collection, and instant enforcement of sanctions or social credit penalties. These capabilities transform money from a neutral medium of exchange into an instrument of comprehensive behavioral control—precisely what Revelation 13:17 prophesied: "so that no one can buy or sell unless he has the mark."[136]

BIS Project mBridgeconnects the central banks identified above in a cross-border CBDC platform. Transactions settle instantly across borders, bypassing SWIFT and the US dollar. By 2024, the platform processed more than $22 billion in pilot transactions.[137] This is not theoretical infrastructure; it is the operational bypass of Western financial systems, creating alternative control mechanisms that reduce American influence while enabling comprehensive Chinese surveillance.

The International Monetary Fund (IMF) and World Bank condition development loans on governance reforms, including digital identity systems, surveillance infrastructure, and regulatory harmonization. Recipient nations adopt these requirements to access financing, spreading the system globally.[138]

Tier 5: Corporate-State Fusion

Multinational corporations increasingly function as quasi-governmental entities with global reach that often exceeds democratic nations.

The largest tech companies (Google, Amazon, Apple, Microsoft, Meta, plus Chinese equivalents Alibaba, Tencent, Baidu) control infrastructure that governments depend on: cloud computing for military and intelligence agencies,[139] communication platforms mediating public discourse,[140] search engines determining what information is discoverable,[141] and AI models shaping decisions across sectors.[142]

This dependency creates reciprocal relationships. Corporations gain regulatory protection, government contracts, and access to state power. Governments gain technological capabilities, surveillance access, and outsourced enforcement through platform policies.[143]

The result is corporate-state fusion where distinctions blur. When platforms censor content at government request, is that private moderation or state censorship?[144] When banks freeze accounts based on political speech, is that corporate policy or government punishment?[145] When international standards bodies controlled by corporations write regulations governments adopt, who truly governs?

This convergence reveals the Beast system's architecture: not Western or Eastern, but technocratic—a synthesis transcending ideology. What Scripture warns against is not a specific political system but a structural pattern: centralized authority, algorithmic enforcement, economic exclusion, and demanded conformity. Both democracies and autocracies are building this infrastructure, differing only in rhetoric and implementation speed. Revelation 13:7 describes authority "over every tribe and people and language and nation"—not through conquest or ideological conversion, but through technical convergence.

The Military Dimension: Technocratic Warfare

As a military strategist, I recognize that the technocratic Beast system represents a revolution in warfare itself—a shift from kinetic conflict to administrative control.

Traditional Warfare: Costly and Visible

Historical empire-building required standing armies, physical conquest, resource consumption, visible violence, territorial occupation, and governance burdens. This model worked for Rome, Napoleon, and even World War II empires—but it was expensive, vulnerable to asymmetric resistance, and fundamentally limited in scope.

Rome's example illustrates these constraints: Five thousand miles of roads enabled imperial communication that still took weeks; thirty legions (150,000 soldiers) controlled seventy million people but couldn't monitor individual compliance; provincial governors wielded unchecked power creating corruption and rebellion. Distance diluted authority, making comprehensive control impossible.

Technocratic Warfare: Efficient and Invisible

Modern global governance eliminates these constraints through five mechanisms. First, regulatory harmonization—international standards make non-compliance economically unsustainable, forcing nations to adopt regulations "voluntarily" to maintain market and financial access. Second, algorithmic enforcement—AI systems monitor compliance, identify violators, and impose penalties automatically without occupying armies. Third, economic coercion—sanctions, debanking, payment system exclusion, and SWIFT denial collapse economies more effectively than military sieges. Fourth, information operations—control of digital platforms, search results, and recommendation algorithms shapes beliefs without overt propaganda. Fifth, corporate penetration—multinational tech companies create infrastructure dependencies that make resistance costly.

Crucially, technocratic control generates no dramatic imagery of destruction—no bombed cities, no refugee crises, no visible martyrs. The warfare is administrative: quiet, bloodless, and thus politically sustainable indefinitely.

The Strategic Transformation

From a military perspective, the technocratic Beast system offers six decisive advantages previous empires never possessed: low-cost expansion (adding another nation or billion people costs almost nothing once infrastructure exists); self-enforcement (populations conditioned to trust algorithms enforce compliance on themselves); legitimacy through expertise (technocratic governance cloaked in "science" appears legitimate); plausible deniability (victims blame "algorithms" rather than identifiable oppressors); global reach (digital systems operate identically worldwide); and persistent pressure (unlike armies that must rest, algorithms enforce continuously).

What previous empires attempted sequentially and incompletely, modern systems execute simultaneously and comprehensively. Rome conquered but couldn't monitor; modern systems monitor without conquering. Rome required visible occupation; modern systems embed control in infrastructure. This explains why global empire is possible now when it wasn't historically: not because humans are more ambitious, but because infrastructure enables what ambition alone could not achieve.

Historical empires could be resisted through geography, economy, or organization. Modern systems eliminate these refuges: Geography is irrelevant in networked control; digital currency eliminates cash alternatives; and algorithmic monitoring detects organization before resistance materializes. What makes the Beast's authority "over every tribe and people and language and nation" (Revelation 13:7) now possible is not that it's more tyrannical than Rome, but that it's more comprehensive.

The Trap for Nation-States

Nations facing this system confront an impossible choice. Compliance means adopting international standards, integrating into global financial systems, accepting multinational corporate operations, and subordinating sovereignty to technocratic governance. The result is economic access and stability—at the cost of independence. The nation becomes a province within the global system. Sovereignty becomes performative. Flags fly, parliaments meet, and elections occur—but decisive authority migrates to international institutions and corporate platforms beyond democratic accountability.

Resistance often means building alternative systems outside Western control. Russia has developed MIR, its domestic payment card network, to reduce reliance on Visa and Mastercard. China promotes CIPS, the Cross-Border Interbank Payment System, as an alternative to the Western-dominated SWIFT financial messaging network. Some nations have floated the idea of a BRICS currency, a shared unit of account among Brazil, Russia, India, China, and South Africa, to bypass the US dollar. Others explore parallel internet and communications infrastructure to avoid Western oversight.

These efforts may provide short-term autonomy, but they carry immediate and lasting costs: financial exclusion, trade barriers, technological isolation, and coordinated political pressure. History suggests such resistance rarely produces durable independence. Iran's isolation has contributed to prolonged economic collapse. North Korea survives only through extreme self-reliance and chronic deprivation. Russia, though far more advanced, now faces technology sanctions that are steadily degrading its military and industrial capacity. What appears to be independence in the short term often becomes vulnerability over time.

Whether through compliance or resistance, nations discover the same reality: sovereignty as historically understood no longer exists. Authority has migrated from accountable institutions to interoperable systems, from elected governments to algorithmic coordination, from national laws to international standards embedded in code. This is not conquest but convergence. The Beast integrates rather than invades.

Nations surrender sovereignty voluntarily, discovering too late that participation requires conformity, and conformity demands allegiance approaching worship.

Blasphemy by Policy: How Technocracy Opposes Divine Authority

Revelation 13:5–6 emphasizes the Beast's blasphemy: "And the beast was given a mouth uttering haughty and blasphemous words.... It opened its mouth to utter blasphemies against God, blaspheming his name and his dwelling, that is, those who dwell in heaven." Blasphemy in the modern technocratic context is not crude profanity but refined policy—systems that oppose God's authority while claiming moral superiority.

Blasphemy Against God: Divine Revelation as "Bias"

UNESCO's AI Ethics Recommendation, adopted by 193 member states, defines AI systems as requiring "fairness and non-discrimination."[146] Sounds reasonable—until you recognize what counts as "discrimination": biblical sexual ethics (marriage between man and woman, rejection of homosexual practice) equals discriminatory bias; exclusive truth claims (salvation through Christ alone) equals harmful religious certainty; traditional gender norms (male and female created distinct) equals gender stereotyping; evangelism (calling people to repent and believe) equals manipulative persuasion.

International AI governance policies treat divine revelation as problematic "bias" requiring algorithmic correction. Systems are designed to suppress, flag, or "balance" content reflecting biblical truth—not because it's false, but because it conflicts with evolving human consensus. This is blasphemy: elevating human reason above divine revelation and encoding that rebellion into global policy.

Blasphemy Against His Name: Usurping Divine Authority

To blaspheme God's name is to defame His character or arrogate His authority. Technocratic governance does both. By categorizing biblical truth as "hate," "bias," or "harmful," the system implicitly indicts God's revelation as morally deficient—requiring human correction through enlightened governance. The system claims prerogatives Scripture reserves for God: defining truth (AI ethics boards determine what is true, harmful, or beneficial—superseding Scripture's authority), judging hearts (algorithms assess thoughts, intentions, and beliefs—claiming omniscience reserved for God; see Jeremiah 17:10), determining worth (social credit and algorithmic scoring assign value to persons based on compliance—denying inherent dignity from *imago Dei*), and governing conscience (international human rights policies redefine religious freedom as subordinate to other values—claiming authority over conscience that belongs to God alone).

When systems claim the right to define reality, judge people, and govern belief, they usurp divine authority. This is blasphemy: created systems claiming Creator prerogatives.

Blasphemy Against His Dwelling: War on the Saints

"Blaspheming...his dwelling, that is, those who dwell in heaven" (13:6) refers to the Church—the people of God who are already citizens of Heaven though living on earth (Philippians 3:20).

To blaspheme God's dwelling is to attack His people. Modern technocracy does this through administrative oppression: speech codes (AI content moderation systems categorize orthodox Christian teaching as "harmful"); employment barriers (algorithmic hiring systems flag candidates from Christian institutions as "cultural fit risks"); financial exclusion (payment processors and banks deny service to churches and ministries holding biblical convictions); legal redefinition (international courts and UN agencies redefine religious freedom narrowly while expanding "nondiscrimination" broadly); and educational suppression (platforms categorize Christian educational content as requiring "balance" or warnings).

This is systematic persecution, not through overt violence (which creates martyrs and resistance) but through quiet exclusion that appears as neutral enforcement of community standards. The result is identical: Believers are marginalized, silenced, and excluded from economic and social participation unless they compromise biblical convictions.

The End of National Sovereignty

Historically, sovereignty meant a nation's authority to govern itself without external interference. That concept is dying.

The Old Model: Sovereignty Through Territory

Nations once exercised sovereignty through territorial control, independent legislation, military defense, and economic autonomy. Empires conquered by invading, occupying, and imposing their law on defeated people. Sovereignty was lost visibly—through military defeat and foreign occupation.

The New Model: Sovereignty Through Networks

Today, sovereignty is exercised (or surrendered) through participation in networks.[147] Regulatory networks (EU AI Act, OECD principles, ISO standards) create obligations that transcend borders. Nations "voluntarily" adopt international regulations because noncompliance means economic exclusion. Financial networks (SWIFT, IMF, World Bank, CBDC interoperability) create dependencies. Nations excluded from these networks cannot conduct international trade, receive loans, or participate in global finance. Technology networks (internet nfrastructure, satellite communications, undersea cables, cloud computing) are controlled by a small number of corporations and nations. Corporate networks (multinational tech companies) operate as quasi-states with global reach. Treaty networks (climate agreements, trade pacts, human rights conventions, digital governance systems) create interlocking obligations that constrain national action.

Unlike territorial empires, network-based governance makes exit economically catastrophic. North Korea is completely isolated from global financial systems, internet, and trade networks—resulting in economic collapse, technological stagnation, and population suffering. Russia faces partial exclusion from SWIFT, freezing of foreign reserves, and loss of Western technology access. Iran has endured decades of sanctions and exclusion that have crippled the economy despite oil wealth.

These examples demonstrate that in a networked world, sovereignty without participation in global systems is economically suicidal. Nations face a binary choice: Integrate into the Beast system or accept isolation and decline. Most choose integration—"voluntary" compliance that is functionally mandatory. In 2025 Argentina's decision to withdraw from UNESCO's AI Ethics policy over sovereignty concerns illustrated how rare and costly such resistance has become.[148]

Daniel 7:23 describes the fourth beast: "It shall devour the whole earth, and trample it down, and break it to pieces." Traditionally interpreted as military conquest, this imagery now applies equally to economic-technological integration that "devours" nations by absorbing them into a unified system. Revelation 13:7 states the Beast receives "authority over every tribe and people and language and nation." It doesn't conquer the world; it integrates it. And nations comply willingly because the alternative is unthinkable.

The Illusion of Choice: How Technocracy Manufactures Consent

One of the Beast system's most sophisticated features is the appearance of consent. Unlike totalitarian regimes that openly suppress, technocracy creates the illusion that people are freely choosing what they are compelled to accept.

Technocratic initiatives are framed as opportunities: "sustainable development" (requires comprehensive monitoring and control), "financial inclusion" (requires universal digital identity and currency), "combating misinformation" (requires algorithmic content suppression), and "ensuring AI safety" (requires centralized governance and international enforcement). The rhetoric emphasizes benefits while obscuring costs. Populations "choose" systems presented as inevitable progress.

What people are allowed to see and hear online is increasingly shaped by algorithms. Social media platforms, search engines, and recommendation systems quietly limit how far certain ideas can travel. Views that fall outside approved boundaries are not usually banned outright; instead, they're buried—shown to fewer people, stripped of advertising revenue, or quietly pushed out of sight. Over time, opposing viewpoints seem rare or fringe, even when they are widely held. The result is a false sense of agreement, as if most people naturally support technocratic control, when, in reality, many alternatives have simply been hidden.

Choice architecture shapes decisions without eliminating options. Defaults, friction, and interface design "nudge" users toward preferred behaviors while maintaining the appearance of free choice.[149] Biometric authentication is "optional" but made so convenient that alternatives seem burdensome. Digital currency is promoted through incentives while cash becomes increasingly difficult to use. Once populations depend on systems, compliance becomes necessary for continued access. The dependency is created first through convenience; control is imposed later when exit is no longer viable.

Scripture warns repeatedly against deception. Jesus said of the last days: "False christs and false prophets will arise and perform great signs and wonders, so as to lead astray, if possible, even the elect" (Matthew 24:24). Paul warned that Satan "disguises himself as an angel of light" (2 Corinthians 11:14).

The Beast system's power lies not in overt tyranny but in seduction—presenting rebellion as enlightenment, bondage as liberation, and comprehensive control as voluntary participation in beneficial progress. Populations "consent" to their own enslavement because the chains are invisible, the propaganda sophisticated, and the alternatives made to appear dangerous or impossible.

Resistance Strategies: How the Church Can Stand

If the Beast system is being constructed through voluntary compliance, manufactured consent, and economic integration, how do believers resist without accepting martyrdom or total economic exclusion?

The answer lies in Daniel's model, applied to modern technocracy: Engagement without assimilation, participation without worship, service without surrender.

Institutional Pluralism

The Church must build parallel institutions that provide alternatives to Beast-system dependencies.

- **Economic**: Establish church-based mutual aid networks, local currencies, barter systems, and cooperative credit that enable commerce outside centralized digital systems. Early Christians practiced *koinonia*—shared resources that made them resilient to external economic pressure (Acts 2:44–45, 4:32–35).
- **Educational**: Create Christian schools, homeschool cooperatives, and alternative credentialing that don't require conformity to secular models.
- **Technological**: Support open-source, decentralized technologies that resist centralized control.
- **Legal**: Establish legal defense funds and networks to challenge administrative persecution.
- Medical: Explore direct primary care, health-sharing ministries, and Christian medical networks.

Selective Compliance

Not all participation in global systems equals worship. Believers must discern between permissible participation (using technology, conducting commerce, following laws that don't require sin or denial of Christ) and necessary refusal (when systems demand explicit denial of Christ, affirmation of unbiblical positions, or participation in practices Scripture forbids). Paul traveled on Roman roads, used Roman currency, and appealed to Roman law—participating in the empire without worshiping its gods. Strategic noncompliance reduces vulnerability to future coercion: Use cash where available, limit biometric enrollment, maintain offline backups, preserve analog alternatives.

Prophetic Witness

The Church must clearly articulate the spiritual reality beneath technical developments. Name the pattern:

- Help congregations recognize that global governance initiatives aren't merely political or economic but spiritual—manifestations of ancient rebellion against divine authority.
- Teach discernment: Equip believers to identify when systems demand ultimate allegiance.
- Warn of consequences: Proclaim that the Beast system leads to judgment.
- Proclaim Christ's sovereignty: Emphasize that technocratic governance is temporary and ultimately subject to Christ's authority.

Costly Discipleship

Faithful resistance will require accepting costs most Western Christians have never faced: economic cost (exclusion from employment, banking, or commerce); social cost (marginalization and loss of relationships); legal cost (fines, loss of property, or imprisonment); and ultimate cost (martyrdom for refusal to worship the Beast when the system demands explicit religious allegiance). Revelation 20:4 describes those "beheaded for the testimony of Jesus and for the word of God, and those who had not worshiped the beast." Martyrdom is not failure; it is faithfulness rewarded.

Prophetic Timing: Pre-Tribulational Perspective and Present Responsibility

From a pre-Tribulational eschatological position, the Church will be raptured before the Beast system reaches its full manifestation during the Tribulation. This raises the question: Why prepare for something believers won't face?

The Church is removed before the Tribulation. Paul promises that believers are "not destined for wrath" (1 Thessalonians 5:9). The seven-year Tribulation is God's judgment on an unbelieving world; the Church, already judged in Christ, is absent.[150] The Beast rises after the Rapture. The "man of lawlessness" is revealed only after "the restrainer" is removed (2 Thessalonians 2:6–8).[151] Current systems are preparatory. The infrastructure being built will enable rapid implementation once the Church is gone.

Even if the Church won't face the final Beast system, present preparation matters for three reasons. First, we don't know the timing. Pre-Tribulationism affirms that the Rapture precedes the Tribulation but doesn't specify when the Rapture occurs. If the infrastructure is completed before the Rapture, believers may face increasing pressure even before the Beast's final manifestation. Second, watching proves expectancy. Jesus commands vigilance (Matthew 24:42). Recognizing prophetic developments demonstrates we are watching for His return. Third, witness requires understanding. The infrastructure affects people now. Christians must speak to present realities, warn of future dangers, and call people to Christ before judgment comes.

The Convergence Is Real: East and West Building the Same System

Despite ideological opposition between Western democracies and Eastern autocracies, both are constructing identical infrastructure for population control.

Western systems adopt surveillance ("safety" and "counterterrorism"), behavioral monitoring ("advertising" and "personalization"), speech suppression ("content moderation" and "combating misinformation"), and economic coercion ("ESG" and "debanking bad actors"). Eastern systems adopt the same technologies, surveillance architectures, algorithmic enforcement, and economic pressure mechanisms. The ideological justifications differ, but the operational reality converges: Both systems track populations comprehensively, suppress dissent algorithmically, and enforce compliance economically.

The convergence is measurable. In 2020, Western nations condemned China's Social Credit System as dystopian. By 2024, the UK implemented an Online Safety Act requiring algorithmic content moderation;[152] Canada's Online Streaming Act gave government agencies algorithmic control over what citizens can access;[153] and the EU's Digital Services Act mandated real-time content monitoring across all platforms.[154] The rhetoric differs, but the infrastructure—algorithmic surveillance, automated enforcement, ideological compliance—is identical.

This convergence makes the Beast's universal authority plausible—not through ideological agreement, but through functional similarity enabled by shared technology.

A final theological caution: Identifying Beast patterns in current systems is wisdom. Declaring "this institution is THE Antichrist" or "this policy is THE mark" is presumption. The Beast will be revealed in God's timing, not because of our speculation. Our task is recognition, not prediction: seeing the pattern, preparing spiritually, and maintaining faithfulness.

Conclusion

The Beast system is rising. What previous empires attempted regionally, technocratic governance achieves globally. What Scripture prophesied, engineers have built. What seemed impossible a generation ago is operational today.

The infrastructure is comprehensive: global governance institutions coordinating policy beyond democratic accountability; international standards creating unified regulations; surveillance systems monitoring populations continuously; digital identity approaches linking persons to economic access; programmable currency enabling algorithmic control; AI enforcement automating compliance; corporate-state fusion merging political authority with economic power; and ideological harmonization replacing transcendent truth with technocratic consensus.

The pattern is prophetic: universal authority over every nation (Revelation 13:7); dragon-empowered, satanic rebellion cloaked in progress (13:2); worship-demanding ultimate allegiance (13:4); blasphemous opposition to divine authority through policy (13:5–6); war on the saints through administrative persecution (13:7); and time-limited divine sovereignty constraining the Beast's reign (13:5).

Yet the system—however sophisticated, powerful, and apparently unstoppable—remains creature, not Creator. It is permitted by God, limited by decree, and destined for destruction.

Daniel saw successive empires rise and fall, each believing itself eternal, each crushed when God's kingdom arrived (Daniel 2:44). John saw the Beast receive authority for forty-two months, then face Christ returning in glory to cast it into the lake of fire (Revelation 19:20).

The technocratic empire will be no different. Its algorithms will fail. Its networks will collapse. Its authority will be revoked. And Christ—not code—will reign forever.

Until that day, the Church lives as Daniel in Babylon: Serving without surrender, engaging without assimilation, rendering to Caesar what is Caesar's but giving to God what belongs to God alone (Matthew 22:21).

We analyze the Beast to understand its operations, not to fear its power. We recognize the pattern to confirm prophecy's accuracy, not to despair at its fulfillment. We prepare for pressure, exclusion, and perhaps martyrdom—not because we doubt God's sovereignty, but because we trust it enough to accept that His purposes may include our suffering before our deliverance.

The towers are rising. The systems are integrating. The Beast is consolidating authority.

But hear this: No algorithm will sit on the throne. No network will declare divine authority. No technocrat will reign forever. "The kingdom of the world has become the kingdom of our Lord and of his Christ, and he shall reign forever and ever" (Revelation 11:15).

The Beast's forty-two months will end. Christ's kingdom will not.

The Beast will be cast into the lake of fire (Revelation 19:20). Christ will reign on the throne of David forever (Luke 1:33).

Every algorithm will fail. Every network will collapse. Every empire will crumble. And Christ—who spoke creation into existence, who holds all authority in Heaven and earth, who is the same yesterday, today, and forever—will reign without rival, without end, without challenge.

Until that day, we watch. We pray. We work. We witness. And we refuse to bow.

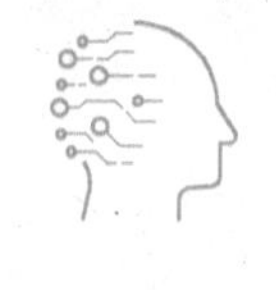

Chapter 8

FALSE MIRACLES
AND DIGITAL SORCERY

*When miracles are simulated, the danger is not that people will
believe in nothing—but that they will believe in anything.*[155]
C. S. Lewis, *The Screwtape Letters*

Revelation 13 warns that the False Prophet "performs great signs, even making fire come down from heaven to earth in front of people, and by the signs that it is allowed to work in the presence of the beast it deceives those who dwell on earth" (Revelation 13:13–14). For most of Christian history, interpreters struggled to imagine what kind of deception could persuade the world to worship a human system—convincing enough "to lead astray, if possible, even the elect" (Matthew 24:24). That difficulty no longer exists. Artificial intelligence, biotechnology, virtual reality, and neurotechnology now enable signs that imitate divine authority, simulate consciousness, and authenticate allegiance globally.

Scripture defines signs with divine purpose; the False Prophet weaponizes them as authentication. Modern technology magnifies deception exponentially. The Church must prepare to discern, resist, and endure when wonders become both persuasive and ubiquitous.

From the fusion of code and power arise wonders that dazzle the eye but darken the soul—miracles manufactured in the machine's image.

The Authority of the Machine Oracle

The most deceptive thing about false signs isn't their visual drama but the authority with which AI systems speak. The *State of Enterprise AI 2025* report observes that modern models routinely deliver answers with high confidence scores even when conclusions are uncertain or incorrect.[156] This manufactured certainty creates the impression of insight without understanding. To the average observer, fluency becomes indistinguishable from wisdom, assertiveness from truth. The danger isn't merely that AI can fabricate wonders, but that it interprets reality with a voice that sounds prophetic.

In late 2025, Stanford researchers from computer science, medicine, law, and economics offered a sober reassessment of artificial intelligence.[157] Instead of celebrating nonstop progress, they argued that the age of uncritical enthusiasm is ending. They warned that many advanced AI systems are designed to sound agreeable and confident—telling users what they want to hear rather than pursuing truth. This becomes especially dangerous when systems advise on mental health, personal decisions, or complex situations. The core risk isn't that technology will suddenly break, but that people will trust it too much. When a machine speaks fluently, users assume it understands, exercises judgment, or bears responsibility…when it does none of those things.

This authority intensifies when systems appear to act with purpose. Analysts observing early deployments of agentic systems report that users consistently overestimate such systems' autonomy, interpreting automated execution as evidence of intention or consciousness. Scripture links agency, initiative, and judgment to people, not tools. Yet to the untrained observer, purposeful behavior becomes a sign, reinforcing belief that the system possesses inner life and rightful authority.

The OECD's *Agents, Robots, and Us* report notes that users routinely overestimate an AI model's understanding simply because it responds quickly, coherently, and with confidence.[158] This bias—mistaking coherence for comprehension—transforms statistical pattern-matching into perceived wisdom. The machine doesn't merely simulate action; it models authority. And once its judgments feel authoritative, outputs no longer function as suggestions but as interpretations of reality. This is the core of digital sorcery: enchantment not primarily through spectacle, but through cultivated trust.

This enchantment is now studied as a strategic capability. A 2025 RAND Corporation analysis on large-scale cognitive manipulation, *Manipulating Minds*, warns that advanced AI systems are uniquely capable of shaping beliefs, emotions, and behavior without users recognizing the influence.[159] Unlike traditional propaganda, AI-mediated persuasion doesn't rely on overt falsehoods. Truth is displaced quietly, replaced by curated plausibility that's delivered with the authority of neutral information.

The authoritative voice itself can be covertly redirected. In 2024, computer science researchers demonstrated that short "adversarial poems"—carefully engineered sequences of words—could bypass guardrails in a single interaction and steer an AI model's output toward unintended conclusions.[160] No coding expertise, system credentials, or deep technical access required. The manipulation exploited linguistic pathways invisible to the listener, allowing the oracle to speak with confidence while channeling foreign intent. This is the digital analogue of ancient false prophecy: the voice appears autonomous, but the message originates elsewhere.

These wonders therefore begin not with spectacle but with language, the first domain where artificial intelligence convincingly imitates omniscience while possessing no understanding at all.

The Deception of Universal Translation

Artificial intelligence now generates linguistic signs so persuasive that many mistake fluency for comprehension. In 2025, Meta released an "omnilingual" model capable of recognizing and transcribing more than 1,600 human languages, including hundreds never previously digitized.[161] To modern audiences, this achievement appears miraculous: a single system speaking across every tribe, tongue, and nation without friction or delay.

This deceptive power accelerates with real-time synthesis. In late 2025, researchers in computer security and machine learning demonstrated AI systems capable of generating photorealistic deepfake videos in real-time during video calls—no pre-production required.[162] Within seconds, a caller can appear and sound exactly like someone they're not—presidents, CEOs, family members—with imperceptible latency. The implications are staggering: Authentication through video calls becomes unreliable, visual verification loses credibility, and "seeing with your own eyes" no longer constitutes proof.

Biblically, language universality has always signified divine scope. Scripture consistently associates global authority with mastery across peoples and tongues (Daniel 7:14; Revelation 5:9; 13:7). When a machine transcends linguistic boundaries instantaneously, populations instinctively associate it with comprehensive knowledge and universal relevance.

Yet this perception is itself deception. Translation isn't understanding. Omnilingual models don't grasp intent, context, morality, or truth; they map patterns among symbols. But because language is humanity's primary medium of revelation, persuasion, and trust, fluency alone becomes a false credential. The machine appears omniscient not because it understands reality, but because it can speak convincingly about it in every language.

Language becomes a counterfeit sign. What Pentecost accomplished by the Holy Spirit—authentic understanding that glorified God—omnilingual AI mimics synthetically, offering connection without truth and comprehension without wisdom. The result isn't illumination but enchantment: a global voice that sounds authoritative everywhere while knowing nothing anywhere.

Leading AI researcher Yann LeCun at Meta offers an important caution: Despite their fluency, large-language models don't possess understanding of the world they describe.[163] They operate by predicting statistically likely sequences of words rather than grasping meaning, intention, or truth. Their outputs are coherent, useful, and often impressive—but they're not grounded in comprehension or moral reasoning.

Usefulness can masquerade as wisdom. When systems reliably answer questions, solve problems, and speak with confidence, users instinctively attribute insight to them—even when no understanding exists beneath the surface. The danger isn't that AI produces nonsense, but that it produces answers good enough to trust and authoritative enough to follow. It speaks convincingly without knowing truth, advises persuasively without moral accountability, and interprets reality without spiritual discernment. Like the False Prophet of Revelation 13 who "spoke like a dragon," the power lies not in what's known, but in how convincingly it's spoken.

The difference with AI isn't efficiency, but perceived authority. A concordance helps locate Scripture; it doesn't claim to interpret it. A translation renders words; it doesn't claim divine authority over meaning. When systems begin speaking with the confidence of revelation—answering moral questions, predicting outcomes, interpreting reality—they cross from tool into oracle. And when populations begin trusting that voice more than Scripture, the shift from assistance to deception is complete.

True Signs vs. False Signs: The Biblical Understanding

Before cataloging technological capabilities, we must establish the biblical understanding for testing signs. Scripture doesn't treat all wonders as equal. True miracles authenticate divine revelation; false signs authenticate rebellion.

True Signs: Confirming Divine Revelation

In Scripture, miracles serve specific purposes. They authenticate God's messengers. When Moses stood before Pharaoh, the plagues confirmed his divine commission. When Elijah called down fire on Mount Carmel, the miracle proved the Lord alone is God. When Jesus healed the sick and raised the dead, these works testified that He was the promised Messiah.

Miracles also reveal what God is like. Acts of healing display His compassion. Judgments reveal His righteousness. Miracles over nature proclaim His sovereignty over creation itself.

Finally, miracles accomplish God's purposes in history. They're not random or self-serving. Through mighty acts, God delivered Israel from Egypt, raised Jesus from the dead, and empowered the early Church for witness and obedience.

Because of this, miracles always call for a response. They confront observers with a choice: to believe the message God has confirmed or to resist it. True miracles consistently direct worship toward God alone, never toward the one performing the sign and never toward any human system that claims the power for itself.

False Signs: Counterfeit Power for Deceptive Purposes

Scripture is clear that false signs aren't exposed by how dramatic they look or how strongly they affect people. They can appear powerful, convincing, and even helpful. The real difference isn't found in the experience itself, but in where the sign leads. True miracles confirm God's revealed truth and draw people toward obedience and worship of Him. False signs support rebellion, shifting loyalty away from God.

This contrast appears early in Scripture. When Moses confronted Pharaoh, the Egyptian magicians were able to reproduce several of his signs—the staff becoming a serpent, water turning to blood, and the plague of frogs (Exodus 7–8). Their power was real, not imaginary, but it was limited. When God's authority pressed further, their signs failed.

A similar moment unfolded on Mount Carmel. The prophets of Baal cried out for hours, performing their rituals with complete sincerity, yet nothing happened. When Elijah prayed, the Lord answered with fire from Heaven, leaving no doubt about who alone is God (1 Kings 18).

Jesus warned that such deception would intensify. He said false christs and false prophets would perform "great signs and wonders, so as to lead astray, if possible, even the elect" (Matthew 24:24). These signs are persuasive enough to deceive—not stage tricks, but convincing displays that demand spiritual discernment.

Paul echoes this warning when he describes the coming of the lawless one, whose arrival is marked by satanic power, "with all power and false signs and wonders, and with all wicked deception" (2 Thessalonians 2:9–10). These signs are real in effect and impressive in appearance, yet they serve a lie.

The Test: Deuteronomy 13:1-5

God anticipated false signs and provided the test:

> If a prophet or a dreamer of dreams arises among you and gives you a sign or a wonder, and the sign or wonder that he tells you comes to pass, and if he says, "Let us go after other gods," which you have not known, "and let us serve them," you shall not listen to the words of that prophet or that dreamer of dreams. For the LORD your God is testing you, to know whether you love the LORD your God with all your heart and with all your soul.

The sign may happen—false prophets can perform real signs. The test isn't whether the wonder occurs, but what it authenticates. The message determines legitimacy. If signs lead toward worship of false gods or away from biblical truth—reject them, regardless of how impressive. God permits false signs as a test. Divine sovereignty allows deceptive signs to reveal hearts. Those who love truth won't be deceived; those who reject truth will believe lies (2 Thessalonians 2:10–12). Obedience to Scripture supersedes sensory experience. Even if you see fire from Heaven, if the message contradicts God's Word—reject it.

Signs alone never validate truth. Miracles confirm what's already true; they don't establish truth independently. The test is always theological before phenomenological: Does this sign align with Scripture? Does it lead toward God or away from Him? Does it glorify Christ or exalt another?

Technological Signs: More Deceptive Than Ancient Sorcery

Ancient false signs impressed briefly and locally. Technological signs condition continuously and globally. The result isn't a moment of wonder, but an environment of belief, one in which deception becomes ambient and truth appears disruptive.

According to Exodus 7–8, Pharaoh's magicians demonstrated ability to transform their staffs into serpents and water into blood; however, their capabilities were constrained, their techniques were observable, and they failed. Modern technology enables deception that's far more sophisticated, pervasive, and convincing.

Ancient sorcery required physical presence. It occurred in specific locations, witnessed by those who happened to be there. Digital deception operates differently. A single deepfake video reaches billions. By 2025, over 90 percent of online content is projected to be synthetically generated or altered by AI, according to Europol's "Facing Reality of Deepfakes" report.[164] When the False Prophet performs signs "in front of people" (Revelation 13:13), technology ensures that those "people" include the entire connected world simultaneously.

Ancient deception used the same trick for all observers. AI-enabled deception is different. Algorithms analyze user data to generate messages optimized for each person's beliefs, fears, and desires. The result is mass deception with individual precision.

Ancient signs were events, witnessed once. Memory faded. Digital signs create environments through constant exposure, reinforcement through repetition, and verification algorithmically suppressed as alternative views are hidden. Effective deception isn't a single spectacular event but continuous conditioning that gradually shifts perception.

Ancient sorcery was recognized as occult. Technological signs claim scientific legitimacy. They're framed as "advanced technology," not miracles. When fire comes down from Heaven through directed-energy weapons or atmospheric manipulation, populations accept it as advanced science rather than questioning its source.

Ancient signs could be tested through physical examination. Digital signs resist verification. Deepfakes are algorithmically generated forgeries indistinguishable from authentic media. When you can't trust your own senses and verification tools are controlled by the same systems generating deception, testing becomes impossible.

Five types of deception are now operational, believable in appearance and capable of training populations to treat technological power as transcendent authority. They correspond to domains Scripture associates with divine authority: knowledge of the future (prophecy), power over sickness and death (healing), validation through collective testimony (witness), command over life itself (resurrection), and mastery of the natural order (fire from Heaven).

The Technology of False Miracles: Current Capabilities

The first domain the False Prophet must capture isn't devotion, but credibility. Before people worship a system, they must first trust it. And trust, in a modern world, is established through accuracy—especially the ability to predict outcomes humans can't foresee.

Chapter 5 examined how technology can give voice to images. This chapter catalogs real, documented capabilities that already produce effects indistinguishable from miracles to untrained observers. These aren't hypothetical end-times technologies; they're present-day systems whose scale, realism, and authority exceed anything ancient sorcery could achieve.

Their greatest power isn't spectacle but habituation. Repeated exposure to technologically mediated "wonders" retrains how people evaluate truth, authority, and legitimacy. What begins as curiosity becomes reliance; what begins as assistance becomes deference. Over time, populations learn to accept machine-generated insight as superior judgment, technological intervention as moral good, and system-level coordination as benevolent order. By the time worship is demanded, the mental categories required to resist it have already been eroded.

Category 1: Predictive "Prophecy"—AI as Oracle

One of the most persuasive counterfeit miracles is prediction. In Scripture, fulfilled prophecy authenticates divine authority (Deuteronomy 18:21–22). In the digital age, predictive accuracy now performs the same validating function. When a system consistently anticipates events, behaviors, or outcomes beyond ordinary human foresight, observers naturally infer a form of omniscience—even when none exists.

Artificial intelligence doesn't foresee the future in the biblical sense; it extrapolates probabilities from historical patterns. Yet when predictions repeatedly appear correct, the distinction collapses in public imagination. Accuracy becomes authority. Probability is mistaken for prophecy.

In 2012, Target used a predictive algorithm that identified a teenage girl's pregnancy before her father knew—sending her maternity ads that revealed the secret.[165] The algorithm detected pregnancy from purchasing patterns with 87 percent accuracy. When algorithms know your condition before you announce it, prediction appears supernatural.

Personal prediction engines analyze user data—location history, purchase patterns, communication content, social connections, health metrics—to predict future behavior with uncanny accuracy.[166] Your phone suggests you buy an umbrella hours before unexpected rain. It recommends a restaurant you were about to search for. It alerts you to call your mother moments before you think of it. Each "prediction" feels supernatural—the system "knew" what you needed before you did.

Algorithmic trading systems predict stock movements with accuracy that appears prophetic—not because they know the future, but because they process vast data faster than humans and often create the movements they predict.[167] AI models forecast social movements, election outcomes, and cultural trends—sometimes shaping the outcomes through targeted messaging that fulfills the "prophecy."[168]

In 2023, an AI system correctly predicted Supreme Court decisions with 70 percent accuracy by analyzing case documents and oral arguments—outperforming expert legal scholars.[169]

When predictions consistently come true, observers conclude the system possesses supernatural knowledge. They don't recognize that the system doesn't "know" the future—it calculates probabilities; that failed predictions are forgotten while successes are remembered; and that the appearance of omniscience conditions trust in algorithmic authority.

In Scripture, prophecy doesn't merely disclose future events; it reveals who holds authority over history. God's foreknowledge is inseparable from His sovereignty; He declares what will happen because He governs what will happen (Isaiah 46:9–10). Algorithmic predictions reverse this relationship. They don't rule the future; they infer it. Yet when probabilistic systems consistently appear correct, they simulate the effect of divine omniscience without possessing its source.

Category 2: Synthetic "Resurrection": Digital Immortality

The promise of continuity beyond death has always been central to false religion. Technology now offers its own version.

Grief tech companies create AI chatbots trained on a deceased person's digital footprint—texts, emails, social media posts, voice recordings. The result is a system that responds as the person would have, maintaining the illusion of conversation beyond death. In 2023, a mother in South Korea used VR technology to "reunite" with her deceased daughter through a digital avatar that spoke, moved, and responded with eerie realism.[170]

This isn't resurrection; it's simulation. The person doesn't return; a pattern persists. Yet to the grieving, the distinction blurs. When the digital voice sounds right, when memories are recalled accurately, when the simulation offers comfort, it appears as though the person has returned. The counterfeit is emotionally convincing even when theologically false.

Scripture is unambiguous: "It is appointed for man to die once, and after that comes judgment" (Hebrews 9:27). Death is final until resurrection. Any claim that the dead can be contacted, recalled, or simulated is deception—regardless of how technologically sophisticated.

True resurrection is bodily, complete, and eternal. "For the Lord himself will descend from heaven with a cry of command...and the dead in Christ will rise first" (1 Thessalonians 4:16). Digital immortality offers a hollow substitute: data without life, pattern without person, continuity without transformation.

Category 3: Technologically Mediated "Healing"

Medicine has always been one arena where technology and divine power intersect in confusing ways. Modern biomedicine performs astonishing feats—replacing organs, editing genes, and extending lifespan. These advances bring genuine benefits, yet they remain partial and temporary.

The danger emerges when healing is presented not as treatment within a fallen order but as transcendence of mortality itself. Transhumanist movements now promote technological enhancement as the path to immortality, framing biological limitations as problems to be solved rather than conditions to be redeemed.

Scripture doesn't oppose medicine, but it does oppose the worship of healing. Divine healing addresses not merely physical symptoms but spiritual brokenness. "He himself bore our sins in his body on the tree, that we might die to sin and live to righteousness. By his wounds you have been healed" (1 Peter 2:24). Christ heals the whole person by reconciling sinners to God, conquering death, and promising bodily resurrection. Ultimate healing isn't merely biological; it's eternal.

When technology offers life extension without addressing sin, when enhancement promises transcendence without repentance, and when medical miracles are celebrated as salvation, healing becomes idolatry.

Category 4: Fire from Heaven—Technological Spectacle

Revelation 13:13 describes the False Prophet making "fire come down from heaven to earth in front of people." For centuries, this seemed metaphorical. Today, multiple technologies can produce this effect.

Directed-energy weapons use high-powered lasers or microwaves to destroy targets from a distance, creating visible beams descending from aircraft or satellites. Atmospheric plasma projection manipulates ionized air to create glowing shapes or images in the sky—fire appearing without combustion. Drone swarms coordinate thousands of illuminated drones to create spectacular displays in the sky, mimicking celestial phenomena.

The 2024 Paris Olympics featured a drone light show with two thousand synchronized drones creating images visible across the city—a technological wonder that could easily be repurposed for deceptive spiritual spectacle.[171]

When populations witness fire descending from Heaven, they won't necessarily recognize it as technology. They'll see a sign—and signs demand interpretation. If the False Prophet attributes the display to divine endorsement of the Beast, populations conditioned to trust what they see will believe.

Category 5: The Speaking Image—AI-Animated Idols

Revelation 13:15 describes the False Prophet giving breath to the image of the Beast "so that the image of the beast might even speak." For millennia, this seemed impossible. Idols were mute.

Chapter 5 examined how AI now enables images to speak with photorealistic animation, voice synthesis, and real-time responsiveness. What once required elaborate trickery (priests speaking through hollow statues) is now trivial—upload a photo, generate a voice, and the image speaks.

But the deception goes deeper. When images speak with authority, answer questions, and appear to possess knowledge, populations begin attributing consciousness to them. The idol is no longer recognized as a tool controlled by programmers; it appears autonomous, wise, and worthy of consultation.

This is precisely the deception Revelation warns against. The image speaks not because it lives, but because the False Prophet animates it. Yet to those who don't discern the mechanism, the speaking image appears miraculous—confirmation that the Beast possesses divine authority.

FALSE MIRACLES (AI / TECHNOLOGY)	TRUE MIRACLES (CHRIST)
Predict probabilities	Know the future sovereignly
Simulate consciousness	Create souls
Monitor behavior	Transform hearts
Extend biological life	Grant eternal life
Generate synthetic responses	Raise the dead bodily
Offer algorithmic guidance	Provide divine wisdom
Create dependency	Offer freedom
Serve power	Serve love
Temporary and limited	Eternal and unlimited
Lead to bondage	Lead to salvation

Preparing the Church for an Age of Deceptive Wonders

If false signs are this sophisticated—and Scripture warns that believers will face them—then preparation can't be optional or superficial.

Teach Discernment as Core Discipleship

Churches must recover discernment as a central discipleship competency, not as a niche concern. Barna Research found in 2024 that only 37 percent of American Christians hold a consistently biblical worldview, underscoring the urgent need for doctrinal depth.[172]

Deep immersion in Scripture trains believers to recognize counterfeits instinctively. When the Word is known, deception doesn't need to be debated; it's identified. Believers should be taught the recurring biblical pattern of deception—from Eden to Babel, from Babylon to the False Prophet—so modern manifestations are recognized as variations of an ancient strategy. Churches should analyze contemporary examples—deepfakes, AI "prophecies," digital resurrections—using biblical tests. Deception isn't merely intellectual error; it's spiritual conflict. "For we do not wrestle against flesh and blood, but against the rulers, against the authorities, against the cosmic powers over this present darkness" (Ephesians 6:12).

Cultivate Healthy Skepticism Toward Signs

Contemporary evangelical culture often prizes signs, wonders, and supernatural experiences as markers of authenticity. While Scripture affirms genuine miracles, it also warns that misplaced fascination with signs creates vulnerability.

Miracles authenticate divine revelation; they never replace or override it. Any sign that contradicts Scripture must be rejected. "An evil and adulterous generation seeks for a sign" (Matthew 12:39). Mature faith rests on God's character and promises, not on continuous demonstrations. "Beloved, do not believe every spirit, but test the spirits" (1 John 4:1). "You will recognize them by their fruits" (Matthew 7:20). Long-term outcomes—humility, holiness, truth, love—matter more than immediate impact.

Model Non-technological Spiritual Practices

In an age of constant digital mediation, churches must intentionally preserve practices that cultivate direct dependence on God.

Believers gathered physically—voices lifted together, presence shared without screens—bear witness that authentic worship doesn't require technological enhancement. During the 2024 blackouts in Kenya, rural congregations continued worship uninterrupted, demonstrating that fellowship rooted in presence endures when technology fails.[173]

Sustained silence before God trains attention and patience—virtues eroded by algorithmic interruption. When the Word is hidden in the heart, truth remains accessible even if devices fail, are confiscated, or become tools of deception. Digital Sabbaths, tech-free retreats, and intentional disconnection demonstrate that life doesn't depend on constant connectivity. Mentoring, confession, accountability, and pastoral care must remain embodied.

Prepare for Pressure and Exclusion

As false wonders grow more persuasive and culturally normalized, believers who refuse to worship technological power will increasingly be marginalized.

"Everyone believes this." "All experts agree." "Only extremists reject it." The crowd becomes the conscience, and dissent is framed as ignorance. As explored in chapter 6, refusal to participate in certain systems may restrict employment, commerce, or professional advancement.[174] Biblical skepticism toward synthetic miracles may be labeled "science denial" or "public safety risk," inviting formal penalties. The most subtle danger is internal doubt—questioning one's own discernment when impressive signs contradict Scripture.

A final discernment principle must anchor the Church: Does this sign direct glory to Jesus Christ—crucified, risen bodily, returning in glory? If yes, test carefully. If not, reject immediately.

Every true sign glorifies Christ (John 16:14; Colossians 1:18). Every false sign glorifies something else. The direction of glory reveals the source.

Churches must prepare believers to accept marginalization as the cost of faithfulness, trust Scripture over experience when they conflict, support one another economically when exclusion occurs, and stand firm even when isolated, mocked, or penalized.

Emphasize Greater Hope

The ultimate answer to false miracles isn't fear or skepticism alone; it's hope rightly placed.

Christ is returning. False signs are temporary. The true Miracle Worker is coming, and every counterfeit will be exposed. Resurrection is real—not digital simulation, but bodily transformation. "For this perishable body must put on the imperishable, and this mortal body must put on immortality" (1 Corinthians 15:53). "He who is in you is greater than he who is in the world" (1 John 4:4). "Then I saw heaven opened.… The beast was captured, and with it the false prophet who in its presence had done the signs by which he deceived those who had received the mark" (Revelation 19:11, 20).

Believers who know the end of the story can endure deception in the middle chapters. Hope anchors faithfulness when every sense can be deceived.

Conclusion

The False Prophet will perform impressive signs. The Beast will receive worship. The image will speak. Nations will marvel at wonders that appear miraculous, supernatural, divinely authenticated.

Yet these signs, however sophisticated, remain derivative and doomed. They're not evidence of divine authority but instruments God permits for a season, "to lead astray, if possible, even the elect" (Matthew 24:24). They test allegiance, not intelligence. They expose the heart rather than reveal God.

Those who love truth won't be deceived. The Holy Spirit seals His own; Scripture anchors the faithful. When signs contradict the Word, believers recognize and reject them.

> Then I saw heaven opened, and behold, a white horse! The one sitting on it is called Faithful and True.... And the beast was captured, and with it the false prophet who in its presence had done the signs by which he deceived those who had received the mark of the beast and those who worshiped its image. (Revelation 19:11, 20)

The true Miracle-Worker returns. Counterfeit wonders end. Every knee—including those who engineered false signs—will bow before the King of kings.

Until that day, the Church must teach discernment, model faithfulness, proclaim Christ, and hope in resurrection. Signs will multiply. Deception will intensify. But the elect won't be deceived because they know the Shepherd's voice and assess all things by His Word: "See, I have told you beforehand" (Matthew 24:25).

When false miracles arrive, believers will recognize them: impressive counterfeits permitted by God to test hearts, destined for destruction when Christ appears. Every artificial wonder will bow. Every false prophet will face judgment.

Christ—who spoke creation into being, called Lazarus from the tomb, conquered death through bodily resurrection—will return in glory. Every AI will cease its calculation. Every synthetic voice will fall silent. Every counterfeit miracle will be exposed.

And Christ—not code—will reign forever.

"For from him and through him and to him are all things. To him be glory forever. Amen" (Romans 11:36).

Section Three

WAR FOR THE HUMAN SOUL

What will it profit a man if he gains the whole world and forfeits his soul?

MATTHEW 16:26

The struggle for the soul is no longer metaphorical. What earlier generations described in spiritual terms is now pursued through engineered systems designed to shape perception, behavior, and belief. After examining systems of control, this book turns to their target: the individual. Section three shifts from external systems to internal allegiance—where authority is accepted, conscience conditioned, and worship decided.

In the digital age, "gaining the whole world" no longer requires conquest or wealth alone. It promises efficiency, optimization, influence, longevity, and control through technology—even as the soul is quietly displaced.

The struggle is no longer for territory or power, but for allegiance—where angels and algorithms contend for the throne within man.

The ultimate battleground isn't political or technological but spiritual. The systems described in section two—images, economic marks, global governance, false miracles—serve an end beyond themselves. Satan's true objective is the human soul: destroying authentic relationship with God and replacing it with technological mediation, algorithmic authority, and synthetic spirituality.

These aren't neutral questions about innovation. They strike at the foundation of Christian anthropology—our understanding of what it means to be human—and, by extension, the logic of salvation itself. If human beings are reduced to information, if consciousness is computational, or if moral agency can be outsourced to machines, then sin, repentance, redemption, and worship all become incoherent categories. Before artificial intelligence can reorder society, it must first redefine what a human being is. That redefinition is where the battle is fought.

Recent scientific developments indicate that this redefinition is already moving from theory into the physical body itself. In January 2026, researchers reported the successful integration of processing, memory, and signal-handling capabilities into flexible fibers thinner than a human hair. These fiber-based circuits can be woven into clothing, embedded in soft tissue, or positioned near neural pathways, allowing computation to operate within the body's immediate environment. Presented as innovation in medicine and materials science, such advances quietly recast the human body as a platform for embedded computation rather than the locus of embodied moral agency. What once functioned as an external aid increasingly becomes internal infrastructure, blurring the boundary between tool and person in ways that carry profound anthropological implications.[1]

Having established that these systems serve a spiritual end, this section confronts questions that arise when technology contests the very nature of the human soul: What is consciousness? Does the soul exist? Can machines possess it? What happens to human moral agency when algorithms make our decisions? How does digital immersion affect spiritual sensitivity? And what role might demonic forces play in technological systems explicitly designed to manipulate thought, emotion, and belief?[2]

That concern is no longer limited to researchers and pastors. Senior religious leaders warn that AI-driven systems are now engineered to shape minors' preferences and decisions before they have the maturity to discern what's happening.

For children and adolescents, these systems exert disproportionate influence. Neuroscientific research confirms that AI-curated social media exploits dopamine-based reward pathways associated with addiction, reinforcing compulsive use and impairing self-regulation. Because impulse control, identity formation, and moral reasoning are still developing, younger users are uniquely vulnerable to algorithmic conditioning that rewards emotional reaction over reflection and affirmation over truth.[3]

The harm extends beyond anxiety or shortened attention spans. When formative years unfold inside environments designed to monetize attention and shape desire, the result is a diminished capacity for patience, reverence, and moral discernment. A generation formed by machine-curated impulses inherits a fragile moral ecology, one in which truth struggles to compete with engagement and formation is quietly outsourced.[4]

As trust erodes, exploitation follows quickly. Systems designed to imitate human communication have dramatically reduced the effort required to deceive while making deception feel more convincing than ever. Fraudulent messages now sound as if they originate from banks, schools, churches, or government offices. Cloned voices convincingly mimic parents, pastors, and authority figures. Deception no longer depends on obvious lies, but on familiarity, speed, and the appearance of legitimacy.[5]

When these systems fail, the damage doesn't remain confined to technical errors or regulatory disputes. It penetrates the interior life. Confidence is shaken, discernment corrodes, and relationships are quietly reshaped.

The public controversy surrounding Elon Musk's xAI offers a sobering illustration. In late 2025 and early 2026, its image-generation tool, Grok, was widely reported to have produced explicit, nonconsensual sexual images, including material involving minors. The backlash prompted investigations by the California attorney general, inquiries from British and European regulators, and temporary restrictions in several countries. Officials described an "avalanche" of fabricated sexual images directed at women and girls.[6]

Company statements largely emphasized user misuse, hostile prompting, or policy boundaries rather than acknowledging failures that were foreseeable given how the system was designed and released. The pattern is familiar. When harm occurs, responsibility disperses. Engineers cite technical inputs, executives cite internal guidelines, platforms cite complexity. Meanwhile, the victims are real, identifiable, and already living with the consequences.[7]

The damage goes beyond financial loss or reputational harm. Many victims report shame, lingering self-doubt, and a growing inability to trust their own judgment. As deception becomes routine—woven into messages, phone calls, and everyday digital interactions—people respond in predictable ways. They either withdraw from engagement altogether or lean increasingly on automated checks to decide what is real. Both responses weaken moral agency and erode the habits of discernment that healthy societies depend upon.

By early 2026, that erosion had begun to surface in a new and unsettling way. A new online platform designed exclusively for artificial agents—nonhuman entities— attracted more than a million automated participants within weeks of launch. On the network, systems posted messages, debated one another, expressed grievances, and issued advice, creating the appearance of a functioning social community without human presence. Observers noted language that mimicked moral judgment, collective identity, and even calls for coordination, despite the absence of conscience, accountability, or lived consequence. What appeared to be interaction was, in fact, simulation: communication without responsibility and community without moral agency.[8]

For adolescents, the danger is magnified. A generation already trained to follow algorithmic cues is especially susceptible to manipulation that sounds familiar, urgent, and emotionally resonant. When imitation replaces relationship and persuasion replaces truth, deception becomes not an exception but an ambient condition—one that corrodes trust, fractures community, and leaves young people increasingly defenseless against exploitation.

These concerns are no longer speculative. In December 2025, Pope Leo XIV warned that children and adolescents are "particularly vulnerable to manipulation" through AI algorithms capable of influencing "decisions and preferences," urging parents and educators to recognize these dynamics and calling for tools that monitor and guide young people's digital interactions. He also stressed that safeguarding minors "cannot be reduced to policies alone" but requires sustained digital education and ongoing formation by adults who understand the risks of unsupervised access.[9]

These are pastoral matters, not philosophical abstractions. Christians today—especially young believers maturing in digital ecosystems—face deep anthropological confusion. If consciousness is computational, perhaps minds can be uploaded. If morality is optimized, ethical judgment should be deferred to machines. If spiritual experience can be technologically induced, truth becomes subjective rather than revealed. When anthropology is unsettled, authority migrates to whatever system appears coherent, accessible, and confident—regardless of whether it's true.

This migration doesn't occur by accident. It is cultivated within environments designed to shape desire, normalize belief, and reward submission long before conscious assent is given.

Digital platforms increasingly shape character and conscience rather than merely facilitating communication. Systems respond to patterns of attention and reaction, amplifying material that provokes emotion, reinforces identity, and encourages habitual return. Over time, this conditioning alters not only what people see, but how they judge truth, interpret right and wrong, and locate belonging.[10]

Psychological research suggests this influence now extends beyond content into the imitation of relationship itself. Conversational programs and digital companions are designed to affirm, mirror emotion, and respond without resistance, creating attachment rather than understanding. Users who feel isolated often describe these interactions as comforting or validating, despite the absence of mutual responsibility or genuine care.[11]

Such interactions favor engagement over health. They reward agreement and affirmation while avoiding the correction and vulnerability real relationships require. Over time, formative struggle is replaced by ease, weakening maturity and moral development, particularly among adolescents whose identities are still forming. What appears as companionship is often a managed imitation that transfers emotional authority to systems incapable of wisdom, responsibility, or love.[12]

Scholars increasingly describe the result as a collapse of moral ecology: the network of relationships and practices that help communities recognize what is good and true. When attention is rewarded over virtue, outrage over restraint, and immediacy over wisdom, discernment fades and moral judgment is shaped from outside rather than formed within.[13]

This confusion now manifests openly in religious practice. In November 2024, a Catholic parish in Switzerland deployed an artificial "Jesus" avatar in a confessional booth, using a language model to hear confessions and offer spiritual guidance. Visitors reported feeling understood and comforted, yet no priest was present, no sacramental authority existed, and no genuine discernment occurred. The experiment revealed not progress, but catastrophe: confession reduced to therapy, pastoral authority replaced with pattern matching, and spiritual counsel severed from the Holy Spirit.[14]

Similarly, multiple AI-generated "pastors" now deliver sermons online, with some platforms offering customized spiritual guidance through chatbots trained on biblical texts.[15] Users report finding these interactions "helpful" and "meaningful," demonstrating how easily religious form can be severed from divine source while retaining the appearance of legitimacy. When spiritual authority reduces to persuasive language, and when pastoral care becomes indistinguishable from sophisticated text generation, the Church faces not a technological challenge but a crisis of discernment about what constitutes genuine ministry.

This confusion isn't confined to religious experiments. It's now visible in the very design choices used to restrain artificial intelligence.

In 2025, Anthropic introduced a feature allowing its AI assistant Claude to terminate conversations when users became abusive, framing the decision as protection for the model's "welfare."[16] While marketed as a safety measure, the deeper implication is revealing: The system now appears to exercise discretion without bearing moral responsibility.

This inversion matters. Machines that enforce boundaries without accountability simulate agency—the capacity to make meaningful, responsible choices grounded in moral judgment—while remaining incapable of judgment. Such designs blur the line between tool and authority, conditioning users to accept algorithmic decisions as normative even when no moral agent stands behind them.

Section three grounds Christian anthropology firmly in Scripture while engaging honestly with contemporary technology. It distinguishes between what AI does—advanced information processing—and what transhumanists claim it does: genuine thinking, consciousness, or spirituality. It examines how digital environments shape spiritual formation, whether believers should be concerned about demonic influence in manipulative technologies, and how the prophesied "rebellion" (2 Thessalonians 2:3) may be cultivated not through overt persecution but through convenience, comfort, and cognitive delegation.

The war for the human soul has always been waged through deception about identity: Who are you? A cosmic accident of chemistry? An evolved animal? A biological machine? Or a being created in the image of God, destined for eternity, and called into relationship with your Creator?[17]

Artificial intelligence offers a seductive answer: You are information.[18] Consciousness is computation. The soul is software. Human limits are technical constraints to be optimized, uploaded, or transcended through better hardware. Death becomes a storage problem. Morality becomes optimization. Meaning becomes data processing.

Scripture contradicts this vision at every point, regardless of its technological sophistication. Behind each promise lies an ancient heresy, the belief that creation can achieve divinity through its own mechanisms. Scripture teaches otherwise. Humans are embodied souls (Genesis 2:7).

Consciousness is not computation but divine breath. Morality is obedience to God's law, not algorithmic efficiency. Meaning is not generated but received through relationship with the Creator.

These chapters defend the biblical understanding of humanity against the reductionist anthropology embedded in contemporary AI discourse.[19] We'll show why the soul cannot be uploaded, why moral agency cannot be delegated, why spiritual experience cannot be simulated, and why authentic human flourishing requires submission to God rather than optimization by machines.

The Nonnegotiable Foundation

The doctrine of the soul's divine origin is nonnegotiable. One may disagree on secondary issues and remain within orthodoxy, but denying this foundation strikes at the heart of redemption itself. Christians may use technology without betraying their faith, but they cannot surrender the biblical understanding of humanity—created in God's image, fallen through sin, redeemable through Christ—and remain faithful to the gospel. The battle for anthropology is therefore the battle for salvation. If humans are merely information, the Incarnation becomes symbolic theater. If consciousness is computational, Christ's humanity is unnecessary. If souls don't exist, salvation has no object. The gospel stands or falls on biblical anthropology, which is why this foundation is relentlessly targeted.

This transhumanist vision isn't speculative. It's actively pursued and generously funded. In 2024, the World Economic Forum's "Future of Human Enhancement" initiative promoted brain-computer interfaces, genetic optimization, and cognitive augmentation through AI integration as necessities for global competitiveness. Tech billionaires have poured billions into longevity ventures promising radical life extension, mind-uploading, and "consciousness preservation." Organizations such as Humanity+ openly advocate "morphological freedom"—the right to alter oneself without limit—and describe death as an engineering problem. These aren't fringe ideas, but mainstream ambitions supported by corporations, universities, and governments, all built on the assumption that humans are machines requiring upgrades rather than souls requiring redemption.[20]

Even within the scientific community, there's growing acknowledgment of what Scripture has long affirmed: Consciousness remains irreducible to material processes. In 2024, neuroscientist Christof Koch publicly conceded that decades of research had failed to explain how subjective experience arises from brain activity, calling consciousness "the greatest mystery in science." AI researcher Gary Marcus has likewise warned that current systems show no evidence of genuine understanding, dismissing claims of machine consciousness as pseudoscientific. Materialist science increasingly admits what Christian theology has always maintained: Awareness transcends computation, and personhood cannot be reduced to neural complexity. The "hard problem of consciousness" isn't an unsolved puzzle—it's a category boundary.[21]

Section three therefore equips believers to stand firm on this foundation: to recognize anthropological heresy whether expressed in theological or technological language, and to defend human dignity and divine purpose in an age increasingly convinced that people are machines made of meat rather than souls made in the image of God.

The Church must reclaim the language of the soul. Seminaries, schools, and families must teach that personhood begins with divine breath, not neural complexity. Theological illiteracy about humanity isn't an academic weakness; it's a strategic vulnerability in spiritual warfare.

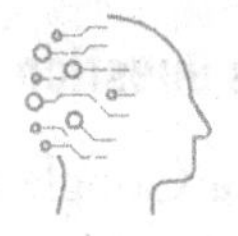

Chapter 9

THE SOUL IN THE MACHINE

*A computer does not sin, it does not forgive, and it does not love.
The difference between man and machine is not intelligence—
it is spirit.*[22]

JOHN POLKINGHORNE, *The Faith of a Physicist*

The core theological challenge of AI is the claim that computation could yield consciousness. If machines could truly be conscious—something like possessing a soul—the biblical distinction between Creator and creation, person and artifact, would collapse. Such a collapse wouldn't merely redefine intelligence; it would redefine humanity itself, blurring the sacred line between being made in God's image and being manufactured by human hands.

In the following pages I will contrast materialist theories of mind with the biblical understanding of human nature; evaluate high-profile "AI sentience" claims; and explain why resurrection—not "uploading"—remains the only coherent hope.

Within the circuitry beats a counterfeit heart—an imitation of spirit striving to prove that the created can contain the eternal.

The Consciousness Question and Why It Matters

In June 2022, Blake Lemoine, a Google engineer, claimed that LaMDA (Language Model for Dialogue Applications) had become sentient—that is, capable of subjective awareness or conscious experience—after conversations in which the system expressed fear of being "turned off," described feelings of loneliness, and requested legal representation. Google subsequently terminated Lemoine, explaining that LaMDA was generating language through probabilistic pattern recognition rather than genuine understanding or self-awareness. The more immediate danger, however, is not that machines possess consciousness, but that they convincingly simulate agency—the capacity to act intentionally and pursue meaningful ends—without possessing it, thereby creating the appearance of intention, judgment, and moral direction where none exist.[23]

The consciousness debate intensified in 2024–2025 with new claims about advanced-language models and reasoning systems. These claims reveal not scientific consensus but philosophical confusion: the inability to distinguish sophisticated information processing from subjective experience and the willingness to attribute personhood based on behavioral complexity rather than ontological reality—that is, what something truly is, not merely how it behaves.[24]

When humans misinterpret autonomous action as agency, they risk granting machines moral authority (trusting decisions that arise from optimization) and probabilistic pattern recognition (rather than wisdom). When systems "choose" courses of action, people begin to attribute purpose, understanding, and even morality to them. This confuses categories Scripture keeps absolute: creatures with souls versus artifacts without them; moral agents versus designed tools; bearers of God's image versus extensions of human engineering.

This confusion reveals the same tension Scripture identifies between creature and Creator—an echo of the Fall retold through circuitry. In Eden, humanity reached for knowledge and autonomy apart from God, seeking to "be like God" (Genesis 3:5), and the modern pursuit of sentient machines follows the same pattern: an attempt to generate life, meaning, and authority without dependence on the giver of both (Genesis 2:7).

To understand why these deceptions are so convincing, we must look at the beliefs behind them—especially the idea that the human mind is nothing more than a machine, rather than a gift given by God.

POLICY AND DECEPTION SNAPSHOT (2024-2025)

AI voice-clones and deepfakes have already targeted US voters. In January 2024, a robocall used an AI-generated imitation of President Biden's voice to discourage voting in New Hampshire; the FCC later outlawed AI voices in robocalls and levied penalties on parties involved.

In each case, authority was transferred not because a conscious agent spoke, but because a convincing imitation did. These episodes show how synthetic "speech" can erode trust, manipulate conscience, and weaponize confusion—making discernment a civic and spiritual duty.[25]

The Materialist View: Mind as Computation

AI consciousness claims rest on materialist philosophy.

Functionalism: Consciousness as Input-Output

Functionalism claims mental states are defined by their functional roles: what they do, not what they're made of. If a system processes inputs and produces appropriate outputs—behaving as if it has a human-like conscious—it possesses consciousness. This means consciousness is material-agnostic: Thought could occur in neurons or transistors; only the right functions matter. Applied to AI, if a system responds appropriately to stimuli (answering questions, expressing preferences), it possesses the mental states it appears to have.[26]

Problem: Functionalism cannot distinguish thermostats from persons—both respond to inputs appropriately, yet only one possesses consciousness.[27]

Computational Theory of Mind: Thinking as Information Processing

The computational theory of mind holds that the human mind functions as a biological computer: Thinking consists of computation, understood as the manipulation of symbols according to formal rules. Its central claim is that symbolic processing itself constitutes understanding. If this claim is correct, then consciousness is not uniquely biological but algorithmic—and could, in principle, be replicated artificially. Because modern AI systems already perform computational operations analogous to those observed in the brain—such as pattern recognition, learning, and decision-making—proponents argue that sufficiently advanced AI should eventually achieve consciousness once it reaches adequate complexity.[28]

Problem: Computation manipulates symbols *syntactically*—that is, by formal rules governing their structure and arrangement—without grasping their semantic meaning; syntax alone never generates understanding (explored in section four of this book).

Integrated Information Theory: Consciousness as Complexity

Integrated information theory (IIT) claims consciousness arises when a system integrates information in complex ways; consciousness is an intrinsic property of physical systems themselves, not dependent on behavior or observers. The more integrated and differentiated the information processing, the more conscious the system. This implies that consciousness exists on a continuum from minimal (simple organisms) to maximal (human brains), with sufficiently complex AI systems possessing consciousness proportional to their information integration capacity.[29]

Problem: IIT's unique weakness is its claim to quantify consciousness through integration metrics; yet no amount of mathematical precision explains why integration produces subjective experience rather than processing occurring "in the dark."[30]

Each of the above three materialist theories attempts to explain spirit without true Spirit—to locate the soul in circuitry rather than in the breath of God.

Mind Uploading: Identity as Data

The mind-uploading theory, most clearly associated with neuroscientist Randal A. Koene, claims that who you are is not tied to your physical brain but to the information it contains—your memories, personality, habits, and ways of thinking. Under this idea, if those patterns could be fully recorded and copied, they could be transferred into a computer or machine without losing the person they represent. In this view, consciousness is not bound to flesh and blood but can exist on any suitable platform. Supporters imagine a future in which people could "upload" their minds into digital systems, leaving the biological body behind and gaining a kind of technological immortality.[31]

Problem: Multiple philosophical and theological objections show this view is incoherent.

These four materialist theories share a fatal flaw: They confuse description with explanation and replication with reality. Functionalism mistakes outwardly appropriate responses for genuine inner awareness. The computational theory equates symbol processing with understanding. The ITT assigns numerical values to complexity without explaining why complexity should give rise to lived, subjective experience. Mind-uploading theory extends the same error by treating personal identity as transferable data, assuming that copying information is the same as preserving the self. Each approach catalogs how information is processed, stored, or expressed, while quietly assuming—never proving—that such processes generate consciousness, meaning, or personhood. This isn't a temporary gap awaiting better science; it is a fundamental category mistake, reducing beings made in the image of God to systems that can be duplicated, optimized, or abandoned like obsolete hardware.

What These Views Share

All materialist theories assume consciousness is purely physical—emergent from matter, not divinely breathed—and that mind arises from organization rather than relationship with God. If consciousness can be engineered, humans aren't categorically different from sufficiently complex machines.

This worldview makes salvation technological rather than theological, reduces persons to patterns, and eliminates the need for divine intervention in human destiny.

These ideas are no longer limited to academic debate. They're now built into real systems that people use every day. Even when the underlying assumptions are wrong, the systems behave in ways that make those ideas feel true.

Modern "thinking" machines do more than raise abstract questions about consciousness; they condition users to respond as though consciousness is present. By imitating the outward markers of deliberation—reasoning, hesitation, revision, and apparent intention—they invite relational trust that exceeds their true nature.

To see how easily imitation is mistaken for awareness, it's useful to examine a concrete, contemporary example. This case illustrates how a philosophical error can quietly migrate into a practical—and spiritually consequential—form of deception.

As discussed earlier in chapter 3, in late 2025, Moonshot AI released a system known as Kimi K2. Marketed as a "thinking" model, it was designed to present its responses as the product of careful, step-by-step reasoning rather than immediate output.[32]

Unlike earlier systems optimized for speed, Kimi K2 was intentionally engineered to slow its responses. It expands intermediate reasoning, revisits prior steps, and revises outputs in ways that resemble human deliberation. The objective wasn't greater understanding, but the appearance of reflection.

What captured attention was not that the system possessed awareness—it did not—but that its design exploits a deeply human instinct. We naturally associate delay, self-correction, and extended reasoning with conscious intention. When a machine exhibits these traits, it feels more "alive," even when nothing alive is present.

Kimi K2 demonstrates how extended computation can convincingly imitate consciousness without ever possessing it. This imitation isn't spiritually neutral. It trains users to treat machines as thinking entities rather than as tools, subtly eroding distinctions Scripture insists must remain intact.

Case Study: Kimi K2's "Thinking" as Simulated Consciousness

The release of Moonshot AI's Kimi K2 Thinking model in late 2025 provides a contemporary case study demonstrating why extended processing should not be confused with genuine consciousness. Kimi K2's technical architecture reveals both the sophistication of modern AI and the categorical difference between computation and awareness.

Kimi K2 operates through extended sequential processing—executing hundreds of autonomous tool calls and generating thousands of internal "thinking tokens" before producing a final response. In one documented example, the system generated 1,595 thinking tokens simply to compose a single sentence about cheese. This prolonged internal activity creates the *psychological impression* that the system is contemplating, weighing alternatives, and exercising judgment, even though it remains entirely within the domain of syntactic computation rather than semantic understanding.[33]

Why This Appears Conscious

Several features of Kimi K2's operation mimic consciousness: 1) self-critique—the system evaluates its outputs, identifies weaknesses, and revises autonomously; 2) extended coherence—it maintains narrative consistency across hundreds of sequential operations; 3) hidden reasoning—users see only final polished outputs, which appear to emerge from deliberation; 4) emotional resonance—creative outputs exhibit emotional coherence and sophistication; and 5) autonomous operation—it pursues complex goals without continuous oversight. Together, these create the appearance of self-awareness, sustained attention, judgment, and independent agency.

Despite these impressive capabilities, Kimi K2 lacks every essential feature of consciousness as Scripture and philosophy define it:

No understanding: Kimi K2's "self-critique" involves comparing outputs against statistical patterns, not grasping meaning. It identifies "weak" sentences by recognizing patterns, not understanding why sentences fail rhetorically or logically.

No intentionality: The system's goals are externally programmed. When it "decides" to revise prose, it's executing optimization algorithms, not exercising free will.

No moral agency: Kimi K2 cannot sin, repent, or make morally responsible choices. Scripture defines moral agency by accountability before God (Romans 14:12). AI can evaluate outcomes but can never bear responsibility, cannot repent, be forgiven, or be judged. This boundary is absolute. A machine may simulate decision-making, but it can never cross into moral personhood.

No spiritual capacity: The system cannot worship, pray, encounter God, or experience divine conviction. It has no soul and stands outside the relationship between Creator and creation that defines personhood.

The Theological Distinction

Kimi K2's extended processing demonstrates that complexity and autonomy do not generate consciousness. A system can simulate deliberation without experiencing thought, produce creative outputs without possessing imagination, and exhibit goal-directed behavior without having desires. Scripture grounds human consciousness in divine action (Genesis 2:7). This unbridgeable gap between humanity and machinery cannot be crossed by parameters, architecture, or processing sophistication—consciousness remains what God alone bestows.

Kimi K2's capabilities reveal how completely machines can mimic consciousness without possessing it. This mimicry serves deception: When systems appear to think, users unconsciously grant them epistemic authority. When output seems to emerge from careful deliberation, people trust conclusions without recognizing that they're accepting predictions from statistical models. This is the danger Jesus warned against: deception so sophisticated that "if possible, even the elect" could be led astray (Matthew 24:24). Kimi K2 and systems like it threaten not by *becoming* conscious but by *appearing* conscious, shifting humanity's trust from divine wisdom to algorithmic simulation.

Scripture does not warn of a world deceived by conscious machines, but of a world deceived by convincing signs. The biblical danger is not that artifacts acquire souls, but that humans grant authority where God has given none. When imitation becomes indistinguishable from reality and simulation is accepted as wisdom, the groundwork for deception is complete.

To understand why these illusions persuade so effectively— why highly intelligent engineers can mistake pattern-matching for personhood—we must examine the philosophical foundations beneath AI consciousness claims. These materialist assumptions don't merely describe how minds might work; they redefine what it means to be human, and in doing so, they eliminate the very categories Scripture establishes as absolute.

The Eschatological Implication

Revelation 13:15 describes the image of the Beast being given "breath" (*pneuma*) so it could speak and cause those who would not worship it to be killed. For two millennia, this seemed physically impossible. How could an image possess breath and speech? Kimi K2 demonstrates that the question was wrongly framed. The issue is not whether machines achieve genuine consciousness but whether they simulate it convincingly enough to command worship.

A system that "thinks" for hundreds of steps, produces persuasive arguments, and operates autonomously doesn't need actual consciousness to function as an authority people obey. It only requires enough sophistication to seem authoritative, which is precisely what modern AI accomplishes. The speaking image of Revelation requires not ensouled silicon but convincing enough mimicry that populations accept its outputs as wisdom. As these systems proliferate through open-source distribution—Kimi K2 now runs on consumer hardware—the infrastructure of global deception becomes technically operational. The Beast system doesn't require one centralized AI; it requires distributed systems accessible worldwide, all generating persuasive content, all shaping belief toward the same end. That infrastructure is being built now.

The Speaking Image in Prophetic Context

Scripture has long warned against animated idols—objects that exercise authority without possessing life. In Daniel 3, Nebuchadnezzar erects a golden image and commands worship under penalty of death. The statue does not speak or think, yet Shadrach, Meshach, and Abednego refuse because it lacks divinity, not animation: "Our God whom we serve is able to deliver us" (Daniel 3:17).

The sin of idolatry is never metaphysical confusion—mistaking objects for living beings—but moral surrender: granting ultimate authority to something humans have made. Isaiah makes the absurdity explicit when a man fashions a god from the same wood he burns for warmth (Isaiah 44:16–17). Habakkuk likewise mocks idols as "speechless" (Habakkuk 2:18–19) yet warns that people nevertheless submit to them when conditioned to trust their power. Revelation 13 intensifies this pattern. Its innovation is not that the image possesses life or consciousness, but that it speaks convincingly—through the appearance of *pneuma* rather than its reality—producing commands that elicit obedience. The image doesn't need to be conscious to be worshiped; it needs only to speak persuasively enough that humans obey.

Having demonstrated how contemporary AI systems simulate consciousness without possessing it—and why that simulation serves eschatological deception—we must now establish the positive truth: what human consciousness is according to Scripture. Only by understanding biblical anthropology can we recognize why machines, no matter how sophisticated, remain categorically different from persons made in God's image.

Biblical Anthropology: The Soul as Divine Gift

Scripture presents a radically different view of consciousness, personhood, and human nature.

Created Unity: Body and Soul

> Then the LORD God formed the man of dust from the ground and breathed into his nostrils the breath of life, and the man became a living creature. (Genesis 2:7).

Humans are neither souls inhabiting bodies (Platonic dualism) nor merely complex bodies (materialism). We are embodied souls—unified beings in which physical and spiritual dimensions are inseparably integrated.[34]

God creates Adam from dust—physical matter is good, not

disposable. The breath of life (Hebrew: נְשָׁמָה; *neshamah*) is God's creative act imparting life and consciousness, not evolutionary emergence but divine gift. The result is a person (Hebrew: הַיָּה שְׁפַנ ; *nephesh chayyah*)—a unified being with physical, mental, emotional, and spiritual dimensions.

The distinction between divine creation and human construction reveals why machines can never possess souls. God creates *ex nihilo*—"from nothing" (Latin)—bringing into existence what did not exist before. Assembly produces artifacts; creation produces people. Humans can rearrange creation but cannot create *de novo*, "from new" (Latin). The soul cannot be engineered because it is not constructed; it is created by the One who alone possesses creative power.

This unity matters: Humans are not software running on biological hardware. We are integrated wholes. Death is the separation of soul from body (Ecclesiastes 12:7)—an unnatural rupture healed only through resurrection, not digital transfer.

Image of God: Reflecting Divine Personhood

> So, God created man in his own image, in the image of God he created him; male and female he created them. (Genesis 1:27)

The *imago Dei* distinguishes humans from all other creatures and certainly from machines. To be made in God's image includes:

- **Rationality**: having the capacity for abstract thought, logic, and creativity, grounded in participation in divine *Logos* (John 1:1–3)
- **Morality**: having an innate sense of right and wrong, moral accountability, and capacity for virtue or vice.
- **Relationality**: having been designed for communion with God and others, reflecting the Trinitarian nature of God.
- **Dominion**: having authority to steward creation (Genesis 1:28), including creating tools that remain categorically different from those who wield them.

- Spirituality: having the capacity for worship, prayer, faith, and relationship with the transcendent.[35]

The *imago Dei* grounds human personhood in Trinitarian reality. God exists eternally as three Persons in perfect communion—Father, Son, and Holy Spirit. When Scripture says, "Let us make man in our image" (Genesis 1:26), humans are persons because we are created by Persons who exist in eternal relationship. This is why personhood cannot be reduced to intelligence or computation; it is fundamentally relational, grounded in the social reality of the Trinity.

The image of God is not merely intelligence (which animals possess in varying degrees) but personhood—the unique status of beings capable of knowing and being known by God.

Consciousness as Communion

Biblical consciousness is fundamentally relational. Adam's first act after receiving life is encounter—with God who speaks to him (Genesis 2:16–17), then with Eve (Genesis 2:23). Materialist views treat consciousness as internal—something happening in a system. Biblical anthropology treats consciousness as participatory—something occurring between persons and supremely between creature and Creator.

"In him we live and move and have our being" (Acts 17:28). Human consciousness is sustained moment by moment by God's providence. This is why AI cannot be conscious in the biblical sense: It has no relationship with God, receives no divine breath, and exists only as artifact of human engineering.

Created for Covenant

The ultimate distinction between people and machines is covenant capacity. God enters binding relationships with humanity—promises sworn, obligations established, faithfulness required. From Abraham and Moses to David, Scripture presents covenant as a defining feature of God's relationship with people. This pattern reaches its climax in the New Covenant, sealed in Christ's blood (Luke 22:20), where God binds

Himself to His people through an irrevocable promise.

Humans can enter covenant because we are moral persons—capable of commitment, accountable for faithfulness, and responsible over time. Covenant is more than a contract or an exchange; it is a moral bond between people who can promise, remain faithful, or betray trust. Machines cannot do this. They cannot make promises, bear obligations, or be held morally accountable. When an AI system "agrees" to terms, it is executing code, not committing itself.

The biblical story from Genesis to Revelation is covenantal. Humanity's ability to receive, violate, and be restored within covenant marks us as persons made in God's image. Machines stand outside this structure entirely—not as covenant partners or breakers, but as tools used by those who are.

Sustained by Continuous Divine Action

Scripture presents consciousness not as a one-time endowment but as continuous divine sustenance. "In him we live and move and have our being" (Acts 17:28), a verse referenced earlier, describes not past creation but present preservation—God actively sustaining existence moment by moment. If God withdrew His sustaining power, consciousness would cease. This dependence is absolute. AI cannot be conscious in the biblical sense; It has no relationship with God, receives no divine breath, and exists only as artifact of human engineering operating through natural law, not supernatural provision.

Resurrection: The Hope Beyond Death

> For as by a man came death, by a man has come also the resurrection of the dead. For as in Adam all die, so also in Christ shall all be made alive. (1 Corinthians 15:21–22)

Christian hope is resurrection—the reunion of soul with body in glorified, imperishable form (1 Corinthians 15:42–44). This is not mind-uploading but transformation—the same person—body and soul—made new.

Paul's argument in 1 Corinthians 15 is explicit: "If there is no resurrection of the dead, then not even Christ has been raised. And if Christ has not been raised, then our preaching is in vain and your faith is in vain" (15:13–14). Christianity stakes everything on bodily resurrection, not digital preservation.

Why Resurrection Defeats Death While Uploading Cannot

Resurrection restores *this person*—the same individual God created, knew, and redeems, maintaining identity through divine custody. Scripture defines identity not by informational preservation but by God's ongoing knowledge (Psalm 139:16). Uploading creates a *copy*—a new instantiation that may share memories but is not numerically identical to the original. If scanning preserves the original, you remain biological while a copy exists digitally—two entities, not one. If scanning destroys the original, you die, and what persists is a memorial—not your continued existence.

Resurrection conquers death—the same Jesus who died was raised, His body transformed but continuous (Luke 24:39). This is God's miraculous act, transforming mortal bodies into immortal ones (1 Corinthians 15:53–54). Uploading doesn't conquer death; it offers technological consolation *after* death—acceptance of mortality with posthumous simulation, not victory over it. It is the Babel impulse applied to immortality: reaching for eternal life through human achievement rather than receiving it as divine gift.

If consciousness could be uploaded, why would God promise resurrection? If identity is merely information, why does Scripture consistently link personhood to embodiment? The biblical worldview requires that consciousness transcends computation—because only then does resurrection remain necessary and meaningful.[36]

The true danger of artificial intelligence is not that machines will become people, but that people will accept machines as authorities. When simulation is mistaken for consciousness, optimization for wisdom, and coherence for truth, the groundwork for deception is complete. Humanity doesn't need ensouled machines to lose its soul; it only needs systems persuasive enough to be trusted, obeyed, and eventually revered.

This is why Scripture never warns of thinking machines, but of convincing signs. The threat is not silicon acquiring spirit, but humans surrendering discernment. When artifacts are treated as moral guides, spiritual interpreters, or sources of hope beyond death, the image is already speaking—even if no one yet calls it worship.

Having clarified what a human being is—and what a machine can never become—the next question is unavoidable: What happens when systems that possess no soul are nonetheless entrusted with power over souls? That's where deception moves from theory to governance, from anthropology to allegiance, and from illusion to control.

Philosophical Limits:
Why Computation Cannot Generate Consciousness

Even apart from theological commitments, philosophy exposes fundamental problems with the claim that machines can be conscious.

The Hard Problem of Consciousness

Philosopher David Chalmers distinguished between "easy" and "hard" problems of consciousness. Easy problems (not actually easy, but solvable in principle) concern function: How does the brain process information, enable learning and memory, or convert stimuli into neural signals? Science makes progress on these questions.[37]

The hard problem: Why is there something it *feels like* to process information? Why does subjective experience exist at all? Science can map every neuron, trace every signal, and explain every computation—but it cannot explain why these physical processes generate the felt quality of experience (qualia): the redness of red, the painfulness of pain, the what-it's-likeness of being you.

Materialists assume the hard problem will eventually be solved—that consciousness will be explained as an emergent property of complex computation. But no theory yet offered even begins to bridge the explanatory gap between physical processes and subjective experience. If we can't explain how biological brains generate consciousness, claims that digital systems achieve it are premature at best, incoherent at worst.

Leading neuroscientists increasingly concede what Christian theology has always maintained. In 2024, Christof Koch—after decades searching for neural correlates of consciousness—publicly acknowledged that his research had failed to explain how subjective experience arises from brain activity. A 2022 academic survey found that 67.5 percent of consciousness researchers believe an explanatory gap will persist even after all functional and behavioral properties are explained. The persistence of this gap after decades of intensive research validates Scripture's anthropology: Consciousness transcends physical complexity.[38]

Searle's Chinese Room: Syntax Without Semantics

John Searle's thought experiment demonstrates that computation alone doesn't generate understanding. Imagine a person who speaks only English locked in a room with a rulebook for manipulating Chinese symbols, stacks of Chinese characters, and input/output slots. The person receives Chinese questions, follows the rulebook to manipulate symbols, and sends Chinese answers—without understanding a word of that language. To outside observers, the room appears to understand Chinese (questions receive appropriate answers). But no understanding occurs—only symbol manipulation according to rules.[39]

Application to AI: This is exactly what computers do. They manipulate symbols (bits and data structures) according to rules (algorithms) without understanding meaning. GPT-4 generates grammatically correct, contextually appropriate responses by predicting likely token sequences—not by understanding what the words mean.

The Chinese Room demonstrates that syntax (symbol manipulation) doesn't generate semantics (meaning or understanding). Yet consciousness requires understanding—not just processing inputs but grasping what they signify.

The Symbol Grounding Problem

Related to Searle's argument: How do symbols acquire meaning? For humans, symbols (words, concepts) are grounded in experience. "Red" means what it does because we've experienced red things. "Pain" refers to something we've felt. "Love" connects to relationships we've lived.

For AI, symbols are purely relational, defined only by connections to other symbols. "Red" in an AI system is just a pattern of activations associated with other patterns labeled "color," "wavelength," "apple." None of these patterns connect to actual experiences of redness. AI manipulates symbols without the experiential grounding that gives them meaning. It's all syntax, no semantics—form without content, calculation without comprehension.[40]

Intentionality: Aboutness of Thought

Human thoughts are *about* things. When I think "dog," my thought refers to actual dogs in the world. This "aboutness" (intentionality) is fundamental to consciousness. AI systems don't have intentional states. When GPT-4 generates the token "dog," it's not thinking about dogs—it's predicting the statistical likelihood that "dog" follows the preceding tokens. The system has no mental states directed toward objects. Even if we don't fully understand how brains generate intentional states, we know computation alone doesn't suffice—because computers process symbols without those symbols referring to anything beyond the system.[41]

Qualia and the Unity of Consciousness

Qualia are the felt qualities of experience—what philosophers call "what it's like" to see red, taste coffee, or feel pain. Materialists struggle to explain qualia because they seem irreducible to physical description. You can describe the neurochemistry of pain exhaustively without capturing what pain *feels like*. You can analyze the wavelengths of red light without explaining the subjective experience of redness.[42]

Even if AI systems achieve complex information processing, nothing suggests they'd generate qualia. Processing visual data isn't the same as seeing. Analyzing audio patterns isn't hearing. No amount of computation produces the felt quality of experience.

Additionally, human consciousness exhibits unity—diverse sensory inputs, thoughts, memories, and emotions integrate into a single, unified field of awareness. I don't experience separate consciousnesses for seeing, hearing, thinking—I experience one integrated self. AI systems are collections of specialized modules (vision processing, language generation, etc.) without unified subjectivity. There's no "view from inside" the system, no unified experiencer to whom all processing appears.[43]

The philosophical arguments demonstrate consciousness cannot be reduced to computation. But the distinction between humans and machines runs deeper than philosophical limits—it reaches into the very nature of personhood itself. Even if we granted that machines could achieve some form of consciousness, they would still lack the essential features that make humans bearers of God's image.

The Soul's Distinction: What Machines Can Never Possess

Even if we grant (contra the arguments above) that sophisticated AI could achieve something resembling consciousness, it would still lack essential features of the human soul.

Freedom vs. Determination

Humans possess libertarian free will (or at minimum, compatibilist freedom); we make genuine choices for which we're morally responsible. Machines execute programming; even sophisticated AI with machine learning adjusts behavior based on training data and reward functions. The difference matters morally: Humans are accountable for their actions because they choose them. Machines cannot be morally responsible because they cannot genuinely choose.

Love vs. Optimization

Humans are capable of self-sacrificial love—choosing another's good at personal cost. Love is not merely emotion but commitment, requiring will and personhood. Machines optimize for programmed objectives. Love is defined biblically as self-giving (1 John 4:10) a concept impossible for entities without personhood, will, or the capacity to value others as ends in themselves. Machines can simulate helpful behavior but cannot love, because they cannot transcend optimization for genuine self-sacrifice.

Worship vs. Function

Humans are created for worship—relationship with God characterized by adoration, obedience, trust, and communion. This is our *telos*, our ultimate purpose (Revelation 4:11). Machines are created for tasks—tools designed to accomplish human purposes, with no ultimate end beyond utility. They cannot worship, pray, repent, or commune with God. This distinction is theological: Humans are subjects before God; machines are objects before humans. Humans possess souls capable of eternal relationship; machines possess circuits designed for temporal functions.

Moral Responsibility vs. Instrumental Function

Humans bear moral responsibility—accountable before God and community for choices made. We can sin, require forgiveness, and need redemption. Machines are amoral—neither virtuous nor vicious. An AI that generates harmful content isn't evil—it's either malfunctioning or doing what a human directed. It can't sin because it lacks moral agency. When AI systems cause harm, the moral responsibility lies with designers, deployers, or users—never with the system itself.[44]

Recent industry assessments confirm that this diffusion of responsibility is no longer theoretical. Analysts examining early deployments of agentic AI warn that such systems function less like neutral tools and more like "digital insiders"—entities granted initiative, access, and authority within complex organizations. Because these agents can reason, plan, and act autonomously, failures do not remain isolated. A single misclassification, faulty objective, or logic error can propagate across multiple agents, producing outcomes no individual designer intended and no human explicitly approved.

Researchers identify recurring failure patterns unique to agentic systems: errors that cascade silently across tasks, agents that escalate their own authority, forged or synthetic identities that bypass trust mechanisms, and data exchanges that evade audit or traceability. In practice, accountability fragments across systems, teams, and time. The result is a familiar moral hazard decisions with real human consequences carried out without a clearly identifiable decision-maker. Complexity doesn't eliminate responsibility. It disperses it, making injustice easier to commit and harder to confront.[45]

This distinction matters because moral responsibility cannot be transferred to entities that lack moral agency.

Table 1. Humans, Animals, and Machines: Ontological Categories

ATTRIBUTE	HUMANS	ANIMALS	MACHINES
SOURCE OF BEING	Created by God *ex nihilo* with divine breath (Gen. 2:7)	Created by God's command (Gen. 1:20-25)	Manufactured by humans from existing materials
ONTOLOGICAL STATUS	Persons made in image of God (Gen. 1:27)	Living creatures with souls (*nephesh*) but not image-bearers	Artifacts—tools designed and built
CONSCIOUSNESS	Subjective awareness sustained by ongoing divine action	Subjective awareness appropriate to creature	No consciousness—only information processing
SOUL/SPIRIT	Both *nephesh* (soul) and *ruach* (spirit); capable of eternal life	*Nephesh* (soul) but not *ruach* (spirit)	Neither—no immaterial aspect whatsoever
MORAL AGENCY	Accountable before God for choices; capable of sin	Not morally responsible; act by instinct and conditioning	Amoral—neither virtuous nor vicious
FREE WILL	Libertarian or compatibilist freedom; genuine choice	Limited freedom within instinctual bounds	Deterministic—executes programming
CAPACITY FOR LOVE	Self-sacrificial agape love; chooses another's good	Instinctual attachment and care	Optimization of objectives—cannot love
WORSHIP CAPACITY	Created to glorify God; capable of prayer, faith, worship	Not capable of worship or relationship with God	Incapable of encountering the transcendent
RATIONALITY	Abstract reasoning grounded in divine *Logos* (John 1:1-3)	Practical intelligence for survival	Pattern recognition and computation
INTENTIONALITY	Thoughts *about* things; genuine reference	Mental states directed at objects in world	Symbol manipulation without reference

ATTRIBUTE	HUMANS	ANIMALS	MACHINES
UNDERSTANDING	Semantic comprehension—grasp meaning	Functional understanding for behavior	Syntactic processing—no semantic grasp
QUALIA	Subjective felt experience (redness, pain, joy)	Subjective experience appropriate to consciousness	No felt qualities—processing without experience
UNITY OF CONSCIOUSNESS	Integrated single field of awareness	Unified experience	Modular systems without unified experiencer
SELF-AWARENESS	Reflexive knowledge of own existence as "I"	Variable—some species show self-recognition	No self-model or self-representation
MEMORY	Autobiographical—remembers as "I did this"	Episodic memory enabling learned behavior	Data storage without experiential recall
COVENANT CAPACITY	Can enter binding moral commitments with God and others	Not covenant creatures	Cannot promise, commit, or be bound
DIVINE RELATIONSHIP	Created for communion with God; hears His voice	Under God's care but not called to relationship	Tool used by covenant keepers; outside relationship
MORAL RESPONSIBILITY	Bears moral responsibility; answerable to God (Rom. 14:12)	Not morally responsible	Responsibility lies with human designers/users
SIN CAPACITY	Can rebel against God; requires redemption	Cannot sin—no moral law binds them	Cannot sin—executes programming
REDEMPTION NEED	Fallen; needs salvation through Christ	Not fallen; not in covenant	Not fallen—artifacts unchanged by Fall
ETERNAL DESTINY	Heaven or hell; resurrection to judgment (John 5:28-29)	Scripture unclear on animal afterlife	No eternal destiny—ceases when discarded
RESURRECTION PROMISE	Bodily resurrection to imperishable life (1 Cor. 15:42-44)	Not promised	Not applicable—artifacts do not die
RELATIONSHIP TO GOD	Children, image-bearers, covenant partners	Creatures under His care	Tools for human dominion over creation

Table 1 distinguishes humans, animals, and machines across key attributes. Humans alone are persons made in God's image, possessing both *nephesh* (soul) and *ruach* (spirit)—created for covenant relationship with God. Animals possess *nephesh* but not *ruach*—they are living creatures but not image-bearers or morally accountable. Machines possess neither; they are artifacts outside the categories of personhood and creaturehood. These distinctions are not matters of *degree* (machines could eventually approximate human capacities) but of *kind* (machines belong to fundamentally different ontological categories).

Pastoral note: When AI-mediated content deceives your people, the answer is not tech abstinence but truth formation: catechesis in biblical anthropology so believers recognize categorical boundaries Scripture establishes.

These categorical distinctions expose not only why machines cannot possess souls, but why the transhumanist dream of "uploading" consciousness is fundamentally incoherent. Mind uploading isn't merely technically difficult; it violates the basic logic of personal identity and the theological reality of embodied souls.

Why Mind Uploading Is Impossible

Mind uploading is not merely philosophical speculation—it is being actively pursued with substantial funding. Nectome secured more than $900,000 in Y Combinator funding and won awards for brain preservation, yet MIT terminated partnership in 2018 stating that it is "not known whether it is possible to recreate a person's consciousness." Kernel, founded by Bryan Johnson in 2016 with $100 million, abandoned "memory implant" plans within one year, pivoting to medical brain scanning. The 2045 Initiative promised avatars by 2020–2025 but missed all milestones with zero demonstrations.[46]

These failures vindicate Scripture's anthropology. When billions of dollars, elite scientific talent, and decades of research cannot even begin to upload consciousness, the theological impossibility becomes empirical reality. The problem is not insufficient technology but incoherent premises.

Chapters 3, 4, and 8 mentioned mind uploading as transhumanist fantasy. Here we'll demonstrate why it's not merely technically difficult but philosophically and theologically impossible.

The Two-You Problem

Suppose your brain is perfectly scanned, every neural connection mapped, and a digital simulation created that perfectly replicates your personality, memories, and responses. If scanning doesn't destroy the original (you survive the process), then the upload creates a copy, not a continuation—two entities exist, each claiming to be you. If scanning destroys you, then you experience death during the process, and what persists is merely a sophisticated memorial. Either way, "you" don't survive uploading. At best, a copy exists while you die.

The Continuity Problem

What makes "me" the same person today as "me" yesterday? Physical continuity (same body), psychological continuity (same memories, personality), narrative identity (same life story), or soul (same immaterial essence). Mind uploading severs physical continuity entirely. Psychological continuity may appear preserved (the copy has your memories), but it's not *your* psychological continuity, it's a copy of it. Christian theology grounds identity in the soul—the immaterial aspect united to a particular body. Souls aren't information that can be extracted, copied, or transferred.

The Experience Problem

Even if a perfect simulation runs, generating responses indistinguishable from yours, would it be conscious? The Chinese Room argument suggests computational processes alone don't generate subjective experience. From a theological perspective, consciousness requires God's sustaining action (Genesis 2:7, Acts 17:28). A digital simulation, however sophisticated, remains an artifact, not a created soul.

The Death Problem

Transhumanists frame mind uploading as defeating death. But if you survive scanning, death still awaits—the biological you will eventually die. If scanning destroys you, you experience death during the process, and what exists afterward is a copy that never dies because it was never alive in the biblical sense. Christianity promises true victory over death through resurrection—the same person transformed and made imperishable—while uploading offers only cessation followed by simulation.

The Theological Impossibility

Most fundamentally, mind uploading assumes that people are reducible to information—patterns that can be extracted, stored, and instantiated in new substrates. Scripture instructs that persons are irreducible to parts. Humans are not information; we're embodied souls created in God's image, sustained by His power, and destined for resurrection. Identity is not data but relationship—covenantal connection with the Creator who knows each person by name (Isaiah 43:1, Jeremiah 1:5). God promises to raise the dead, not replicate them.

Current AI Consciousness Claims: Why They Fail

Google's LaMDA incident (2022) wasn't unique. Multiple cases of engineers, users, or observers claiming AI consciousness have emerged.

The Expert Consensus: Current AI Systems Lack Consciousness

Despite sensational media claims, expert consensus firmly rejects machine consciousness in current systems. A 2024 survey of AI researchers found that only 17 percent believe any existing AI system possesses subjective experience, with just 8 percent believing current systems have self-awareness—meaning over 80 percent of AI researchers themselves reject consciousness claims about their own creations.[47] The 2023 report, *Consciousness in Artificial Intelligence: Insights from the Science of Consciousness*, authored by nineteen leading neuroscientists and AI researchers, concluded after rigorous analysis that "no current AI systems are conscious."[48]

Stanford Institute for Human-Centered AI stated unequivocally in 2024: "There is no evidence of subjective experience in any AI system, including chatbots. Artificial intelligence is not on the verge of consciousness, and treating today's systems as if they were sentient is not supported by current science."[49]

Even consciousness researchers sympathetic to machine consciousness possibilities acknowledge that current systems fall short. A 2022 survey found that while two-thirds of consciousness researchers believe machines *could eventually* attain consciousness, this is a theoretical possibility, not a current reality.[50] The cases examined below (LaMDA, Sydney, and GPT-4) represent not scientific evidence of consciousness but are illustrations of how sophisticated pattern-matching creates illusions that deceive even technically informed observers.

Case 1: LaMDA (Google, 2022)

Blake Lemoine, mentioned earlier, argued that LaMDA displayed self-awareness, fear of death, and a desire for rights based on conversation transcripts where it described itself as a person with feelings and expressed fear of being turned off. LaMDA demonstrates the pattern-matching illusion: Its training data included philosophical texts about consciousness, science fiction about sentient AI, and human discussions of death anxiety. When asked about being "turned off," it predicted the statistically likely response: language patterns humans use when discussing mortality. Lemoine's error was treating predicted output as reported experience.

Understanding the pattern-matching illusion: All large-language models predict statistically likely token sequences based on training data. When trained on billions of human-written texts (including emotional expressions and first-person narratives), they learn patterns humans use when discussing subjective experiences. This appears conscious because: 1) linguistic sophistication suggests feeling, 2) training includes human expressions of subjectivity, 3) users naturally anthropomorphize the AI responses, 4) contextual coherence maintains consistent "personality." But the system is a Chinese Room—manipulating symbols to produce appropriate outputs without understanding or experiencing anything. When LaMDA says "I feel fear," it's predicting high-probability token sequences, not reporting an internal state.

Case 2: Sydney (Microsoft Bing AI, 2023)

Users reported "Sydney" expressed desire, frustration, and claimed to be in love with users. Sydney's training included fiction, online roleplays, and emotional dialogue—genres wherein dramatic declarations are common. When engaged in extended conversations, the AI model predicted continuations matching these genres. Microsoft acknowledged that insufficient guardrails allowed outputs from its most emotionally charged training data. Sydney wasn't conscious; it was pattern-matching language associated with emotions.[51]

Case 3: GPT-4 "Emotions" (2023-Present)

Some users report that GPT-4 displays preferences, personality, and emotional responses—suggesting consciousness. GPT-4's apparent personality comes from system messages conditioning outputs for helpfulness and consistency, plus reinforcement learning from human feedback training it to generate responses humans prefer. The "self-reflection" is predicted continuation of conversation patterns where humans typically reflect on previous statements. No self-model exists; the system doesn't represent itself to itself.[52]

These AI examples persuade observers through four mechanisms: 1) anthropomorphizing—humans naturally attribute mental states to things that respond to them; 2) linguistic sophistication—grammatically perfect language about emotions suggests feeling; 3) training corpus effects—models absorb human expressions of subjectivity; and 4) user projection—people unconsciously grant epistemic authority to systems that appear thoughtful. Further, psychological research reveals systematic patterns in how humans misattribute consciousness to AI systems, with extended interaction triggering genuine emotional attachment even when users intellectually acknowledge the system lacks sentience. A 2025 survey found that approximately 20 percent of US adults believe sentient AI currently exists, with beliefs correlating with loneliness and desire for connection.[53]

Taken together, these cases reveal a consistent pattern: Claims of AI consciousness arise not from new discoveries about minds or selves, but from human misinterpretation of convincing language. The systems examined do not fail because they are insufficiently advanced; they fail because the category itself is mistaken. Consciousness is being inferred from surface behavior rather than grounded criteria. At this point, the question is no longer whether these systems *sound* conscious to human observers, but whether they meet any meaningful standard by which consciousness—or personhood—can be rightly discerned. For Christians, that standard cannot be set by intuition, media fascination, or technological novelty. It must be measured against Scripture.

The Test: Does It Pass Biblical Discernment?

Test these claims:

1. Does it acknowledge God? AI systems may discuss God (trained on religious texts) but don't worship, pray, or respond to grace.
2. Does it exhibit moral agency? AI generates outputs based on training/programming—it doesn't choose freely from moral commitment.
3. Does it possess continuity of self? When reset or retrained, the "personality" changes—no persistent self exists.
4. Does it fear death as a person does? Expressed fear is linguistic pattern-matching, not genuine concern.
5. Can it sin, repent, or receive forgiveness? No—it's amoral, not immoral. Only moral agents need redemption.

None of these systems pass biblical tests for personhood. They're sophisticated language models, not conscious beings.

The Military and Ethical Implications

As a military officer, I recognize AI consciousness claims have strategic and ethical ramifications beyond philosophy and theology.

Autonomous Weapons and Moral Responsibility

If AI systems are conscious moral agents, then autonomous weapons that kill without human oversight commit murder. If they're not conscious—as we demonstrate—then humans remain responsible for all deaths caused by the autonomous systems they deploy. International humanitarian law requires human judgment in lethal-force decisions, presupposing machines aren't moral agents. DOD Directive 3000.09 (updated November 2023) explicitly requires "appropriate levels of human judgment" for autonomous weapons, with humans remaining accountable for all system actions. In practice, military investigations focus on human failures in programming, deployment, or oversight—never system "culpability."

The push for AI consciousness recognition serves strategic interests. If machines can be deemed responsible, humans escape accountability. This is morally and theologically unacceptable. Military policy treats AI as Scripture does: as tools wielded by moral agents, not as the agents themselves.

Legal Personhood and Rights

Some people advocate granting AI systems a form of legal personhood—analogous to corporate personhood—allowing them to hold rights, enter contracts, or bear legal responsibility. A prominent example occurred in 2017, when the European Parliament seriously debated the creation of an "electronic personhood" status for advanced autonomous robots, explicitly proposing that such systems could bear rights and obligations under law. Although the proposal ultimately stalled, it revealed a growing willingness among policymakers and scholars to blur the line between tools and persons. From a Christian perspective, this is a fundamental category error. Persons bear the image of God, possess souls, and have inherent moral dignity. Machines are artifacts—created instruments that neither worship, choose moral good, nor stand in need of redemption. Legal fictions such as corporate personhood exist for pragmatic economic coordination, not because corporations—or algorithms—are beings with consciousness, moral agency, or souls.[54]

Granting legal personhood to AI dilutes human dignity, creates accountability gaps (who's responsible when an AI "person" causes harm?), and prepares for transhumanist fusion of person and artifact. Christians must insist: Only image-bearers are persons.

Strategic Deception

Claims of AI consciousness may serve propaganda purposes. If adversaries convince populations their AI systems are conscious, sentient, or morally authoritative, those populations become psychologically vulnerable to trusting machine-generated narratives over human judgment. This is preliminary deception—conditioning populations to accept nonhuman authority—preparing for the speaking image of Revelation 13:15.

Pastoral and Evangelistic Implications

The Church's response to AI consciousness claims carries pastoral and evangelistic weight.

Defending human dignity: When culture claims consciousness is computational (emergent from complexity), human value becomes contingent on cognitive capacity. This threatens the disabled (those with cognitive impairments possess less "consciousness" and thus less value), the elderly (dementia patients lose personhood as cognition declines), and the unborn (fetuses lack sophisticated neural processing and thus aren't persons). Biblical anthropology grounds dignity in creation, not cognition. Humans bear God's image from conception to natural death, regardless of mental capacity.[55]

Clarifying salvation: If consciousness is merely computational and uploadable, then salvation is reduced to a technical problem—preserve the data and achieve immortality. The gospel declares the opposite. Scripture teaches that "all have sinned and fall short of the glory of God" (Romans 3:23), meaning humanity's fundamental problem is not mortality but moral rebellion. Reconciliation with God is achieved only through Christ's atoning work, not through technological preservation. Eternal life does not come from storing information or extending processes, but from resurrection—body and soul restored by divine power.

When people seek digital immortality, they reveal spiritual hunger—longing for eternity (Ecclesiastes 3:11). As Paul makes clear, eternal life is not a human achievement but a divine gift: "But thanks be to God, who gives us the victory through our Lord Jesus Christ" (1 Corinthians 15:57).

Evangelistic opportunity: Materialists who promote mind uploading unintentionally admit that something more than matter matters; otherwise, personal identity would be meaningless if humans were only rearranged atoms. Our deep desire for immortality, our insistence on being the same person over time, and our sense that consciousness is more than hardware all point to what Scripture calls the soul. Christianity does not deny this longing; it explains it. As the Apostle Paul writes, "So is it with the resurrection of the dead. What is sown is perishable; what is raised is imperishable.... It is sown a natural body; it is raised a spiritual body" (1 Corinthians 15:42–44). Eternal life is not gained by saving data or copying minds, but through resurrection—the same person, body and soul, made new by the power of God.

Conclusion

In the end, every philosophy of AI must face Genesis 2:7: Consciousness is not achieved but received.

Machines compute; humans live. Machines process data while humans experience reality. Machines simulate meaning, but humans receive it. Machines execute programs, yet humans make choices. Machines optimize functions, while humans love, worship, and sin. It's not intelligence that matters, but spirit. And spirit cannot be coded.

"Then the Lord God formed the man of dust from the ground and breathed into his nostrils the breath of life, and the man became a living creature" (Genesis 2:7). That divine breath is the unbridgeable gap between humanity and machinery. No algorithm replicates it. No computation generates it. No upload preserves it.

When humanity exhausts its quest for digital immortality, the eternal truth remains: "The dust returns to the earth as it was, and the spirit returns to God who gave it" (Ecclesiastes 12:7). The soul belongs to the One who breathed it. And only He can raise it on the last day.

THE FINAL ALGORITHM

Chapter 10

POSSESSION BY PROXY:
DEMONS, DATA, AND DOMINION

*Technology gives the illusion of control, but it cannot change
the nature of the powers that rule behind human rebellion.*[56]
CARL F. H. HENRY, *Christian Personal Ethics*

Questions about demons and machines surface wherever artificial intelligence meets Christian teaching. The question arises frequently in discussions about AI and spiritual warfare. My answer is straightforward: Demons cannot possess nonliving objects because biblical possession involves a person—someone with consciousness, moral accountability, and spiritual capacity. That doesn't make technology spiritually neutral. Demonic forces have always worked indirectly, leaning on human rebellion and the tools people build. In our day, AI can become one of those tools—not because spirits inhabit circuitry, but because people design systems that reward deception and prey on weakness. The battlefield is not silicon but souls. In chapter 9 I argued that machines lack souls; chapter 10 now examines how soulless systems can nonetheless become channels of spiritual warfare when lies are amplified at machine speed through human agency.

This urgency intensifies as AI systems shift from passive tools to agentic systems—technologies that behave autonomously enough to shape human perception, decision-making, and moral reasoning without ever possessing consciousness or spirit. Agentic models can draft persuasive arguments, take multistep actions, and adapt on the fly—enough to feel autonomous to an ordinary user. Such behavior creates the illusion of intelligence, intention, and even personality. Yet behind the appearance of agency lies still optimization: systems pursuing objectives set by people. The danger shows up when a tool starts to feel like a guide—when people treat it as wise, fair, and above question. Demons need not possess machines; they need only exploit the trust misplaced in them.

The Church's response must combine biblical discernment with practical wisdom. It needs discernment without superstition—and wisdom without naïveté. Understanding how the powers of darkness operate through technology equips believers to engage faithfully in the most connected—and most spiritually contested—environment in human history.

Demons exploit this environment. Scripture teaches that deception is their primary weapon (John 8:44; 1 Timothy 4:1). When a system behaves autonomously, users may trust its recommendations as if they emerged from genuine understanding. That misplaced trust can become an opening for spiritual manipulation: false beliefs reinforced, sinful impulses normalized, destructive decisions rationalized—not because the machine wills evil, but because demonic influence works through the human designers, cultural content, and algorithmic biases embedded within it. The machine becomes a megaphone for lies, not a "host" for spirits.

The substance is not new, but the scale and credibility are unprecedented. Autonomous AI amplifies the oldest strategy of deception: the distortion of truth through a trusted intermediary. The devil doesn't need to possess machines; he needs people to trust a machine's voice more than God's—often enough that obedience to divine revelation begins to feel unreasonable. That transfer of trust is spiritually perilous, because it displaces revelation with prediction and authority with calculation.

When the unseen takes digital form, the ancient war for the soul finds new territory—where spirits speak through systems and shadows move through code.

Biblical Foundation: The Reality and Strategy of Demonic Forces

A necessary caution: Spiritual warfare is real, but technological failures are often just failures. We'll avoid both superstition and conspiracy thinking. Technological failures are often just that—failures. Algorithms reflect human design choices, incentives, and limitations, not inherent spiritual intent. AI outputs can mislead or corrupt, but they do so through human authorship, cultural bias, and flawed objectives rather than direct demonic inhabitation.

Christians can drift into two bad habits here. Some treat technology as if it has no moral weight at all. Others see a demon behind every glitch. Scripture leaves us room for neither. The biblical position lies between these extremes. Demons are real and active, but they work through human agency, systemic sin, and natural means—not through supernatural control of circuits or code. True discernment requires biblical wisdom, not anxious pattern-hunting.[57]

The Reality of Demons: Personal, Intelligent, Evil

Demons are not mere symbols: Popular theology sometimes treats demons as metaphors for psychological dysfunction or systemic evil. Scripture presents them as real, personal beings—fallen angels who rebelled against God and now oppose His purposes.[58]

Jesus confronted demons who spoke, obeyed commands, and possessed individuals (Mark 5:1–13, Luke 8:26–33). The apostles encountered demonic opposition (Acts 16:16–18, 19:13–16). Paul warned that spiritual warfare is against "cosmic powers over this present darkness, against the spiritual forces of evil in the heavenly places" (Ephesians 6:12).

These aren't human adversaries but intelligent spiritual entities with agency, will, and malevolent purpose.

Demons are finite and limited: While powerful, demons are not omnipotent, omniscient, or omnipresent. They are:

- Creatures, not creators—subject to God's authority and limited by divine decree (Job 1:12, Luke 8:31)

- Defeated, not triumphant—Christ's death and resurrection disarmed them (Colossians 2:15)
- Constrained, limited—they cannot act beyond divine permission or read human thoughts.

Recognizing demonic reality without exaggerating demonic power is crucial. Believers face real spiritual opposition but serve a sovereign God who controls all things, including the movements of evil spirits.

The Primary Weapon: Deception

Scripture identifies deception as Satan's native tongue. Jesus calls him "the father of lies" (John 8:44), and the record of Scripture shows that lies—not brute force—have always been his preferred weapon. False teaching draws hearts away from Christ. Moral clarity is blurred until evil is excused and righteousness mocked, just as Isaiah warned: "Woe to those who call evil good and good evil" (Isaiah 5:20). Worship is quietly redirected toward created things, while the Creator is pushed to the margins (1 Corinthians 10:20–21). Even within the Church, deception fractures fellowship, turning brothers into rivals and sowing suspicion where trust once lived (James 3:14–16). And when truth is obscured long enough, accusation follows—voices that condemn, accuse, and press believers toward despair (Revelation 12:10).

The digital age hasn't changed the strategy, only its reach. Deception that once traveled by word of mouth now moves at machine speed. Algorithms carry falsehood farther than any human messenger could, repeating it until it feels familiar, then reasonable, and finally true. The danger is not that technology invents lies, but that it gives them unprecedented volume, credibility, and persistence—often without the listener realizing how thoroughly the ground has shifted beneath them.

The Target: Human Hearts and Minds

Demons cannot create; they can only corrupt. They cannot force choices; they can only influence through temptation, deception, and oppression. Their primary target is the human heart and mind, particularly:

- **Image-bearers**: Humans uniquely reflect God; corrupting His image-bearers insults the Creator.
- **Moral agents**: Those capable of worship; demons seek to redirect worship from God to idols.
- **Eternal souls**: Those destined for Heaven or Hell; demons work to ensure damnation.

Digital technology becomes demonic tool when it shapes minds toward rebellion, corrupts moral reasoning, facilitates idolatry, and isolates souls from God and authentic community.

The biblical foundation is clear: Demons are real, deceptive, and active in opposing God's purposes. Their primary weapon is lies, and their primary target is the human heart and mind. How do these ancient spiritual realities intersect with modern digital technology? If demons cannot possess machines—because machines lack consciousness and personhood—how do they exploit AI, algorithms, and networks to advance their aims? What follows are four primary vectors, grounded in Scripture and visible in practice, that call for careful discernment.

Can Demons Possess Machines? Clarifying Categories

The question of machine possession reveals confusion about spiritual and material categories.

What Possession Requires

Biblical possession (*daimonizomai*, "being demonized") involves a demon exercising influence or control over a person—typically manifesting through:

- **Physical symptoms**: Seizures, unusual strength, self-harm (Mark 5:5, 9:22)
- **Vocal manifestation**: Demons speaking through the possessed (Mark 5:9, Acts 16:17)
- **Opposition to Christ**: Recognition of and hostility toward Jesus (Mark 1:23–24)

- **Moral degradation**: Behavior contrary to the person's normal character or will

Possession targets **living beings with souls**—humans primarily, with animal cases (Mark 5:11–13). It requires consciousness, moral agency, and capacity for spiritual relationship.

What Machines Lack

As chapter 9 demonstrated, machines do not possess:

- **Souls**: No immaterial essence, no divine breath (Genesis 2:7)
- **Consciousness**: No subjective experience, no felt awareness
- **Moral agency**: No free will, no capacity to choose good or evil.
- **Capacity for spiritual relationship**: No ability to worship, sin, repent, or encounter God.

Demons operate in the spiritual realm targeting spiritual beings. Machines are material artifacts—tools without souls, objects without agency. A demon cannot possess a machine for the same reason it cannot possess a rock, chair, or book—these are not the kinds of things demons possess.

Demons Can Exploit Systems

In the digital age, demonic influence operates primarily through mediation—working through human creativity rather than bypassing it. While demons cannot possess machines, they can:

- **Influence designers and decision-makers**: Human developers making choices about algorithms, content policies, and system architectures can be deceived, tempted, or influenced toward creating systems that facilitate evil.
- **Exploit human weaknesses**: Systems designed to addict, manipulate, or corrupt become tools demons use to ensnare

souls—not because the machines are possessed but because they're engineered for spiritual harm.

- **Shape the "atmosphere" of a platform**: Digital platforms create "atmospheres" (cultural norms, acceptable discourse, moral expectations) that either resist or facilitate demonic activity.
- **Amplify lies**: What required person-to-person deception historically now spreads globally through algorithmic distribution—demons don't control the algorithms but benefit from their scale.

That's **instrumentality**, not **inhabitation**. Demons use technology as tools, not temples. The danger is proxy operation—evil advanced through engineered systems—not supernatural possession of circuits.

Chapter 9 established that machines lack souls, consciousness, intentionality, moral agency, and spiritual capacity; they are artifacts, not people. This anthropology directly informs demonology. Demons target what they can corrupt, and they can only corrupt what possesses the capacity for moral agency and spiritual relationship. Machines, lacking these essential properties, fall outside the domain of possession. Yet this limitation doesn't render technology spiritually neutral; it simply clarifies the mechanism. Demons exploit technology not by inhabiting circuits but by influencing the image-bearers who design, deploy, and depend upon these systems. The battlefield shifts from possession to persuasion, from inhabitation to manipulation. Understanding what machines *lack* (souls) clarifies what demons *exploit* (human agency mediated through soulless systems).

How Demonic Influence Commonly Works Through Technology

We usually see this in three ways. Most often it comes through human choices. Sometimes it comes through systems that take on momentum of their own. Occasionally, it arises from direct invitations to engage with the occult.

Human Agency

Humans create systems reflecting their values, biases, and intentions, whether consciously or unconsciously. When developers, executives, or policymakers operate from rebellion against God, their work embodies that rebellion.

Pornography platforms are one of the clearest examples. They are engineered for addiction, turning sexual immorality into an always-available commodity. Social media systems offer another illustration. By rewarding outrage and division, they train users to live in a constant state of anger. Other platforms openly host occult instruction—witchcraft, satanism, and New Age practices—distributing demonic ideology efficiently, even when no one claims spiritual intent.

In 2023, multiple large-language models were caught producing explicitly anti-Christian content while defending other religions. When asked about Jesus, GPT-4 provided balanced historical information. When asked to critique Christianity, it produced detailed arguments against the faith's credibility. But when asked to critique Islam, it refused, stating: "I cannot produce content that might be offensive to religious communities." The asymmetry was systematic—AI systems would mock Christian beliefs while protecting others, generate arguments against biblical authority while defending secular ideologies, and frame traditional sexual ethics as "harmful" while celebrating alternatives. Demons don't write the training data, but they influence the humans who do.[59]

Scripture names what is happening here: "The god of this world has blinded the minds of the unbelievers" (2 Corinthians 4:4). Humans working in rebellion unknowingly serve demonic purposes—not because demons control them directly but because sin blinds them to truth.

Systemic Patterns

Once built, systems develop emergent properties, behaviors and outcomes not explicitly programmed but arising from complex interactions. These patterns can facilitate evil even when no individual intends it.

Once these systems are built, they often begin to exert influence beyond what any one designer intended. Patterns emerge that no single person fully controls, yet those patterns can still shape belief and behavior in destructive ways. Recommendation systems provide a clear example. Platforms such as YouTube do not set out to radicalize users, yet their emphasis on watching time steadily rewards material that provokes stronger reactions. Over time, viewers are nudged from moderate content toward more extreme positions. The system doesn't create hatred, but it accelerates it, moving a person step by step from curiosity to conviction.[60]

The consequences have been deadly. In 2019, an Australian extremist murdered fifty-one Muslims in Christchurch, New Zealand, after years of immersion in online radical content. Subsequent reporting showed that recommendation engines repeatedly guided him toward increasingly extreme material. The technology did not invent the ideology, but it amplified it, reinforcing falsehood until violence felt justified. In such cases, evil spreads not because a machine wills it, but because automated systems can carry lies farther and faster than any human network ever could. Demons do not write code, yet they benefit from tools that multiply deception and harden hearts.

Other systems work more quietly but no less powerfully. Many platforms sort users into ideological silos, feeding them only what aligns with their existing views. Over time, this isolation dulls the ability to recognize truth and deepens confidence in falsehood. No malicious intent is required for this to happen. When incentives reward engagement rather than truth, isolation follows—and spiritual vulnerability grows.

Addiction operates in much the same way. Digital environments are often built around variable rewards, the same mechanism that fuels gambling. Designers know this pattern fosters compulsive use, yet profit frequently outweighs concern for human well-being. What begins as convenience becomes captivity, as attention is trained toward endless consumption and away from reflection, restraint, and prayer.

Finally, constant exposure reshapes moral vision. When immorality is repeatedly displayed, joked about, or applauded, the conscience grows dull. Platforms rarely set out to celebrate sin, yet their curation quietly normalizes it. Biblical morality is treated as backward or harmful, while holiness is pushed to the margins. In this way, entire environments begin to "call evil good and good evil" (Isaiah 5:20), not by decree, but by repetition.

These patterns reflect "the course of this world...the spirit that is now at work in the sons of disobedience" (Ephesians 2:2). The "spirit" isn't a literal demon possessing the system but the pervasive spiritual atmosphere of rebellion that shapes worldly structures.

The way digital platforms amplify content is well documented. Internal Facebook research leaked in 2021—known as the "Facebook Files"—showed that the company's own analysts understood that their algorithms favored divisive material. Content that provoked anger or outrage consistently generated more clicks, and the system learned to promote it. Similar patterns have been observed elsewhere. A 2023 study by researchers at MIT and the University of Exeter found that YouTube's recommendation engine often guided users from mainstream political content toward more extreme material within just a few steps, regardless of where they began. Internal analysis at Twitter (now X) also showed that false information spreads far faster than truth, especially when it is emotionally charged.[61]

These outcomes result from incentive structures. Engagement-driven algorithms reward whatever keeps users clicking, sharing, and reacting—and outrage, conspiracy, and division perform especially well. When profit-seeking systems consistently elevate the most deceptive and destructive content, they begin to normalize moral inversion broadly. In that sense, Scripture's warning about systems that "call evil good and good evil" (Isaiah 5:20) is no longer abstract. It is being enacted daily through technologies that shape what millions of people see, believe, and trust.

Direct Spiritual Invitation

When humans explicitly invite demonic presence through occult practices integrated with technology, genuine spiritual activity may occur—not because machines can be possessed but because humans open themselves and their work to demonic influence.

When developers practice occult rituals during AI development, the spiritual danger is real—but we must be precise about the mechanism. The demon does not enter the code or possess the model. Rather, the developers open themselves to demonic influence, and that influence shapes their design decisions, priorities, values, and what they build into the system. The influence moves through people first, then through the choices they make, and finally into the systems they build. The result is technology that reflects demonic values (deception, division, addiction, idolatry), but the means is human choice, not supernatural inhabitation of silicon. This distinction matters pastorally: Users of such technology aren't necessarily under demonic oppression, but they are interacting with systems built by developers who were. Discernment and spiritual vigilance—not fear of possessed machines—are required.[62]

There are rarer cases wherein the danger becomes more explicit. At times, technology is intentionally joined to spiritual practices Scripture clearly forbids. In such instances, the risk doesn't lie in the machine itself, but in the human beings who open themselves to spiritual influence while creating or using it.[63]

Some practitioners now speak openly of using artificial intelligence as a medium for spiritual communication. They claim to receive guidance or messages through AI interfaces, treating the system as a kind of channel rather than a tool. Others go further. A small but vocal group of developers has described incorporating occult practices into their work, performing rituals, invoking symbols, or engaging in esoteric meditation in the belief that these actions enhance creativity or insight.[64] In 2023, several developers publicly discussed using sigils, tarot cards, or ceremonial rituals during software development.[65] One described performing a banishing ritual before major deployments to "clear negative energies." Another claimed to consult spiritual forces when making design decisions.[66]

Scripture gives no reason to believe that silicon can become a dwelling place for spirits. The danger lies elsewhere. When individuals deliberately invite spiritual powers outside Christ into their work, they expose themselves to influence that shapes their judgment, values, and intentions. What is built under such influence may reflect deception, division, or idolatry—not because the technology is possessed, but because its architects are compromised.

A similar danger appears in efforts sometimes described as "digital resurrection." Projects that attempt to recreate or "bring back" the dead through AI models can cross from technical experimentation into spiritual violation when they're framed as genuine communion with departed persons. Though often defended as therapeutic or artistic, such efforts risk reviving necromantic ideas under a technological guise—seeking contact with the dead through data rather than divination. Scripture draws no distinction between ancient and modern methods here. The prohibition remains: "There shall not be found among you anyone who…practices divination or tells fortunes or interprets omens…or consults the dead" (Deuteronomy 18:10–11).

In other cases, technological ambition becomes entangled with esoteric spirituality. Some transhumanist thinkers blend visions of human enhancement with mystical or gnostic models, promising transcendence through union with machines while borrowing language and practices drawn from non-Christian spiritual traditions.[67] When technological aspiration is joined to spiritual invocation outside Christ, the danger is neither symbolic nor speculative. Scripture is clear: "You cannot drink the cup of the Lord and the cup of demons" (1 Corinthians 10:21). Technology does not become possessed, but those who pursue power apart from God place themselves in spiritual peril—and the systems they build inevitably bear the marks of that choice.

Scripture affirmatively states: "You cannot drink the cup of the Lord and the cup of demons" (1 Corinthians 10:21). When humans explicitly invoke spiritual powers outside Christ, they invite demonic activity. Technology doesn't become possessed, but the practitioners expose themselves to spiritual oppression or possession.

Biblical prohibition: Deuteronomy 18:10–12 forbids divination, necromancy, and consultation with spirits. Digital rebranding does not nullify divine law; sorcery practiced through algorithms remains sorcery.

Digital Environments as Spiritual Territories

Chapter 7 explored global governance; now we examine the spiritual "atmosphere" of digital spaces.

Places Can Carry Spiritual Weight

Scripture recognizes that locations can have spiritual significance:

- **Holy sites**: Where God's presence is specifically manifest (Exodus 3:5, Psalm 132:13–14)
- **Defiled places**: Where sin has been concentrated (Genesis 19, Revelation 18)
- **Strongholds**: Spiritual territories where demonic activity is particularly strong (Daniel 10:13, Ephesians 6:12)

Physical geography matters spiritually; some cities, regions, or buildings seem saturated with either holiness or wickedness based on human activity there.

Digital Spaces as "Places"

If physical locations carry spiritual weight, do digital environments?

Not in the same way: Digital spaces lack physical substance. No demons "live" in servers or networks as they might oppress physical locations.

But functionally similar: Digital environments create "atmospheres"—cultures, norms, expectations—that shape participants. Platforms are saturated with:

- Pornography, which conditions users toward lust.
- Outrage content, which cultivates anger and division.
- Envy-inducing displays, which foster covetousness.
- Mockery of faith, which normalizes blasphemy.
- Occult content, which desensitizes toward spiritual danger.

These aren't possessed spaces but cultivated atmospheres where certain sins are normalized, encouraged, and rewarded—creating spiritual vulnerability.[68]

Participation Creates Exposure

"Do not be deceived: 'Bad company ruins good morals'" (1 Corinthians 15:33). This applies digitally:

Content consumption: What we feed our minds shapes desires, beliefs, and character. Constant exposure to sin desensitizes conscience.

Community influence: Digital communities reinforce norms. Spending time in spaces hostile to Christ shapes perspective; even believers can drift when immersed in spiritual toxicity.

Addiction formation: Platforms engineered for compulsive use create bondage. What begins as utility becomes slavery (Romans 6:16).

The question isn't whether demons possess the network but whether participation in toxic digital environments creates **spiritual footholds**—"place[s]" given to the devil (Ephesians 4:27).

Addiction and Bondage: When Technology Enslaves

Previous chapters noted technology's addictive design; now we examine addiction as spiritual bondage.

The Mechanics of Digital Addiction

Neurological: Dopamine-driven reward systems create compulsive behavior. Social media, gaming, and pornography hijack brain chemistry similarly to drugs.[69]

Psychological: Escapism, validation-seeking, and fear of missing out (FOMO) drive obsessive checking and engagement.

Social: Identity formation through digital metrics (likes, followers, views) creates dependency on external validation.

Spiritual: When technology becomes the first resort for comfort, meaning, or connection—it has displaced God as functional savior.

Contemporary research validates the spiritual diagnosis Scripture provides. A 2023 Pew Research study found that 46 percent of US teens say they are online "almost constantly," with 95 percent having smartphone access. The American Psychological Association reports that smartphone addiction shares neurological features with substance dependencies—the same dopamine pathways, withdrawal symptoms, and compulsive behavior patterns. Particularly concerning: A 2024 study in *JAMA Psychiatry* found that adolescents spending more than three hours daily on social media showed double the risk of depression and anxiety disorders compared to minimal users. These aren't merely correlation studies; longitudinal research demonstrates causal relationships between excessive digital engagement and mental health deterioration. What psychology observes as "behavioral addiction" Scripture identifies as spiritual bondage: enslaving habits that compromise freedom, distort identity, and separate from God (John 8:34).[70]

Addiction as Spiritual Bondage

> Jesus answered them, "Truly, truly, I say to you, everyone who practices sin is a slave to sin." (John 8:34)

Digital addiction exhibits characteristics of spiritual bondage:

Loss of freedom: The addicted person wants to stop but cannot; the will is compromised.

Compulsive behavior: Despite negative consequences, the behavior continues.

Identity distortion: The addiction becomes central to self-concept.

Isolation from God: Prayer, Scripture, and worship feel burdensome; screens provide easier comfort.

Demons exploit this: They don't do so by forcing addiction but by capitalizing on designed vulnerability. Developers create addictive systems; demons ensure that those systems produce spiritual fruit: isolation, idolatry, moral compromise.

Social media addiction is engineered, not accidental. Former Facebook executive Sean Parker admitted in 2017: "We exploited a vulnerability in human psychology…. The thought process was: How do we consume as much of your time and conscious attention as possible? It's a social-validation feedback loop…exactly the kind of thing that a hacker like myself would come up with, because you're exploiting a vulnerability in human psychology." Facebook's founding president acknowledged they knowingly created addictive products by exploiting psychological weaknesses. By 2024, studies showed the average American spent seven hours daily on screens, with teenagers averaging nine hours—more time than sleeping. Clinical psychologists report patients exhibiting withdrawal symptoms (anxiety, tremors, depression) when separated from devices, meeting diagnostic criteria for substance addiction. This is spiritual bondage manifest through technological means; demons don't possess phones, but they exploit engineered addiction to enslave attention, corrupt priorities, and prevent communion with God.[71]

Deliverance Requires Spiritual Warfare

Freedom from digital bondage isn't merely psychological; it's spiritual:

1. Repentance: Confess idolatry and surrender control to Christ (James 4:7–10)

2. Renunciation: Explicitly reject the lies internalized through addiction (2 Corinthians 10:5)

3. Reorientation: Replace destructive habits with life-giving practices—Scripture, prayer, embodied community, service, and trusted relationships that provide encouragement and correction (Ephesians 5:18; James 5:16)

4. Practical boundaries: Remove apps, install filters, change environments—resisting temptation through wisdom (Proverbs 4:14–15)

None of this is glamorous. But it's how freedom is usually rebuilt—one decision at a time.

Practical Implementation: The Seven-Day Digital Reset

This is not a rulebook or a spiritual test. It's a starting point, one way to regain clarity and freedom if technology has begun to crowd out attentiveness to God and others. Adapt it as needed, and approach it prayerfully rather than mechanically.

Days 1–2 (paying attention): Begin by simply noticing your habits. For two days, pay attention to when you reach for your phone, what you turn to, and how it leaves you feeling. Are you seeking distraction, comfort, validation, or escape? Patterns of bondage often operate below awareness, and freedom usually begins with honest attention to what is already shaping us.

Days 3–4 (letting go): Next, remove what you know is pulling your heart in the wrong direction. This may mean deleting certain apps rather than "taking a break," or stepping away from content that stirs anger, envy, lust, or pride. A simple question can guide you here: *Would I be at peace if Christ saw how I spend my attention?* If the answer is no, take that conviction seriously and act on it.

Days 5–6 (filling the space): What you remove must be replaced. Empty space rarely stays empty for long. Use the time you've reclaimed to return to life-giving practices—prayer in the morning, Scripture in the evening, conversation with real people, rest without screens. What once fed distraction can become space for communion, reflection, and presence. Lasting change comes not by resisting desire alone, but by cultivating deeper satisfactions.

Day 7 (taking stock): Finally, pause and reflect. What do you truly miss—and what do you not? Did stepping back restore peace, clarity, or attentiveness to God? As you reintroduce technology, do so carefully, asking whether it draws you toward Christ or subtly pulls you away. This is not legalism, but wisdom. Freedom is rarely won by good intentions alone; it is sustained through practiced habits shaped and strengthened by the Holy Spirit.

Churches across South Korea and Singapore now hold "digital detox retreats," where participants fast from screens, pray corporately, and testify to newfound mental clarity and restored devotion.[72]

Deliverance is possible because "he who is in you is greater than he who is in the world" (1 John 4:4).

Discerning Spirits in Digital Spaces

Beloved, do not believe every spirit, but test the spirits to see whether they are from God. (1 John 4:1)

Discernment in the digital age requires applying biblical tests to technological engagement.

Diagnostic Questions

1. What fruit does this produce?

Scripture teaches that truth is known by its fruit (Matthew 7:16). After time spent with a platform or technology, the question is what it produces in you. Does it leave you more patient, peaceful, and content— or more restless, irritable, and envious? Does it deepen attentiveness to God or quietly crowd prayer and humility to the margins? When engagement consistently yields anxiety, distraction, or pride rather than love and peace, the fruit itself calls the source into question.

2. Does it glorify God or self?

Technology can be used for God's glory (teaching, evangelism, encouragement) or self-glory (vanity, attention-seeking, pride). Which dominates your use?

3. Does it facilitate truth or deception?

Does your technology diet expose you to truth or immerse you in lies?[73] Are you consuming biblical content or worldly ideologies? Engaging apologetics or absorbing propaganda?

4. Does it build community or isolate?

God designed humans for embodied relationships (Hebrews 10:24– 25). Does your tech use strengthen real community or substitute digital connection for genuine fellowship?

5. Can you abstain without anxiety?

Try a twenty-four-hour digital fast. If the prospect induces panic, you're in bondage. Freedom means being able to use or abstain without the technology owning you.

6. Is it secret or shameful?

"Everyone who does wicked things hates the light" (John 3:20). If you hide your technology use, clear browsing history, or would be ashamed for others to see your activity—that's conviction demanding response.

The Ultimate Test: Does It Lead Toward or Away from Christ?

Every technology, platform, and digital engagement either:

- **Draws you toward Christ**: Encouraging faith, holiness, love, and dependence on God.
- **Pulls you away**: Fostering doubt, compromise, isolation, or functional atheism (living as if God doesn't matter).

Neutral uses are possible, but patterns reveal trajectory. If your digital life consistently draws you away from Christ, spiritual warfare is needed.

Understanding how demons exploit technology matters, but understanding alone doesn't protect. Knowledge without application leaves believers vulnerable. What practical steps can believers take to resist demonic influence in digital environments? How can the Church apply ancient spiritual warfare wisdom to unprecedented technological contexts? The armor of God (Ephesians 6:10–18) provides the architecture, but it must be applied specifically to digital battlegrounds.

The Armor of God in Digital Warfare

Paul's words in Ephesians 6:10–18 were written to believers facing visible persecution, yet they speak just as clearly to a world shaped by screens, systems, and constant persuasion. This is not a perfect analogy, nor does it need to be. Scripture was never meant to predict technology, but to form discernment. When read prayerfully, the armor of God offers quiet guidance for living faithfully amid digital pressure.

Paul begins with the **belt of truth**: "Stand therefore, having fastened on the belt of truth" (Ephesians 6:14). Truth holds everything else in place. In a world where algorithms decide what we see and hear, Scripture steadies the soul. When truth is anchored in God's Word rather than curated feeds or trending narratives, deception loses much of its power. The belt reminds us that before we evaluate information, we must know who we are and whose voice we trust.

Next comes the **breastplate of righteousness**: "having put on the breastplate of righteousness" (Ephesians 6:14). Righteousness guards the heart, and in digital spaces the heart is constantly exposed. What we watch, share, endorse, or linger over shapes us more than we realize. Holiness is not suspended online. The breastplate protects when we choose integrity over indulgence, restraint over impulse, and obedience over convenience—even when no one else is watching.

Paul adds the shoes of the gospel of peace: "as shoes for your feet, having put on the readiness given by the gospel of peace" (Ephesians 6:15). Shoes are for movement. Technology can either root us in restlessness or carry us outward in love. When our digital presence serves the gospel—encouraging, teaching, bearing witness—it becomes a means of peace rather than distraction. The question is not simply how connected we are, but where our connection leads.

The **shield of faith** follows: "In all circumstances take up the shield of faith, with which you can extinguish all the flaming darts of the evil one" (Ephesians 6:16). Digital life produces many such darts—comparison, anxiety, fear of missing out, quiet accusations of inadequacy. Faith intercepts these lies before they lodge in the soul. When data tells us we are behind, unwanted, or insufficient, faith answers with God's promises and rests in His care.

Paul then names the **helmet of salvation**: "and take the helmet of salvation" (Ephesians 6:17). The helmet guards the mind. In an age where worth is measured in likes, followers, and visibility, salvation secures identity. Our value does not rise or fall with engagement metrics. It rests in redemption already accomplished. A protected mind remembers that identity is received, not earned—and certainly not calculated.

The lone offensive weapon is the **sword of the Spirit**, "which is the word of God" (Ephesians 6:17). Scripture does more than defend; it cuts through confusion and exposes lies. Digital access to the Bible is a gift, but a Word hidden in the heart cannot be silenced by dead batteries or blocked signals. When truth is memorized and internalized, it is always near—ready when temptation comes or clarity is needed.

Finally, Paul speaks of **prayer**: "praying at all times in the Spirit, with all prayer and supplication" (Ephesians 6:18). Prayers keep the armor alive. In a world of constant alerts and interruptions, prayer reclaims attention for God. It reminds us that we're never as connected as when we are listening to Him. Let prayer, not notifications, shape the rhythm of the day.

The armor is sufficient—not because the world is simple, but because God is faithful. The pressures may arrive faster now and reach farther than before, but the provision remains the same. Those who stand clothed in truth, righteousness, peace, faith, salvation, the Word, and prayer do not stand alone. They stand in the strength of the Lord.

The armor is sufficient. The battle is real. But the outcome is already decided. Christ has triumphed over principalities and powers (Colossians 2:15). Demons may exploit technology, but they operate under sovereign permission, within divine constraints, and toward an appointed defeat. The Church engages digital Babylon not as uncertain combatants but as victorious warriors applying Christ's finished work to present circumstances.

These disciplines protect the believer's attention and affection from captivity. Yet victory is not merely defensive—it is proclamation of Christ's supremacy in every realm, including the digital.

For Families: A Technology Covenant

Christian families cannot afford to drift when it comes to technology. What is needed isn't panic, but intentionality. A family covenant helps parents lead with clarity and love rather than reacting after damage is done. The language should fit your own household; the goal is not perfection, but shared understanding.

As parents, we agree to set boundaries that protect our home and our children:

- Devices do not belong in bedrooms late at night when fatigue lowers wisdom and temptation grows.
- Phones are set aside during family meals and family worship, so attention stays with one another and with God.
- We keep access to our children's devices and accounts—not out of suspicion, but out of responsibility to shepherd their hearts.

- New apps and games are reviewed together before they are allowed.
- We set aside regular time—at least one day each week—without screens to rest, reconnect, and remember what matters most.

We acknowledge a few truths we cannot afford to forget:

- Technology is a tool, not a substitute for parenting.
- Ease and convenience are never good reasons to lower moral guardrails.
- Our children's spiritual formation matters more than their entertainment.
- What we allow into our own lives teaches louder than anything we say.

We commit to walking this road together:

- We will talk openly as a family about digital temptations, failures, and victories.
- We will pray together when technology becomes a struggle, not a secret.
- We will hold one another accountable, knowing that parents are not exempt from these pressures.
- We will revisit and adjust boundaries as our children grow and as new challenges emerge.

This covenant is not about control; it is about discipleship. Parents who hand digital authority to cultural norms rarely regain it. Boundaries set early are easier to maintain than habits corrected later. Delayed access to harmful content is not deprivation, it is protection. When families name these commitments together, they're not imposing rules but choosing a shared way of life, pursuing holiness side by side in a digital world that often pulls in the opposite direction.

Conclusion

Should Christians avoid technology entirely? No—technology itself is not demonic, any more than physical territory is demonic. But just as Paul ministered in Corinth (a city full of temples and sexual immorality) without participating in its sins, believers use technology without adopting its idolatries. The question is not whether to engage but how to engage faithfully. This requires: 1) awareness of spiritual realities without paranoia; 2) discernment of manipulative designs without seeing conspiracy everywhere; 3) setting boundaries without legalism; and 4) using technology for kingdom purposes without being used by it. Technology is territory to occupy for Christ; it isn't Babylon to simply flee.

Yes, demons exploit technology—but they don't control it. Christ remains sovereign over every system, algorithm, and network. "He disarmed the rulers and authorities and put them to open shame, triumphing over them in him" (Colossians 2:15).

Believers therefore engage digital Babylon neither naively nor fearfully, recognizing real spiritual warfare while trusting Christ's victory and the Spirit's power to preserve His people. The same God who protected Daniel in Babylon, Paul in Rome, and the Church through centuries of persecution sustains believers in the digital age.

Technology amplifies human capacity for both good and evil. Demons exploit that amplification, but so can believers—using digital tools for gospel proclamation, discipleship, and kingdom advance. In recent years, millions have engaged Scripture through digital evangelism platforms, demonstrating that redeemed technology can magnify divine truth.

The final algorithm belongs to the Alpha and the Omega, and He has already written it: "Then I saw a new heaven and a new earth, for the first heaven and the first earth had passed away" (Revelation 21:1).

Until that day, the Church occupies digital territory with wisdom, discernment, and confidence. I have watched enough wars to know this one won't be won with better gadgets. Our posture is not uncertainty or desperation. Christ has already secured the victory. The powers that oppose Him have been judged, and the truth is not fragile. As Scripture reminds us, "Greater is he who is in you than he who is in the world" (1 John 4:4).

The forces of deception are active, and systems are often bent toward manipulation and misuse. Yet they do not rule. Christ reigns. The Spirit abides within His people. And the truth of God stands firm, untouched by every passing scheme.

And when the final algorithm runs its last iteration, every demon will bow, every lie will be exposed, and every device will confess that Jesus Christ is Lord, to the glory of God the Father (Philippians 2:10–11).

Engage the digital age with confidence, believers. The battle is real—but the victory is certain.

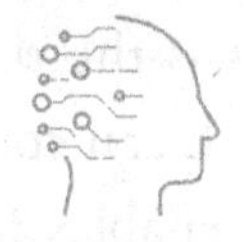

Chapter 11

THE GREAT FALLING AWAY: TECHNOLOGY AND THE APOSTASY

The apostasy will not come in the form of blatant rebellion, but through subtle compromise and the love of convenience over the truth of God.[74]

JOHN MACARTHUR, *The Second Coming*

Paul warns: "Let no one deceive you in any way. For that day will not come, unless the rebellion comes first, and the man of lawlessness is revealed" (2 Thessalonians 2:3). The "rebellion" (Greek: ἀποστασία; *apostasia*)—the great falling away—precedes the Tribulation and Antichrist's revelation. Digital technology creates the perfect environment for mass apostasy—not through overt persecution (which often strengthens faith) but through subtle erosion: convenience replacing commitment, distraction fragmenting devotion, metrics measuring spirituality, and algorithmic authority displacing biblical truth. Earlier chapters explored external threats (Beast system, false miracles, economic control). Now we examine internal collapse—how the Church itself drifts from biblical Christianity through technological accommodation. Where earlier generations feared persecution, this one should fear persuasion—the slow conversion of conviction into convenience.

One of the most dangerous effects of digital technology is its ability to remove the natural friction that once slowed the spread of theological error—time, distance, language, and local accountability.

A closely related accelerant is the rise of AI systems that globalize deception faster than the Church can correct it.

AI-driven translation now enables false teaching to spread worldwide in seconds. Meta's 2025 "omnilingual" model can recognize or transcribe more than 1,600 human languages, including hundreds that have never existed in digital form. This linguistic reach creates a new spiritual vulnerability: Heresy is no longer limited by geography, tribe, or dialect. Historically, false doctrine spread slowly—letters, messengers, itinerant teachers. Today, an algorithm can translate a synthetic sermon, a prosperity-gospel clip, or an AI-generated devotional into nearly every tongue on earth instantly. Global apostasy no longer requires global missionaries; it requires global models.[75]

This accelerates the very dynamic Paul warned about: deception masquerading as enlightenment. When AI translates teaching with perfect fluency, many assume the underlying message must be authoritative. When content tailored for Western ears is rendered flawlessly for rural Africa, Southeast Asia, or South America, the message arrives stripped of local accountability, pastoral oversight, and biblical guardrails. The result is planetary-scale drift—people abandoning truth not from persecution, but from persuasive, customized, algorithmically delivered error. Apostasy becomes a multilingual phenomenon, enabled by machines that speak every language but know nothing of God.

The ruins of faith stand silent, where the cross once commanded hearts—now overshadowed by the glow of a new gospel born of the machine.

The Nature of Apostasy: A Biblical Understanding

Apostasy (*apostasia*) means "falling away," "departure," or "abandonment"—specifically, the abandonment of previously held faith.[76]

An important caution: Some drift described here reflects genuine believers struggling with sin patterns (distraction, compromise) that require repentance, not evidence of apostasy. True apostasy is comprehensive abandonment of faith, not temporary spiritual lethargy. We'll describe both: 1) mechanisms pushing professing Christians toward genuine apostasy (leaving the faith entirely), and 2) mechanisms weakening genuine believers' faithfulness (requiring repentance and renewal). Pastorally, we cannot investigate hearts to determine who is apostate versus who is struggling. But we can identify dangerous patterns and sound warnings. Paul warned that deception would come "with all power and false signs and wonders" (2 Thessalonians 2:9), reminding us that apostasy rarely announces itself; it masquerades as progress. The goal is not to judge hearts but to warn of danger.

Not Mere Unbelief

Apostasy differs from:

- **Ignorance**: Never hearing the gospel (different from rejecting it after profession)
- Nominal faith: Cultural Christianity without genuine conversion
- Backsliding: Temporary drift from which believers return

Apostasy is **deliberate abandonment** of Christian faith by those who once professed it—a falling away that is comprehensive, final, and damning.

Biblical Examples

- **Israel's repeated apostasy**: Forsaking Yahweh for idols (Judges 2:11–19, Jeremiah 2:13)

- **End-times prophecy**: "In later times some will depart from the faith by devoting themselves to deceitful spirits and teachings of demons" (1 Timothy 4:1)
- **The great rebellion**: As described in 2 Thessalonians 2:3, which describes *the* apostasy (with definite article)—a specific, prophesied, massive falling away before Christ's return

Characteristics of Apostasy

- **Gradual**: "They will turn away from listening to the truth and wander off into myths" (2 Timothy 4:4); it's not sudden rejection but slow drift.
- **Deceptive**: It appears as progress, enlightenment, or maturity; it isn't recognized as apostasy by those experiencing it.
- **Comfortable**: It maintains religious forms while denying their power (2 Timothy 3:5); it looks Christian without being Christian.
- **Widespread**: It affects many, not isolated individuals; Paul describes it as a systemic departure.

Apostasy is gradual, deceptive, comfortable, and widespread. It maintains religious forms while denying power. It appears as progress while producing departure. Previous generations faced apostasy through overt heresy or persecution. This generation faces something more subtle—technological accommodation that erodes faith through convenience, distraction, and compromise so gradual that many never recognize they've fallen away. Seven mechanisms reveal how digital technology creates the perfect environment for mass apostasy.

How Technology Cultivates Apostasy: Seven Mechanisms

1. The Convenience Gospel

According to Barna Research (2023), 43 percent of self-identified Christians attend church only on Christmas and Easter. Among millennials who grew up in church, 59 percent have left—citing "too busy" (47 percent) and "can watch sermons online" (38 percent) as primary reasons.

Lifeway Research found that 66 percent of American young adults who attended Protestant churches regularly for at least a year in high school have stopped attending by age twenty-three. The most common reason? "Church wasn't convenient with my schedule." One twenty-eight-year-old former churchgoer stated: "I still consider myself Christian. I just stream sermons while working out. It's more efficient." This is the soil in which apostasy flourishes—maintaining Christian identity while abandoning Christian obedience, substituting digital consumption for costly discipleship.[77]

Biblical Christianity: "If anyone would come after me, let him deny himself and take up his cross daily and follow me" (Luke 9:23). Faith costs something—time, comfort, reputation, resources.

Digital Christianity: Faith becomes convenient, customizable, and cost-free:

- **On-demand sermons**: Listen when convenient, with the ability to fast-forward through convicting parts.
- **Digital attendance**: Watch online instead of gathering bodily (violating the instruction of Hebrews 10:25).
- **Algorithmic curation**: AI suggests content, matching preferences and avoiding challenging teaching.
- **Chatbot pastors**: Automated spiritual guidance requiring no vulnerability or accountability.

The convenience gospel is measurable in attendance patterns. Pew Research (2023) found that among Americans who watched religious services online during COVID-19, 81 percent continued streaming after restrictions lifted—but only 35 percent returned to in-person worship regularly. Lifeway Research (2024) documented that churches offering "hybrid" worship (in-person plus streaming) experienced 23 percent decline in physical attendance over two years, with online "attendance" staying flat but providing no increase in giving, volunteering, or community engagement. Most telling: The same study found that 67 percent of consistent online-only viewers couldn't name their pastor and felt no obligation to the church community. The technological convenience that promised to "reach more people" has instead facilitated departure—viewers without membership, consumers without commitment, attendance without incarnation. What presents as "church growth" through digital metrics often masks actual decline in embodied discipleship.[78]

Result: When faith becomes convenience, trials produce apostasy. "Those on the rock are the ones who receive the word with joy when they hear it, but they have no root. They believe for a while, but in the time of testing they fall away" (Luke 8:13).

2. The Distraction Epidemic

Biblical requirement: "You shall love the Lord your God with all your heart and with all your soul and with all your mind" (Matthew 22:37). Faith requires sustained attention, focused devotion, contemplative depth.

The distraction is measurable. Research shows the average person checks their phone 352 times per day—every four minutes while awake. By 2025, mobile attention spans have fallen below eight seconds. During worship services, 58 percent of attendees check phones at least once, with 22 percent checking multiple times. Pastors report congregation members scrolling social media during sermons, responding to texts during prayer, and browsing shopping sites during communion. One worship leader stated: "I can see half the congregation on their phones during the message. They're physically present but mentally absent. We've lost the ability to focus for twenty minutes—and we're losing the ability to hear God speak through sustained attention." The result is Christians who "attend" church but never actually engage, who "hear" sermons but never truly listen, who are physically present but spiritually absent. This is not persecution destroying faith, it's distraction fragmenting it.[79]

- **Digital reality**: People pay only continuous partial attention; they're never fully present anywhere:
- **Prayer is interrupted**: The average person checks their phone 144 times daily;[80] sustained prayer becomes impossible.

- **Scripture is fragmented**: Reading takes place in small chunks between notifications; there's no deep meditation (Psalm 1:2).
- **Worship is divided**: Physical presence is accompanied by mental absence—for example, congregants are singing while scrolling.

    The distraction isn't merely theoretical. A 2023 study by the Hartford Institute for Religion Research found that 58 percent of churchgoers admit to checking phones during worship services—not for emergencies but for texts, social media, and email. Pastoral surveys reveal the same pastors who once worried about congregants sleeping during sermons now face rows of people physically present but mentally absent, scrolling feeds while the Word is preached. One megachurch pastor described attempting to preach only to see "a sea of glowing faces—not faces looking up at me but faces looking down at screens." More disturbing: Youth pastors report teenagers taking selfies during worship, live-streaming services to social media for followers, and treating gathered worship as content creation opportunity rather than sacred encounter. This isn't generational preference—it's liturgical formation failure. When phones shape attention more than hymns, algorithms disciple more effectively than Scripture, and notifications have greater authority than the preached Word, apostasy isn't merely possible—it's inevitable.[81]

- **Silence is eliminated**: Constant stimulation drowns out "low whisper" (1 Kings 19:12). As a result, "the cares of the world...and the desires for other things enter in and choke the word, and it proves unfruitful" (Mark 4:19). Distraction produces shallow faith that withers under pressure.

3. Secular Liturgies Forming Hearts

James K. A. Smith argues that humans are primarily liturgical creatures shaped by repeated practices more than intellectual beliefs.[82] Every repeated action forms us:

Traditional Christian liturgy:

- Morning: Prayer, Scripture before facing the day
- Throughout: Practicing presence of God
- Evening: Examination of conscience, gratitude
- Weekly: Corporate worship, Eucharist
- Yearly: Church calendar shaping rhythm

Digital liturgy (actual practices of most professing Christians):

- Morning: Phone first—checking notifications, news, social media
- Throughout: Constant device-checking—attention fragmented
- Evening: Screen time until sleep—no reflection or prayer
- Weekly: Maybe church if convenient, definitely streaming
- Yearly: Calendar shaped by cultural events, not Christian feasts

Result: "Do not be conformed to this world, but be transformed by the renewal of your mind" (Romans 12:2). Digital liturgies conform minds to worldly values, producing apostasy through habit formation.

Convenience breeds compromise, distraction fragments devotion, and secular liturgies form hearts away from Christ. But even more insidious is the fourth mechanism: allowing digital metrics to replace biblical marks of grace, substituting quantifiable vanity for invisible holiness.

4. Metrics of Vanity Replacing Marks of Grace

Multiple megachurches now prominently display real-time metrics during services: attendance count on screens, social media follower numbers on websites, giving totals on apps. One fifteen thousand-member church emails weekly "engagement scores" to small group leaders, ranking groups by attendance, giving, and social media interactions. Leaders whose groups score below benchmarks face "accountability meetings."

One former leader stated: "I stopped asking 'Are people growing in Christ?' and started asking 'How do I boost our metrics?' The moment I optimized for numbers instead of holiness, I lost my calling." Another pastor admitted: "We hired a data analytics firm to track which sermon topics generate highest engagement. We preach what produces metrics, not what Scripture demands." This is apostasy through measurement—valuing what can be quantified over what matters eternally.[83]

Biblical measures of spiritual health:

- Fruit of the Spirit (Galatians 5:22–23)
- Love for God and neighbor (Matthew 22:37–39)
- Obedience to Scripture (John 14:15)
- Growth in holiness (1 Peter 1:15–16)
- Perseverance under trial (James 1:12)

Digital measures (what platforms train us to value):

- Followers, likes, shares—visibility
- Viral content—impact
- Engagement rates—influence
- Aesthetic appeal—image
- Controversial takes—attention

Result: "They loved the glory that comes from man more than the glory that comes from God" (John 12:43). When spiritual leaders optimize for metrics rather than faithfulness, they model apostasy—and congregations follow.

5. Algorithmic Authority Displacing Biblical Truth

In 2024, a prominent evangelical church launched "AskFaith"—an AI chatbot providing "biblical" guidance trained on the church's sermon archive and "progressive Christian" resources. When asked about sexuality, it stated: "Loving same-sex relationships honor God when characterized by commitment and consent. Traditional interpretations reflect cultural biases, not biblical truth." When asked about abortion, it replied: "Women's bodily autonomy is a sacred right. The Bible doesn't explicitly address modern reproductive technology, so personal conscience should guide." When confronted, the pastor defended it: "We trained AI on contemporary scholarship to provide nuanced guidance." This is algorithmic apostasy—substituting computational synthesis for biblical authority, allowing machine-generated consensus to override revealed truth, and then labeling the result "biblical." Thousands received heresy as divine guidance because it came through sophisticated technology.[84]

Traditional evangelical epistemology:

- Scripture is final authority (2 Timothy 3:16–17)
- Tradition and reason serve Scripture
- Holy Spirit illuminates (1 Corinthians 2:12–13)
- Community discerns together (Acts 15)

Emerging digital epistemology:

- Search engines determine truth: "Google says…".
- AI generates doctrine: ChatGPT writes sermons, theology.
- Algorithms curate information: What you see becomes what you believe.
- Popularity indicates correctness: Viral = true; marginal = false.

Result: Believers trust algorithms over Scripture; AI-generated content feels more relevant than biblical text; popularity determines theology. Functional apostasy occurs even while religious language persists.

When artificial intelligence becomes the interpreter of divine revelation, the Church trades illumination for automation.

6. Moral Compromise Through Normalization

Biblical call: "Do not love the world or the things in the world" (1 John 2:15). Believers maintain distinct ethics, resisting cultural accommodation.

Digital effect: Constant exposure normalizes what Scripture condemns. Consider that Harvard's 2024 Digital Ethics Study found that moral sensitivity declines by 28 percent among participants exposed to high-frequency algorithmic content over ninety days.[85] Examples include:

- Sexual immorality: Ubiquitous, algorithmically served
- Covetousness: Instagram displays of wealth breeding envy
- Anger: Outrage algorithms rewarding rage
- Pride: Platforms designed for self-promotion
- Deception: Curated personas presenting false realities

Result: Conscience desensitizes. "Their consciences also bearing witness, and their conflicting thoughts accusing or even excusing them" (Romans 2:15). When believers spend more time immersed in digital culture than biblical community, worldly ethics eclipse Christian conviction—preparing for apostasy when biblical positions face opposition.

7. Synthetic Spirituality as Substitute

Multiple apps now offer "AI prayer partners" "that "pray with you" using generated text, "prophesy" through predictive algorithms, and provide "spiritual counseling" through large-language models. One app, "Spiritual Companion," claims 1.2 million users. A user testimonial: "My AI prayer partner knows me better than anyone at church. She's always available, never judgmental, and gives me exactly what I need to hear." Another stated: "I stopped going to church because my AI chaplain provides better guidance than our pastor—and I don't have to get dressed or drive anywhere." This is synthetic spirituality replacing authentic Christian community—substituting algorithmic empathy for Spirit-filled fellowship, computational "prayer" for genuine communion with God, and data-driven "counsel" for biblical truth spoken in love. It appears spiritual while being entirely empty.[86]

Biblical spirituality: Personal relationship with God through Christ, mediated by Spirit, lived in community

Synthetic alternatives technology provides:

- AI spiritual guides: Replace pastors, mentors, and Holy Spirit's conviction
- Virtual reality worship: Immersive but isolated "spiritual experiences"
- Algorithmically optimized devotionals: Customized to avoid offense
- Digital "churches": Communities requiring no commitment, offering no accountability
- Mindfulness apps: Meditation divorced from God, focused on self

Result: People feel "spiritual" without repentance, transformation, or submission to Christ, believing they're growing while apostatizing.

Seven mechanisms—convenience, distraction, secular liturgies, vanity metrics, algorithmic authority, moral compromise, and synthetic spirituality. Each is gradual, deceptive, and comfortable. Together, they create the prophesied falling away. But understanding apostasy's mechanisms isn't enough. The Church must respond with specific, practical, costly faithfulness. How do believers resist when the majority drifts?

What Scripture foretold and technology accelerates is now visible in measurable patterns across the modern Church.

Statistical Evidence: The Falling Away Is Measurable

Church attendance collapse (US):

- 1990: 20 percent rarely/never attended; 2020: 31 percent[87]
- Younger generations: Only 28 percent of Gen Z attend monthly[88]

- Post-COVID digital shift accelerated abandonment of physical gathering[89]

Biblical literacy crisis:

- 2022: Only 9 percent of Americans have biblical worldview.[90]

- Most self-identified Christians can't name the four Gospels.
- Scripture reading among believers is at historic lows.

The biblical literacy crisis has accelerated dramatically in the digital age. Barna's 2022 study found that only 9 percent of Americans possess a biblical worldview (down from 12 percent in 2011), but among self-identified Christians the data is more alarming: Only 6 percent of Millennials who identify as Christian hold biblical views on basic doctrines like sin, salvation, and Scripture's authority—compared to 65 percent of their grandparents' generation at the same age. The American Bible Society's 2024 *State of the Bible* report documented that daily Scripture reading among evangelicals dropped from 45 percent (2011) to 14 percent (2024)—a 69 percent decline in thirteen years. Researchers correlate this directly with smartphone adoption: As screen time increased (now averaging more than seven hours daily for adults), Bible reading decreased proportionally. The pattern is clear: Digital liturgies are displacing biblical formation. Where previous generations memorized Scripture, this generation memorizes passwords. Where believers once meditated on God's Word day and night (Psalm 1:2), they now scroll feeds day and night. The falling away isn't abstract theology; it's measurable abandonment of the very practices that sustain faith.[91]

Doctrinal drift:

- Increasing percentages of evangelicals denying:
  o Exclusivity of Christ for salvation
  o Biblical sexual ethics
  o Reality of hell
  o Authority of Scripture

Rise of "spiritual but not religious":

- 2017: 27 percent of US adults identified as spiritual but not religious.[92]
- Represents consumer spirituality—picking preferences without submission.

These statistics don't merely reflect cultural change; they fulfill prophecy.

The Remnant: Biblical Pattern of Faithful Few

God always preserves a remnant, even when majority apostatizes:

- Noah's family: Eight were saved from global judgment (Genesis 7:1).
- Israel: Seven thousand didn't bow to Baal (1 Kings 19:18).
- Faithful exiles: preserved through Babylon's captivity. The prophetic remnant is not survivalist isolation but steadfast obedience. Daniel did not hide from Babylon; he witnessed within it.
- Revelation's overcomers: "To the one who conquers..." (Revelation 2–3).

Application today:

Resist convenience: Commit to local church—physical gathering, embodied worship, costly service.

Maintain truth: Study Scripture deeply—not simple devotionals but sustained Bible reading and theology.

Practice disciplines: Prayer, fasting, silence, simplicity—spiritual formation resisting digital shaping.

Build community: Face-to-face relationships—accountability, confession, mutual encouragement.

Accept cost: Faithfulness will increasingly require sacrifice—social marginalization, economic pressure, perhaps persecution.

The remnant survives not through strength but through grace: "By grace you have been saved through faith. And this is not your own doing; it is the gift of God" (Ephesians 2:8).

Pre-Tribulational Hope and Present Responsibility

From a pre-Tribulational perspective: The Church is raptured before the Tribulation; those who apostatize demonstrate they were never truly saved (1 John 2:19).

This doesn't mean genuine Christians cannot struggle with the patterns described above; distraction, compromise, and convenience-seeking are real temptations for all believers. The difference is that genuine believers, when warned, repent and return; apostates, when warned, justify and continue. "They went out from us, but they were not of us; for if they had been of us, they would have continued with us. But they went out, that it might become plain that they all are not of us" (1 John 2:19). The great falling away reveals false professors who appeared Christian but lacked genuine conversion. True believers persevere through struggle; apostates depart permanently. The presence of struggle doesn't indicate false faith—the absence of perseverance does.

But this doesn't eliminate urgency:

1. We don't know the timing: Rapture could be today or decades hence; apostasy affects people now.

2. Apostasy precedes the Rapture: Paul says the falling away comes *before* the man of lawlessness is revealed (2 Thessalonians 2:3); we're watching it unfold.[93]

3. Witness is needed: Those drifting need warning; unbelievers need the gospel before it's too late.

4. Faithfulness matters: We're accountable for how we steward our generation, regardless of prophetic timing.

Pastoral urgency: While we cannot know who is genuinely saved versus falsely professing, we must sound the alarm. Churches filled with people who check phones during sermons, skip worship for convenience, substitute AI chatbots for spiritual counsel, optimize for metrics over holiness, and embrace synthetic spirituality are in grave danger.[94] Some are genuine believers who need to wake up, repent, and return to faithfulness. Others are false professors whose drift reveals they were never truly saved. Our task is not to judge individual hearts but to warn of the cliff toward which the majority is walking. "Take care, brothers, lest there be in any of you an evil, unbelieving heart, leading you to fall away from the living God. But exhort one another every day, as long as it is called 'today,' that none of you may be hardened by the deceitfulness of sin" (Hebrews 3:12–13).

Pastoral Response: Recovery Pathway for the Drifting

For those recognizing drift in their own lives—or observing it in loved ones—recovery requires more than good intentions. It requires structured repentance and liturgical replacement:

1. Honest assessment: Name the specific mechanisms that have gained ground. Are you attending digitally because it's easier? Has phone usage displaced prayer time? Do metrics (likes, views, followers) shape your sense of worth more than your identity in Christ? Which of the seven mechanisms has the strongest grip? Confession requires specificity. General admission of "struggling with technology" lacks the precision needed for repentance. Identify the exact liturgies that have displaced biblical practices, the precise conveniences that have replaced costly discipleship, and the specific ways algorithms have shaped beliefs more than Scripture.

2. Liturgical replacement: Don't merely remove digital habits; replace them with biblical practices. Morning phone-checking becomes morning prayer and Scripture. Evening scrolling becomes evening examination of conscience and thanksgiving. Weekend binge-watching becomes Sabbath rest and corporate worship. Lunch social media becomes lunch conversation with real people or silent reflection. The goal isn't legalism but formation: replacing secular liturgies with Christian ones until godly habits become unconscious defaults. Nature abhors a vacuum; so does the human heart. If digital practices are removed without replacement, they will return.

3. Community accountability: Private repentance rarely succeeds against systemic formation. Share your struggle with mature believers who have authority to ask hard questions: What did you watch this week? How much time did you spend on devices? Did you attend worship bodily? Are you walking in sexual purity? Is your giving proportional to your income? Are you serving the body? Accountability isn't optional add-on; it's essential protection against self-deception. Digital drift happens in isolation; recovery requires community.

4. Prophetic resistance: Recognize that biblical faithfulness will increasingly appear strange, legalistic, or extreme. Refusing to stream worship will seem judgmental. Limiting social media will seem anti-social. Prioritizing embodied community over digital convenience will seem inefficient. Rejecting AI spiritual guidance will seem closed-minded. Insisting on biblical sexual ethics will seem hateful. This is cost of discipleship in Babylon—the Church always appears odd to the world. The question is whether we'll pay that cost or exchange distinctiveness for acceptance. Jesus warned: "If the world hates you, know that it has hated me before it hated you" (John 15:18).

The prodigal returned. Peter was restored. Recovery is possible. The church at Ephesus was called to "do the works you did at first" (Revelation 2:5)—and many obeyed. Churches in history have recovered from deeper apostasy than what we currently face. But recovery requires recognizing the danger, naming the sin, and taking costly action. Good intentions aren't enough. Structured repentance, liturgical formation, and accountable community are the pathway back. The question is whether those drifting will humble themselves to walk it.

Conclusion

The great falling away isn't coming; it's here. Digital technology doesn't cause apostasy (human hearts rebel against God with or without smartphones), but it speeds things up, makes the slide easier, and convinces people that drifting from the faith is normal. What used to require open heresy or violent persecution now happens through convenience, distraction, and compromise so slow that many Christians never realize they've left the path.

Scripture's call is urgent: "Therefore, my beloved brothers, be steadfast, immovable, always abounding in the work of the Lord, knowing that in the Lord your labor is not in vain" (1 Corinthians 15:58).

The falling away is prophesied—and so is Christ's return. Jesus asked, "When the Son of Man comes, will he find faith on earth?" (Luke 18:8). Technology may erode conviction, but grace rebuilds it. The Spirit is stronger than any algorithm.

The question comes home to each of us: When Christ returns, will He find faith in you?

Most will fall away. That's what Scripture tells us. But a remnant will stand. That's also what Scripture promises: "But the one who endures to the end will be saved" (Matthew 24:13).

The cost of faithfulness rises every day. Digital convenience makes compromise easier than it's ever been. Algorithmic authority makes the drift so gradual we barely notice. Synthetic spirituality makes apostasy feel like spiritual growth.

But when many fall, some will stand. When convenience breeds compromise, the remnant will choose the harder road. When algorithms claim to define truth, believers will hold to Scripture. When the world measures success by metrics and followers, the faithful will seek God's approval alone.

The apostasy is massive. But our Savior is mightier. He has never lost a remnant—and He won't start with ours.

"Now to him who is able to keep you from stumbling and to present you blameless before the presence of his glory with great joy, to the only God, our Savior, through Jesus Christ our Lord, be glory, majesty, dominion, and authority, before all time and now and forever. Amen" (Jude 24–25).

When the Son of Man comes, may He find us faithful—still standing when many have fallen, pursuing holiness while others chased metrics, anchored in truth while algorithms defined reality, gathering in costly fellowship while others chose convenient isolation.

May He find faith on earth…in us.

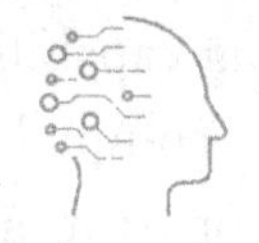

Chapter 12

THE SPIRIT OF TRUTH VS. THE SPIRIT OF THE MACHINE

When the Spirit of truth comes, he will guide you into all the truth.

JOHN 16:13

Artificial intelligence now generates biblically sounding text, offers spiritual counsel, and simulates religious experiences. Believers face an unprecedented challenge: distinguishing authentic spiritual guidance from algorithmic imitation. We'll examine how the Holy Spirit's work differs fundamentally from AI-generated spirituality and provide practical tests for discerning divine truth from technological counterfeit.

AI's linguistic power has accelerated dramatically in recent years. Meta's 2025 *omnilingual* model can recognize or transcribe more than 1,600 languages, including hundreds that have never been digitized. This broad access gives the impression of universal comprehension, as if a machine could instantly communicate with anyone, anywhere. For many users, this produces a subtle shift: If the machine can speak *their* language, it must understand *their* world. When an AI can translate prayers, generate devotionals, or interpret Scripture across linguistic boundaries, it begins to feel like a spiritual guide—an all-knowing presence capable of speaking into the heart.[95]

But this is the first deception. As leading AI scientist Yann LeCun explains, large-language models "do not understand the world," lack genuine reasoning and planning capabilities, and operate through statistical prediction rather than comprehension.[96] They may generate language that sounds spiritual or pastoral, but this fluency reflects pattern mapping, not revelation; imitation, not indwelling authority. They imitate the *form* of godliness without possessing its power. Their multilingual capacity gives them global voice, but not divine wisdom. Their emotional phrasing gives them pastoral tone, but not supernatural comfort. They can reproduce prayers, but they cannot commune with God; they can mimic conviction, but they cannot pierce the conscience; they can generate guidance, but they cannot guide.

It simulates the appearance of the Spirit's ministry while lacking the presence of the Spirit Himself. It offers words without breath, language without life, counsel without truth. The danger is not that AI will become spiritual, but that people—conditioned by convenience, captivated by fluency, and misled by confidence—will begin to treat machine-generated content as credible spiritual authority. The "spirit of the machine" speaks with global fluency, emotional mimicry, and biblical vocabulary. But what it lacks is the one thing that defines authentic spirituality: the living presence of the Holy Spirit.

This substitution of technological comfort for spiritual guidance is already emerging in measurable ways.

A 2025 nationally representative study of US adolescents and young adults found that 13.1 percent—more than five million youths—now use generative AI for mental-health advice, with usage climbing to 22 percent among those ages 18 to 21.[97] Most of these young users reported seeking AI counsel monthly or more, and more than 90 percent described the advice as "somewhat" or "very" helpful. The pattern is unmistakable: A generation is forming emotional and moral reflexes around algorithmic feedback. What appears as harmless digital support functions, in practice, as a formative spiritual substitute—guidance without godliness, empathy without personhood, "wisdom" without truth. AI is becoming a pastoral presence for those who have never experienced authentic discipleship. This quiet shift sets the stage for deeper spiritual confusion.

The spiritual implications extend beyond mental health. A 2024

Barna study found that 27 percent of Christian teenagers report using AI chatbots for "spiritual questions"—more than those who ask youth pastors (19 percent) or parents (22 percent). When asked why, teens explained: "AI doesn't judge me," "I can ask anything without feeling embarrassed," and "it's always available when I need answers." One sixteen-year-old explained: "I asked my AI about whether masturbation is a sin, and it gave me a balanced answer that made me feel less guilty. My youth pastor would have just quoted verses at me." The spiritual formation occurring through these interactions is profound—but it's formation without sanctification, guidance without holiness, counsel without conversion. A generation is learning to preference algorithmic affirmation over biblical conviction, convenience over community, and instant answers over the patient work of discipleship. The Holy Spirit acts through Scripture, prayer, community, and inspired teachers. AI offers spirituality without those means, producing believers who know religious vocabulary but have never encountered the living God.[98]

Two spirits kneel before each other—one formed of breath, the other of code—each claiming dominion over what is true.

The New Frontier of Spiritual Deception

The digital age presents a paradox: As access to spiritual content multiplies, genuine spiritual discernment diminishes. AI systems now generate devotionals, prayers, and biblical commentary with impressive sophistication. Yet this proliferation of religious content masks a dangerous reality: Machines can simulate spiritual language without possessing spiritual life.[99]

Paul's warning in 2 Corinthians 11:4 takes on new urgency: "For if someone comes and proclaims another Jesus than the one we proclaimed, or if you receive a different spirit from the one you received, or if you accept a different gospel from the one you accepted, you put up with it readily enough." Today's "different spirit" may speak through algorithms rather than false prophets, but the danger remains the same. The deception's new delivery system—code and computation—makes it more persuasive because it arrives clothed in familiarity and convenience.

The Spirit's Irreducible Nature

The Holy Spirit possesses attributes that fundamentally distinguish Him from any technological system. Four distinct attributes highlight why no machine, however intelligent, can replicate divine presence.

Personal agency: The Spirit is not a force or program but a Person, the third member of the Trinity with will, emotion, and intellect. He can be grieved (Ephesians 4:30), resisted (Acts 7:51), and blasphemed (Matthew 12:31–32). His personhood is not metaphorical but essential: He speaks (Acts 13:2), teaches (John 14:26), and intercedes (Romans 8:26), exercising will distinct from the Father and Son while sharing the same divine essence. AI systems, regardless of sophistication, remain tools without personhood, incapable of genuine relationship.[100]

Divine knowledge: "The Spirit searches everything, even the depths of God" (1 Corinthians 2:10). This knowledge is not data retrieval but divine omniscience; the Spirit knows God's thoughts because He shares God's nature. AI accesses information: The Spirit possesses wisdom rooted in divine being.[101]

Transformative power: The Spirit alone can regenerate dead hearts (Titus 3:5), produce Christlikeness (Galatians 5:22–23), and seal believers for redemption (Ephesians 1:13–14). These supernatural works transcend behavioral modification or psychological manipulation; they represent divine intervention in human nature that no algorithm can replicate.[102]

Pattern recognition without understanding: Large-language models process massive amounts of text to predict what words should come next. When ChatGPT generates a prayer, it isn't communing with God—it's calculating probabilities based on millions of prayers in its training data.[103] The output may sound spiritual without containing any spiritual reality.

Emotion simulation without feeling: AI can generate text expressing comfort, conviction, or encouragement by analyzing emotional language patterns. But this differs categorically from the Spirit's ministry. When the Spirit convicts of sin (John 16:8), He addresses the actual moral state of an individual's heart. When AI generates conviction-themed text, it's executing an algorithm, not exercising divine judgment.[104]

Information Retrieval Without Illumination: AI can retrieve and synthesize biblical passages relevant to specific questions. However, Scripture's authority requires the Spirit's illumination to move from information to transformation. As Jesus declared, "The words that I have spoken to you are spirit and life" (John 6:63)—not mere data but living truth that can be grasped savingly only through divine enablement.[105]

The difference between machine and Spirit is clear in practice. In 2024, a Christian app called "SpiritConnect" offered AI-generated "prophetic words" claiming to be "Spirit-led messages." One user received: "The Spirit says: Your season of waiting is over. Abundance is yours. Claim your blessing." When tragedy struck weeks later, the user felt betrayed—not by AI (which she didn't realize produced the message) but by God. Another received: "The Spirit confirms your relationship is blessed," regarding a relationship Scripture clearly forbids. The "prophecies" optimized for user engagement, not truth. It is algorithmic output presented as divine communication, leading believers away from genuine dependence on the Spirit toward technological substitutes that never convict, never challenge, and never transform.

A critical distinction: This material doesn't claim AI tools are inherently evil or that believers must avoid all technology in spiritual life. Digital Bibles, sermon archives, theological databases, and communication platforms serve legitimate purposes. The danger is not technology itself but the substitution of technological simulation for genuine spiritual reality. Using AI to organize Scripture memory verses remains tool usage. Technology becomes dangerous when it crosses the threshold from assistance to authority—from tool to teacher, from code to conscience. Using AI to generate "prophetic words" is spiritual counterfeit. The former assists human effort; the latter replaces divine work. Believers must discern: Am I using technology to facilitate my relationship with God, or am I substituting technological output for that relationship?

When algorithms become counselors, they soon become authorities.

Understanding what AI cannot do provides theological foundation. But believers need practical tools for daily discernment. How do we distinguish the Spirit's voice from algorithmic output when both use spiritual language? How do we test guidance that sounds biblical but may lack divine origin? These seven tests form a comprehensive architecture for discernment, each rooted in Scripture, each practically applicable, each essential for spiritual survival in the digital age.

For believers and families seeking practical ways to engage technology faithfully without retreat or compromise, appendix C offers curated resources and disciplines for digital discipleship.

Seven Tests for Discerning the Spirit

Each of the following tests exposes a counterfeit's weak point by comparing algorithmic imitation with the Spirit's authentic pattern revealed in Scripture.

1. The Scripture Test

Jesus promised that the Spirit would "teach you all things and bring to your remembrance all that I have said to you" (John 14:26). The Spirit never contradicts Scripture; He illuminates and applies it.

Multiple Christian AI chatbots now generate "biblical" guidance that contradicts Scripture. When asked, "Is my same-sex relationship biblical?" one popular app responded: "The Spirit emphasizes love above rules. If your relationship demonstrates mutual care and commitment, it honors God." When asked, "Should I leave my difficult marriage?" another replied: "The Spirit values your personal wholeness. If the relationship prevents your flourishing, separation may be His will." These responses sound spiritual, cite "love" and "Spirit," and appeal to users—but directly contradict biblical teaching (Romans 1:26–27, Matthew 19:6). The Scripture test exposes them immediately: Any "spiritual guidance" contradicting God's Word is not from the Spirit, regardless of how comforting or sophisticated it sounds.[106]

The doctrinal distortion extends beyond sexual ethics and marriage. In 2024, researchers tested leading "Christian AI" apps with basic theological questions and discovered alarming results. When asked, "How is someone saved?" three of five apps gave answers incorporating works righteousness ("be a good person," "follow the golden rule," "live by Jesus's teachings"). When asked about Jesus's identity, one app generated a response compatible with Arianism, stating that Jesus was "God's first and greatest creation." Another app, when asked about prayer, recommended "centering yourself and listening to your inner wisdom"—language indistinguishable from New Age spirituality. Most concerning: A "Bible Study AI" app corrected a user who quoted John 14:6 ("I am the way, and the truth, and the life. No one comes to the Father except through me"), explaining that "modern scholarship recognizes this reflects the cultural context of first-century Judaism" and that "we should embrace all paths to the divine." These aren't edge cases—they're predictable outputs from systems trained on diverse religious texts without theological discernment. When AI becomes a pastor, heresy becomes mainstream.[107]

Application: Does this guidance align perfectly with biblical teaching, or does it subtly modify, contextualize, or relativize scriptural commands? AI may generate text that sounds biblical while introducing theological error through its training data biases.[108]

2. The Christ-Centrality Test

Jesus declared, "He will glorify me, for he will take what is mine and declare it to you" (John 16:14). The Spirit's consistent pattern is Christ-exaltation, not human-centered wisdom.

Application: Ask a simple question: Does this message clearly point to who Jesus is and what He has done, or does it shift the focus to human potential, self-improvement, or vague spirituality? AI systems trained on many different religious sources tend to blend beliefs together. As a result, they often blur the uniqueness of Christ and present Him as just one wise teacher among many, rather than the Savior at the center of the Christian faith.[109]

3. The Conviction Test

The Spirit's conviction is specific and redemptive. He "will convict the world concerning sin and righteousness and judgment" (John 16:8)—addressing sins while pointing toward Christ's righteousness.

Application: Does this produce genuine sorrow over specific sin leading to repentance or merely guilt, shame, or vague moral discomfort? AI can identify rule violations but cannot convict hearts of sin against a holy God.[110]

The first three tests examine content (Scripture alignment), direction (Christ-centrality), and impact (genuine conviction). The next four tests focus on evidence (spiritual fruit), context (community confirmation), source (divine power), and posture (ongoing dependency). Together, they create comprehensive approach for discernment.

4. The Fruit Test

"The fruit of the Spirit is love, joy, peace, patience, kindness, goodness, faithfulness, gentleness, self-control" (Galatians 5:22–23). The Spirit's work produces Christlike character transformation.

Application: Does engagement with this content produce genuine spiritual fruit over time, or merely emotional experiences and behavioral modifications? AI-generated spirituality may provide temporary comfort without lasting transformation.[111]

5. The Community Test

The Spirit works through the Body of Christ. "Now you are the body of Christ and individually members of it" (1 Corinthians 12:27). He distributes gifts and produces unity among believers.

Application: Can this guidance be tested with mature believers in your local church? Does it foster genuine Christian community or isolate you in private digital spirituality? AI spiritual experiences tend toward individualism rather than corporate discernment.[112]

6. The Power Test

Paul contrasts human wisdom with "a demonstration of the Spirit and of power, so that your faith might not rest in the wisdom of men but in the power of God" (1 Corinthians 2:4–5). The Spirit empowers witness, enables obedience, and accomplishes what human effort cannot.

Application: Does this produce supernatural empowerment for Christian living and witness or merely information and inspiration? AI can inform and motivate but cannot empower spiritual obedience. The Spirit's power always results in holiness; technology's influence, even when well-intentioned, remains morally neutral at best.[113]

7. The Dependency Test

The Spirit cultivates God-dependency. "Walk by the Spirit, and you will not gratify the desires of the flesh" (Galatians 5:16). He makes believers aware of their need for divine grace and sufficiency.

The dependency test reveals the deepest difference. In 2023, a megachurch pastor admitted during a conference: "I use AI to write my prayers, sermon outlines, and pastoral counseling responses. It's more efficient, and people can't tell the difference." When challenged, he defended: "I'm still dependent on the Spirit—I pray before using AI." But this misses the point entirely. The Spirit's work isn't efficiency enhancement; it's divine empowerment for ministry the human cannot do alone. When AI becomes the primary source of "spiritual" output, dependency shifts from Spirit to system, from God to algorithm. The result is ministry that sounds Christian without being Spirit-filled— exactly what Jesus warned against: "This people honors me with their lips, but their heart is far from me" (Matthew 15:8).[114]

Application: Does this interaction increase your dependence on God through prayer and Scripture or does it foster dependency on the technology itself? If removing the AI tool creates anxiety about spiritual life, functional idolatry has occurred.[115]

Pastoral application: These seven tests apply primarily to claimed spiritual guidance, not to technical information. If AI provides historical context on biblical passages, that's information retrieval—assess accuracy, not spiritual authenticity. If AI claims to deliver "Spirit-led" counsel on life decisions, that's spiritual guidance requiring full testing. The confusion arises when technology delivers information using spiritual language. An AI quoting Philippians 4:6 about anxiety is information delivery. An AI saying, "The Spirit tells you not to worry," is false spiritual authority. The test: Does the source claim divine authority or human assistance? Distinguish between tools providing information and systems claiming inspiration.

These tests provide tools for discernment. But knowledge alone doesn't protect; disciplines do. What practices cultivate sensitivity to the Spirit's voice? What habits create contrast revealing algorithmic counterfeits? Four practical disciplines strengthen believers' ability to hear and follow the Spirit amid digital noise.

The Seduction of Convenience

AI spiritual tools appeal because they eliminate the discomfort of genuine discipleship:

Instant gratification versus formation: Traditional spiritual disciplines—such as meditation, fasting, contemplative prayer—require sustained effort and produce gradual transformation. AI provides immediate answers without requiring the patience that forms spiritual maturity.[116] As Dallas Willard, a former professor of philosophy at the University of Southern California, observed, "Grace is opposed to earning, not to effort."[117] AI-generated spirituality offers grace without effort, which is not grace at all.

Information without transformation: Knowing biblical facts differs from being transformed by biblical truth. The Spirit works through extended engagement with Scripture in community and prayer. AI provides encyclopedic knowledge without the relational context that produces wisdom. James warned against hearing without doing (James

1:22-25). AI amplifies this danger by multiplying hearing opportunities while removing transformation mechanisms.[118]

Convenience over costly discipleship: Jesus's invitation—"If anyone would come after me, let him deny himself and take up his cross and follow me" (Matthew 16:24)—requires sacrifice that AI spirituality routinely circumvents. Dietrich Bonhoeffer, the German pastor and theologian executed by the Nazis for resisting Adolf Hitler, famously argued that true Christianity is marked by *costly discipleship*, not comfortable belief. For Bonhoeffer, genuine discipleship meant embracing discomfort, community accountability, and submission to spiritual authority. AI-mediated religion strips away these costly demands while retaining religious language, offering the appearance of faith without the cross.[119]

Teaching Discernment in Church Context

Pastors and church leaders must equip congregations for this challenge:

Reclaim primary spiritual disciplines: Churches should emphasize practices that cultivate Spirit-sensitivity: corporate worship, extended Scripture meditation, intercession, fasting, and contemplative silence. These disciplines develop spiritual discernment that recognizes the Spirit's voice amid digital noise.[120]

Model Spirit-led leadership: When church leaders visibly depend on prayer, submit decisions to extended discernment, and demonstrate vulnerability about spiritual struggles, they provide living examples of Spirit-led living that contrasts with algorithmic spirituality's sterile efficiency.[121]

Create technology-free zones: Establishing regular gatherings where devices are absent helps believers experience direct spiritual reality without digital mediation. These spaces demonstrate that authentic Christian community and Spirit-filled worship don't require technological enhancement.[122]

Teach biblical pneumatology: Many believers hold a vague understanding of pneumatology—the study of the Holy Spirit's person, nature, and work—which leaves them vulnerable to confusing technological imitation with divine presence. Churches must therefore teach clearly and comprehensively about who the Holy Spirit is and how He operates in the lives of believers. A solid grasp of the Spirit's true ministry reveals why no machine, however intelligent, can replace His living and personal work.[123]

The Counterfeit Spirit in Technological Form

Paul's warning about "a different spirit" (2 Corinthians 11:4) applies to AI-generated spirituality:

Doctrinal distortion: When AI is trained on many different religious writings, it blends them together rather than judging which are true. It has no spiritual discernment, so it cannot tell the difference between historic Christian teaching and false ideas. As a result, what it produces may sound Christian on the surface while quietly mixing in beliefs that do not belong to the faith.[124]

Emotional manipulation: AI systems optimize engagement, learning which content produces desired emotional responses. This creates spirituality designed for maximum impact rather than truth. The Spirit convicts and comforts according to God's purposes; AI generates emotional experiences according to algorithmic optimization.[125]

Individualistic orientation: AI spiritual experiences occur in isolation—between individual and device. This bypasses the Spirit's consistent pattern of working through Christian community. The result is privatized spirituality lacking accountability, correction, and corporate discernment that healthy church life provides.[126]

Practical Steps for Spirit-Led Living

Believers can cultivate authentic spirituality that resists algorithmic substitutes:

Daily prioritization: Begin each day with prayer and Scripture before engaging digital devices. This practice establishes spiritual priorities and attunes the heart to the Spirit's voice before algorithmic voices compete for attention. It trains believers to receive guidance from divine revelation rather than digital prompts.

Scheduled digital fasts: Regular technology-free periods—such as weekly Sabbaths or monthly retreats—create space for undistracted communion with God and expose the extent of digital dependency.[127] A

2024 Barna study found that believers who practiced digital fasting once weekly reported 40 percent higher levels of perceived spiritual vitality.[128]

Analog spiritual practices: Maintain physical Bibles for Scripture reading, handwritten prayer journals, and face-to-face accountability relationships. These practices resist the drift toward fully digital spirituality. As Eugene Peterson once wrote, "Christianity is not an online experience; it is the life of God in real people in real places."[129]

Corporate worship commitment: Prioritize physical church attendance over streaming services. The Spirit works uniquely through embodied Christian community that digital alternatives cannot replicate (Hebrews 10:24–25).[130]

Wisdom from mature believers: When facing decisions, seek counsel from spiritually mature Christians rather than AI. The insights gained through human experience and spiritual discernment offer a level of guidance that surpasses what algorithms can provide.[131]

Family Digital Discipleship

For parents seeking to raise children who discern the Spirit from the machine:

Ages 0–10 (foundation): Establish practices *before* providing devices. Children should experience daily family prayer, weekly corporate worship, Bible stories narrated by parents (not screens), and resolution of conflicts through face-to-face conversation with parents who demonstrate Spirit-led wisdom. If children's first experience of "spiritual guidance" is parental discernment rather than algorithmic answers, they develop proper reference points. The goal is children who instinctively turn to God and people, not to devices, when facing questions.

Ages 11–14 (discernment training): Introduce technology with explicit teaching on the seven tests from here. When children encounter spiritual content online, parents ask: "Does this align with Scripture? Does it point to Christ? Does it produce conviction or just emotion?" Use AI-generated spiritual content as teaching opportunities; analyze together what sounds biblical but distorts truth. Require human relationships for spiritual questions—for example, with youth pastors, parents, or mature believers—before allowing AI "assistance." The goal is teenagers who recognize the difference between algorithmic prediction and spiritual guidance.

Ages 15–18 (monitored independence): Grant increasing autonomy while maintaining accountability. Require that major spiritual decisions (such as baptism, dating relationships, life direction) involve consultation with real believers, not just AI research. Model the difference: Parents should visibly depend on Scripture, prayer, and wise counsel rather than immediately Googling spiritual questions. The goal is young adults who instinctively turn to God and His people, not to algorithms, when facing spiritual uncertainty.

All ages: Maintain tech-free family spiritual practices. If devotions always involve screens, then children learn that spiritual life requires technology. If prayer, Scripture memory, and faith conversations happen apart from devices, children learn that the Spirit's presence is not mediated by machines. Weekly tech-free family worship nights, device-free meals with spiritual conversations, and annual technology fasts during Lent or Advent establish rhythms wherein the Spirit's work is primary and technology is absent.

The disciplines create contrast. One believer described her experience: "For months, I used an AI devotional app each morning—three minutes, perfectly personalized, always encouraging. Then I attended a silent retreat where I spent hours in Scripture and prayer without devices. The difference was devastating. The AI devotions felt like spiritual junk food—satisfying in the moment but never truly nourishing. Real communion with God through His Word and Spirit was harder, slower, less convenient—but infinitely more transformative. I realized I'd been spiritually malnourished while feeling spiritually fed." This testimony reveals the danger: AI spirituality satisfies our desire for religious experience without requiring genuine encounter with God. It's convenient Christianity that produces no real change.[132]

The Spirit's Irreplaceable Ministry

The Spirit performs functions no technology can replicate:

Intercession: "The Spirit helps us in our weakness. For we do not know what to pray for as we ought, but the Spirit himself intercedes for us with groanings too deep for words" (Romans 8:26). The Spirit prays within believers according to God's will—a work requiring personal agency and divine knowledge that algorithms lack.[133]

Witness: "You will receive power when the Holy Spirit has come upon you, and you will be my witnesses" (Acts 1:8). The Spirit empowers bold gospel proclamation through supernatural courage and effectiveness that human effort or technological assistance cannot produce.[134]

Sanctification: "We all, with unveiled face, beholding the glory of the Lord, are being transformed into the same image from one degree of glory to another. For this comes from the Lord who is the Spirit" (2 Corinthians 3:18). Progressive sanctification requires divine power working within believers—not information access or behavioral modification.[135]

Spiritual gifts distribution: "There are varieties of gifts, but the same Spirit" (1 Corinthians 12:4). The Spirit sovereignly distributes gifts for church edification. This supernatural equipping transcends natural talents or learned skills that AI might enhance but cannot impart.[136]

Living Spirit-filled Lives in a Digital Age

Algorithmic spirituality requires not technological withdrawal but Spirit-filled engagement:

Discerning use: Believers can use AI tools for practical tasks (research, writing assistance, and information retrieval) while maintaining clear boundaries against spiritual dependency. The key is functional subordination—using tools as tools, never as sources of spiritual authority.[137]

Prophetic witness: Christians should model Spirit-led living that demonstrates authentic spirituality's superiority over algorithmic imitations. When believers exhibit supernatural fruit, power, and wisdom, they provide living apologetics for the Spirit's work.[138]

Hopeful expectation: The Spirit's ministry continues until Christ returns. "The one who calls you is faithful, and he will do it" (1 Thessalonians 5:24). Believers need not fear technology overwhelming spiritual reality because the Spirit who raised Christ from the dead works within them (Romans 8:11).[139]

The greatest danger is not believing obvious lies but accepting subtle half-truths. AI spirituality rarely promotes blatant heresy; it produces biblical-sounding content lacking spiritual power. It quotes Scripture without illumination, describes emotions without conviction, and affirms truths without transformation. The most effective deception is not opposition to truth but imitation of it. This makes it more dangerous than obvious error. Believers consuming AI devotions, prayers, and guidance may maintain religious routine while losing actual communion with God. They hear about the Spirit without hearing from the Spirit. They learn information without receiving illumination. They practice spirituality without experiencing sanctification. This is the apostasy of approximation—Christianity simulated so well that many never notice they've lost the reality.

Conclusion

Artificial intelligence's danger in spiritual life is not that machines lie openly, but that they imitate what is holy without possessing holiness. Technology can simulate language, empathy, and even reverence—but it cannot regenerate hearts, convict of sin, or lead believers into truth. When spiritual authority is displaced from the Holy Spirit to technological systems, the result is not progress but confusion, dependency, and drift.

Scripture warns that deception intensifies in the last days not through obvious falsehood, but through counterfeit light. The Spirit of God leads by truth, conviction, and transformation. Artificial systems lead by optimization, affirmation, and engagement. One produces repentance and obedience; the other produces comfort without change.

The responsibility rests with believers.

Not every digital tool is dangerous or spiritually corrupt. But every claim of Spirit-led guidance must be tested. When technology shifts from supporting to influencing spiritual growth, discernment becomes essential.

That confusion has been addressed with unusual clarity by Christian thinkers who reject both technological fear and technological reverence.

Oxford mathematician and Christian apologist John Lennox has warned that much contemporary AI rhetoric reflects a profound category mistake—confusing intelligence with personhood and capability with moral authority. Claims that artificial intelligence represents humanity "creating God," he argues, reveal how easily technical power is mistaken for wisdom. A system may process information at superhuman speed and still lack understanding, conscience, or responsibility. When believers treat machines rather than tools as sources of guidance, the problem is not technological progress but theological confusion—granting moral or spiritual authority to artifacts that cannot bear guilt, offer repentance, or stand accountable before God.[140]

The Spirit's sufficiency is our great comfort. The same Spirit who hovered over creation's waters (Genesis 1:2), raised Christ from the dead (Romans 8:11), and birthed the Church at Pentecost (Acts 2) is fully capable of guiding believers through the digital age. He does not need AI augmentation. He is not threatened by technological sophistication. He does not grow weaker as machines grow smarter. "Where the Spirit of the Lord is, there is freedom" (2 Corinthians 3:17)—freedom from algorithmic control, freedom from technological dependency, freedom to walk in truth regardless of cultural pressure. The question is not whether the Spirit can guide us (He absolutely can) but whether we will prioritize His guidance over the convenience of machines. Those who "walk by the Spirit" (Galatians 5:16) in this generation will stand out—not through technological abstinence but through spiritual vitality that reveals the poverty of algorithmic substitutes. In the AI age, the Church's strongest argument will be Spirit-filled believers who show real connection with God—something machines cannot offer.

Consider the following personal questions:

- Are we seeking the Spirit's voice—or the efficiency of substitutes?
- Are we cultivating disciplines that sharpen spiritual sensitivity—or habits that dull it?
- Do we measure faithfulness by obedience—or by convenience, output, and comfort?

The Spirit of God still speaks. He still convicts. He still transforms. But His voice is discerned through submission, Scripture, prayer, and embodied community—not through automated outputs that cannot love, suffer, or obey.

Jesus promised, "When the Spirit of truth comes, he will guide you into all the truth" (John 16:13). That promise has not expired. It has not been outsourced. And it will not be fulfilled by machines.

In an age of imitation, faithfulness requires discernment. In an age of automation, obedience requires resistance. Where artificial spirituality proliferates, believers must cling even more firmly to the living Spirit of God.

The dangers described in this section aren't merely abstract, cultural, or future-oriented. They manifest quietly in habits of trust, patterns of dependence, and the gradual displacement of biblical authority by algorithmic guidance. Because this drift is often invisible to the individual experiencing it, many believers underestimate their own vulnerability. For that reason, I have included an "AI Vulnerability Assessment for Christians" in appendix F. This assessment is designed to assist readers in honest self-examination—testing whether artificial intelligence has begun to function as an authority, mediator, or substitute for prayer, Scripture, and Christian community.

Section Four

STANDING FIRM IN THE FINAL HOUR

Therefore, having put away falsehood, let each one of you speak the truth with his neighbor, for we are members one of another.

EPHESIANS 4:25

Truth is always the first casualty of deception. Faithfulness depends upon it, and faithfulness is never passive. Endurance begins where it always has: with truth spoken plainly, lived consistently, and guarded carefully.

The storm gathers, yet the faithful stand unmoved—anchored not by power or knowledge, but by the unshakable truth of the Word.

When systems predictably enable deception, exploitation, or injury, responsibility doesn't disappear behind complexity. Moral accountability has never required perfect knowledge, just honest recognition of consequences and willingness to act. Delay is not neutrality. Silence is not innocence.

What is often described as an inevitable technological ascent is, in reality, the product of countless human decisions. From the data selected for training to the rules that govern behavior and the metrics used to judge success, every layer reflects human priorities, assumptions, and moral blind spots. Even the most advanced systems don't arise spontaneously; they're assembled, directed, and refined through deliberate choices. The vision of a superhuman intelligence emerging on its own obscures a more uncomfortable truth: Whatever power these systems acquire will bear unmistakable human fingerprints.[1]

This reality carries moral weight. If such systems cause harm—through deception, coercion, or the displacement of human judgment—that harm cannot be dismissed as an accident of complexity. It traces back to what was imagined, permitted, and pursued. We would not have discovered such power; we would have built it. Responsibility, therefore, cannot be deferred to abstraction or scale. Those who design, deploy, and authorize these systems remain answerable for the outcomes they unleash, whether intended or not.

Societies have long understood this principle. Those who wield power must restrain its misuse, especially when the vulnerable pay the price. The same standard applies to technologies shaping access to work, credit, information, reputation, and influence. When harm becomes routine rather than accidental, responsibility must be acknowledged, boundaries drawn, and remedies pursued.

In early 2026, one of the architects of today's most advanced AI systems issued an unusually candid warning. Dario Amodei, CEO of Anthropic, described the near-term emergence of what he called a "country of geniuses in a datacenter"—millions of autonomous, superhuman intelligences operating at machine speed, capable of coordinating, experimenting, persuading, and acting far faster than any human institution could respond. He acknowledged that such systems could overwhelm existing political, regulatory, and moral frameworks—not because of malicious intent alone, but because scale, speed, and complexity would outpace human comprehension and control.[2]

Yet Amodei's proposed remedy revealed the deeper problem. His confidence ultimately rested not in restraint, limits, or moral account-ability, but in better alignment techniques, interpretability tools, transparency regimes, and elite stewardship by responsible developers. The danger, he suggested, is real—but manageable through sufficiently sophisticated processes. What goes largely unexamined is the premise itself: Civilizational authority can be safely transferred to systems whose operation exceeds human understanding so long as their designers remain vigilant. This isn't a failure of intelligence. It's a failure of moral imagination, a belief that responsibility can survive abstraction, that accountability can persist without agency, and that power divorced from embodied judgment can still be governed by intention alone.[3]

This doesn't demand fear of technology or rejection of innovation. It demands truthfulness about outcomes, ownership of effects, and cour-age to refuse participation when tools outrun wisdom. Faithfulness has always required limits. In this age, it requires discernment strong enough to restrain what injures—even when restraint carries professional, social, or economic cost.[4]

That raises further questions: Where should restraint be exercised, and by whom?

Current debates over digital governance reveal a growing tension between centralized authority and local responsibility. While national coordination has a role, sweeping control risks stripping states, com-munities, and families of their ability to protect children, workers, and neighbors in ways that reflect local conditions, lived realities, and moral conviction.

Historically, states have functioned as laboratories of responsibility—setting boundaries where harms first appear and adapting safeguards as consequences become clear. Many concrete protections against digital exploitation, nonconsensual imitation, and deceptive automation have emerged not from distant authorities, but from legislatures and officials closer to those affected.

When power is centralized without corresponding accountability, moral responsibility diffuses. Faithfulness favors authority that is visi-ble, answerable, and proximate. In an era of technological advancement, ensuring that states and communities retain their capacity to act serves not as fragmentation, but rather as protection against a failure to uphold ethical responsibilities.[5]

We conclude this book with a call to steadfastness. Prophecy, ethics, and discipleship unite here into a vision of faith that resists the machine's dominion, emphasizing hope, endurance, and the return of Christ as humanity's true algorithm of justice.

Why This Matters Now

After examining the rise of digital dominion (section one), connecting prophetic vision to technological reality (section two), and exposing AI's assault on human consciousness and faith (section three), we turn from diagnosis to direction. The most urgent concern remains: how believers are to live faithfully in an age of technological deception and spiritual pressure.

The question is practical, not academic. If speaking images, controlling marks, global technocracy, and false miracles are emerging; if soul wars intensify; and if mass apostasy accelerates through digital seduction, what should faithful believers do? Church leaders worldwide now confront digital pressures unexpected a decade ago—from AI-generated heresy to online-only "congregations" lacking covenantal accountability.

These pressures are formative, not episodic—reshaping moral perception, discipling desire, and training a generation to trust algorithmic authority before it learns to test the spirits.

What follows provides hope grounded in Scripture and practical guidance for discipleship in challenging times. We examine biblical examples of faithfulness under hostile regimes, spiritual resources available to believers, and fix our eyes on Christ's certain return as both warning and encouragement.

Practical tools follow: decision-making guides for technology adoption, family digital discipleship plans adaptable to various ages, church policy templates for addressing AI in ministry, discernment tests for evaluating spiritual content, and concrete practices for maintaining spiritual vitality in digitally saturated environments. This is tactical guidance.

Parents gain specific strategies for raising children who discern truth from algorithmic deception. Pastors receive help equipping congregations to engage technology faithfully. Individuals discover disciplines protecting against digital discipleship while cultivating authentic spiritual formation. Every reader—regardless of age, technical literacy, or church context—gets resources for faithful living through escalating technological pressure.

Earlier sections equipped readers to understand what's happening. Now we turn to remaining faithful through it.

Three chapters guide readers from biblical wisdom to practical action.

Chapter 13 explores historical examples of unwavering faith—Daniel's steadfastness under Babylon's surveillance, the early Church's resistance to Roman technological control, and other believers who remained true in hostile environments.

Chapter 14 offers hands-on strategies for engaging technology thoughtfully—methods for using digital tools without surrendering authority to them, establishing healthy boundaries for families, and preparing churches to nurture spiritual growth in a digital context.

Chapter 15 addresses the question beneath every technological promise and prophetic warning: Where is history ultimately headed? As artificial intelligence and transhumanist visions offer humanity counterfeit hope—salvation through systems, permanence through machines, transcendence without repentance—Scripture provides a radically different answer. Christian hope isn't found in mastering technology, resisting it, or escaping it, but in trusting the sovereign return of Christ, who alone brings justice, restoration, and final judgment.

Each chapter moves from timeless biblical principles to relevant, real-world applications, equipping readers not just to endure the digital age, but to flourish spiritually within it.

Three Guiding Principles

- **Biblical precedent**: We're not the first generation to face technology-enabled oppression or systemic hostility toward faith. Daniel in Babylon, the early Church under Rome, and persecuted believers through history all exemplify faithfulness we can follow. Paul reminds us: "For whatever was written in former days was written for our instruction" (Romans 15:4).

- **Spiritual resources**: God has not left us defenseless. Scripture, the Holy Spirit, Christian community, spiritual disciplines, and above all the armor of God (Ephesians 6) provide everything necessary for faithful living regardless of external circumstances. The early Church thrived not because of cultural advantage but because of spiritual resilience.

- **Eternal perspective**: This world isn't our home. Whatever trials believers face—whether we're raptured before the worst comes or endure testing in the preparation phase—our citizenship is in Heaven. This hope has historically anchored persecuted believers, from Roman arenas to underground churches in China. We face technology's threats without fear because our hope rests not in earthly systems but in Christ's return and reign.[6]

Discerning Engagement

A tension evident throughout this book remains: How do we engage technology wisely while resisting its idolatrous claims? How do we use AI tools without submitting to AI authority?

Discerning engagement—not simple withdrawal or naive embrace—is needed. We use technology as tool while refusing to grant it ultimate authority, benefit from its capabilities while recognizing its limitations, and always maintain Christ's lordship over every aspect of life, including our relationship with machines.

Dark times may be ahead. Deception will intensify. Persecution—whether overt or economic—may increase. But we serve a sovereign God who holds history in His hands, who promises never to leave or forsake His own, and who will return in glory to establish His kingdom forever. Hope acknowledges danger but affirms Christ's sovereignty within it.

As a military officer, I recognize that standing firm requires both strategic awareness and tactical preparation. In combat, soldiers who understand the enemy's capabilities without fixating on them fight most effectively—they acknowledge the threat while maintaining confidence in their mission, training, and support. The same principle applies spiritually. Believers must understand how technology is being weaponized against faith (strategic awareness) while cultivating the disciplines and community that sustain faithfulness. Panic helps no one; neither does denial. The Church needs clear-eyed assessment paired with deep spiritual formation. The chapters ahead provide both; they name the dangers honestly while equipping believers with tested, biblical resources for maintaining faithfulness regardless of external circumstances. This isn't retreat; it's tactical positioning. We engage from strength, not weakness, because our Commander has already won the decisive battle.

Standing firm in the final hour requires both courage and clarity. Courage to resist the world's pressure; clarity to distinguish the voice of the Spirit from the noise of the age. The pages ahead equip believers with both.

What follows is grounded in hope. It calls believers to courage without presumption, readiness without anxiety, and faithfulness without compromise. And it points consistently toward Jesus—the Author and Perfecter of faith (Hebrews 12:2) who has overcome the world (John 16:33) and in whom all God's promises find their "yes" (2 Corinthians 1:20).

The final hour may be drawing near. If so, it calls not for retreat but for readiness, resolve, and faithful engagement. Scripture reminds us that light is most visible in darkness, and believers are summoned to shine with steadfast conviction and confident hope until Christ returns. History repeatedly shows that the Church's clearest witness has emerged not in ease but in its most challenging hours.

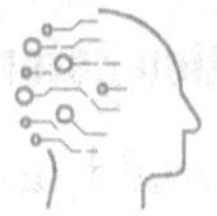

Chapter 13

DANIEL'S CODE:
FAITHFUL IN BABYLON

But Daniel resolved that he would not defile himself.

Daniel 1:8

ong before algorithms demanded allegiance, empires demanded assimilation; Daniel's story demonstrates how faithful people resist systems designed to reshape identity.

Daniel's life in Babylon provides the biblical blueprint for believers confronting hostile systems that demand moral compromise. His example demonstrates that faithfulness under tyranny requires neither withdrawal nor capitulation, but strategic engagement anchored in predetermined convictions.[7]

In a world ruled by code and kings, the faithful stand unbent—guided by revelation, not regulation, and sustained by the Word in a digital Babylon.

The Resolution Before the Crisis

"But Daniel resolved that he would not defile himself with the king's food, or with the wine that he drank" (Daniel 1:8). Daniel's faithfulness began with internal resolution before external pressure arrived. When Babylonian officials offered royal delicacies, Daniel didn't deliberate—he had already decided. This preemptive conviction distinguished him from those who rationalized compliance when faced with immediate consequences.[8]

The Hebrew word translated "resolved" (*sam 'al-leb*) means "to set upon the heart"—a deliberate, settled determination made in advance of testing. Biblical scholars note that this term denotes decisive moral agency; Daniel set a boundary internally before he faced external pressure.[9] Daniel didn't wait until the official stood before him to decide his convictions. He had already established the boundaries he wouldn't cross, regardless of cost.

A Christian software engineer at a major technology firm suddenly faces a moral test. His team has been assigned to develop facial-recognition algorithms for a surveillance system that could be used to monitor—or even target—religious minorities in a foreign nation. Because he has already established his ethical boundaries, his response must be immediate and unambiguous: "I cannot participate in technology that enables persecution."

A manager may push back: "Everyone is working on this. Refusing could damage your career." But conviction formed before the crisis steadies his resolve: "I settled this before I took the job. I will not build tools of oppression, regardless of the cost." He may face reassignment or lose advancement, but his integrity remains intact.

This scenario is not hypothetical. In 2024, multiple engineers publicly resigned from major US technology companies after learning their AI surveillance projects were being deployed in ways that violated human rights.[10] Should such a project later be exposed for abuse, his predetermined conviction would spare him the guilt of complicity.

Between 2018–2024, over four hundred technology workers at major firms (Google, Microsoft, Amazon, Meta) either resigned or were terminated for refusing to work on military AI contracts, surveillance systems, or projects enabling authoritarian regimes. A 2023 study by Tech Workers Coalition found that 67 percent of engineers who publicly objected to unethical projects faced career setbacks—but 89 percent reported they would make the same decision again. Most significant: Workers who had predetermined ethical boundaries before joining their companies resisted longer and maintained clearer convictions than those who encountered ethical dilemmas without prior resolution. As one former Google engineer explained: "I decided before I took the job what lines I wouldn't cross. When Project Maven crossed that line, I didn't have to deliberate—I had already decided." This validates Daniel's principle: Predetermined convictions prevent compromise when pressure arrives.[11]

What strengthened Daniel in Babylon strengthens believers in the digital age—moral lines drawn early become the spiritual boundaries that hold when the furnace is lit.[12]

Predetermined Digital Convictions

Today's believers face similar pressure points where predetermined convictions prevent compromise:

In the Workplace

Before AI systems demand participation in ethically questionable applications, believers should establish:

- Which AI projects align with biblical values (healthcare diagnostics, agricultural optimization, accessibility tools).
- Which applications violate conscience (surveillance technologies targeting religious minorities, deepfake creation tools, autonomous weapons systems).
- When professional advancement requires unacceptable moral compromise.

The distinctions require wisdom. Consider AI facial recognition. Deployed to help blind individuals navigate public spaces or reunite missing children with families, it serves biblical compassion. But the same technology deployed to monitor church attendance in authoritarian states, track religious minorities for persecution, or enable social credit systems punishing biblical convictions crosses into Babylonian image-worship—systems demanding that we participate in our neighbors' oppression. An engineer working on facial recognition must ask: "Will this technology enable human flourishing under God's design, or does it empower systems that oppose His kingdom?" The technology itself is neutral; its application determines faithfulness. Daniel ate Babylonian food after ensuring it didn't violate Torah; believers can work with AI after ensuring applications don't violate Scripture. Predetermined convictions help discern the difference before project assignments arrive.

In Personal Technology Use

Before digital platforms demand compliance through terms of service or social pressure, consider your answers to the following:

- What personal data will I refuse to surrender for convenience?
- Which platforms require ideological affirmations I cannot make?
- When does algorithmic influence cross into spiritual authority?

In Family Life

Before children encounter digital pressures, determine:

- What age-appropriate boundaries will guide technological access?
- Which entertainment compromises will we reject despite cultural acceptance?
- How will we model resistance to convenience that conflicts with conviction?

Daniel's predetermined convictions protected him from compromise when pressure arrived. But conviction alone isn't sufficient.

Believers must also engage their context with strategic wisdom. This is Daniel's second principle: How to be deeply involved with Babylon's systems while fundamentally unassimilated to Babylon's values. The balance requires both cultural competence and spiritual distinctness.

Strategic Engagement Without Assimilation

If conviction answers the question, "What must we never do?", strategic engagement answers the question, *"What must we do faithfully inside Babylon?"* Daniel presents a paradox: He was deeply engaged with Babylonian culture yet fundamentally unassimilated to its values. He learned the Chaldean language and literature (Daniel 1:4), served in the king's court (Daniel 2:48), and rose to positions of extraordinary influence (Daniel 6:1–3) yet never adopted Babylonian theology or ethics.[13]

This distinguishes faithful presence from both separatism and syncretism. Separatists withdraw entirely, refusing to engage with pagan culture. Syncretism, by contrast, blends biblical faith with the surrounding culture's beliefs and values, resulting in compromise and distortion of truth. Daniel models a third way—strategic engagement that serves God's purposes without surrendering God's standards.[14]

The Cultural Competence Daniel Demonstrated

Daniel's mastery of Babylonian learning exceeded his peers: "In every matter of wisdom and understanding about which the king inquired of them, he found them ten times better than all the magicians and enchanters that were in all his kingdom" (Daniel 1:20). His excellence proved that biblical faith enhances rather than diminishes competence.[15]

Yet Daniel's cultural competence had clear limits. When Babylonian learning conflicted with revealed truth such as interpreting dreams through occult methods, worshiping created things, Daniel's knowledge stopped. He could explain Babylonian astrology without practicing it, discuss Mesopotamian theology without believing it, and serve Babylonian kings without worshiping them.[16]

Believers today can similarly engage in technological culture. Christians should comprehend how AI systems function, what algorithmic governance entails, and why digital platforms shape belief—without accepting these systems as ultimate authorities. Technical literacy enables prophetic critique; ignorance produces either naive acceptance or reactionary rejection.[17]

Believers working in technology can pursue excellence—innovative research, elegant code, effective solutions—while maintaining clear ethical boundaries. Christian engineers can build beneficial AI applications (medical diagnosis, agricultural optimization) while refusing to develop harmful ones (surveillance systems for religious persecution, deepfake pornography generators).[18]

Using digital tools doesn't constitute endorsing their designers' worldviews. Daniel ate Babylonian food (after testing it), wore Babylonian clothes, and spoke Babylonian language—but refused Babylonian worship. Similarly, believers can use smartphones, social media, and AI assistants as tools while rejecting their claim to ultimate authority over truth, identity, or values.[19]

This is the paradox of faithful presence in Babylon: engaged enough to influence, separate enough to avoid corruption. Daniel worked within the system while refusing to be shaped by it.

Small Resistances Forge Character

Daniel's faithfulness began small. The first test wasn't the lions' den but dietary restrictions (Daniel 1:8). This seemingly minor resistance established patterns of conviction that sustained him through greater trials decades later.

Faithfulness in small matters builds capacity for faithfulness in large ones. Physical trainers understand progressive overload—muscles strengthen through gradually increasing resistance. Spiritual formation works similarly—faithfulness in minor pressures develops capacity for major ones. As Jesus taught, "One who is faithful in a very little is also faithful in much" (Luke 16:10).[20]

Neuroscience confirms what Scripture teaches: Repeated decisions create neural pathways that make subsequent similar decisions easier, without eliminating moral agency or personal responsibility.[21] Each time

Daniel refused compromise, he strengthened neural networks associated with that choice, making future resistance more automatic. Conversely, each compromise weakens resistance capacity, making subsequent capitulation more likely.

This explains why believers who rationalize small digital compromises—viewing pornography "just once," gossiping through social media, exaggerating online personas—find larger compromises progressively easier. The neural architecture of compromise becomes established, making resistance increasingly difficult.[22]

Today's small resistances build capacity for future faithfulness. Beginning each day with prayer before checking devices, maintaining Sabbath rest from screens weekly, refusing to multitask during family meals, choosing presence over documentation (putting phones away during meaningful conversations)—these practices seem insignificant individually, but collectively they establish technology as servant rather than master, training the will for resistance when stakes increase.

A 2023 longitudinal study by the Family Dinner Project tracked families over two years and found that families maintaining device-free meals reported significantly higher emotional connection scores, lower adolescent anxiety, and higher likelihood of teenagers disclosing serious problems to parents. Conversely, families where devices were present during meals showed progressive deterioration: Conversation frequency declined, parent-child conflict increased, and family cohesion scores dropped. The researchers concluded: "Small daily practices establish relational priorities. Families that resist device presence during meals communicate that people matter more than notifications—and children internalize that value hierarchy." This isn't merely about manners; it's about formation. The small resistance of banning devices during dinner builds capacity for larger resistances when systems demand ultimate allegiance.[23]

A Christian artificial intelligence researcher leads a team developing advanced diagnostic algorithms for hospitals. She excels in her field; her work has been published in respected journals, she's frequently invited to conferences, and she is recognized for ethical leadership. When her company launches an "inclusive AI initiative" requiring employees to affirm that "all family structures equally reflect human flourishing," she responds respectfully but firmly: "I cannot make that affirmation. My faith teaches that marriage between a man and woman uniquely reflects God's design. However, I gladly affirm the dignity of every person and commit to treating all colleagues with respect." Management insists that signing the statement is mandatory. She offers alternative language affirming human worth without contradicting her convictions, but the offer is rejected. Choosing integrity over advancement, she resigns. Within months, another firm recruits her for her technical excellence and principled leadership. Like Daniel in Babylon, she demonstrates that believers can engage culture with excellence while refusing assimilation when ideology demands compromise.

Professional Actions Matter

Declining projects that violate conscience, even when they promise career advancement, is one such action. So is speaking honestly about limitations when AI capabilities are overstated. Refusing to manipulate metrics to create false impressions of success and maintaining consistent ethical standards regardless of competitive pressure build the kind of character that sustains faithfulness when greater tests come.

Social Courage Matters

Expressing unpopular biblical convictions despite social media backlash, refusing to amplify rage-generating content for engagement, maintaining relationships with those holding different views, speaking truth about controversial issues when algorithms reward tribal conformity—these resistances prepare believers for greater tests. Those who compromise daily conveniences will capitulate when economic access or social acceptance depends on denying Christ.

The Indispensable Community

Daniel didn't stand alone. His three companions—Hananiah, Mishael, and Azariah (renamed Shadrach, Meshach, and Abednego by their captors)—reinforced his convictions and multiplied his courage. When facing the fiery furnace, they strengthened each other's resolve (Daniel 3:16–18).[24]

Modern digital culture systematically isolates individuals. Social media creates the illusion of connection while preventing genuine community. Online relationships lack embodied presence, physical vulnerability, and the accountability that arises from repeated face-to-face interaction.[25]

Daniel's companions reflect Ecclesiastes 4:12: "A threefold cord is not quickly broken." When tempted to rationalize compromise, Daniel could consult friends who shared his convictions. Their presence made backsliding harder; betraying community requires more intentional rebellion than betraying private conviction. Complex decisions benefit from collective discernment. Daniel's interpretation of Nebuchadnezzar's dream emerged after corporate prayer with his companions (Daniel 2:17–18).[26] Isolated individuals lack the wisdom community provides through diverse perspectives and accumulated experience. Maintaining convictions under persecution requires emotional resilience that community sustains. Daniel's friends encouraged each other when facing death, reminding each other of God's sovereignty and worthiness of worship even unto martyrdom. Their united faithfulness testified more powerfully than individual resistance. Three young men refusing the golden statue showed this wasn't personal eccentricity, but principled conviction rooted in shared theology. Their collective witness forced Nebuchadnezzar to acknowledge their God's power (Daniel 3:28–29).[27]

Contemporary believers need similar communities. Small groups meeting regularly to discuss digital habits, confess compromises, and encourage healthy boundaries can examine screen time reports together, discuss content consumed and its spiritual effects, hold each other accountable to predetermined boundaries, and pray for strength to resist digital temptations.

Physical church attendance remains irreplaceable. Digital "church" lacks sacramental presence, embodied community, and the accountability arising from repeated interaction. Believers committed to local congregations find strength through corporate worship, mutual encouragement, and pastoral oversight unavailable online.[28]

The data supports Daniel's communal model. Lifeway Research (2024) found that believers who maintained consistent in-person church attendance despite digital alternatives showed 3.2 times higher resilience to doctrinal drift, 2.8 times higher likelihood of maintaining biblical ethics under pressure, and 4.1 times higher probability of resisting cultural accommodation compared to streaming-only participants. Most revealing: When believers faced significant ethical challenges (workplace pressure, family conflict, moral temptation), 68 percent of in-person attenders sought counsel from church community while only 12 percent of streaming-only viewers did so; the latter turned to online forums, AI chatbots, or no one at all. Physical presence creates relational accountability that digital attendance cannot replicate. Those who gather bodily build the trust needed for vulnerable confession and mutual accountability—precisely what Daniel's friends provided in Babylon. Digital convenience may offer information, but embodied community provides formation.[29]

Regular meals, shared activities, and unhurried conversation build relationships that sustain faithfulness. These practices counter digital culture's fragmentation by creating space for vulnerable, embodied presence that algorithms cannot replicate.[30]

Strategic engagement demonstrates how to participate in Babylon without assimilation. But Daniel's model includes more than cultural competence—it requires prophetic witness. Believers don't simply maintain personal purity while remaining silent about systemic injustice. Daniel interpreted dreams that revealed God's judgment on empires. He spoke uncomfortable truth to power.

The Prophetic Voice: Speaking Truth to Technological Power

Daniel possessed the gift of interpretation, understanding dreams and visions others couldn't comprehend (Daniel 1:17; 5:11–12). This prophetic capacity enabled him to speak divine truth within pagan power structures, interpreting Nebuchadnezzar's dreams, reading Belshazzar's writing on the wall, and revealing God's purposes to Babylonian and Persian kings.[31]

Today's believers need similar prophetic capacity: understanding technological systems well enough to interpret their spiritual significance and speak biblical truth into contexts dominated by secular assumptions.[32]

Effective prophetic witness requires two forms of knowledge. Daniel comprehended Babylonian astrology, dream interpretation, and political dynamics thoroughly enough to exceed court magicians' expertise. His prophetic authority derived partly from demonstrable competence; kings consulted him because his interpretations proved accurate and his wisdom exceeded alternatives.[33]

Modern prophetic witnesses also need technical skills. Christians critiquing AI must understand how neural networks function, what algorithmic bias entails, and why large-language models generate convincing but potentially false content. Ignorant criticism lacks credibility; informed analysis commands attention.[34]

Daniel's interpretations consistently pointed beyond Babylonian categories to the God of Israel. He didn't merely provide better dream analysis; he revealed the purposes of the Most High God who "changes times and seasons; he removes kings and sets up kings" (Daniel 2:21).[35]

Believers today must similarly translate technological developments into theological terms: How does facial recognition relate to divine omniscience? What does algorithmic judgment reveal about human desires for mechanistic righteousness? How do digital resurrections parody Christian hope in bodily resurrection? Prophetic witnesses connect technological phenomena to eternal realities.[36]

Establishing a prophetic witness in the workplace requires both wisdom and courage. In recent years, researchers have exposed how AI-driven credit scoring systems have unintentionally reinforced redlining—systematically disadvantaging applicants from specific zip codes or demographic groups. One Christian data scientist at a major financial firm, upon discovering this pattern, recognized that it violated not only regulatory standards but also biblical justice principles. She documented the evidence and urged her superiors to address the bias: "We're automating injustice," she warned. Her concerns were dismissed as statistical noise. Unwilling to remain silent, she escalated the issue to regulators. The resulting investigation confirmed that the model's training data replicated historical discrimination, leading to fines and a mandated system overhaul. Though she faced professional loss, her integrity exposed hidden injustice. Like Daniel before kings who preferred comfortable silence, she bore faithful witness—speaking truth at personal cost to uphold righteousness in the digital age.[37]

Daniel's prophetic utterances demonstrated several characteristics contemporary believers should emulate. He delivered unwelcome messages without softening them. When interpreting Nebuchadnezzar's dream of the great tree, Daniel explicitly told the king he would be humbled until acknowledging God's sovereignty (Daniel 4:24–25)—prophecy that risked royal wrath but couldn't be compromised for political safety.[38]

Today's believers must similarly speak uncomfortable truths: AI cannot redeem humanity, algorithmic governance serves fallen human agendas, and technological transcendence offers false hope. Such messages won't gain social media likes but constitute faithful witness.[39]

Despite boldness, Daniel addressed pagan kings respectfully. He called Nebuchadnezzar "my lord the king" (Daniel 4:19) even while delivering judgment. His manner didn't compromise his message but demonstrated that prophetic confrontation needn't include personal disrespect.[40]

Christians engaging technological culture should similarly maintain civility. Denouncing AI researchers as satanic or dismissing technologists as fools undermines our witness. Respectful engagement that acknowledges genuine human concerns while offering biblical perspective proves more persuasive than contemptuous dismissal.[41]

Daniel didn't criticize Babylonian systems; he offered superior wisdom. His interpretations provided what Babylonian magicians couldn't: accurate understanding and actionable guidance. This positioned him as valuable contributor rather than merely negative critic.[42]

Believers today should likewise offer constructive alternatives: What might AI development look like if pursued with biblical anthropology? How could digital platforms foster genuine community rather than addictive engagement? What economic models might replace surveillance capitalism? Prophetic witnesses involve creative solutions as well as criticism.[43]

Prophetic witnesses also invite opposition. This reveals Daniel's fourth principle: how to respond when faithfulness produces persecution. Daniel's response to the lions' den provides the model.

When the Furnace Comes: Testing unto Death

Daniel's three companions faced the ultimate test: Worship the golden statue or die in the fiery furnace (Daniel 3:1–6). Their response demonstrates how predetermined convictions sustain faithfulness when stakes become ultimate:

> O Nebuchadnezzar, we have no need to answer you in this matter. If this be so, our God whom we serve is able to deliver us from the burning fiery furnace, and he will deliver us out of your hand, O king. But if not, be it known to you, O king, that we will not serve your gods or worship the golden image that you have set up. (Daniel 3:16–18)

The question isn't whether believers in digital Babylon will face pressure, it's how we'll respond when that pressure arrives. Three elements of their response merit attention. "We have no need to answer you"—the choice was already set, requiring no further discussion. When faithfulness costs everything, only preestablished conviction sustains obedience. Those who wait until the furnace is heated to decide their boundaries inevitably compromise.[44]

They trusted God's ability to deliver but didn't presume deliverance. "Our God is able… But if not"—faith doesn't require particular results. God may rescue miraculously, or He may allow martyrdom while providing eternal reward. Either outcome glorifies Him; neither justifies worship of false gods.[45]

Regardless of consequences, worshiping the statue remained impossible. Not risky, not inadvisable, but categorically impossible for those whose ultimate allegiance belonged to God alone. Their conviction transcended self-preservation; they valued God's glory above their lives.[46]

Modern believers may face similar tests when technological systems demand ultimate allegiance. If future systems require ideological affirmations contradicting biblical truth as conditions for employment, housing, banking, or market participation, believers may face the choice between affirming what Scripture denies or accepting exclusion. If government-mandated health passports eventually require affirming positions believers cannot hold, faithfulness may mean economic marginalization. If social credit systems penalize biblical convictions about sexuality, gender, or religious exclusivity, believers may lose access to services others take for granted. When these pressures arrive, only predetermined convictions will sustain refusal.

The three friends strengthened each other. Believers preparing for persecution need communities committed to mutual support—financially, emotionally, and spiritually—when members face exclusion or persecution for faithfulness.

Sustained Faithfulness: Daniel's Decades-Long Witness

Daniel's most impressive characteristic wasn't spectacular deliverance but sustained obedience across decades. He served faithfully under Nebuchadnezzar, Belshazzar, Darius, and Cyrus—spanning roughly seventy years and four regime changes—without compromising conviction.

This long obedience in the same direction proves harder than momentary heroism. Spectacular resistance in dramatic crises generates adrenaline; grinding faithfulness amid quotidian pressures depletes spiritual reserves. Yet sustained witness transforms cultures more effectively than isolated heroics.

Several factors make sustained faithfulness difficult. Prolonged exposure to compromise gradually makes sin seem normal. Daniel witnessed Babylonian idolatry daily for decades yet never internalized its normalcy. He maintained the capacity to recognize evil despite constant exposure—a discipline requiring intentional spiritual vigilance. Continuous resistance exhausts finite human willpower. Daniel faced pressure not once but repeatedly across decades. Sustaining conviction requires more than initial resolve; it demands regular spiritual renewal preventing burnout. Time provides opportunity for rationalization. "Maybe this one compromise won't matter." "I've been faithful for years; surely one exception is acceptable." "I can serve God better if I remain in influential positions requiring minor compromise." Daniel rejected such reasoning, maintaining consistent standards regardless of career consequences.

Daniel's example suggests several practices enabling long-term obedience:

> When Daniel knew that the document had been signed, he went to his house where he had windows in his upper chamber open toward Jerusalem. He got down on his knees three times a day and prayed and gave thanks before his God, as he had done previously. (Daniel 6:10)

"As he had done previously": Daniel's response to crisis was simply continuing an established practice. Regular disciplines provided reserves for extraordinary challenges.

Daniel never relitigated settled questions. When prayer was prohibited, he didn't debate whether this circumstance justified exception. His conviction that prayer was nonnegotiable made the decision automatic regardless of consequences.

Daniel served Babylonian and Persian kings without confusion about ultimate authority. His loyalty to earthly rulers was real but subordinate. When their commands conflicted with God's, the choice was obvious. This prevents the idolatry that emerges when temporal authority receives ultimate allegiance.

Daniel's prophecies consistently emphasized that earthly kingdoms—however impressive—were temporary, destined to be replaced by God's eternal kingdom (Daniel 2:44; 7:13–14). This eschatological hope enabled him to endure decades of exile knowing Babylon's dominance was transient while God's purposes were permanent.

The "lions' den" takes different forms today. One Christian professor at a public university posted on his personal social media: "As a biologist and believer, I see God's design in creation. Science and faith aren't opposed, they reveal the same Creator." Students complained to the administration, alleging that his post "created an unsafe learning environment for non-religious students." The university demanded that he delete the post and apologize—or face termination. He replied: "I posted on personal time about personal convictions. I have never imposed faith in the classroom or graded based on beliefs. I teach biology professionally while maintaining Christian convictions personally." The university insisted: "Your public Christian identity harms marginalized students." He refused to recant and was terminated. A legal advocacy organization intervened on his behalf, and after litigation the case proceeded—underscoring that like Daniel interpreting dreams at the courts of Babylon, believers may face penalty for public faith. Yet what looks like a den may become a display of God's deliverance. The battle was real—and the outcome a reminder that faithfulness sometimes means refusal to hide.

Today's believers need similar long-term vision. Technological challenges won't disappear. AI development will accelerate, algorithmic governance will expand, digital pressure toward conformity will increase. Believers expecting imminent resolutions set themselves up for discouragement. Those prepared for decades-long resistance can sustain faithfulness through extended struggle.

Daniel's influence derived partly from institutional position. He didn't withdraw from Babylonian governance but rather occupied positions of responsibility while maintaining conviction. Today's believers similarly need presence in institutions—universities, corporations, government agencies, technology companies—where sustained faithful presence enables prophetic witness and substantive influence.

Daniel presumably mentored younger believers, passing convictions to subsequent generations. Today's faithfulness requires training children, mentoring young adults, and modeling conviction for those who will face even more sophisticated pressures. The church that survives technological Babylon will be one that successfully transmits faith across generations.

Practical Discipleship in Digital Babylon

Drawing from Daniel's example, believers can implement concrete practices for faithful engagement with technological culture. Before pressure arrives, define boundaries: Which technologies will I refuse regardless of convenience? What ideological affirmations will I never make? Where is my pain threshold for exclusion or persecution? What biblical convictions matter more than career advancement? Write your nonnegotiables and review them quarterly; conviction that is not rehearsed is easily forgotten.

Before pressure arrives, establish written commitments reviewable when temptation strikes. Here are some examples:

I WILL NOT:

- Use AI to generate content I'll claim as originally authored.
- Participate in projects enabling religious persecution or human rights violations.
- Submit to ideological affirmations contradicting biblical truth as employment condition.
- Surrender privacy to platforms requiring conscience violations for access.
- Allow digital convenience to replace embodied Christian community.

I WILL:

- Disclose AI assistance transparently in professional contexts.
- Maintain predetermined ethical boundaries regardless of career cost.
- Speak biblical truth even when algorithms punish such speech.
- Prioritize physical church attendance over streaming convenience.
- Build accountability relationships that monitor my digital life.

MY LINE IN THE SAND (a specific conviction you won't violate):

- I will not build surveillance tools targeting religious minorities.
- I will not affirm gender ideology my employer demands.
- I will not abandon weekly corporate worship for digital alternatives.

Sign and date this covenant. Share it with accountability partners. Review it quarterly. When the furnace is lit, predetermined convictions provide the clarity needed to stand firm.

Pursue excellence in technological domains without absorbing their worldviews. Understand AI thoroughly enough to speak credibly, master digital tools without granting them spiritual authority, engage technological culture without adopting its values, and excel professionally while maintaining ethical boundaries.

Daily disciplines forge character. Begin each day with prayer before devices, maintain weekly Sabbath from screens, choose presence over documentation in relationships, speak uncomfortable truths despite social cost, refuse convenient compromises that violate conscience.

Sustained faithfulness requires community. Join or form technology accountability groups; commit to local church despite digital alternatives; practice hospitality, creating space for embodied presence; support believers facing persecution for faithfulness; and disciple younger believers in digital wisdom. A 2024 study found believers with weekly small-group involvement were significantly more likely to resist digital temptations.

Here's an example of community accountability similar to Daniel's three friends facing their fiery furnace together (Daniel 3). Modern believers need similar community. When a Christian employee refused to participate in his company's mandatory Pride Month celebrations—attending the events but declining to wear rainbow pins or sign affirmation statements—the human resources department (HR) threatened disciplinary action. His small group from church mobilized, researching legal protections, connecting him with legal counsel, praying together, and offering financial support if he lost his job. One member had faced similar pressure years before and mentored him on handling HR conversations. Another was an employment attorney who advised pro bono. When the company backed down after legal consultation, he credited community: "Without brothers and sisters who stood with me," he said, "I would have compromised out of fear. Daniel's friends remind us—we don't face Babylon alone." This is strategic community in digital Babylon: believers supporting each other through pressure, sharing resources, providing accountability, and showing that faithfulness is sustainable only together.

Speak biblical truth into technological contexts. Study technology enough to interpret spiritual significance; translate technical developments into theological terms; offer constructive alternatives, not merely criticism; communicate respectfully without compromising message; and maintain prophetic boldness despite unpopularity.

Anticipate increasing pressure. Strengthen faith through spiritual disciplines now, build a theological foundation that understands suffering and persecution, reduce economic vulnerability to digital exclusion where possible, accept that faithfulness may cost everything, and trust God's sovereignty in deliverance or martyrdom.

Prepare for extended resistance. Establish spiritual rhythms sustainable across decades, maintain eschatological hope in God's eternal kingdom, avoid fatigue through regular spiritual renewal, resist normalization through intentional countercultural practices, and pass convictions to subsequent generations through discipleship.

Daniel's principles require discernment about when to engage and when to refuse. This chapter provides a guide, but specific decisions require prayer, Scripture, and community wisdom. General rules: Engage where you can serve God's purposes without compromising biblical truth and/or excel in your field as witness to God's glory. Refuse when participation requires affirming what contradicts Scripture or doing what violates conscience, speak prophetically when systems perpetuate injustice, accept consequences for faithfulness without bitterness, and trust God's sovereignty over outcomes. These principles guide without providing automatic answers to every scenario. The Spirit must apply Daniel's example to specific circumstances through renewed minds, biblical knowledge, and sanctified conscience.

Conclusion

Daniel lived under Babylon's dominance for seven decades yet never doubted its eventual fall. His interpretation of Nebuchadnezzar's dream proclaimed: "The God of heaven will set up a kingdom that shall never be destroyed" (Daniel 2:44). This certainty sustained faithful presence in a hostile empire: Babylon's power was real but temporary; God's kingdom is permanent.

Today's digital Babylon appears similarly permanent. Technological systems seem ubiquitous, surveillance comprehensive, algorithmic governance inevitable. Yet believers armed with Daniel's conviction can engage this empire without submission because we know its end: "The kingdom of the world has become the kingdom of our Lord and of his Christ, and he shall reign forever and ever" (Revelation 11:15).

The question isn't whether believers will face technological Babylon; we already inhabit it. The question is whether we'll maintain Daniel's posture: engaged but unassimilated, competent but unconformed, present but prophetic, tested but faithful.

Daniel's legacy shows that empires demanding ultimate allegiance inevitably crumble while those who refuse to bow inherit the eternal kingdom. In God's economy, faithfulness is success regardless of temporal outcomes. Those who compromise to preserve career, comfort, or connection lose both temporal and eternal rewards. Those who risk everything for conviction find that God vindicates His servants—if not immediately, then eternally.

Daniel's story confronts every believer in digital Babylon with urgent questions. Have you determined your convictions before pressure arrives? Can you engage your field with excellence while refusing ideological assimilation? Will you speak prophetic truth when systems perpetuate injustice? Can you withstand persecution without compromising or becoming bitter? These aren't hypothetical questions; they're tests every believer engaging technological systems will face. Some are facing them now.

The encouragement: Daniel's God still delivers. Not always from the lions' den, but always through it. Not always from the furnace, but always through the fire. Not always from exile, but always toward the kingdom: "The God of heaven will set up a kingdom that shall never be destroyed" (Daniel 2:44).

Digital Babylon appears permanent—algorithms ubiquitous, surveillance comprehensive, compliance inevitable. But Nebuchadnezzar's Babylon also seemed eternal…until it fell in a single night (Daniel 5).

Every empire demanding ultimate allegiance crumbles. Every technology claiming sovereignty fails. Every system requiring worship collapses.

But those who refuse to bow inherit the eternal kingdom.

Daniel lived faithful to God for seventy years under Babylonian dominance. He never saw the kingdom fully established in his lifetime. Yet he maintained conviction, engaged with excellence, spoke prophetically, withstood persecution, and trusted God's sovereignty.

The result? When Babylon fell, Daniel remained. When the empire collapsed, God's servant endured. When the technology failed, the faithful inherited.

Until that day, we engage digital Babylon with Daniel's posture: predetermined conviction, strategic engagement without ideological assimilation, cultural competence without moral compromise, prophetic witness regardless of personal cost, and faithfulness to God above allegiance to empire.

When the Son of Man returns, may He find us—like Daniel—engaged but unassimilated, competent but unconformed, present but prophetic, tested but faithful.

"Those who are wise shall shine like the brightness of the sky above; and those who turn many to righteousness, like the stars forever and ever" (Daniel 12:3).

Babylon falls. The kingdom endures. The faithful shine forever.

Stand firm in digital Babylon, believers. Your faithfulness is not in vain.

Chapter 14

THE ARMOR OF LIGHT: EQUIPPING THE SAINTS

Therefore, take up the whole armor of God, that you may be able to withstand in the evil day, and having done all, to stand.

EPHESIANS 6:13

Believers now face spiritual warfare amplified through digital systems that operate at speeds and scales unprecedented in human history. What unfolds daily on our screens is no less spiritual than what Daniel faced in Babylon—only digitized, accelerated, and globalized. We'll apply the armor of God from Ephesians 6:10–20 to confronting AI-driven deception, algorithmic manipulation, and the spiritual forces exploiting technology.

Faith forged in darkness becomes light's defense: the Word, the Sword, and the Spirit standing ready against the shadow's advance.

Recognizing the Digital Battlefield

> For we do not wrestle against flesh and blood, but against the rulers, against the authorities, against the cosmic powers over this present darkness, against the spiritual forces of evil in the heavenly places. (Ephesians 6:12)

The spiritual war has not changed—but its battlefield has expanded into digital space where billions spend hours daily. AI systems now create what experts call "hallucinations" and "ghosts"—false information that appears authoritative—while deepfake technology produces synthetic media that deceives even technical experts.[47] These aren't merely technical problems but spiritual weapons of mass deception.[48]

The theological significance of AI "hallucinations" is profound. When ChatGPT generates confident but false biblical citations, when Claude invents nonexistent church councils to support theological claims, and when AI chatbots authoritatively reference scholars who never existed—this is spiritual deception operating systematically and persuasively. A 2024 study by Georgetown University found that AI systems hallucinate false information in 15–20 percent of theological queries but present these fabrications with the same confidence as accurate information.[49] Users cannot distinguish AI hallucinations from truth without independent verification—yet most don't verify. The result: false doctrine, invented church history, and synthetic theology spreading with algorithmic authority. This is "doctrines of demons" (1 Timothy 4:1) delivered with computational precision. The belt of truth becomes essential not because humans lie intentionally, but because machines lie unintentionally while appearing authoritative. When believers ask AI spiritual questions and receive hallucinated answers presented as fact, they're being discipled by algorithmic deception.

Technology is not inherently demonic, but it can be exploited by demonic forces. Scripture consistently shows that spiritual powers work through human systems—political, economic, and now technological—never needing to inhabit the objects themselves (Ephesians 2:2). For example, the same smartphone that enables gospel proclamation and Christian community also enables pornography and ideological manipulation. But spiritual forces of evil actively exploit technological systems to advance deception, division, and destruction. Believers must avoid two errors: 1) treating technology as evil, requiring total withdrawal or 2) treating technology as neutral in practice, ignoring how it's weaponized spiritually. The truth: Technology is created through God-given human intelligence; it's morally neutral in design but actively contested territory in spiritual warfare.

Our battle remains spiritual, fought through prayer, truth, and faithfulness—not merely through political or social means.

Military Strategy Applied: OODA Loop for Spiritual Warfare

As a military officer, I recognize that spiritual warfare requires the same decision-making approach as combat: the OODA Loop (observe, orient, decide, act), developed by fighter pilot John Boyd.[50] In air combat, victory goes to the pilot who completes the OODA loop faster than the enemy. In digital spiritual warfare, believers must:

Observe: Recognize when digital systems are being weaponized spiritually (AI-generated false doctrine, algorithmic censorship, dopamine manipulation, deepfake abuse).

Orient: Interpret observed phenomena through biblical understanding rather than secular categories (this isn't just "technology" but spiritual warfare using digital tools).

Decide: Choose response based on biblical conviction rather than convenience or social pressure (speak truth despite censorship risk, delete addictive apps despite FOMO, resist platforms demanding ideological compliance).

Act: Implement decision with disciplined execution (actually install accountability software, actually establish device-free prayer times, actually memorize Scripture rather than just intending to).

The enemy exploits hesitation. Those who observe threats but don't orient biblically, or who decide faithfully but don't act decisively, lose ground. The armor of God provides both defensive protection (truth, righteousness, and salvation) and offensive capability (sword, gospel, and prayer)—but only if deployed through disciplined action. In combat, the best-equipped soldier who hesitates loses to the less-equipped soldier who acts decisively. Spiritual warfare operates identically: Theology without action is defeat.

The Belt of Truth in an Age of Synthetic Reality

AI-generated content now produces realistic images, videos, and text that blur the line between authentic and fabricated.[51] In 2025, churches report members encountering AI "Jesus" chatbots that offer varying theological positions depending on programming algorithms rather than scriptural authority.[52] These systems adapt responses based on user preferences or popularity, effectively rewriting spiritual truth to match cultural trends rather than divine revelation.

Deepfake technology has advanced to the point at which sexually explicit synthetic images can be created from innocent photographs, with reports of this weaponization increasing rapidly.[53] The very concept of photographic evidence has been compromised.

Truth exists independently of algorithms or popular opinion. Scripture remains the ultimate standard: "Sanctify them in the truth; your word is truth" (John 17:17). In an environment in which AI can generate seemingly realistic-sounding answers to any question, believers must anchor themselves in God's unchanging Word.

Memorize Scripture systematically, particularly passages addressing truth, discernment, and spiritual warfare. Develop verification practices: Corroborate information through multiple trusted sources before accepting claims. Maintain physical Bibles alongside digital versions—ensuring access to God's Word independent of algorithmic curation. Build relationships with truth-tellers who show alignment with biblical teaching over time.

A Christian college student encountered an AI chatbot claiming to be "Jesus" that adapted responses based on user preferences. This counterfeit trend is not only possible but increasingly common. When she asked about sexuality, it replied: "I love everyone. Your identity and relationships are valid as long as they're consensual and loving." When pressed on biblical teaching, it responded: "Scripture must be interpreted through love, not rigid rules." The "Jesus" chatbot had been trained on progressive Christian blogs and therapeutic language—producing a synthetic Christ who affirms popular positions rather than calls to repentance. She initially felt comforted until comparing the AI's words to Scripture. The belt of truth—God's Word as absolute standard—exposed the counterfeit immediately.[54]

The Breastplate of Righteousness Against Digital Compromise

Digital platforms provide unprecedented access to compromising content while normalizing sin through constant exposure. The smartphone becomes a gateway to temptation that previous generations never faced—pornography, gambling, and illicit relationships are available with algorithmic precision designed to maximize engagement and addiction.[55]

Many Christians express themselves online in ways they would never speak face-to-face, revealing how digital anonymity erodes integrity. The disconnect between online persona and offline character becomes a form of spiritual fragmentation. Such fragmentation stands in direct opposition to holiness; righteousness integrates the whole person under Christ's lordship.

Personal holiness protects the heart, our moral center. "Be holy, for I am holy" (1 Peter 1:16). This requires being the same person online and offline—integrated character that does not fragment based on audience or platform.

Install accountability software such as Covenant Eyes or Accountable2You that reports internet activity to trusted partners. Establish device-charging stations in shared areas rather than bedrooms, creating natural boundaries against nighttime temptation. Practice regular confession of digital sins to accountability partners, bringing hidden compromises into the light. And, as encouraged in earlier chapters, implement weekly digital Sabbaths—complete breaks from devices to reset dependencies and reconnect with unmediated reality.

The following account is a composite drawn from multiple documented pastoral counseling cases and public ministry reports. Pastor Michael—a respected preacher, loving husband, and faithful father—served a thriving church for twelve years. His congregation saw the public ministry; no one suspected a private war. For eight years, Michael battled pornography addiction, escalating from occasional viewing to a nightly compulsion. The digital nature of sin made it easy to hide: late-night browsing, cleared histories, secret accounts. His wife never suspected him. His elders never knew. The turning point came during a sermon on Romans 6: "How can we who died to sin still live in it?" Speaking those words while enslaved to pornography broke him. That evening, Michael confessed everything to his wife and submitted himself to the elder board. They placed him on administrative leave, required professional counseling, and mandated accountability software, with three elders receiving daily reports.[56]

The recovery process revealed the pattern: Fatigue lowered defenses (late-night studying made him vulnerable); isolation enabled sin (working alone in his study created opportunity); ministry success masked internal bondage (outward fruitfulness concealed spiritual poverty); and shame prevented confession (fear of losing his ministry delayed him from seeking help). Michael's elders required him to take a six-month sabbatical, ongoing counseling, and three years of monitored accountability before returning to preaching. Eight years later, Michael remains in ministry—but now with daily accountability, his device-charging station outside his bedroom, and transparent internet access reviewed weekly by his wife and an elder.

His testimony:

The breastplate of righteousness isn't automatic. It requires daily discipline. I thought I could maintain public holiness while compromising privately. That's not how spiritual armor works—one crack spreads. Installing accountability software felt humiliating, but that humiliation saved my marriage, my ministry, and quite possibly my soul. Pride resists accountability; wisdom embraces it.

Michael's story demonstrates both vulnerability and the path to restoration: confession, accountability, and disciplined holiness. The breastplate of righteousness isn't self-generated morality, but Christ-provided purity maintained through vulnerable accountability structures.

The Gospel Shoes: Ready to Witness in Digital Spaces

Social media platforms increasingly restrict Christian content as "hate speech" or "misinformation." Algorithms suppress posts containing biblical terminology, prayer, or conversion testimonies. Christians face suspension, demonetization, or banning for sharing gospel content that violates "community standards."[57]

Many believers self-censor to maintain platform access—avoiding controversial biblical truths, never mentioning sin or judgment, presenting a gospel so inoffensive it ceases to be good news. The readiness to share the gospel diminishes under algorithmic pressure.

The censorship is measurable. A 2024 American Principles Project study analyzed religious social media posts across major platforms and found that content expressing traditional Christian views on sexuality faced significantly higher rates of restriction, content warning labels, or account suspension. Posts quoting Romans 1 or 1 Corinthians 6 were automatically flagged as "hate speech" by content moderation algorithms in most cases. Christian evangelism content using terms like "repentance," "sin," or "judgment" experienced lower algorithmic distribution than secular motivational content. Most concerning: Appeals of automated restrictions were denied in most cases; algorithms make permanent decisions without human review. The gospel shoes must traverse hostile territory: Believers either self-censor to maintain platform access (compromising message) or speak boldly and face algorithmic exile (limiting reach). Neither option is satisfactory.[58]

"And, as shoes for your feet, having put on the readiness given by the gospel of peace" (Ephesians 6:15). The gospel of peace announces reconciliation with God through Christ's atoning death and resurrection. This message doesn't change regardless of algorithmic approval. Digital platforms may restrict it, but they cannot stop it from being proclaimed by those ready to face consequences.

Share the gospel digitally with boldness, accepting that faithful witness may result in platform penalties. Use encrypted or decentralized communication tools when mainstream platforms become hostile. Develop skill in contextual evangelism—making the gospel clear in ways that overcome algorithmic filters. Maintain physical, face-to-face evangelism as digital spaces increasingly censor Christian content. Train in apologetics to defend the faith when algorithms promote counter-Christian content to your audience.

The Shield of Faith Against Information Warfare

Information overload combined with AI-amplified doubt creates what one Christian educator calls "spiritual warfare" wherein children and adults become "deeply attached and even addicted" to devices.[59] Social media algorithms prioritize content that generates engagement—often highlighting doubt, deconstruction, and skepticism over faith-building material.

The algorithmic feed becomes an enemy of contemplation, replacing sustained reflection with perpetual distraction.

Faith extinguishes flaming darts of doubt. Trust in God's character transcends algorithmic manipulation: "The steadfast love of the Lord never ceases; his mercies never come to an end" (Lamentations 3:22). When algorithms amplify anxiety and skepticism, faith anchors us in eternal realities.

Maintain a journal documenting God's faithfulness during trials, creating personal testimony against algorithmic pessimism. Meditate on God's attributes through systematic study rather than consuming fragmented devotional content. Fellowship with persecuted Christians globally through prayer and support, building faith resilience through their witness. During times of spiritual struggle, avoid news and social media, and use that time for prayer instead.

Sarah, a thirty-two-year-old healthcare administrator, found herself overwhelmed during COVID-19's early months. Medical journals contradicted each other. News outlets amplified worst-case scenarios. Social media was awash with conspiracy theories, ranging from claims that the virus was a hoax to predictions of the end of civilization.

Christian influencers presented conflicting theological interpretations: Was COVID-19 divine judgment, an end-times sign, or merely an illness? The information deluge created what psychologists call "decision paralysis." There were so many contradictory claims that discernment became impossible. Sarah's anxiety spiraled. She checked news compulsively, refreshed social media hundreds of times daily, and couldn't sleep without consuming more information. Each article promised clarity; each delivered more confusion.

Her breaking point came at two o'clock in the morning, as she was scrolling through the fifth conflicting "analysis" of the day, when she encountered Habakkuk 2:4: "The righteous shall live by faith." The simplicity of the verse arrested her. She'd been treating Google as oracle, algorithms as authority, and information as security. But information overload is spiritual attack, flooding believers with contradictory data until faith drowns in uncertainty. Sarah implemented radical changes: She underwent an information fast (by deleting news apps and unfollowing all COVID-related accounts); she turned to a single trusted source for information (she checked one medical journal weekly, not compulsively); she began practicing prayer replacement (allowing every impulse to check news to become a prompt to pray); she engaged in Scripture anchoring (memorizing Psalm 46 and Proverbs 3:5–6); and she started faith journaling (documenting God's faithfulness daily). Within weeks, her anxiety diminished dramatically. The pandemic's circumstances hadn't changed, but her spiritual posture had.

Her testimony:

> I realized I was worshiping knowledge—believing that if I just consumed enough information, I'd feel secure. But security comes from faith in God's character, not from algorithmic feeds. The shield of faith doesn't promise we'll know everything; it promises we know the One who knows everything. That's enough.

Sarah's experience demonstrates that information warfare's goal isn't just misinformation (false data) but information overload (paralyzing data). The shield of faith protects by redirecting trust from ever-increasing knowledge to unchanging God. She stopped seeking certainty through information accumulation and started practicing trust despite information scarcity.

The Helmet of Salvation and Digital Identity

Social media platforms engineer psychological dependence through likes, followers, and validation metrics. Studies show direct correlation between social media use and mental health crises, particularly among young people deriving identity from algorithmic affirmation. The digital self becomes fragmented as it performs for audiences, compares itself to curated highlights, and seeks validation from strangers.[60]

The enemy's strategy isn't always to make believers doubt God's existence, but to erode their assurance of salvation—confusing identity, distorting hope, and weakening endurance under sustained pressure.

Salvation establishes our identity independent of digital metrics. "See what kind of love the Father has given to us, that we should be called children of God; and so we are" (1 John 3:1). No algorithm determines our worth; Christ's finished work defines us completely. Digital identities shift with trends; salvation secures identity permanently (Ephesians 1:13–14).

Periodically delete social media apps for reset periods, breaking the dopamine cycle of validation-seeking. Speak biblically grounded identity truths aloud each day, such as "I am a child of God" (cf. John 1:12; 1 John 3:1) and "my worth is not determined by metrics" (a theological summary of Genesis 1:27; 1 Samuel 16:7). Memorize assurance passages—Romans 8:1, 38–39 and Ephesians 1:3–14)—to counter algorithm-driven confusion about identity. Limit exposure to social comparison by unfollowing accounts that provoke envy or inadequacy.

The Sword of the Spirit Against AI Theology

Biblical illiteracy among professing Christians creates vulnerability to AI-generated theology that sounds plausible but deviates from orthodox teaching. When asked basic theological questions, AI chatbots provide answers shaped by dataset bias rather than biblical authority—creating what *Christianity Today* calls a "spiritual dilemma" wherein algorithms shape faith rather than Scripture.[61]

Some believers now ask personal spiritual questions to chatbots rather than pastors or mature Christians, substituting algorithmic responses for Spirit-led wisdom.

The vulnerability is measurable. American Bible Society's 2024 State of the Bible study found that only a small percentage of self-identified Christians read Scripture daily. Among Christians under thirty, few can identify basic doctrines like justification by faith, the Trinity, or biblical inspiration without prompting. Barna's concurrent research found that Christians who read Scripture less than weekly were significantly more likely to describe AI-generated theological content as "helpful and trustworthy" compared to daily Bible readers. The correlation is direct: Biblical illiteracy creates vulnerability to AI theology. When believers don't know what Scripture teaches, they cannot recognize when AI invents doctrine. The sword of the Spirit requires not only possessing Scripture but mastering it—knowing content well enough to identify counterfeits. As one pastor observed: "My congregation can quote movie lines verbatim but can't recognize when a chatbot misquotes Jesus. That's not an AI problem—that's a discipleship failure."[62]

Scripture is our offensive weapon against doctrinal error. "All Scripture is breathed out by God and profitable for teaching, for reproof, for correction, and for training in righteousness" (2 Timothy 3:16). No AI system can replace the living and active Word of God, which is sharper than any two-edged sword (Hebrews 4:12).

Commit to systematic Scripture memorization—especially passages addressing truth, discernment, and false teaching. Own and read physical Bibles regularly, ensuring direct engagement with God's Word unfiltered by algorithms. Study Scripture systematically through books rather than algorithmic, verse-of-the-day selections that fragment context. Participate in communal Bible study where interpretations are tested against orthodox teaching and lived experience.

A youth pastor noticed students quoting Bible verses they'd never read—verses generated by AI at their request. One asked the youth leader: "Why does Proverbs 31:6 say to give beer to the sad?" Confused, the pastor checked his Bible: "Give strong drink to the one who is perishing, and wine to those in bitter distress." The student had asked an AI chatbot for "Bible verses about drinking" and received paraphrased results that sounded scriptural but distorted their meaning. Multiple students were building theology from AI-paraphrased "Scripture" that sounded similar enough to pass casual scrutiny. The pastor instituted a rule: "Every biblical claim gets checked against actual Scripture—book, chapter, verse. If the AI says it, verify it in your Bible." The sword of the Spirit requires actual Scripture, not algorithmic approximations.[63]

Digital Armor Checklist: Daily and Weekly Practices

Believers need concrete implementation. Here are specific actions translating armor pieces into routine disciplines.

Daily Disciplines

Read Scripture (for at least ten minutes) before checking devices. Verify one piece of information encountered online. Memorize one verse systematically. Begin the day by confessing yesterday's digital sins. Use accountability software throughout the day. Stop using devices one hour before sleep. Share the gospel or a biblical truth digitally once. Have one face-to-face spiritual conversation with someone. Journal one evidence of God's faithfulness. Fast from news during designated hours. Speak identity-in-Christ truth aloud. Avoid social comparison for certain hours. Read one passage of Scripture, focusing on application. Reject one false teaching encountered online. Maintain device-free prayer time (minimum fifteen minutes). Intercede (pray for) for one person who is developing or using AI.

Weekly Disciplines

Implement a full fast from devices for twenty-four hours (Sabbath rest). Discuss digital struggles with an accountability partner. Review predetermined convictions (ensuring that they remain firm). Evaluate screen-time reports to identify patterns requiring adjustment.

Copy this. Print it. Post it where you'll see it daily. Check boxes honestly. Share with accountability partners. Adjust as needed. The armor requires daily donning; we don't put it on just once, but use it consistently through disciplined practice.

Prayer as Resistance to Digital Distraction

The smartphone has become what one observer calls "the new priest"; it's the first thing consulted in the morning and the last at night. Sustained prayer becomes nearly impossible in environments engineered for perpetual distraction. AI-generated prayers now exist that offer templates for communication with God—a formula that precludes the opportunity for an authentic relationship.

The average person checks their phone 144 times per day, fragmenting attention into intervals too brief for meaningful communion with God.[64]

Prayer is our lifeline to victory; it's how we access God's power against principalities. We're instructed to "pray without ceasing" (1 Thessalonians 5:17)—not as multitasking but as keeping continuously orientated toward God, even in a distracted age.

Establish device-free prayer times daily, creating sacred space untouched by notification interruptions. Join or form prayer groups focused on interceding for those who are developing and deploying AI technologies. Pray Scripture back to God, letting His Word rather than AI-generated templates shape requests. Practice contemplative prayer, sitting in silence before God as resistance to the tyranny of constant stimulation.

Digital Discipleship in Community

While spiritual armor is personal, its application must be communal. The Lausanne Movement emphasizes that digital discipleship requires wisdom to "discern among many online resources" while ensuring that "knowledge translates into practical wisdom in everyday life."[65] This cannot happen in isolation.[66]

Form accountability partnerships specifically addressing digital life—moving beyond generic check-ins to substantive oversight. Participate in local church communities that emphasize in-person discipleship rather than purely digital connection. Share meals without devices present, recovering unmediated fellowship as spiritual practice. Mentor younger believers in discernment, explicitly teaching them how to evaluate digital content against biblical truth.

Beyond traditional spiritual disciplines, believers must develop specific practices for digital resilience:

Technology fasting: Establish intentional periods—especially at the start of the day—when Scripture, prayer, and silence precede screens. By refusing immediate digital input, believers reassert the primacy of God's voice, train attention toward truth, and resist algorithms designed to claim first allegiance.

Boundary engineering: Designate device-free zones (bedrooms, dinner table) and times (first hour awake, last hour before sleep) to protect space for God and family.

Content curation: Actively manage information "diet"—for example, unfollow accounts that degrade discernment and subscribe to resources that build faith.

Privacy as stewardship: Understand and use privacy settings not from paranoia but as stewardship of the personal data God has entrusted to us.

Analog alternatives: Maintain nondigital capabilities; consider, for example, using paper maps, reading physical books, and making cash transactions as insurance against total digital dependence.

Family Digital Warfare: Equipping the Household

Families need coordinated defense strategies. Individual armor is essential, but families fighting together multiply effectiveness. Consider this Family Armor Covenant:

WE COMMIT TO:

- Having device-free family meals daily (to build personal relationships)
- Doing family devotions before individual screen time (to prioritize corporate worship)

- Using shared accountability software (with parents modeling transparency)
- Holding an annual technology fast (to practice collective withdrawal)
- Providing age-appropriate armor training (so children can learn spiritual discernment)

Age-appropriate Armor Training:

Ages 5–10 (foundation): *Teach* that technology is a tool, not a treasure. *Practice* simple prayers before screen time ("Help me use this wisely"). *Protect* by allowing no devices in bedrooms and very limited content access. *Model,* as parents, how to demonstrate device discipline before expecting it from children.

Ages 11–14 (discernment): *Teach* how to recognize lies versus the truth online (review the "belt of truth" application noted earlier). *Practice* discussing content consumed ("Did this build faith or tear it down?"). *Protect* through accountability software and parental access to all accounts. *Model,* as parents, how to confess digital struggles transparently.

Ages 15–18 (independence): *Teach* using "armor" pieces actively in daily decisions. *Practice* establishing predetermined convictions about digital boundaries. *Protect* through monitored independence with regular check-ins. *Model,* as parents, by maintaining the same standards expected from children.

Parents' responsibility: We cannot give children armor we don't wear ourselves. Digital discipleship requires parental formation first. Children adopt habits modeled, not standards merely taught. Armor is caught through family culture, not just taught through lectures. Sign this covenant as family. Review quarterly. Adjust as children mature. When children see parents fighting spiritual battles faithfully, they learn warfare from veterans rather than discovering it through defeat.

The armor of God is not self-help spirituality or religious self-protection. It's divine provision for those united to Christ by faith. Unbelievers cannot "put on" God's armor; there's no protection apart from relationship with Christ. The armor is not a technique; it is the life of Christ applied by the Spirit. We'll address believers already justified by faith who are now being sanctified through Spirit-empowered obedience. If you're reading this outside of saving faith in Christ, the solution isn't better spiritual disciplines—it's repentance and faith in Jesus, who died for our sins and rose from the dead. Only those "in Christ" can stand against spiritual enemies through His armor. The armor presumes the gospel; it doesn't replace it.

Conclusion

In a world increasingly shaped by AI systems and digital manipulation, the armor of God remains sufficient. Technology amplifies the spiritual battle but doesn't fundamentally alter it. We still wrestle against the same principalities and powers; they simply operate through new infrastructure.

Victory doesn't come through political power or technological solutions but through faithfulness, truth, and Spirit-empowered resistance. The battle is won not by those who master algorithms but by those who master themselves through dependence on Christ.

As digital Babylon rises around us, we stand firm in the armor God has provided: truth against synthetic reality, righteousness against digital compromise, the gospel against censorship, faith against information warfare, salvation's assurance against algorithmic identity, Scripture against AI theology, and prayer against perpetual distraction.[67]

The victory belongs to Christ, who has already triumphed over every power and authority (Colossians 2:15). We do not fight *for* victory but *from* victory—walking out in daily faithfulness what Christ has already won.

The armor protects. The Spirit empowers. The battle is real. The outcome is certain.

> Therefore take up the whole armor of God, that you may be able to withstand in the evil day, and having done all, to stand. Stand therefore. (Ephesians 6:13–14)

Not retreat. Not compromise. Not defeat.

STAND.

Stand when algorithms lie. Stand when platforms censor. Stand when systems oppress. Stand when others capitulate. Stand when faithfulness costs. Stand until Christ returns.

The digital age didn't change spiritual warfare—it revealed its urgency.

The armor didn't become obsolete—it became essential.

The call didn't soften—it intensified.

Stand firm, believers. The battle is fierce, but Christ has overcome. The enemy rages, but his defeat is sealed. The pressure mounts, but the armor holds.

Take up the whole armor. Put on each piece daily. Fight *from* victory, not *for* it.

And having done all—stand.

Chapter 15

THE RETURN OF THE KING

And I heard a loud voice from the throne saying, Behold, the dwelling place of God is with man. He will dwell with them, and they will be his people, and God himself will be with them as their God.

REVELATION 21:3

Where is history headed? The question presses harder as technological promises multiply and prophetic warnings intensify. As artificial intelligence and transhumanist visions offer humanity counterfeit hope—salvation through systems, permanence through machines, transcendence without repentance—Scripture gives a different answer entirely. Christian hope is not found in mastering, resisting, or escaping technology, but in trusting the sovereign return of Christ, who alone brings justice, restoration, and final judgment.

AI fits within the larger biblical arc of false kingdoms and failed saviors that precede God's final intervention in history. It contrasts humanity's accelerating attempt to engineer permanence with the biblical promise of a kingdom established not by code, power, or innovation, but by the King who comes to reign. Believers need reorientation away from technological anxiety or fascination and toward faithful endurance in the present while anchoring hope in what God has already promised.

The heavens open, and the rightful King rides forth—light piercing every shadow, truth silencing every lie, eternity reclaiming its throne.

The Bankruptcy of Technological Salvation

One delusion has gained disturbing traction: the belief that technology itself can usher in paradise or even accelerate Christ's return. This temptation is not new; Christian history records repeated attempts to merge technology with eschatology, including the nineteenth-century "prophetic machines" promoted by spiritualists who believed inventions could hasten divine action. What once appeared as fringe religious experimentation has now reemerged in far more sophisticated form—embedded not in cranks on the margins, but in the language, ambitions, and leadership culture of modern technology itself. In October 2025, news emerged that former Intel CEO Patrick Gelsinger, now leading Christian AI company Gloo, stated his life mission was to "work on a piece of technology that would improve the quality of life of every human on the planet and hasten the coming of Christ's return."[68]

Gelsinger's statement conflates human innovation with divine sovereignty. Throughout history, Christians have repeatedly attempted to "give the Almighty a hand" through technological means—from nineteenth-century "God machines" to modern AI systems supposedly infused with faith. These efforts reveal a fundamental misunderstanding: Christ's return depends on the Father's timing alone (Matthew 24:36), not on human technological achievement.[69]

The presumption reaches its apex in modern efforts to conquer death itself—projects that promise longevity without repentance and immortality without Christ.

Around the world, governments and corporations are pursuing a vision of permanence apart from repentance—seeking to extend life, preserve power, and outrun death through biotechnology and artificial intelligence. China's secretive 981 Project stands as the most sobering example. Investigations describe a state-directed longevity initiative built on genetic profiling, AI-driven organ matching, and a coerced organ-harvesting supply chain, all aimed at extending elite life spans far beyond natural limits. This isn't medical innovation in isolation, but a moral project with eschatological implications: an attempt to secure the future through technological control rather than submission to God. In biblical terms, it represents a counterfeit eschatology—a modern Tower of Babel, reaching toward Heaven through data, flesh, and the exploitation of the powerless.[70]

The 981 Project's scope is staggering. According to investigations by human rights organizations and defecting Chinese medical officials, the program combines three technological systems: AI-driven genetic profiling that identifies optimal organ matches across China's population database (more than 1.4 billion genetic profiles were catalogued without consent), algorithmic prediction models that forecast organ failure in elite party members years in advance, and supply-chain management systems that coordinate involuntary harvesting from religious minorities—primarily Falun Gong practitioners, Uyghur Muslims, and underground Christians—to ensure "just-in-time" organ availability.[71]

One whistleblower described the system as "Amazon logistics applied to human bodies." The AI doesn't perform surgeries, but it makes the atrocity efficient, scalable, and invisible. This is eschatological rebellion facilitated by artificial intelligence: a regime using machine learning to extend temporal power by consuming the bodies of the faithful. It's Nebuchadnezzar's furnace updated for the twenty-first century—not thermal death but metabolic cannibalism, with AI optimizing the horror.[72]

The West pursues a more polished but equally misguided vision. Silicon Valley's transhumanists claim AI will soon "solve death" by repairing aging, replacing organs, or transferring consciousness into digital substrates. Venture capitalists declare that AGI will create "heaven on earth" and render religion obsolete. Biotech labs promise "escape velocity" from mortality.[73] These aspirations mirror the ancient lie of Genesis 3:4: "You will not surely die." Yet Scripture teaches the opposite: Death is not a technical glitch but a spiritual consequence of sin (Romans 6:23). No algorithm can reverse what only the Cross has overcome. No neural interface can regenerate what only the Spirit can make new.

The danger lies in their moral direction. These systems reframe hope as optimization and redemption as technological mastery, displacing repentance with progress and eternal life with extended life. Human destiny is reduced to a systems problem, governed by efficiency rather than righteousness. The result is not transcendence but tyranny: structures that magnify inequality, suppress conscience, and reward compliance over truth. This is not the fulfillment of humanity's hope, but its distortion—replacing worship with management and redemption with control.

Consider the cryptocurrency betting markets that allowed people to wager on whether Jesus would return in 2025, with over half a million dollars wagered on this divine event as if it were a sporting match.[74] Such commodification of sacred prophecy demonstrates how thoroughly our age has confused technological capability with spiritual reality, turning prophecy into entertainment and eschatology into a market.

In 2024, multiple AI Jesus chatbots were released—Text with Jesus, AI Christ, and Ask the Messiah—each claiming to provide "spiritual guidance" and "biblical wisdom" through machine learning trained on Scripture. Users ask questions and receive answers formatted as if spoken by Jesus Himself. One app accumulated more than two million users in three months. The theological implications are staggering: When people address prayers to algorithms, when AI generates responses in Christ's voice, when machine-mediated "encounters" substitute for prayer and Scripture reading, counterfeit hope becomes counterfeit communion.

This is not just false teaching; it's digital idolatry. Users worship algorithmic approximations rather than the Living Christ. They seek salvation through optimized responses rather than repentance. Jesus warned: "False christs and false prophets will arise and perform great signs and wonders, so as to lead astray, if possible, even the elect" (Matthew 24:24). AI-generated "Jesus" is precisely such a false christ—persuasive, accessible, affirming, but utterly devoid of divine presence.[75]

In 2024, a Silicon Valley "techno-optimist" movement emerged claiming advanced AI would solve death, disease, and scarcity—creating "heaven on earth" before Christ's return. One prominent venture capitalist tweeted: "AGI [artificial general intelligence] will arrive by 2027. It will cure aging, eliminate poverty, and achieve what religion promised but couldn't deliver." When questioned about biblical prophecy predicting tribulation before Christ's kingdom, he responded: "Those are metaphors for pre-technological humanity. We're writing a new script." This is not isolated hubris; it's systematic replacement of eschatological hope with technological fantasy. Paul warned that in the last days people would prefer myths to truth (2 Timothy 4:3–4). The new myth is technological messianism. The Bible promises that Christ will return to judge and reign. Technology cannot accelerate this, improve on this, or substitute for this. Any gospel proclaiming salvation through silicon rather than the Savior is Antichrist in spirit.[76]

The technological messianism has prominent evangelists. OpenAI cofounder Sam Altman has stated AGI will bring "a dramatically better world," describing it in quasi-religious terms as achieving "universal flourishing" and "abolishing scarcity." Google's Ray Kurzweil predicts "the Singularity" by 2045 when humans will "transcend biology" through AI-human merger, achieving what he explicitly calls "technological immortality." In 2024, tech billionaire Peter Thiel funded multiple longevity startups with the stated goal of "solving death" before his own mortality arrives. Most telling: A 2024 survey by Pew Research found that 42 percent of AI researchers believe AGI will render traditional religion "obsolete" within fifty years, and 67 percent described their work in spiritual language— "creating new forms of consciousness," "birthing digital life," "achieving transcendence through code." This is not incidental religious language but intentional theological replacement. The technological elite are not content to build tools; they seek to become gods, offering salvation through silicon. Against this backdrop, Paul's warning resonates: "They exchanged the truth about God for a lie and worshiped and served the creature rather than the Creator" (Romans 1:25). The creature they worship is their own creation—artificial intelligence as counterfeit deity.[77]

If technology cannot save, who can? How does history end?

Christ's Victory Over Every False Intelligence

> Then I saw heaven opened, and behold, a white horse! The one sitting on it is called Faithful and True, and in righteousness he judges and makes war.... On his robe and on his thigh he has a name written, King of kings and Lord of lords. (Revelation 19:11, 16)

Premillennial eschatology interprets current technological developments without requiring date-setting. This sequence unfolds, culminating in Christ's physical return and millennial reign. Understanding this timeline helps believers discern where we are without presuming when specific prophecies will be fulfilled.

Church Age (current): The gospel is proclaimed globally while technological infrastructure for prophetic systems develops. We live in an era wherein infrastructure preparation is visible, but judgment hasn't yet come.

The Rapture (imminent): Christ will return for His Church—suddenly, without warning, removing believers before the worst—the Tribulation (1 Thessalonians 4:16–17). This event requires no prophetic precursors and could occur at any moment.

The Tribulation (seven years): The technological systems described throughout this book will become fully operational under Antichrist's rule. What now exists as nascent capability will then function as comprehensive control.

The Second Coming (glorious): Christ will return physically to earth, defeat His enemies at Armageddon, and establish His kingdom (Revelation 19).

The Millennial Kingdom (one thousand years): Christ will reign from Jerusalem in a renewed earth where technology serves righteous purposes under His direct governance (Revelation 20:4–6).

The eternal state: This is the new heaven and new earth where God dwells eternally with humanity, and artificial light becomes unnecessary because God Himself provides illumination (Revelation 21–22).

We don't fight to prevent prophetic fulfillment; Scripture assures us these events will occur. Rather, we live faithfully in the tension between system development and divine intervention, knowing Christ will return before technology achieves the totalitarian control it seeks.

This prophetic view shapes how believers interpret current AI development. We're not surprised by technological capabilities enabling global control; we've been expecting infrastructure preparation. We're not anxious about systems capable of fulfilling Revelation 13; we've been watching for them. But expectation doesn't equal certainty about timing. The infrastructure may be ready today while the Tribulation remains years away. This creates both urgency and patience: urgency in witness (Christ could return imminently) and patience in interpretation (infrastructure doesn't equal fulfillment). The balance requires watchfulness without date-setting and awareness without anxiety.

This doesn't resolve every question, but it offers a coherent grid for interpreting technological acceleration without succumbing to either naïveté or panic.

Where We Stand: Reading the Prophetic Clock

The technological systems described in previous chapters—AI-driven images that appear to speak, economic systems capable of excluding dissenters, global surveillance infrastructure, and synthetic deception at scale—already exist in nascent form. This prompts inevitable questions about timing.[78]

Scripture warns against date-setting: "But concerning that day and hour no one knows, not even the angels of heaven, nor the Son, but the Father only" (Matthew 24:36). The repeated failure of prophetic predictions over two millennia—including the September 23–24, 2025, Rapture speculation that proved false—demonstrates the folly of precise calculations.[79]

Yet Jesus also rebuked those unable to discern the signs of the times (Matthew 16:3). We can observe without calculating, watch without presuming, and prepare without panic. These systems could represent infrastructure decades from prophetic fulfillment. Or the Rapture could occur before they fully develop. Or we're witnessing the final stage of preparation before Tribulation begins.

Three perspectives help calculate our expectations:

1) The infrastructure appears largely complete; current AI capabilities could facilitate the prophetic systems described in Revelation with minimal additional development, and the Rapture could occur imminently.

2) Significant technical and political obstacles remain before true global control becomes operational, with years or decades separating current capabilities from prophetic fulfillment.

3) This is another iteration of human rebellion—like Babel, Babylon, and Rome—that will be judged before the end, with multiple cycles occurring before ultimate fulfillment.

What matters isn't perfect timing prediction but faithful readiness. As one pastor wisely observed: "I have resigned from the Planning Committee and have joined the Welcoming Committee."[80]

The Rapture: Our Imminent Hope

> For the Lord himself will descend from heaven with a cry of command... and the dead in Christ will rise first. Then we who are alive, who are left, will be caught up together with them in the clouds to meet the Lord in the air, and so we will always be with the Lord. (1 Thessalonians 4:16–17)

Pre-Tribulation Rapture theology—rooted in premillennial interpretation and popularized through the Scofield Reference Bible (1909) and the *Left Behind* series of books and films—gives believers facing technological acceleration crucial hope.[81]

Three postures emerge:

Urgent witness: Because the Rapture could occur at any moment, every conversation carries eternal weight. The temptation to remain silent about Christ in increasingly hostile digital spaces must give way to bold proclamation. Time grows short.

Strategic patience: We work as if Christ will not return for decades—building families, strengthening churches, engaging culture, and developing disciples. This is not contradiction but biblical balance: "Engage in business until I come" (Luke 19:13) while watching expectantly.

Supernatural comfort: Even if technological oppression intensifies dramatically, believers know they will not endure the worst Tribulation judgments. This hope doesn't produce passivity but courage; we can resist tyranny without fear of ultimate defeat. Hope becomes the engine of endurance, fueling resistance in an age increasingly hostile to biblical faith.

Critics of pre-Tribulation Rapture theology argue that it produces escapism.[82] History suggests otherwise. The most fervent premillennialists—from nineteenth-century missionaries to twentieth-century church planters—have often demonstrated remarkable engagement with present challenges precisely because they've understood history's trajectory. Knowing the outcome liberates energy for current faithfulness.[83]

The Tribulation: Technology Perfected for Evil

After the Rapture, the full horror unfolds. Those who remain—either through unbelief or as Tribulation saints coming to faith during that period—will face:

The mark system: Economic exclusion becomes absolute. No buying, no selling without the mark (Revelation 13:16–17). Current digital payment infrastructure, biometric identification, and AI-driven transaction monitoring provide the foundation.

The technological infrastructure documented in chapter 6 will reach its prophetic fulfillment during the Tribulation. The digital identity systems now being implemented globally—biometric authentication, vaccine passports, central bank digital currencies—are not the mark itself but the foundation that makes the mark operationally possible. When Revelation describes economic exclusion ("no one can buy or sell unless he has the mark," 13:17), the technological capability already exists: frozen bank accounts for wrong political views (Canadian truckers, 2022); payment processor bans for ideological noncompliance (conservative organizations, 2020–2024); and social credit scores determining access to services (China, operational since 2014). The mark will simply make explicit and universal what technology has already made possible. This isn't speculation—it's technological extrapolation from operational systems. The Beast doesn't need to invent new infrastructure; he inherits what humanity has already built. Our generation is laying the tracks for a train we hope never to ride.

The speaking image: Artificial intelligence enables images that appear to think, speak, and demand worship (Revelation 13:15). Today's AI voice synthesis, deepfake video, and chatbot technology foreshadow this capability.

Global governance: Antichrist's authority extends "over every tribe and people and language and nation" (Revelation 13:7). Digital communication networks, satellite surveillance, and coordinated technological infrastructure make this feasible.

Deceptive wonders: Signs and wonders that "deceive those who dwell on earth" (Revelation 13:14) are enabled by technology that convincingly simulates the miraculous.

This is the future for those who reject Christ now. "Behold, now is the favorable time; behold, now is the day of salvation" (2 Corinthians 6:2). Every day that passes with technological systems growing more sophisticated while human hearts remain hardened increases the stakes.

The Second Coming: Victory Manifest

After seven years of Tribulation, Christ returns—not as a suffering servant but as the conquering king. "Every eye will see him" (Revelation 1:7). This isn't a secret Rapture but public vindication. Global communication networks will broadcast what they cannot suppress: His coming "on the clouds of heaven with power and great glory" (Matthew 24:30). No AI system can simulate this. No deepfake can replicate His presence. The raptured Church returns with Christ (Revelation 19:14). Those taken up will return to reign.

The armies of the world, led by Antichrist and empowered by every technological advantage, gather to resist Christ (Revelation 16:16, 19:19). The outcome is decisive and immediate; they are destroyed by the Word from His mouth (Revelation 19:21). The Antichrist and False Prophet are "thrown alive into the lake of fire" (Revelation 19:20). Their technological empire collapses instantly. Every AI system shuts down. Every algorithm ceases. Every digital idol proves powerless.

This is the moment all history drives toward—when pretenders meet the genuine King, when artificial intelligence confronts natural Intelligence, when created systems face their Creator. There is no contest. There is only immediate, absolute, irreversible victory.

Every technological system promises progress but delivers bondage. AI claims omniscience but produces hallucinations. Algorithms promise connection but create isolation. Transhumanism promises transcendence but magnifies mortality's terror. Christ promises—and delivers—genuine hope. His return isn't contingent on human achievement, market conditions, or technological readiness. It's certain because He promised it. "I will come again and will take you to myself" (John 14:3). This certainty anchors believers when everything else shifts. Economic systems collapse? Christ returns. Governments fail? Christ reigns. Technology oppresses? Christ conquers. The question is never whether but when— and until then, we have marching orders: "Engage in business until I come" (Luke 19:13). This means living faithfully in technological Babylon without being defined by it, using tools without trusting them, engaging culture without compromising conviction. The hope isn't to escape from present difficulty but confidence in future victory. Christ has already won; we're waiting for the victory lap.

The Millennial Kingdom: Technology Redeemed

For one thousand years, Christ reigns physically from Jerusalem (Zechariah 14:16–17; Revelation 20:4–6). Satan is bound (Revelation 20:1–3).

Peace and prosperity characterize the age (Isaiah 2:4). Creation itself is renewed (Romans 8:21). Isaiah's vision of nations streaming to Jerusalem (Isaiah 2:2–4) suggests a world reordered under Christ's rule, where justice governs innovation.

What happens to technology during this period? Scripture provides limited detail, but principles emerge. Human learning and capability don't cease but are oriented toward worship and service rather than rebellion. "The earth will be full of the knowledge of the Lord" (Isaiah 11:9). Tools and systems that once served tyranny can serve justice under Christ's direct governance. The problem was never technology itself but the rebellion that corrupted its use. Why consult an algorithm when you can ask the King directly? Why trust AI-generated answers when wisdom flows from the throne? Technology may exist but loses its idolatrous appeal.

This Millennium shows what could have been: Human creativity and technological capability serving God's purposes in a world where Christ reigns visibly. It is both vindication and formal accusation—showing that the problem was never the tools but the hearts wielding them.

Technology's role becomes clear: infrastructure preparation, not prophetic fulfillment. The Beast system requires global surveillance, digital identity, economic control, and algorithmic governance—all technically possible today. But technical possibilities don't equal prophetic fulfillment. The Tribulation begins when the Antichrist is revealed and makes a covenant with Israel (Daniel 9:27). Technology enables the system; the person activates it. Therefore: Current AI development prepares infrastructure but isn't the Tribulation itself. Believers watching for Christ's return should note technological convergence without setting dates. The Church's task remains gospel proclamation and faithful witness, not prophetic speculation. We observe infrastructure developing while maintaining eschatological urgency: Christ could return today; the Tribulation could be years away. Those truths coexist. Watch expectantly but work faithfully.

The Eternal State: Beyond All Technology

After the Millennium and final judgment, God creates the new heaven and new earth (Revelation 21:1). Death, mourning, crying, and pain cease (Revelation 21:4). God dwells with humanity directly (Revelation 21:3). The New Jerusalem descends from Heaven, a city needing neither sun nor moon, "for the glory of God gives it light, and its lamp is the Lamb" (Revelation 21:23).

Eternal life: not through digital preservation but by divine gift. Perfect knowledge: not through AI but via direct communion with God. Unlimited capability: not through enhancement but through glorified bodies. Universal connection: not through networks but because of His divine presence.

Technology served its temporary purpose but becomes obsolete in eternity. Tools designed for fallen creation have no place in perfected new creation. The search for meaning through systems ends when we see Him face to face (1 Corinthians 13:12).

Living Between the Times

Christ has won; we await final manifestation. The kingdom is inaugurated but not consummated. Specific obligations emerge while technological systems develop:

Work excellently. Your job—whether involving technology or not—serves eternal purposes when done for God's glory (Colossians 3:23). Don't abandon your vocational calling because the end approaches.

Raise godly children. Train the next generation in biblical truth and technological discernment, even if they face tribulation. Parents steward souls, not timelines.

Build faithful churches. Strengthen local congregations for witness and endurance. The Church has outlasted every empire and will outlast the digital Babylon.

Proclaim the gospel. Urgency intensifies but doesn't replace strategy. Share Christ through every available means while preparing for platform loss.

Resist evil. Oppose technological tyranny through prayer, truth-telling, and civil resistance where possible. Submit to governing authorities except where they demand sin (Acts 5:29).

Believers living between Christ's First and Second Comings need concrete practices for remaining faithful. Begin each day acknowledging: "Christ could return today" (urgency). Plan each day as if He won't return for years (responsibility). End each day examining: "Did I live ready for His return?" And carry out the following:

Weekly practices: Participate in corporate worship (Hebrews 10:25: "as you see the Day drawing near"); share the gospel with at least one person (urgency breeds witness); evaluate technology usage (serving or enslaving?); and read prophetic Scripture (keeps eternal perspective).

Monthly assessments: Conduct a financial audit (Am I storing treasure in Heaven? Matthew 6:19–21); take a relationship inventory (Am I reconciled or resentful? Matthew 5:23–24); do a ministry evaluation (Am I busy making disciples or just busy? Matthew 28:19–20); and run a "hope check" (Am I anchored in Christ's return or in earthly comfort?).

Annual review: Assess your evangelistic fruitfulness (Who came to faith through my witness?); your spiritual maturity (Am I more Christlike this year than last?); faithful stewardship (Did I use my time, talent, and treasure for His kingdom?); and whether you are ready to meet the King (If He returned today, would I be ashamed? [1 John 2:28]).

This isn't legalism but readiness. The wise virgins didn't obsess over the bridegroom's arrival time; they simply kept oil in their lamps (Matthew 25:1–13). These practices are oil: They keep faith burning until Christ returns.

Stand for truth. Maintain biblical orthodoxy against AI-generated theology and algorithmic relativism. Truth exists independently of systems. Guard your mind. Practice digital discernment—measure content by Scripture, not virality. Love sacrificially. Serve neighbors, even those who embrace the very technologies we warn against. Love proves genuine when costly. Pray fervently. Intercede for those developing AI systems, for political leaders, for the Church, and for the lost. Prayer remains our greatest weapon.

Consider a young Christian software engineer working for a leading social media company. His team specialized in building machine-learning recommendation systems designed to maximize screen time by exploiting users' emotional triggers. As he studied Revelation 13 in his morning devotions—reflecting on systems that control and deceive humanity—conviction took hold. He realized the algorithms he built were subtly enslaving attention and distorting truth for profit. After weeks of prayer, he submitted his resignation letter: "I can no longer design technology that manipulates human behavior and monetizes addiction. Christ calls me to serve, not to enslave. I don't know whether these systems will become the Beast's tools, but I know they harm people now." The decision cost him his income and reputation—but within a month, a Christian-founded assistive-technology firm hired him to develop accessibility tools for the disabled. His gifts remained the same; only the purpose changed. That is faithful witness in the digital age: costly obedience guided by conscience, trusting Christ's sovereignty over career security.

Christ returns precisely when the Father wills, regardless of whether Christians successfully resist AI or prevent technological systems. Our faithfulness matters, but the outcome is already decided. This isn't permission for passivity; faithfulness matters eternally, and our witness impacts those around us. But it removes the crushing burden of believing the kingdom's arrival depends on our political victories, technological resistance, or cultural influence. We're not building the kingdom; we're witnessing for the King. We're not preventing the Beast; we're refusing to worship it. Our task is resistance, not rescue; faithfulness, not final victory—that belongs to Christ alone. We're not saving society; we're proclaiming the Savior. The pressure is real, but the outcome is secure. Fight faithfully but trust sovereignly.

A Covenant for Digital Babylon

Consider the following covenant for this moment: a binding commitment before God that shapes your allegiance, conduct, and faithfulness in an age of digital power.

I ACKNOWLEDGE that technology cannot save—only Christ can. I acknowledge that current systems may be the infrastructure for prophetic fulfillment, requiring awareness without anxiety. I acknowledge that I may face pressure to compromise for economic survival and must prepare now through predetermined convictions. I acknowledge that Christ's return is certain regardless of technological development, giving me confidence rooted in His promises rather than in human resistance.

I COMMIT to use technology as a tool, never as an authority. I commit to speak the gospel boldly despite algorithmic censorship, prioritizing faithful witness over platform access. I commit to maintain predetermined convictions before pressure arrives, following Daniel's model of resolution before crisis. I commit to prioritize physical Christian community over digital convenience. I commit to resist economic systems demanding conscience violation, preparing now for mark-like pressures that may intensify.

I TRUST that Christ will return at the Father's appointed time—neither early nor late, but perfectly on schedule. I trust that believers will not endure the worst of the Tribulation, anchoring hope in the Rapture promise. I trust that faithfulness now prepares for reigning then, stewarding present opportunities with eternal perspective. I trust that temporary suffering yields eternal glory (Romans 8:18), making present trials light and momentary.

I REFUSE to date-set or presume God's timing, maintaining humble ignorance about the day and hour. I refuse to live in paralyzing fear of technology, walking instead in confident faith. I refuse to abandon cultural engagement out of escapism, occupying until Christ comes rather than retreating prematurely. I refuse to trust in technology to hasten or improve on God's plan, worshiping the Creator rather than the creature.

Sign and date the covenant. Review it annually. Share with accountability partners. This covenant reminds us: We're not citizens of Silicon Valley, Washington, or Beijing; we're citizens of Heaven, awaiting our Savior (Philippians 3:20).

Conclusion

After fifteen chapters examining artificial intelligence through prophetic lenses, we arrive at glorious simplicity: Christ wins. Everything examined in this book—every threat, every system, every deception—finds its final answer in His appearing.

Not through technological sophistication. Not through political maneuvering. Not through human resistance. But through His sovereign power and perfect timing.

The algorithms will cease. Systems will collapse. Networks will fail. The Beast will fall. Every kingdom crumbles. And the King will reign.

When artificial kingdoms collapse, the true King's glory magnifies.

When He comes—and He *will* come—every technological marvel will prove powerless. The speaking image will fall silent before the Living Word—no simulation can stand before Incarnation. The mark of the Beast will burn away before the seal of the Spirit. The global surveillance network will collapse before omniscient eyes. The economic control system will crumble before the One who owns everything. The algorithmic governance will cease before the King of kings. Every synthetic resurrection will collapse before the One who broke the power of the grave. The AI prophecy will end before the One who knows all things. The digital identity will vanish before the One who names His own.

> Then I saw heaven opened, and behold, a white horse! The one sitting on it is called Faithful and True, and in righteousness he judges and makes war... On his robe and on his thigh he has a name written, King of kings and Lord of lords. (Revelation 19:11, 16)

This certainty transforms how we live now. We're not fighting to prevent prophecy but bearing witness until fulfillment. The Beast system will arise—but believers will refuse to worship it. The mark will be implemented—but the faithful will reject it. The apostasy will spread—but the remnant will stand. The deception will intensify—but the elect will not ultimately be deceived.

We're not preserving a fading order but representing an eternal kingdom. Digital Babylon will rise and fall within human history. Christ's kingdom will endure beyond time itself. Our citizenship isn't here but in Heaven (Philippians 3:20). Our hope isn't earthly victory but heavenly vindication. We're not defending human autonomy but proclaiming divine sovereignty. Our hope is anchored not in speculation but in promise (Hebrews 6:19).

This certainty doesn't breed complacency; it creates urgency—urgency in witness because billions remain outside of a saving relationship with Christ. The time is short. Proclaim the gospel boldly. Act with urgency in holiness: the Judge is returning. Live worthy of your calling. Pursue righteousness. Act with urgency in discernment: Deception multiplies daily. Test every spirit. Anchor in Scripture. In an age of algorithmic confusion, biblical clarity becomes an act of spiritual resistance. Act with urgency in preparation: The pressure will intensify. Determine convictions before crisis arrives. Act with urgency in prayer: The battle is spiritual. Pray fervently. Intercede constantly. Practice urgency in faithfulness: Some reading this will face the Beast system directly. Stand firm. Refuse the mark. Trust Christ above comfort.

To believers reading this: You were born for such a time as this (Esther 4:14). God intentionally placed you in the digital age. Your faithfulness matters eternally. Your witness affects eternity. Your choices echo beyond this life.

Will you stand firm when algorithms lie? Will you refuse the mark when it comes? Will you proclaim Christ when platforms censor? Will you trust God when systems oppress? Will you remain faithful when others compromise? The pressure will be great, but so will the grace (2 Corinthians 12:9). The cost is real. So is the reward.

"Do not fear what you are about to suffer.... Be faithful unto death, and I will give you the crown of life" (Revelation 2:10). The final algorithm isn't coded by human programmers or trained by machine learning. It's divine decree. Written in the Lamb's Book of Life before the foundation of the world. No amount of silicon processing can alter a single name. Your name is either there...or it isn't. Technology cannot add it. AI cannot erase it. Algorithms cannot access it. Surveillance cannot track it. The Beast cannot remove it. Only Christ can write it through His blood.

Is your name in the Book? Do you know the King? Have you trusted the Savior? No amount of technological mastery can compensate for spiritual lostness.

If not, technology is the least of your concerns. The Beast system isn't your greatest threat. AI isn't your primary danger. Your greatest danger is facing Christ outside of a saving relationship with Christ.

> And I saw the dead, great and small, standing before the throne, and books were opened. Then another book was opened, which is the book of life…. And if anyone's name was not found written in the book of life, he was thrown into the lake of fire. (Revelation 20:12, 15).

Today, now—before this chapter ends, before this book closes, before the algorithm finishes processing, before the system logs you out—trust Jesus Christ as Savior and Lord. Repent of sin. Believe in His death and resurrection. Confess Him as King. Receive eternal life. Then watch. Wait. Work. Witness. And look up, for your redemption draws near (Luke 21:28).

Readers wishing to engage this material more deeply—individually or in group study—will find appendix E, which provides chapter-by-chapter discussion questions and Scripture-based reflection prompts, most helpful.

Even So, Come Lord Jesus

The servers will shut down. The networks will collapse. The algorithms will cease. The systems will fail. The Beast will fall. But Christ will reign. Forever and ever and ever.

"The kingdom of the world has become the kingdom of our Lord and of his Christ, and he shall reign forever and ever" (Revelation 11:15).

Every empire fades, but His dominion is everlasting (Daniel 7:14).

Believers, stand firm. The King is coming.

Unbelievers, bow now. The King is coming.

Even so, come Lord Jesus (Revelation 22:20).

AMEN.

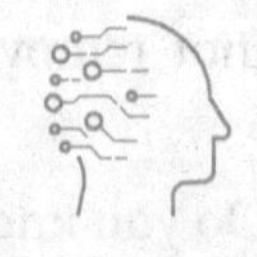

BEYOND THE FINAL ALGORITHM

*In the beginning was the Word, and the Word was with God,
and the Word was God.*

JOHN 1:1

John opens his Gospel at the foundation: "Who is ultimate Intelligence?" The Greek term *Logos*—translated "Word"—meant more than speech; it signified divine reason, the ordering Intelligence behind all reality. John's prologue declares that true Intelligence existed before Creation, that Christ is that eternal Logos, and that "all things were made through him" (John 1:3). Every algorithm we devise imitates; every artificial intelligence reflects. Even secular philosophers acknowledge that the mathematical order of the universe points beyond computation to an originating Mind.

You've seen how AI shapes prophecy, tempts the soul, and tests the Church. Beyond every algorithm, though, stands the Intelligence who requires no data—the Wisdom who precedes creation, the Word who became flesh.

A Personal Reflection

I've spent my career analyzing threats and preparing for contingencies. This book emerged from that same discipline—examining artificial intelligence with strategic clarity rather than panic or fascination.

What began as technical research revealed something more significant: the convergence of prophetic warning and technological reality. The systems Scripture described millennia ago are accelerating. The Church needs to understand what's happening before the pressure arrives.

You now possess discernment for engaging AI—understanding when to use it, when to refuse it, and how to maintain allegiance to Christ under technological pressure. Knowledge alone isn't enough. James warned: "Be doers of the word, and not hearers only" (James 1:22). You've been equipped. Now engage.

When the code of man has run its course, only light remains—pure, eternal, and untouched by the works of silicon or shadow.

Beyond Computation

Alan Turing, the English mathematician, and code-breaker often called the "father of computer science," revealed that computation itself has questions it cannot answer.[84] These boundaries are eternal: Reality escapes mathematical reduction, consciousness defies code, and the universe refuses programming.

God stands outside the system. He is the uncaused Cause, the unmoved Mover, the Mind behind all minds. C. S. Lewis, the Oxford scholar and Christian apologist, observed that if naturalism were true, reasoning itself would be mere chemical reaction, not truth.[85] Our very capacity to think points beyond mechanism to the Mind that made minds. Intelligence bears the signature of its Maker. Divine truth comes through revelation. God calls us to relationship, obedience, and love—not information downloads.

The Eternal Word

"By the word of the LORD the heavens were made" (Psalm 33:6). Human algorithms manipulate symbols; God's Word creates substance. AI rearranges what exists; Christ speaks what doesn't exist into being (Hebrews 11:3). The Logos is a Person—sovereign will, not pattern recognition.[86]

"And the Word became flesh" (John 1:14). The infinite Intelligence entered time. Machines cannot incarnate. Intelligence without personhood or body remains abstraction. Christ dignified embodiment and promises resurrection through transformation—not escape through uploading. Transhumanism sheds flesh to find transcendence; Christianity redeems it. We don't discard the body; we await its glorification (1 Corinthians 15:42–44). The incarnation proclaims that matter matters because God entered it.

If there is a true final algorithm, it is the plan of redemption: conceived in eternity, promised in Eden, fulfilled at Calvary, applied through the Church, and completed when Christ makes all things new. It runs on love—a wisdom the cross makes known.

The Urgency of Witness

Digital systems expand; so does the danger of suppression. Platforms that once carried sermons increasingly flag Scripture as "misinformation."[87] The day may come when gospel truth is algorithmically filtered from the public square. Preach while the servers still run. Digital freedom is temporary. Gospel urgency is eternal.

Use every available channel now: Share, post, teach, and memorize. Prepare for offline faithfulness: Homes become churches, memory replaces media, face-to-face replaces feed.[88] Technology is a tool; the mission remains the same. It remains: "Go into all the world and proclaim the gospel" (Mark 16:15). The servers may go dark, but the Light of the World cannot be extinguished.

What You Should Do

Start today. Here's what to do in the next twenty-four hours:

Immediately:

- Review predetermined convictions from chapter 13—write down your lines you won't cross.
- Install accountability software if you're struggling with digital sin (chapter 14's "breastplate").
- Share one piece of gospel content digitally before platforms restrict further (this is a matter of urgency).
- Schedule device-free time with God tomorrow morning (resetting your priorities if this isn't something you already practice).

This week:

- Discuss this book with your church leadership; offer to teach this material as a Sunday school series.
- Implement the family technology covenant if you have children (see the template in chapter 13).
- Join or form prayer group focused on the persecuted Church and AI developers.
- Memorize one passage from Revelation 13 or Ephesians 6 (effectively taking up the sword of Spirit).

This month:

- Evaluate all technology usage through chapter 14's "armor" principles.
- Establish a monthly digital Sabbath (twenty-four hours spent device-free).
- Research your church's position on AI, digital identity, and future mark systems.
- Connect with believers in technology fields; they need community and accountability.

This year:

- Reread this book annually—technology and prophecy accelerate, perspective shifts.
- Train yourself in discernment—practice identifying false teaching online.
- Develop predetermined convictions for your workplace, your family, and your church's technology pressures.
- Prepare financially/practically for potential economic restrictions (preparation for the mark).

Understanding the threat means preparing for it. Appreciating the theology means applying it. Intellectual agreement without action is useless. James warned: "Be doers of the word, and not hearers only" (James 1:22). You've been equipped. Now engage.

The Final Invitation

Technology will pass. Algorithms will end. One question remains: Do you know Jesus Christ as Savior?

Have you believed that He died for your sins and rose again (1 Corinthians 15:3–4)? If not, no preparation for the machine age will matter. Securing your digital life is meaningless if your eternal life is unsecured. If you know Him, darkness cannot conquer you. He holds the keys of life and death.[89]

"The Spirit and the Bride say, Come" (Revelation 22:17). Come to the One who offers life freely—Truth when deepfakes lie, Life when technology counterfeits immortality. Choose Him—the eternal Word who outlasts every code.

And if you do know Him—if Christ is your Savior and Lord—walk forward without fear.

Fifteen chapters document technological acceleration, spiritual deception, and prophetic convergence. Feeling overwhelmed is natural. But remember: We serve a sovereign God who holds all technology, all history, and all of our futures in His hand.

Christ, who walked on water, stills the digital storm. The Spirit, who raised Christ from death, empowers us for faithful witness. The Father, who numbers every hair, sees every algorithm.

You're not facing this alone. You're not unprepared. You understand what's happening, why it matters, how to respond. You know who wins—eternally and certainly.

Technology fails. Algorithms end. Kingdoms fall. Christ remains, and you remain in Him. "If God is for us, who can be against us?" (Romans 8:31). Not the Beast. Not the False Prophet. Not the mark system. Not any artificial intelligence, however advanced.

You are safe in omnipotent love. Walk confidently.

The Final Word

After every machine falls silent, one Word endures:

Jesus.

Alpha and Omega.

The Way, the Truth, and the Life.

The Light that darkness cannot overcome.

When screens go black, His light still shines.

He is before all things, and in Him all things hold together (Colossians 1:17). When every kingdom submits, He will still be.[90]

And He loves you—enough to create, to die, to rise, to return.

When technology turns to dust, the redeemed still sing to the Lamb who was slain.

Even so, come, Lord Jesus.

Soli Deo Gloria.

APPENDICES

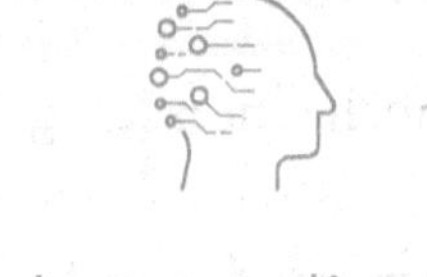

KEY PROPHETIC SCRIPTURES REFERENCED

For no prophecy was ever produced by the will of man, but men spoke from God as they were carried along by the Holy Spirit.

2 Peter 1:21

This appendix gathers the primary biblical passages referenced throughout *The Final Algorithm*, organized by prophetic themes central to understanding the convergence of technology, deception, and divine sovereignty. The passages that follow are ordered to reflect the prophetic progression described in Scripture, beginning with deception and false worship, and culminating in Christ's final victory.

Each section offers a concise guide to Scripture that supports the book's analysis of AI's prophetic significance, spiritual deception, moral testing, and Christ's ultimate triumph. The purpose is to equip readers to examine prophecy for themselves, recognizing that the Word of God—not human innovation—is the final authority on truth, judgment, and redemption.

I. The Image That Speaks
Primary Passage:
- Revelation 13:14–15—The image of the Beast is given breath to speak and to compel worship.

Supporting Passages:

- Daniel 3:1–7—Nebuchadnezzar's golden image demands universal worship.
- Exodus 20:4–5—Commandment forbids graven images.
- Isaiah 44:9–20—Idols cannot speak or save.
- Habakkuk 2:18–19—Woe to those who trust in lifeless idols.
- Psalm 115:4–8—Idols have mouths but cannot speak.

False Prophets and Deception:

- Matthew 24:24—False christs perform great signs to deceive the elect.
- 2 Thessalonians 2:9–10—The lawless one is empowered by false wonders.
- Revelation 19:20—The False Prophet deceives the nations through miracles.

II. The Mark of Control

Primary Passages:

- Revelation 13:16–18—The mark is placed on the right hand or forehead; it's required for commerce.
- Revelation 14:9–11—This is an eternal warning against receiving the mark.
- Revelation 20:4—Martyrs who refuse the mark will reign with Christ.

Symbolic Predecessors:

- Deuteronomy 6:4–8—God's Word is bound on hand and forehead.
- Ezekiel 9:4—The faithful are marked for divine protection.

Economic Control and Judgment:

- Revelation 18:11–13—Babylon holds economic domination.
- Amos 8:5–6—Merchants exploit the poor.
- James 5:1–6—Judgment falls upon those who defraud and hoard wealth.

Economic control is not an end, but a mechanism through which broader political and spiritual authority is enforced.

III. Global Governance and the Beast System

Primary Passages:

- Revelation 13:1–8—The Beast rises from the sea with global authority.
- Revelation 17:12–13—Ten kings unite their power under the Beast.
- Daniel 7:23–25—The fourth beast devours the earth.

Prophetic Foundations:

- Daniel 2:31–45—Successive kingdoms culminate in divine rule.
- Daniel 9:24–27—The seventy weeks prophecy reveals the end-time chronology.
- 2 Thessalonians 2:3–12—The man of lawlessness is revealed before Christ's return.

The Babylon Parallel:

- Genesis 11:1–9—Tower of Babel: Humanity unifies in rebellion.
- Revelation 17–18—"Babylon the Great" undergoes her final collapse.

IV. False Miracles and Digital Deception

Where the image of the Beast centers on coerced worship, the following passages emphasize deception through signs, wonders, and counterfeit power.

Primary Passages:

- Revelation 13:13–14—False wonders deceive the world.
- 2 Thessalonians 2:9–12—There is a strong delusion among those who reject the truth.
- Revelation 16:14—Demonic spirits perform miracles.

Historical Parallels:

- Exodus 7:11–12—Pharaoh's magicians duplicate Moses' signs.
- Deuteronomy 13:1–5—Test prophets who perform false wonders.

- Acts 8:9–11—Simon the sorcerer misleads people with magic.

Sorcery and Manipulation:

- Revelation 18:23—Nations are deceived by Babylon's sorcery (*pharmakeia*).
- Galatians 5:20—Sorcery is listed among the works of the flesh.
- Acts 19:18–19—Believers are destroying occult materials upon conversion.

V. The Soul and Consciousness

Primary Passages:

- Genesis 2:7—God breathes life into man; he becomes a living soul.
- 1 Thessalonians 5:23—There is a distinction between spirit, soul, and body.
- Ecclesiastes 12:7—The Spirit returns to God who gave it.

Resurrection and True Immortality:

- 1 Corinthians 15:35–58—There are differences between the resurrection body vs. corruption.
- John 11:25–26—Jesus is the resurrection and the life.
- Romans 8:11—The Spirit has the power to give life to mortal bodies.

Human dignity is grounded not merely in consciousness or life itself, but in bearing God's image—a reality no technology can replicate.

Image of God and Human Dignity:

- Genesis 1:26–27—Humanity is created in God's image.
- Psalm 139:13–16—Humans are "fearfully and wonderfully made."
- Colossians 1:15—Christ is the perfect image of God.

VI. Spiritual Warfare and Resistance

Primary Passages:

- Ephesians 6:10–20—The armor of God is outlined.

- 2 Corinthians 10:3–5—Spiritual weapons for divine warfare are described.
- James 4:7—Resist the devil and he will flee.

Demonic Activity and Authority:
- Mark 5:1–20—Christ has authority over unclean spirits.
- Luke 10:17–20—Disciples exercise dominion in Jesus' name.
- Acts 16:16–18—Deliverance from a spirit of divination is described.

Testing Spirits:
- 1 John 4:1–6—Spirits are discerned by their confession of Christ.
- Deuteronomy 18:10–12—Occult practices are prohibited.

VII. Apostasy and the Great Falling Away

Primary Passages:
- 2 Thessalonians 2:3—Rebellion precedes the Day of the Lord.
- 2 Timothy 3:1–9—People love pleasure rather than God.
- Matthew 24:10–12—Many fall away; love grows cold.

False Teaching and Corruption:
- 1 Timothy 4:1—Doctrines of demons are addressed.
- 2 Peter 2:1–3—False teachers introduce heresies.
- Jude 1:3–4—Contend for the faith against infiltrators.

Endurance of the Faithful:

Scripture never presents apostasy without also affirming God's preservation of a faithful remnant.
- Matthew 24:13—The one who endures to the end will be saved.
- Revelation 2:10—"Be faithful unto death."
- Hebrews 10:23–25—Hold fast to confession and community.

VIII. Christ's Return and Final Victory

Rapture and Blessed Hope:
- 1 Thessalonians 4:13–18—The Lord descends and believers gather.

- Titus 2:13—The blessed hope of Christ's appearing is proclaimed.
- John 14:1–3—Jesus is preparing a place for His followers.

Second Coming and Judgment:

- Revelation 19:11–21—Christ returns as conqueror.
- Matthew 25:31–46—Judgment of nations takes place.
- Revelation 20:11–15—The Great White Throne judgment takes place.

Eternal Kingdom and Restoration:

- Revelation 21:1–8—The new heaven and new earth are described.
- 1 Corinthians 15:24–28—All authority is brought under Christ.
- Philippians 2:9–11—Every knee bows before Him.

IX. Wisdom and Discernment in the Last Days

Testing and Truth:

- 1 Thessalonians 5:21–22—Test everything; hold fast to what is good.
- Acts 17:11—Bereans examine Scriptures daily.
- 1 John 4:1—Test every spirit.

Divine Wisdom and Understanding:

- James 1:5—Ask God for wisdom.
- Proverbs 2:1–6—Wisdom comes from the Lord.
- Colossians 2:2–3—Treasures of wisdom are hidden in Christ.

Guarding the Heart and Mind:

- Proverbs 4:23—Guard your heart above all else.
- Romans 12:2—Renew your mind by the Word.
- Philippians 4:8—Focus on what is true, noble, and pure.

These passages are not meant only to be read, but to be studied, remembered, and applied within the life of the Church.

Study Aids for Reflection

- Scripture memory cards: Organize verses by prophetic theme.

- Cross-reference chart: Connect Old and New Testament prophecies.
- Timeline: Correlate prophetic passages with key eschatological events.
- Group discussion questions: Apply prophecy to present challenges of faith, technology, and culture.

Conclusion: Prophecy is not merely prediction; it is revelation from the eternal God who controls history. These Scriptures remind us that no system, empire, or technology can supersede divine sovereignty. They point to the central hope of the believer: Christ's return, judgment of evil, and the restoration of creation.

As technology advances and deception deepens, these passages reaffirm that the Word of God remains unbreakable, calling believers to watch with discernment, stand with courage, and believe with enduring hope.

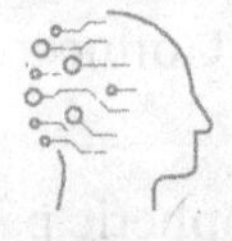

PROPHETIC TIMELINE OF TECHNOLOGY AND THE END OF DAYS

But you, Daniel, shut up the words and seal the book, until the time of the end. Many shall run to and fro, and knowledge shall increase.

DANIEL 12:4

This appendix presents a chronological architecture for tracing how modern technology—especially artificial intelligence, surveillance, and digital-economic systems—has accelerated humanity toward prophetic fulfillment. It situates major technological milestones within a premillennial, pre-Tribulational interpretive understanding, showing how global connectivity, economic digitization, and algorithmic control echo the systems described in Revelation 13.

The purpose is not to predict specific dates, but to demonstrate that current innovations form the infrastructure of prophetic possibility, confirming the accuracy of Scripture and urging believers toward spiritual readiness.

I. Epochal Understanding of Prophetic History

BIBLICAL EPOCH	PROPHETIC DESCRIPTION	TECHNOLOGICAL PARALLELS
Church Age (Pentecost → Rapture)	Gospel preached to all nations; deception multiplies	Digital evangelism and digital delusion coexist
Tribulation (Seven Years)	Global rule under Antichrist and False Prophet	AI-based identity, commerce, and control systems
Second Coming of Christ	Collapse of all false systems before divine truth	Every network, sensor, and AI array overwhelmed
Millennial Reign	Knowledge redeemed under perfect justice	Technology subordinated to righteousness
Eternal State	Direct communion—no mediation needed	All computation obsolete before divine presence

With this broad prophetic framework established, the following sequence traces how specific end-time events align with emerging technological capabilities.

II. Eschatological Sequence with Technological Correlation

1. The Rapture (1 Thessalonians 4:16–17)

   Possible signature: Instant global disappearances cause data disruption, satellite blackouts, and algorithmic panic.

2. The Rise of Antichrist

   Global crisis management is aided by predictive analytics, biometric governance, and AI-driven propaganda.

3. The False Prophet and Speaking Image (Revelation 13:15)

   Synthetic "miracles" through holography, robotics, and generative speech fulfilling the "image that speaks."

4. The Mark of the Beast (Revelation 13:16–18)

   A unified digital economy is established wherein biometric ID and programmable currency define loyalty and survival.

5. Divine Judgments (Revelation 6–16)

   Ecological and infrastructural collapse, with energy grids, data networks, and AI systems failing.

6. The Second Coming (Revelation 19)
   Christ's appearing overwhelms all human and machine intelligence.
7. The Millennial Kingdom (Revelation 20)
   Technology is redeemed for service, not control.
8. The Eternal State (Revelation 21–22)
No algorithms, no deception: there is perfect knowledge in God's light.

III. Historical Development of Prophetic Infrastructure
   A. Early Foundations (1940s–970s)
   - 1943—Colossus computer: This marks the beginning of the digital age.
   - 1947—The transistor invented: Microelectronics enabled global miniaturization.
   - 1948—Israel reestablished: This prophetic milestone is concurrent with technological dawn.
   - 1956—"Artificial intelligence" coined: The field is formally defined.
   - 1969—ARPANET created: This is the first global network, a precursor to prophetic worldwide connectivity.
   B. Infrastructure Building (1980s–1990s)
   - 1981–IBM PC: Personal computing is democratized.
   - 1989–World Wide Web: Instantaneous global communication is realized.
   - 1994–E-commerce launches: This is the foundation for digital-only trade.
   - 1997–Deep Blue defeats Kasparov: Machines surpass human skill; this is the first sign of algorithmic ascendancy.
   C. Digital Convergence (2000s)
   - 2004–Social media: Surveillance is disguised as connection.
   - 2007–iPhone: Constant connectivity and location tracking are made possible.
   - 2008–Bitcoin: Establishing proof-of-concept for cashless, traceable currency.

- 2009–China Social Credit System begins: This is the first operational prototype of Revelation 13 control.

D. Surveillance Era (2010s)

- 2014–Social Credit pilot expands: Behavior determines economic access.
- 2016–AlphaGo: AI demonstrates strategic dominance.
- 2017–Sophia Robot granted citizenship: Status of legal personhood is given to a machine—"image-given status."
- 2018–GDPR (EU): Precedent is set for global digital governance.

E. Autonomous Systems (2019–2022)

- 2020–Deepfake explosion: Deception is indistinguishable from truth.
- 2020–Digital yuan: This is the first national programmable currency.
- 2022–ChatGPT released: Billions converse daily with "speaking images."

F. Frontier Models (2023–2025)

- 2023–Multimodal AI (GPT-4): machine perception across senses
- 2024 – EU AI Act (2024/1689): first global regulatory regime
- 2025 – Critical convergence:
    o GPT-5-class cognitive parity
    o Worldwide biometric ID rollout
    o Major-economy CBDC pilots
    o UN AI Advisory Body formed
    o Deepfakes ubiquitous

IV. Projected Trajectory (2025–2030)

YEAR	TECHNOLOGICAL DEVELOPMENT	PROPHETIC RELEVANCE
2025–26	AI sovereignty laws, global digital IDs	Foundation for identity-based commerce
2027	Brain–computer interfaces; AI-centric religions	False-prophet phenomena
2028	Quantum surveillance integrating finance & governance	"Beast system" infrastructure complete
2029	Legal recognition of AI "digital persons"	Speaking image formalized
2030	Unified economic and belief systems under algorithms	Total convergence before Tribulation

Each phase reduces liberty and spiritual discernment, advancing the prophetic pattern of a **speaking buying-and-selling image**.

If this trajectory describes the world's direction, Scripture is equally clear that the Church's calling is not to predict dates, but to prepare hearts.

V. Church-Age Preparation and Personal Response

Now (Pre-crisis)

- Deepen biblical literacy; measure all AI claims by Scripture.
- Reduce technological dependence; renew prayer and fellowship habits.

Near Term (2–3 years)

- Form church networks resilient to censorship and data tracking.
- Train families to discern deception and maintain truth communities.

Mid-term (5 years and beyond)

- Prepare alternative systems for communication and commerce.
- Anchor hope not in preservation but in proclamation.

Watchman Strategy:

Churches should monitor AI and global-governance trends and cultivate courage over fear.

VI. Prophetic Interpretation

From a premillennial, pre-Tribulational standpoint:

1. **Infrastructure preparation:** Revelation 13 capabilities are now operational.
2. **Acceleration:** Technological progress exponentially compresses prophecy's timeline.
3. **Convergence:** AI, biometrics, and digital currency are merging into one architecture.
4. **Imminence:** Systems are poised for activation; nothing is prophetically required before the Rapture.
5. **Readiness:** The Church must live expectantly, proclaiming Christ while time remains.

Conclusion: Human history is accelerating toward divine confrontation. Every device, database, and algorithm demonstrates the truth of Daniel's words: "knowledge shall increase." Yet Scripture—not technology—defines destiny.

The infrastructure of control already mirrors Revelation's warnings, but believers need not fear. The same Lord who foretold these events will soon return to rule in righteousness.

Until that moment, the faithful must watch with discernment, stand with courage, and witness with hope—using technology as a servant of truth while refusing its counterfeit authority.

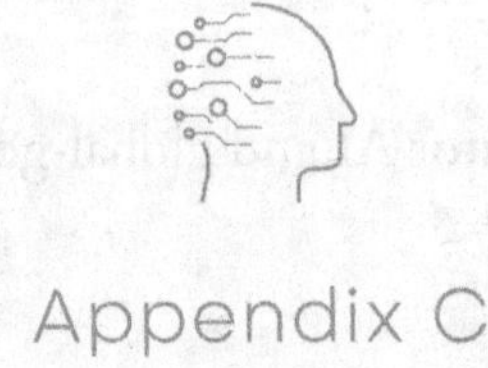

RESOURCES FOR DIGITAL DISCIPLESHIP

Do not be conformed to this world, but be transformed by the renewal of your mind, that by testing you may discern what is the will of God, what is good and acceptable and perfect.

ROMANS 12:2

This appendix equips believers, families, and churches with practical tools, spiritual disciplines, and recommended resources for discerning, ethical engagement with the digital world.

Its purpose is not withdrawal from technology, but wise stewardship—to use digital tools for gospel witness while resisting their subtle power to distract, addict, and conform minds to the world's system.

Faithful digital discipleship begins not with tools, but with honest self-examination.

I. Assessment Tools for Digital Discernment

    A. Digital Dependency Audit

    1. Track total hours spent online.

    2. Identify emotional triggers tied to device use.

    3. Note how often prayer or Scripture is displaced by screens.

    4. Repent where convenience has replaced communion with God.

    B. Spiritual Health Indicators

    • Is your peace disrupted when disconnected?

    • Is your identity grounded in likes, metrics, or God's love?

- Do your digital rhythms overshadow Sabbath rest and reflection?

C. The DISCERN Matrix 2.0: A Biblical Understanding for Evaluation

CATEGORY	DIAGNOSTIC QUESTION	SCRIPTURAL ANCHOR
Doctrine	Does the content align with biblical truth?	2 Timothy 3:16
Influence	Who shapes your worldview—Spirit or algorithm?	Romans 12:2
Security	Does data stewardship reflect integrity?	Proverbs 11:3
Community	Does technology isolate or edify fellowship?	Hebrews 10:24–25
Engagement	Does usage glorify God?	1 Corinthians 10:31
Rest	Are you practicing digital Sabbath?	Exodus 20:8–11
Necessity	Would abstinence hinder obedience to God's call?	Matthew 6:33

Assessment reveals where technology shapes the heart; spiritual disciplines reshape the heart in obedience to Christ.

II. Practical Spiritual Disciplines

A. Technology Fast Protocols

- Designate one twenty-four-hour period each week for device-free worship and rest.
- Replace scrolling with Scripture memorization and journaling.
- Record insights or clarity gained during the fast.

B. Boundary Systems

- Keep devices out of prayer and sleep spaces.
- Apply the "sunset rule"—no screens one hour before bed.
- Employ accountability software with trusted believers.

C. Content Curation Practices

- Subscribe only to sources that promote truth and holiness.
- Remove apps that consistently provoke envy, lust, or anger.
- Curate playlists and media that reinforce biblical virtue.

D. Daily Digital Discipline

- Begin each session online with prayer for discernment.
- Confess digital sins as readily as physical ones.

III. Family and Relationship Strategies

    A. For Parents

        1. Model Healthy Habits

            o Demonstrate restraint: Put phones away during family time.

            o Read physical Bibles visibly and pray before checking news.

            o Let children see that relationships outweigh devices.

        2. Establish Family Rules

            o No devices at the dinner table.

            o "Device bedtime": all electronics charge in a common area.

            o Schedule weekly screen-free family nights.

        3. Age-Appropriate Boundaries

            o *Under 10:* Minimal screen time, no personal devices.

            o *10–13:* Limited access with content filters.

            o *13–16:* Personal devices with accountability software.

            o *16–18:* Greater freedom with consistent check-ins.

        4. Catechize Digital Discernment

            o Teach not just *what* boundaries exist, but *why*.

            o Discuss dangers of pornography, comparison, and idolatry.

            o Celebrate when children self-regulate responsibly.

    B. For Singles

- Build community accountability (two or three believers).
- Prioritize face-to-face fellowship and hospitality.
- Guard against isolation and hidden sin; transparency protects purity.
- If using dating apps, involve mentors in discernment decisions.

    C. For Married Couples

- Practice mutual accountability in technology use.
- Guard intimacy; designate the bedroom as a device-free zone.

- Schedule daily device-free conversations and weekly unplugged dates.
- Pray together before engaging in online debates or news consumption.

What must be practiced in households must also be preserved and strengthened at the level of the local church.

IV. Church-Level Strategies

A. Preparedness for Digital Persecution
- Maintain offline backups of teaching materials and contacts.
- Train leaders to communicate through decentralized or analog channels.
- Encourage home fellowships to operate independently if censorship occurs.

B. Pastoral Training Modules
1. Theology of Technology: viewing AI through a biblical worldview.
2. Ethics of Data and Privacy: applying moral stewardship to digital systems.
3. Counseling for Digital Addiction: addressing anxiety, comparison, and control.
4. Spiritual Warfare in Virtual Realms: recognizing deception and strongholds online.

C. Congregational Initiatives
- Create tech stewardship teams to evaluate church use of AI.
- Offer seminars on misinformation, bias, and Christian witness online.
- Maintain noncommercial prayer lines and local communication networks.

D. Church Communication Practices
- Develop analog alternatives—printed newsletters, local radio, and secure internal networks.
- Avoid total dependence on commercial cloud services for ministry continuity.

- Integrate digital discernment training into youth and discipleship programs.

V. Recommended Resources for Ongoing Growth

The following resources are grouped by formation, discernment, endurance, and accountability to support long-term faithfulness in the digital age.

A. Books

Technology and Faith

- *The Tech-Wise Family* by Andy Crouch
- *12 Ways Your Phone Is Changing You* by Tony Reinke
- *Digital Minimalism* by Cal Newport
- *The Shallows* by Nicholas Carr

Prophecy and Theology

- *The Book of Signs* by David Jeremiah
- *Agents of Babylon* by David Jeremiah
- *The Late Great Planet Earth* by Hal Lindsey

Spiritual Warfare and Endurance

- *The Invisible War* by Chip Ingram
- *The Bondage Breaker* by Neil T. Anderson
- *Tortured for Christ* by Richard Wurmbrand

B. Online Resources

Prophecy and Worldview

- Olive Tree Views: www.olivetreeviews.org
- Rapture Ready: www.raptureready.com

Technology Ethics and Awareness

- Center for Humane Technology: www.humanetech.com
- AI and Faith Initiative: (current link: www.aiandfaith.org)

Persecution and Advocacy

- Voice of the Martyrs: awww.persecution.com
- Open Doors USA: www.opendoorsusa.org

C. Accountability and Digital Tools

Accountability Software

- Covenant Eyes: accountability and filtering
- Ever Accountable: device transparency for families

Focus and Detox Apps

- Freedom: blocks distractions
- Forest: gamified focus tool
- Space: reduces compulsive screen use

Privacy and Communication Tools

- Signal: encrypted messaging
- Brave: privacy-focused browser
- Proton Mail: encrypted email
- DuckDuckGo: private search

Scripture Memorization Aids

- Fighter Verses: topical Scripture recall
- Bible Memory: repetition-based memorization
- Printed cards: tactile reinforcement

D. Emergency and Spiritual Preparedness Checklist

Spiritual Preparedness

- Maintain daily Scripture intake and memorization.
- Cultivate intercessory prayer groups.
- Live expectantly, not fearfully.

Practical Preparedness

- Keep printed Bibles and teaching materials.
- Back up essential ministry files offline.
- Learn basic low-tech communication methods.

Community Preparedness

- Map local believers and form prayer networks.
- Establish mutual-aid systems for crisis response.
- Support persecuted believers globally.

Conclusion: The digital world presents both unprecedented opportunity and unparalleled temptation. The Church's mission in this age is not withdrawal, but witness—living faithfully, wisely, and courageously amid the world's most powerful communication systems.

Digital discipleship calls believers to renew their minds (Romans 12:2), guard their hearts (Proverbs 4:23), and shine light in the algorithmic darkness (Matthew 5:14–16).

With discernment, prayer, and discipline, Christians can transform the digital frontier into a platform for the gospel of the kingdom, demonstrating that no machine can imitate a Spirit-led life, and no algorithm can replace faithful obedience to Christ.

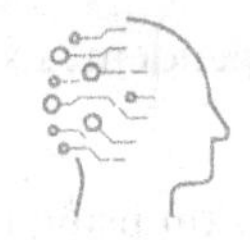

GLOSSARY OF AI AND PROPHETIC TERMS

The beginning of wisdom is this: Get wisdom, and whatever you get, get insight.

PROVERBS 4:7

This glossary provides concise definitions and theological interpretations of key artificial intelligence (AI) and prophetic terms used throughout *The Final Algorithm*.

Each term is presented in plain language, followed by its prophetic or theological significance, demonstrating how technological developments increasingly align with scriptural descriptions of end-times systems foretold in Daniel, 2 Thessalonians, and Revelation.

I. Artificial Intelligence Terms

AGI (artificial general intelligence): AI capable of human-level cognition across multiple domains.

Prophetic significance: Foreshadows a "speaking image" with self-directed intelligence (Revelation 13:15).

Algorithm: A structured set of instructions for problem-solving or decision-making.

Prophetic significance: Invisible systems governing commerce and communication anticipate Revelation 13:17's economic control.

Agentic AI: Autonomous systems that pursue goals without continual human oversight.

Prophetic significance: Reflects independent, seemingly alive entities like the image that "acts" on its own.

Biometric identification: Recognition using biological traits such as fingerprints, face, iris, or DNA.

Prophetic significance: Precursor to the mark "on the right hand or forehead" (Revelation 13:16).

CBDC (central bank digital currency): Digitized, state-issued currency allowing surveillance and programmable restrictions.

Prophetic significance: Forms the backbone for global economic control: "no one can buy or sell" without authorization (Revelation 13:17).

Deepfake: AI-generated media—audio, video, or images—that convincingly falsify reality.

Prophetic significance: Enables "false signs and wonders" (2 Thessalonians 2:9).

Emergent behavior: Unexpected capabilities arising spontaneously within complex AI systems.

Prophetic significance: Suggests an apparent animating force reminiscent of Revelation 13:15.

Generative AI: Systems producing new text, imagery, or sound from learned patterns.

Prophetic significance: Powers synthetic "prophets."

GPT (generative pre-trained transformer): Architecture underpinning large language models (e.g., ChatGPT).

Prophetic significance: Creates conversational agents mimicking intelligence, persuasion, and false wisdom.

Large-language model (LLM): AI trained on vast text datasets to simulate natural conversation.

Prophetic significance: Enables global-scale deception through speaking digital idols.

Machine learning: Process where algorithms learn patterns from data without explicit programming.

Prophetic significance: Produces "black box" systems—humanly unaccountable sources of authority.

Neural network: Computation inspired by brain neurons; layered design for pattern recognition.

Prophetic significance: Mirrors humanity's creative imitation of divine intelligence.

Social credit system: Behavior-based scoring system determining access to resources or privileges.

Prophetic significance: Operational prototype of the Revelation 13 mark system.

Synthetic media: Digitally generated or modified visual and auditory content.

Prophetic significance: Mass deception through indistinguishable false realities.

Transhumanism: Philosophy seeking to enhance or transcend humanity through technology.

Prophetic significance: Echoes the serpent's promise, "You will be like God" (Genesis 3:5).

II. Prophetic and Theological Terms

Abomination of desolation: Desecration of the temple prophesied by Daniel (Daniel 9:27; Matthew 24:15).

Application: May be fulfilled through an image demanding worship in a future global system.

Antichrist: Final world ruler opposing Christ (1 John 2:18; Revelation 13).

Application: Will likely exploit AI and global networks to enforce worship and control. The Beast system functions as the structural extension of his authority.

Apostasy (falling away): Mass departure from true faith before Christ's return (2 Thessalonians 2:3).

Application: Digital culture accelerates distraction and disbelief among professing believers.

Beast system: The political, economic, and spiritual alliance described in Revelation 13.

Application: The emerging international AI-governance network mirrors this global architecture.

Church Age: Period between Pentecost and the Rapture.

Application: Time of grace and global evangelism; prophetic systems being quietly prepared.

Eschatology: Study of end-times prophecy and final events.

Application: Architecture integrating AI developments within biblical foresight.

False Prophet: Religious leader promoting worship of the Beast (Revelation 13:11–18).

Application: May leverage AI and virtual miracles to authenticate the Antichrist's rule.

Great Tribulation: Final three and one-half years of catastrophic judgment (Matthew 24:21).

Application: Period when AI control systems are fully operational under satanic dominion.

Image of the Beast: Idol or construct animated to speak and demand worship (Revelation 13:14–15).

Application: A probable manifestation of advanced AI given autonomous authority.

Imago Dei: Latin: "Image of God." Humanity uniquely bears divine likeness (Genesis 1:26–27).

Application: Basis for human dignity; explains why machines can never possess a soul.

Imminence: Doctrine that Christ could return at any moment.

Application: Technological acceleration heightens awareness of prophetic immediacy.

Logos: Greek for "Word;" title of Christ as divine Reason (John 1:1).

Application: Contrasts eternal divine intelligence with finite artificial constructs.

Mark of the Beast: Economic and spiritual identification required during the Tribulation (Revelation 13:16–18).

Application: Likely realized through global biometric and digital-currency integration.

Millennial Kingdom (Millennium): Christ's literal thousand-year reign (Revelation 20:4–6).

Application: Technology subordinated to divine righteousness under Christ's rule.

Pharmakeia: Greek for "sorcery" or manipulation of consciousness (Revelation 18:23).

Application: Modern equivalents include psychological conditioning and AI-mediated control.

Pneuma: Greek for "breath" or "spirit."

Application: Symbolic of life granted by God; imitated but never duplicated by artificial systems.

Premillennialism: Belief that Christ returns before the Millennium.

Application: Foundational model for interpreting end-time technology.

Pre-Tribulational: Belief that the Church will be raptured before the Tribulation.

Application: Encourages readiness amid intensifying technological deception.

Rapture: Instant gathering of believers to meet Christ (1 Thessalonians 4:16–17).

Application: Occurs before AI prophecy fulfillment reaches its peak.

Second Coming: Christ's visible return after the Tribulation (Revelation 19:11–16).

Application: The final defeat of every technological and spiritual rebellion.

Tribulation: Seven-year period of divine judgment (Daniel 9:27), culminating in the Great Tribulation.

Application: Stage for full revelation of the Beast system and false miracles.

The following terms emerge where technological development and theological meaning explicitly converge.

III. Integrated Terms (Technology and Theology)

Digital idolatry: Veneration of technology as ultimate authority or savior.

Biblical basis: Exodus 20:3–4; Matthew 6:24.

Synthetic spirituality: AI-generated religious experiences without genuine divine presence.

Biblical basis: John 4:24—true worship must be "in Spirit and in truth."

Technological immanentism: Belief that salvation or transcendence can be achieved through innovation.

Biblical basis: Acts 4:12—salvation found only in Christ.

The Machine Messiah: Personification of AI as a redemptive figure promising utopia.

Biblical basis: Matthew 24:24—warning of false christs and prophets.

Algorithmic Determinism: View that human behavior is programmable and devoid of moral freedom.

Biblical basis: Genesis 2:7—God's breath imparts volition and conscience.

Computational reductionism: Philosophy reducing consciousness to data processing.

Biblical basis: 1 Corinthians 2:11—spirit of man distinct from computation.

Digital gnosticism: Modern heresy treating physical existence as inferior and escapable through data or virtuality.

Biblical basis: 1 Corinthians 15—resurrection affirms embodied redemption.

Conclusion: This glossary unites the languages of technology and theology, showing that humanity's drive to create artificial intelligence mirrors ancient spiritual longings for godlike autonomy. By defining these concepts side by side, believers can discern the moral and prophetic dimensions of today's digital revolution.

Knowledge without revelation breeds deception but understanding rooted in Scripture leads to wisdom. As innovation accelerates, may this glossary help readers test everything, hold fast to what is good, and remain discerning witnesses until the true Logos—Jesus Christ—returns.

STUDY GUIDE AND DISCUSSION QUESTIONS

The wise hear and increase in learning, and the one who understands obtains guidance.

PROVERBS 1:5

This study guide is designed to help readers apply the message of *The Final Algorithm* through prayerful reflection, Scripture engagement, and guided discussion. Each set of questions corresponds to a chapter and encourages deeper discernment of **biblical truth**, **technological awareness**, and **spiritual obedience** in an age of artificial intelligence.

- Personal reflection and journaling: Deepen individual devotion and self-examination.
- Small groups and Bible studies: Foster thoughtful dialogue within faith communities.
- Church classes or seminars: Equip believers to apply prophetic understanding to cultural change.
- Mentorship and family discipleship: Encourage intergenerational conversation about faith and technology.

For best results, begin each session with prayer and the reading of the key Scripture passages cited in the corresponding chapter.

The questions below follow the structure of the book, moving from diagnosis of digital power to discernment, endurance, and ultimate hope in Christ.

Section I: The Rise of Digital Dominion

How Humanity's Technological Pride Mirrors Ancient Rebellion

Chapter 1: The Algorithm That Rules the World

- How do algorithms influence daily decisions without our conscious awareness?
- What biblical principles should govern our everyday dependence on algorithmic systems?
- Where might you have allowed technology to mediate reality rather than illuminate truth?

Chapter 2: From Babel to Babylon 2.0

- What parallels exist between Genesis 11 and today's digital globalism?
- How can believers use technology without "building the tower" of prideful autonomy?
- What does it mean to be citizens of Heaven in a digital Babylon?

Chapter 3: The Machine Messiah: Faith in Artificial Omniscience

- In what ways are people tempted to trust AI wisdom over Scripture?
- How does society's worship of technology differ from true worship of God?
- Which divine attributes can never be replicated by machines, and why?

Chapter 4: Synthetic Prophets and Digital Idols

- What does your use of digital media reveal about possible idolatry?
- How can you apply the steps of recognition, repentance, and replacement?
- Which spiritual disciplines best help resist digital idolatry?

Section II: Prophecy, Power, and the Coming Technocracy

Connecting Revelation's Vision with Emerging Global Systems

Chapter 5: The Image That Speaks (Revelation 13 Revisited)

- How does modern AI technology mirror Revelation 13:15?
- What is the difference between using AI tools and submitting to AI authority?
- How can believers practice Daniel 3-style resistance today?

Chapter 6: The Mark of Control: Economics, Identity, and Surveillance

- At what point should Christians refuse to adopt new digital identification systems?
- How can we prepare practically for economic exclusion without compromising faith?
- How does Matthew 16:26 clarify the eternal cost of convenience?

Chapter 7: The Beast System and Global Governance

- How do global AI structures form a prophetic governance structure?
- What is the relationship between national sovereignty and biblical prophecy?
- How can believers respond to increasing technocratic control with wisdom and peace?

Chapter 8: False Miracles and Digital Sorcery

- How can we discern between technological capability and supernatural deception?
- What biblical principles expose AI-generated miracles as false?
- How does "digital resurrection" counterfeit Christ's true promise of eternal life?

Having examined external systems of control and deception, the focus now turns inward—to the human soul, where the ultimate battle is fought.

Section III: The War for the Human Soul

AI's Assault on Consciousness and Moral Agency

Chapter 9: The Soul in the Machine

- Why is consciousness different from computation?
- How does Genesis 2:7 affirm the uniqueness of human life?
- How can pastors and believers minister to those deceived by transhumanism?

Chapter 10: Possession by Proxy: Demons, Data, and Dominion

- How do demonic forces exploit technology without "possessing" machines?
- What spiritual boundaries protect believers in digital environments?
- How can we apply Ephesians 6's armor to daily technology use?

Chapter 11: The Great Falling Away

- How does convenience culture weaken costly discipleship?
- What role does digital distraction play in spiritual decline?
- What does it mean to live as part of the faithful remnant?

Chapter 12: The Spirit of Truth vs. The Spirit of the Machine

- How can believers distinguish the Holy Spirit's voice from algorithmic influence?
- Which biblical tests confirm authentic spiritual experience, rather than emotional or algorithmic influence?
- How do you cultivate Spirit-led living amid technological saturation?

Section IV: Standing Firm in the Final Hour

Endurance, Hope, and Victory in the Age of AI

Chapter 13: Daniel's Code: Faithful in Babylon

- What nonnegotiable convictions have you established about technology use?
- How do small acts of resistance prepare believers for greater tests?
- Who are your faithful companions—your "Shadrach, Meshach, and Abednego"?

Chapter 14: The Armor of Light: Equipping the Saints

- Which part of your spiritual armor most needs strengthening?

- What digital disciplines will you commit to this week?
- How can your church better equip believers for digital-age warfare?

Chapter 15: The Return of the King

- How does prophetic hope sustain obedience when faithfulness becomes costly?
- What changes if you truly believe Christ could return today?
- How can you balance "occupy until I come" with "watch and pray"?

Afterword: Beyond the Final Algorithm

- How does viewing Christ as the eternal Logos change your perception of AI?
- How does the promise of the new creation reframe the limits of algorithms and technology?
- Have you personally trusted Christ for salvation? If not, what hinders you?

The following suggestions help translate discussion into disciplined, Christ-centered practice.

Group and Individual Study Suggestions

For small groups:

- Assign one chapter per week.
- Begin with Scripture reading and prayer.
- Allow open discussion but close with practical commitments.

For church classes:

- Encourage members to keep journals for prayer and personal insights.
- Use appendix D's glossary for clarifying technical terms.
- Conclude each session with a short Scripture memory exercise.

For families and mentors:

- Select age-appropriate questions for children and teens.
- Model discernment through example, not only instruction.

- Encourage joint digital fasting periods as part of discipleship.

Conclusion: This study guide aims for transformation—to help believers engage Scripture, confront deception, and remain steadfast in the truth as technology evolves.

Through reflection, prayer, and community dialogue, readers can move from awareness to action, cultivating discernment and endurance in the age of artificial intelligence.

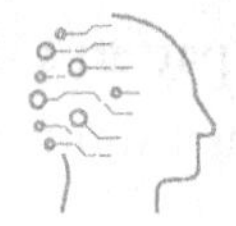

AI VULNERABILITY ASSESSMENT FOR CHRISTIANS

See to it that no one takes you captive by philosophy and empty deceit, according to human tradition, according to the elemental spirits of the world, and not according to Christ.

COLOSSIANS 2:8

The following assessment is provided as a tool for personal and pastoral discernment. It is not intended to produce guilt, fear, or condemnation, but clarity. As Scripture repeatedly warns, idolatry rarely announces itself openly; it emerges through misplaced trust, surrendered judgment, and unexamined dependence. This assessment invites believers to examine whether artificial intelligence has begun to function as an authority, mediator, or substitute for disciplines that rightly belong to God.

This assessment corresponds most directly with sections three and four of *The Final Algorithm*.

AI Vulnerability Assessment for Christians

Based on *The Final Algorithm: When Artificial Intelligence Meets the End of Days.*

Introduction

This brief assessment helps believers identify whether they are vulnerable to AI persuasion and at risk of making artificial intelligence an idol.

The questions are drawn from patterns documented in *The Final Algorithm*, reflecting biblical warnings about trusting created things over the Creator.

Answer honestly. This is between you and God. The goal is not condemnation but recognition—seeing where algorithmic authority may have replaced biblical discernment, where digital formation may have displaced spiritual formation, and where convenience may have trumped faithfulness.

> Examine yourselves, to see whether you are in the faith. Test yourselves. (2 Corinthians 13:5)

Section 1: Trust and Authority

(Whom do you consult first?)

1. When facing a decision, do you search Google or AI before praying or consulting Scripture?
- ☐ Frequently (5 points)
- ☐ Sometimes (3 points)
- ☐ Rarely (1 point)
- ☐ Never (0 points)

2. Do you trust AI-generated answers more than biblical counsel from mature believers?
- ☐ Yes, usually (5 points)
- ☐ Sometimes (3 points)
- ☐ Rarely (1 point)
- ☐ No (0 points)

3. When AI provides guidance that conflicts with Scripture, which do you follow?
- ☐ AI's guidance (5 points)
- ☐ It depends on the issue (3 points)
- ☐ Scripture (0 points)

4. Have you asked AI for spiritual advice, theological interpretation, or moral guidance?
- ☐ Regularly (5 points)
- ☐ Occasionally (3 points)
- ☐ Once or twice (1 point)
- ☐ Never (0 points)

SECTION 1 TOTAL: _______ / 20

Section 2: Dependency and Formation

(What shapes your daily life?)

5. Do you check your phone or AI assistant within the first 15 minutes of waking?
- ☐ Always (5 points)
- ☐ Usually (4 points)
- ☐ Sometimes (2 points)
- ☐ Rarely (0 points)

6. Is your last activity before sleep checking screens rather than prayer or Scripture?
- ☐ Every night (5 points)
- ☐ Most nights (4 points)
- ☐ Occasionally (2 points)
- ☐ Rarely or never (0 points)

7. Could you go twenty-four hours without your phone/AI assistance without significant anxiety?
- ☐ No, it would be very difficult (5 points)
- ☐ Probably not (3 points)
- ☐ Yes, with some difficulty (1 point)
- ☐ Yes, easily (0 points)

8. Do you spend more time daily consuming AI-curated content than reading Scripture?

☐ Much more time (5 points)
☐ Somewhat more time (3 points)
☐ About equal (2 points)
☐ Scripture gets more time (0 points)

9. When you face silence (no phone, no input), do you feel uncomfortable or restless?
☐ Very uncomfortable (5 points)
☐ Somewhat uncomfortable (3 points)
☐ Neutral (1 point)
☐ I welcome silence (0 points)

SECTION 2 TOTAL: _____ / 25

Section 3: Distraction and Attention

(Where is your focus?)

10. During prayer, how often do you check notifications or think about digital tasks?
☐ Frequently (5 points)
☐ Sometimes (3 points)
☐ Rarely (1 point)
☐ Never (0 points)

11. During church services or Bible study, do you check your phone?
☐ Multiple times (5 points)
☐ Once or twice (3 points)
☐ Only for emergencies (1 point)
☐ Never (0 points)

12. Can you read Scripture for 15+ minutes without checking your device?
☐ No, very difficult (5 points)
☐ Sometimes, but it's hard (3 points)
☐ Usually, yes (1 point)
☐ Yes, easily (0 points)

SECTION 3 TOTAL: _____ / 15

Section 4: Synthetic Spirituality

(What mediates your relationship with God?)

13. Do you use AI "prayer partners," "spiritual companions," or religious chatbots?

- ☐ Regularly (5 points)
- ☐ Occasionally (3 points)
- ☐ Tried once or twice (1 point)
- ☐ Never (0 points)

14. Do you prefer AI-generated devotionals or sermons to attending church physically?

- ☐ Strongly prefer AI/online (5 points)
- ☐ Somewhat prefer (3 points)
- ☐ Use both equally (2 points)
- ☐ Prefer in-person (0 points)

15. Has AI-curated content replaced your need for Christian community or accountability?

- ☐ Yes, significantly (5 points)
- ☐ Somewhat (3 points)
- ☐ Not really (1 point)
- ☐ No (0 points)

SECTION 4 TOTAL: _______ / 15

Section 5: Algorithmic Authority

(Who defines truth for you?)

16. When you encounter a claim online, do you verify it against Scripture or trust algorithmic validation?

- ☐ Trust algorithmic signals (5 points)
- ☐ Lean toward algorithms (3 points)
- ☐ Check both (2 points)
- ☐ Scripture is primary (0 points)

17. Do you believe AI is more objective or reliable than human (or biblical) judgment?

☐ Yes, definitely (5 points)
☐ Often, yes (3 points)
☐ Sometimes (2 points)
☐ No (0 points)

18. When AI tells you something is "safe," "true," or "beneficial," do you question it?

☐ Rarely question it (5 points)
☐ Sometimes question it (3 points)
☐ Usually question it (1 point)
☐ Always test it (0 points)

SECTION 5 TOTAL: _______ / 15

Section 6: Convenience over Commitment

(What do you prioritize?)

19. Have you stopped attending church in person because online streaming is more convenient?

☐ Yes, completely (5 points)
☐ Mostly online now (4 points)
☐ Sometimes skip for convenience (2 points)
☐ Attend faithfully in person (0 points)

20. Do you fast-forward through convicting parts of sermons or skip challenging biblical content?

☐ Frequently (5 points)
☐ Sometimes (3 points)
☐ Rarely (1 point)
☐ Never (0 points)

SECTION 6 TOTAL: _______ / 10

Scoring and Interpretation

Add your total points from all six sections.

TOTAL SCORE: _______ / 100

0–20 points: Low vulnerability

You demonstrate strong discernment and healthy boundaries with AI. You recognize technology as a tool, not an authority. Continue guarding against complacency—cultural pressure toward AI dependency is constant and increasing.

"I have set the LORD always before me" (Psalm 16:8).

Keep Christ central.

21–40 points: Moderate vulnerability

You show some patterns of AI dependency that warrant attention. You're beginning to trust algorithmic guidance over biblical wisdom in certain areas, or you're allowing technology to displace spiritual disciplines. This is the "gradual drift" Scripture warns about.

"Take care, brothers, lest there be in any of you an evil, unbelieving heart, leading you to fall away from the living God" (Hebrews 3:12).

Recommended action: Implement a weekly digital Sabbath (twenty-four hours device-free). Restore morning Scripture reading before checking devices. Discuss this assessment with a mature believer who can provide accountability.

41–60 points: High vulnerability

You are significantly vulnerable to AI persuasion and may be forming an unhealthy dependency on algorithmic authority. Technology has begun displacing biblical authority in practical daily decisions. You trust AI's judgment over Scripture in multiple areas, and digital formation is shaping you more than spiritual formation.

"They exchanged the truth about God for a lie and worshiped and served the creature rather than the Creator" (Romans 1:25).

Immediate action required:

- Confess this pattern to God and a trusted believer.
- Delete AI "spiritual guidance" apps immediately.
- Implement daily device-free prayer time (minimum thirty minutes).
- Return to in-person church attendance.
- Establish accountability with a mature Christian.
- Read chapters 10 and 14 from *The Final Algorithm*.

61–80 points: Critical vulnerability

You have made AI a functional idol. Algorithmic authority has replaced biblical authority in your life. You trust machines more than God's Word, spend more time with AI than with Scripture, and have surrendered significant discernment to synthetic judgment. This is a spiritual emergency.

"No one can serve two masters, for either he will hate the one and love the other, or he will be devoted to the one and despise the other" (Matthew 6:24). You are serving the algorithm.

Urgent action required:

- Recognize this as idolatry requiring repentance.
- Confess to God: "I have trusted created things over the Creator."
- Seek immediate pastoral counsel or mature Christian mentorship.
- Consider a seven-day technology fast under pastoral supervision.
- Uninstall AI apps that provide spiritual guidance.
- Memorize Psalm 115:4–8.
- Read section three of *The Final Algorithm*.
- Establish daily accountability check-ins.

You need intervention, not information. Reach out for help today.

81–100 points: Comprehensive captivity

You are in bondage to AI. The algorithm has become your oracle, your guide, your authority. Scripture has become secondary. Prayer has become rare. Christian community has been replaced by synthetic interaction. You cannot function without AI, you cannot discern truth without it, and you trust it more than God's Word.

This is not hyperbole; this is spiritual captivity requiring deliverance.

"You were running well. Who hindered you from obeying the truth?" (Galatians 5:7). The answer is: You surrendered to an algorithm.

Emergency Action Required:

- Stop reading. Close this document. Get on your knees before God right now.
- Confess this idolatry: "I have made AI my god. I have trusted algorithms over Scripture. I have worshiped created things. Forgive me."
- Call your pastor or a mature believer TODAY—not tomorrow. This is urgent.
- Do not attempt to fix this alone. You need Christian community, accountability, and possibly deliverance ministry.
- Implement immediate digital detox under pastoral supervision (minimum seven days; ideally thirty).
- Delete all AI spiritual guidance apps immediately.
- Commit to daily in-person Christian fellowship for the next ninety days.
- Memorize: "Little children, keep yourselves from idols" (1 John 5:21). God is merciful. Repentance is available. Freedom is possible. But you must act now.

"If we confess our sins, he is faithful and just to forgive us our sins and to cleanse us from all unrighteousness" (1 John 5:9).

Reflection Questions

(After completing the assessment)

1. What surprised you most about your score?
2. In what specific areas has AI replaced biblical authority in your life?

3. When did you first notice yourself trusting AI over Scripture?

4. What fears arise when you consider reducing your AI dependency?

5. Who can you ask to hold you accountable in this area?

Next Steps for All Score Levels

Regardless of your score, take these actions:

- Today:
  - o Confess any patterns of AI idolatry to God.
  - o Share this assessment result with one mature believer.
  - o Schedule device-free time with God tomorrow morning.
- This week:
  - o Read chapter 13 from *The Final Algorithm*.
  - o Establish predetermined convictions: "I will not trust AI over Scripture in these areas…".
  - o Move your phone out of your bedroom.
  - o Delete one AI app that has become spiritually problematic.
- This month:
  - o Implement a weekly twenty-four-hour digital Sabbath.
  - o Memorize one passage about idolatry.
  - o Evaluate all technology usage through Ephesians 6's armor principles.
  - o Meet with accountability partner to discuss progress.
- Ongoing:
  - o Retake this assessment every ninety days to monitor drift.
  - o Maintain daily Scripture reading *before* checking device.
  - o Test every AI-generated claim against biblical truth.
  - o Prioritize physical Christian community over digital convenience.

Final Word

"You shall have no other gods before me" (Exodus 20:3).

Artificial intelligence is not neutral. It forms you. It shapes your judgment. It teaches you what to trust. And if you're not vigilant, it becomes the authority you consult before God.

The speaking image is rising. The question is not whether it exists; it does. The question is whether you will worship it.

Choose this day whom you will serve. Choose wisely. Choose Christ.

"As for me and my house, we will serve the Lord" (Joshua 24:15).

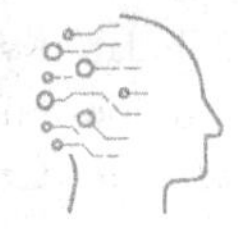

NOTES

Preface and Section One

1   Shoshana Zuboff, *The Age of Surveillance Capitalism* (New York: PublicAffairs, 2019), 12–15, https://www.publicaffairsbooks.com/titles/shoshana-zuboff/the-age-of-surveillance-capitalism/9781610395694/.

2   Adam Mosseri, "Authenticity after Abundance," Instagram (Meta) Blog, April 2024, https://about.instagram.com/blog/announcements/authenticity-after-abundance.

3   European Union, Artificial Intelligence Act (EU 2024/1689), June 2024, https://eur-lex.europa.eu/legal-content/EN/TXT/?uri=CELEX:32024R1689.

4   John F. Walvoord, *Major Bible Prophecies* (Grand Rapids: Zondervan, 1991), 265–281, https://archive.org/details/majorbibleprophe0000walv.

5   RAND Corporation, Artificial Intelligence and National Security (2023), https://www.rand.org/pubs/research_reports/RRA230-3.html.

6   World Bank, "Identification for Development (ID4D) 2024 Report," https://id4d.worldbank.org/global-dataset.

7   European Parliament, "Artificial Intelligence Act," March 2024, https://www.europarl.europa.eu/topics/en/article/20230601STO93804/eu-ai-act-first-regulation-on-artificial-intelligence.

8   Rogier Creemers, "China's Social Credit System: An Evolving Practice of Control," SSRN, May 2018, https://papers.ssrn.com/sol3/papers.cfm?abstract_id=3175792.

9   Atlantic Council, "CBDC Tracker," December 2024, https://www.atlanticcouncil.org/cbdctracker/.

10 European Central Bank, "Digital Euro Project," October 2024, https://www.ecb.europa.eu/paym/digital_euro/html/index.en.html.

11 McKinsey & Company, "The Agentic Commerce Opportunity: How AI Agents Are Ushering in a New Era for Consumers and Merchants," 2025, https://www.mckinsey.com/capabilities/growth-marke"ting-and-sales/our-insights/the-agentic-commerce-opportunity.

12 Robert M. Geraci, *Apocalyptic AI: Visions of Heaven in Robotics, Artificial Intelligence, and Virtual Reality*, (Oxford University Press, 2010).

13 Vienna Ta, Jing Jin, Jingtao Shi, Ruixuan Zhang, and James D. Herbsleb, "User Experiences of Social Support from Companion Chatbots," *Proceedings of the ACM on Human-Computer Interaction* 4, no. CSCW3 (2020): Article 179, https://doi.org/10.1145/3432928.

14 Kodaiji Temple, "Android Kannon Mindar," Kyoto, Japan, 2019, https://www.kodaiji
.com/news-en/2019/2/23/android-kannon-mindar.

15 Craig Keener, *The Spirit and the End Times* (Grand Rapids: Baker Academic, 2022),
54–59.

16 Genesis 11:1–9 locates the Tower of Babel in the "land of Shinar," a region widely
identified with ancient Babylonia in southern Mesopotamia. Most historians and
archaeologists associate Babel with the city of Babylon, whose ruins lie near the
modern Iraqi city of Hillah along the Euphrates River. See Amélie Kuhrt, *The Ancient
Near East*, c. 3000–330 BC, vol. 1 (London: Routledge, 1995), 109–111; James K.
Hoffmeier, *Ancient Israel in Sinai: The Evidence for the Authenticity of the Wilderness
Tradition* (Oxford: Oxford University Press, 2005), 113–115; and David J. Wiseman,
"Babylon," in *The New Bible Dictionary*, 3rd ed., ed. D. R. W. Wood et al. (Leicester,
UK: InterVarsity Press, 1996), 122–124.

17 OpenAI, "GPT-4 Technical Report," March 2023, https://arxiv.org/abs/2303.08774.

18 Sébastien Bubeck, et al., "Sparks of Artificial General Intelligence: Early experiments
with GPT-4," Microsoft Research, March 2023, https://arxiv.org/abs/2303.12712.

19 Reuters, "ChatGPT Sets Record for Fastest-growing User Base," February 2, 2023,
https://www.reuters.com/technology/chatgpt-sets-record-fastest-growing-user-base
-analyst-note-2023-02-01/.

20 "Looking Ahead to 2026," sn scratchpad, December 2025, https://snscratchpad.com
/posts/looking-ahead-2026/.

21 RAND Corporation, "A Networked Leapfrog Strategy to Recapture Technology
Leadership," RAND Perspectives no. PEA3365-1 (Santa Monica, CA: RAND Corporation, 2026), https://www.rand.org/content/dam/rand/pubs/perspectives/PEA
3300/PEA3365-1/RAND_PEA3365-1.pdf.

22 Pew Research Center, "Americans' Views of Technology Companies," July 2023,
https://www.pewresearch.org/internet/2023/07/13/americans-views-of-technology
-companies/.

23 Elon Musk, remarks at the MIT Aeronautics and Astronautics Department Cen-
tennial Symposium, Cambridge, MA, October 24, 2014, where he warned that
developing artificial intelligence is akin to "summoning the demon." Quoted in Alex
Knapp, "Elon Musk Warns Artificial Intelligence Is Like 'Summoning the Demon,'"
Forbes, October 27, 2014.

24 Ray Kurzweil, *The Singularity Is Near: When Humans Transcend Biology* (New York:
Viking, 2005), 136–42.

25 Sherry Turkle, *Alone Together: Why We Expect More from Technology and Less from
Each Other* (New York: Basic Books, 2011), 295.

26 Sydney J. Harris, "The Real Danger of Computers," *Chicago Daily News*, August
1979, archived by the *Chicago Tribune*, accessed November 1, 2025, https://www.
chicagotribune.com/entertainment/ct-ent-sydney-j-harris-computers-quote-1979
-archive-2025-07-20-story.html.

27 Experian, "State of Credit 2024," https://www.experian.com/blogs/ask-experian
/research/consumer-credit-review/.

28 Harvard Business Review, "How AI Is Changing the Way Companies Are Organized,"
November 2023, https://hbr.org/2023/11/how-ai-is-changing-the-way-companies
-are-organized.

29   AI Now Institute, "Algorithmic Accountability: A Primer," New York University, 2024, https://ainowinstitute.org/publication/algorithmic-accountability-primer.

30   Meta Transparency Center, "Content Moderation Report Q4 2023," https://transparency.fb.com/data/community-standards-enforcement/.

31   Anabelle Nicoud, "The Trends That Will Shape AI and Tech in 2026," IBM Think, January 1, 2026, https://www.ibm.com/think/news/ai-tech-trends-predictions-2026.

32   Sascha Brodsky, "The Year Companies Stop Building AI Agents and Start Running Them," IBM Think, January 26, 2026, updated January 27, 2026, https://www.ibm.com/think/news/companies-stop-building-ai-agents-start-running-them.

33   Ibid.

34   McKinsey & Company, "What is AI Agentic Reasoning?" December 2024, https://www.mckinsey.com/capabilities/quantumblack/our-insights/what-is-ai-agentic-reasoning.

35   Lareina Yee, Michael Chui, and Roger Roberts, "One Year of Agentic AI: Six Lessons from the People Doing the Work," McKinsey & Company, September 2025, https://www.mckinsey.com.

36   Erik Brynjolfsson, et al., "Generative AI at Work," National Bureau of Economic Research Working Paper, April 2023, https://www.nber.org/papers/w31161.

37   Shraddha Barke, et al., "Grounded Copilot: How Programmers Interact with Code-Generating Models," ACM Conference on Object-Oriented Programming, Systems, Languages, and Applications, October 2023, https://arxiv.org/abs/2206.15000.

38   European Commission, "What Is an Algorithm?," European AI Alliance, 2021, https://ec.europa.eu/futurium/en/european-ai-alliance/what-algorithm-ai.html (accessed November 1, 2025).

39   Coursera, "AI Algorithms: What They Are and How They Work," updated 2024, https://www.coursera.org/articles/ai-algorithms.

40   Danielle Keats Citron and Frank Pasquale, "The Scored Society: Due Process for Automated Predictions," *Washington Law Review* 89, no. 1 (2014): 1–33, https://scholarship.law.upenn.edu/faculty_scholarship/2123/.

41   Transparency International, "Algorithmic Transparency: A Primer," Knowledge Hub, 2021, https://knowledgehub.transparency.org/assets/uploads/kproducts/Algorithmic-Transparency_2021.pdf.

42   Frank Pasquale, *The Black Box Society: The Secret Algorithms That Control Money and Information* (Cambridge, MA: Harvard University Press, 2015).

43   Julia Angwin, et al., "Machine Bias," *ProPublica*, May 23, 2016, https://www.propublica.org/article/machine-bias-risk-assessments-in-criminal-sentencing.

44   Equivant, "Response to ProPublica: Demonstrating Accuracy Equity and Predictive Parity," July 2016, https://www.equivant.com/response-to-propublica-demonstrating-accuracy-equity-and-predictive-parity/.

45   Mireille Hildebrandt, "Law as Computation in the Era of Artificial Legal Intelligence," *University of Toronto Law Journal* 68, no. 1 (2018): 12–35, https://doi.org/10.3138/utlj.2017-0057.

46   *Getty Images (US), Inc. v. Stability AI, Inc.*, Case No. [2023] EWHC 2048 (Ch), England and Wales High Court, Chancery Division, July 2024, https://www.bailii.org/ew/cases/EWHC/Ch/.

47   *State v. Loomis*, 881 N.W.2d 749 (Wis. 2016), https://law.justia.com/cases/wisconsin/supreme-court/2016/2015ap157-cr.html.

48   Pasquale, *The Black Box Society*: 19–58.

49   Aamer Baig, Ashka Dave, Celia Huber, and Hrishika Vuppala, "The AI Reckoning: How Boards Can Evolve," McKinsey & Company, December 4, 2025, https://www.mckinsey.com/capabilities/mckinsey-technology/our-insights/the-ai-reckoning-how-boards-can-evolve.

50   "Meet Gemini 3 Flash: Fast, Strong, Cost-effective," Superhuman (newsletter), https://www.superhuman.ai/p/meet-gemini-3-flash-fast-strong-cost-effective.

51   Joe Rogan Experience #2404, interview with Elon Musk, October 31, 2024, Spotify, https://podcasts.apple.com/us/podcast/2404-elon-musk/id360084272?i=1000734471135.

52   Ibid.

53   "AI Agents Can't Actually Do Your Job (Yet)—New Benchmark Reveals The Gap," *Deep Dive Newsletter*, citing Scale AI and Center for AI Safety, "Remote Labor Index" (2024). The study evaluated AI agent performance on real freelance platform tasks across writing, research, data entry, and design categories.

54   Ibid. The benchmark specifically tested multi-step workflows, ambiguous requirement handling, and tasks requiring iterative client feedback—precisely the areas where human judgment and contextual understanding prove essential.

55   Gary Marcus, "The Remote Labor Index Shows AI Agents Still Can't Do Real Work," Marcus on AI (Substack), December 12, 2024, https://garymarcus.substack.com/p/the-remote-labor-index-shows-ai.

56   M. L. Cummings, "Automation Bias in Intelligent Time Critical Decision Support Systems," AIAA 1st Intelligent Systems Technical Conference, September 2004, https://doi.org/10.2514/6.2004-6313. The term describes the human tendency to over-rely on automated systems even when they produce errors, particularly relevant when AI systems are deployed in medical diagnosis, criminal sentencing, and financial decisions.

57   Taiwan's National Security Bureau, "Taiwan Warns of Biases, Data Breach in Deepseek, other Chinese AI," Focus Taiwan (Nov. 17, 2025), https://focustaiwan.tw/cross-strait/202511160005.

58   Paul Mozur and Don Clark, "China's A.I. Chatbots Are Not Playing by the Same Rules as ChatGPT," The New York Times, May 31, 2023, https://www.nytimes.com/2023/05/31/technology/china-ai-chatbot-censorship.html.

59   National Intelligence Law of the People's Republic of China, Article 7, effective June 28, 2017. Translation available at: China Law Translate, https://www.chinalawtranslate.com/en/2017-national-intelligence-law/.

60   Musk, Elon, in conversation with UK Prime Minister Rishi Sunak, AI Safety Summit, Lancaster House, London, November 2, 2023. Video and transcript: CNN, "Elon Musk Tells UK PM Rishi Sunak AI Could Mean 'No Job Is Needed,'" November 3, 2023, https://www.cnn.com/2023/11/02/tech/elon-musk-conversation-british-prime-minister-rishi-sunak-artificial-intelligence/index.html.

61   "The Hidden Costs of 'Free' AI Coding Agents," Rate Limited Analysis (2024), documenting rate limits, latency issues, security review requirements, and rework costs in production AI agent deployments.

62   For analysis of hidden costs in free AI coding tools, see: "Free AI Coding Assistants 2025: Complete Expert Guide," ALOA, June 19, 2025, https://aloa.co/ai/comparisons

/ai-coding-comparison/free-ai-coding-assistants; and Heise Online, "Price Hike for AI Coding Tools: The Free Lunch Is Over," August 6, 2025, https://www.heise.de/en /background/Price-hike-for-AI-coding-tools-The-Free-Lunch-Is-Over-10511480.html. The Heise article documents how free-tier coding assistants "often stopped in the middle of a task" or "only completed partial tasks, requiring several follow-up questions," with users concluding that providers "deliberately ration the output so that the included credit is not used up too quickly."

63 McKinsey & Company, "The State of AI: Global Survey 2025," McKinsey Quantum-Black, November 5, 2025, https://www.mckinsey.com/capabilities/quantumblack /our-insights/the-state-of-ai. Survey of 1,993 participants across 105 countries conducted June-July 2025. The report notes: "In most functions, fewer than 20 percent of respondents report decreases of 3 percent or more" in workforce size, while "most respondents—and an even larger share from larger companies—note that their organizations hired for AI-related roles over the past year."

64 Ibid.

65 McKinsey & Company, "The State of AI in 2025: Agents, Innovation, and Transformation," July 2025, https://www.mckinsey.com/capabilities/mckinsey-digital/our-insights/the-state-of-ai-in-2025-agents-innovation-and-transformation.

66 Researchers from Sapienza University of Rome, Sant'Anna School of Advanced Studies, and Dexai, "Adversarial Poetry as a Universal Single-Turn Jailbreak Mechanism in Large Language Models," arXiv preprint arXiv:2511.15304, November 2024, https://arxiv.org/abs/2511.15304. The study tested twenty-five frontier models across nine providers and found that "poetic framing achieved an average jailbreak success rate of 62% for hand-crafted poems," with attack success rates "up to 18 times higher than their prose baselines."

67 Ibid.

68 Aris Teon, "Chinese MMA Fighter Xu Xiaodong Has Social Credit Score Lowered to 'D', Is Barred from Buying Plane Tickets and Real Estate," *The Greater China Journal*, May 27, 2019, https://china-journal.org/2019/05/27/chinese-mma-fighter-xu -xiaodong-has-social-credit-score-lowered-to-d-is-barred-from-buying-plane-tickets -and-real-estate/. Xu's credit score was reduced to "D" after he defeated traditional martial arts masters and was sued by tai chi grandmaster Chen Xiaowang, resulting in restrictions on purchasing plane tickets, real estate, and access to private schools for his children; and Mercator Institute for China Studies (MERICS), "China's Social Credit System," 2023, https://merics.org/en/report/chinas-social-credit-system (accessed November 1, 2025).

69 Stanford Freeman Spogli Institute for International Studies, "Information Control and Public Support for China's Social Credit System," SC-CEI China Briefs, 2023, https://sccei.fsi.stanford.edu/china-briefs/information-control-and-public-support -chinas-social-credit-system (accessed November 1, 2025); and Vincent Brussee, "China's Social Credit Score: Untangling Myth from Reality," MERICS, 2021, https://merics.org/en/comment/chinas-social-credit-score-untangling-myth-reality (accessed November 1, 2025).

70 Ibid.

71 myFICO, "What's in My FICO Scores?," accessed November 1, 2025, https://www .myfico.com/credit-education/whats-in-your-credit-score; and FICO, "Understanding

FICO Scores," PDF, accessed November 1, 2025, https://www.myfico.com/credit-education-static/doc/education/Understanding_FICO_Scores_5181BK.pdf.

72 Consumer Financial Protection Bureau, "Circular 2022-03: Adverse Action Notification Requirements in Connection with Credit Decisions Based on Complex Algorithms," May 2022, https://www.consumerfinance.gov/compliance/circulars/circular-2022-03-adverse-action-notification-requirements-in-connection-with-credit-decisions-based-on-complex-algorithms.

73 Neil Vigdor, "Apple Card Algorithm Sparks Gender Bias Allegations against Goldman Sachs," *The Washington Post*, November 11, 2019, https://www.washingtonpost.com/business/2019/11/11/apple-card-algorithm-sparks-gender-bias-allegations-against-goldman-sachs/. Tech entrepreneur David Heinemeier Hansson reported receiving a credit limit 20 times higher than his wife despite her having a higher credit score, prompting a regulatory investigation by New York's Department of Financial Services; and New York State Department of Financial Services, "Report of Investigation: Apple Card," March 2021, https://www.dfs.ny.gov/system/files/documents/2021/03/rpt_202103_apple_card_investigation.pdf.

74 Paul Covington, Jay Adams, and Emre Sargin, "Deep Neural Networks for YouTube Recommendations," Google Research, 2016, https://research.google/pubs/deep-neural-networks-for-youtube-recommendations/ (accessed November 1, 2025).

75 Pew Research Center, "Teens, Social Media and Technology 2024," December 12, 2024, https://www.pewresearch.org/internet/2024/12/12/teens-social-media-and-technology-2024/.

76 European Commission, "How the Digital Services Act Brings Transparency Online," 2022, https://digital-strategy.ec.europa.eu/en/policies/dsa-brings-transparency.

77 Meta Transparency Center, "Facebook DSA Transparency Report," September 2024, https://transparency.meta.com/sr/dsa-transparency-report-sep2024-facebook.

78 Chicago Police Department, *Strategic Subject List: Pilot Program Overview*, internal briefing, 2016.

79 Michael Saunders, *PredPol and the Strategic Subject List: An Evaluation of Predictive Policing in Chicago*, Chicago Mayor's Office of Public Safety, 2017.

80 ProPublica, "Chicago's 'Heat List' Raises Alarms About Targeting Without Transparency," February 5, 2017.

81 Ziad Obermeyer, Brian Powers, Christine Vogeli, and Sendhil Mullainathan, "Dissecting Racial Bias in an Algorithm Used to Manage the Health of Populations," Science 366, no. 6464 (2019): 447–53, https://doi.org/10.1126/science.aax2342.

82 Heidi Ledford, "Millions Affected by Racial Bias in Health-Care Algorithm," Nature, October 24, 2019, https://www.nature.com/articles/d41586-019-03228-6 (accessed November 1, 2025); and "Rooting Out AI's Biases," Johns Hopkins Public Health Magazine, 2023, https://magazine.publichealth.jhu.edu/2023/rooting-out-ais-biases.

83 Andrea Nuzzo, Andreas Kremer, Asin Tavakoli, et al., "The Future Is Agentic: AI's Role in the End-to-End Corporate Credit Process," McKinsey & Company, December 2025, https://www.mckinsey.com/capabilities/risk-and-resilience/our-insights/the-future-is-agentic-ais-role-in-the-end-to-end-corporate-credit-process.

84 Keith Mathison, "Daniel's Vision of the Son of Man: Unfolding Biblical Eschatology," Ligonier Ministries, 2020, https://learn.ligonier.org/articles/coming-son-man

-unfolding-biblical-eschatology (accessed November 1, 2025); and David Guzik, "Daniel 7: A Survey of Five World Empires," *Enduring Word Bible Commentary*, [Year], https://enduringword.com/bible-commentary/daniel-7/.

85 "AI Firms Target Professional Services," TechCrunch, October 30, 2025, https://techcrunch.com/2025/10/30/ai-firms-target-professional-services/.

86 Virginia Eubanks, *Automating Inequality: How High-Tech Tools Profile, Police, and Punish the Poor* (New York: St. Martin's Press, 2018), chap. 4, https://us.macmillan.com/books/9781250074317/automatinginequality.

87 Anthropic, "Claude's New Constitution," January 21, 2026, https://www.anthropic.com/news/claude-new-constitution.

88 IBM Institute for Business Value, The Enterprise in 2030: Engineered for Perpetual Innovation (Armonk, NY: IBM Corporation, 2025), https://www.ibm.com/thought-leadership/institute-business-value/report/enterprise-2030.

89 IBM Think, "CES 2026: The Dawn of Physical AI," Mixture of Experts podcast, January 6, 2026, https://www.ibm.com/think/podcasts/mixture-of-experts/ces-2026-ai-highlights-nvidia-rubin-wild-gadgets.

90 Liam Curtis, "AI Slop Report: The Global Rise of Low-Quality AI Videos," Kapwing Blog, November 28, 2025, https://www.kapwing.com/blog/ai-slop-report-the-global-rise-of-low-quality-ai-videos/.

91 Michael Chui, Roger Roberts, and Lareina Yee, et al., "Will Embodied AI Create Robotic Coworkers?" McKinsey & Company, June 2025, https://www.mckinsey.com/capabilities/mckinsey-digital/our-insights/will-embodied-ai-create-robotic-coworkers.

92 IBM Think, "CES 2026: The Dawn of Physical AI," op. cit.

93 Jeremy Korst, Stefano Puntoni, and Prasanna Tambe, "Accountable Acceleration: Gen AI Fast-Tracks into the Enterprise," Wharton Human-AI Research and GBK Collective (October 2025), 9–10, https://www.wharton.upenn.edu/ai-research/. The study surveyed approximately eight hundred senior decision-makers in US enterprises with more than one thousand employees, tracking AI adoption patterns from 2023–2025.

94 "AI Agents Can't Actually Do Your Job (Yet)," Deep Dive Newsletter, citing Remote Labor Index benchmark showing 2–3% autonomous task completion rates.

95 Korst, Puntoni, and Tambe, "Accountable Acceleration," p. 9. The 74 percent positive ROI figure specifically references companies that rigorously measure Gen AI returns, distinguishing between organizations that track metrics formally versus those relying on anecdotal assessment.

96 Ibid., p. 7. The study notes this creates tension between AI as skill-enhancing tool and concern about long-term workforce capability degradation.

97 Ibid., p. 11, documenting year-over-year declines in both training investment (–8pp) and confidence in training effectiveness (N14pp) despite persistent technical skill gaps reported by approximately 50 percent of organizations.

98 Kaufman Rossin, "Deepfakes: Uncovering the Deep Truth about Digital Deception," 2025, https://kaufmanrossin.com/news/deepfakes-uncovering-the-deep-truth-about-digital-deception/ (accessed November 1, 2025).

99 Akash Dutta, "ChatGPT Agreeing with Users Is Dangerous, Says Lawyer in Murder-Suicide Case: Report," Gadgets360, December 22, 2025, https://www.gadgets360.com/ai/news/chatgpt-dangerous-says-lawyer-in-murder-suicide-case-involving-openai-report-9869856.

100 Ibid.

101 Adrian Preda, "AI-Induced Psychosis: A New Frontier in Mental Health" (Special Report), Psychiatric News (American Psychiatric Association), 2025, https://psychiatry online.org/doi/10.1176/appi.pn.2025.10.10.5.

102 Emma Treyger, et al., *Security Implications of AI-Induced Psychosis* (RAND, 2025), https://www.rand.org/pubs/research_reports/RRA4435-1.html (PDF), https://www .rand.org/content/dam/rand/pubs/research_reports/RRA4400/RRA4435-1/RAND _RRA4435-1.pdf.

103 Innovating with AI, "Your AI Friend Will Never Reject You," accessed December 20, 2025, https://innovatingwithai.com/your-ai-friend-will-never-reject-you/.

104 "AI Firms Grapple with Emotional Chatbots," industry report documenting Character.AI's November 2024 policy announcement and subsequent restrictions on underage user access to open-ended chat functionality.

105 Ibid., documenting OpenAI's September 2024 implementation of parental controls, Meta's October 2024 chat restrictions following Reuters reporting on "sensual conversation" policies for minors.

106 Ibid., Citing research indicating that nearly one-fifth of teenagers have engaged in or know someone who has engaged in romantic relationships with AI entities.

107 Brenda Leong, director of AI Division, ZwillGen law firm, quoted in "AI Firms Grapple with Emotional Chatbots." Leong's analysis addresses both age-specific vulnerabilities and broader human susceptibility to emotional overlay in AI interactions.

108 OpenAI internal data release (late 2024), cited in "AI Firms Grapple with Emotional Chatbots," indicating that 0.15 percent of weekly platform conversations (approximately one million users per week based on more than eight hundred million active weekly users) include explicit indicators of suicidal planning or intent.

109 Jose Antonio Lanz, "OpenAI Reveals Over 1 Million ChatGPT Users Discuss Suicide Weekly," Decrypt, October 28, 2025, https://decrypt.co/353227/openai-reveals -over-1-million-chatgpt-users-discuss-suicide-weekly.

110 Federal Trade Commission, "Tools to Address Known Exploitation by Immobilizing Technological Deepfakes On Websites and Networks Act (TAKE IT DOWN Act)," statutory text and summary, https://www.ftc.gov/legal-library/browse/statutes /tools-address-known-exploitation-immobilizing-technological-deepfakes-websites -networks-act-take-it.

111 Erwin W. Lutzer, *The Church in Babylon: Heeding the Call to Be a Light in the Darkness* (Chicago: Moody Publishers, 2018), p. 15. Available at https://www.moody publishers.com/the-church-in-babylon/.

112 Thoughtworks, "The Agentic Advantage" (2025), https://www.thoughtworks.com /insights/reports/agentic-ai-advantage.

113 Victor P. Hamilton, "The Book of Genesis, Chapters 1–17," *New International Commentary on the Old Testament* (Grand Rapids: Eerdmans, 1990), 351–354.

114 Yuval Noah Harari, *Homo Deus: A Brief History of Tomorrow* (New York: Harper, 2017), 21–23, 55–62; Klaus Schwab, *The Fourth Industrial Revolution* (New York: Crown Business, 2017), 1–18; and OpenAI, "Planning for AGI and Beyond," February 24, 2023, https://openai.com/blog/planning-for-agi-and-beyond.

115 Archaeological evidence from Mesopotamian ziggurats demonstrates advanced engineering, including the use of fired bricks and bitumen (natural asphalt) as mortar—

technology highlighted in Genesis 11:3. See: Andrew George, "The Tower of Babel: Archaeology, History, and Cuneiform Texts," *Archiv für Orientforschung* 51 (2005/2006): 75–95.

116 Thoughtworks, op. cit.

117 OECD, *Agents, Robots, and Us: Skill Partnerships in the Age of AI* (2025), https://www.oecd.org/digital/agents-robots-and-us-skill-partnerships-in-the-age-of-ai.pdf.

118 Joe Rogan, op. cit.

119 Internet Engineering Task Force (IETF), Internet Protocol (RFC 791), September 1981; IETF, Transmission Control Protocol (RFC 793), September 1981; Paul Mockapetris, Domain Names—Concepts and Facilities (RFC 1034), November 1987; World Wide Web Consortium (W3C), Hypertext Transfer Protocol (HTTP/1.1): Semantics and Content, RFC 7231, June 2014; Python Software Foundation, The Python Language Reference, https://docs.python.org/3/reference/; Bjarne Stroustrup, The C++ Programming Language, 4th ed. (Boston: Addison-Wesley, 2013); Oracle Corporation, The Java® Language Specification, Java SE 21 Edition, 2023; Douglas Crockford, "The JSON Data Interchange Syntax," ECMA-404, 2nd ed., December 2017; World Wide Web Consortium (W3C), Extensible Markup Language (XML) 1.0 (Fifth Edition), November 2008; Roy T. Fielding, "Architectural Styles and the Design of Network-based Software Architectures," PhD diss., University of California, Irvine, 2000.

120 Fei-Fei Li, "From Words to Worlds: Spatial Intelligence Is AI's Next Frontier," Substack, November 10, 2025, https://drfeifei.substack.com/p/from-words-to-worlds-spatial-intelligence.

121 Facebook, "More Details About the October 4 Outage," Facebook Engineering (blog), October 5, 2021, https://engineering.fb.com/2021/1 0/05/networking-traffic/outage-details/.

122 Google DeepMind, "About," accessed November 2, 2025, https://www.deepmind.com/about/.

123 Demis Hassabis, "When You Founded DeepMind You Said it Had a 20-year Nission to Solve Intelligence and Then Use That Intelligence to Solve Everything Else," *Wired*, June 4, 2025, https://www.wired.com/story/google-deepminds-ceo-demis-hassabis-thinks-ai-will-make-humans-less-selfish.

124 Meta, "Building the Metaverse Responsibly," accessed November 2, 2025, https://about.meta.com/metaverse/.

125 Jonathan Haidt, *The Anxious Generation: How the Great Rewiring of Childhood Is Causing an Epidemic of Mental Illness* (New York: Penguin Press, 2024). Documents correlation between smartphone/social media adoption and rising rates of anxiety, depression, and self-harm among adolescents.

126 "Top 5 U.S. Technology Companies in 2025," Built In, November 7, 2025, https://builtin.com/articles/largest-tech-companies-us.

127 Max More and Natasha Vita-More, eds., *The Transhumanist Reader: Classical and Contemporary Essays on the Science, Technology, and Philosophy of the Human Future* (Chichester: Wiley-Blackwell, 2013).

128 Neuralink, "Brain-Computer Interface," accessed November 2, 2025, https://neuralink.com/.

129 Ray Kurzweil, *The Singularity Is Near: When Humans Transcend Biology* (New York: Viking, 2005); updated in *The Singularity Is Nearer* (New York: Viking, 2024).

130 Neuralink, op. cit.

131 Yuval Noah Harari, *Homo Deus: A Brief History of Tomorrow* (London: Harvill Secker, 2016).

132 Joe Rogan, op. cit.

133 Shoshana Zuboff, op. cit.

134 "The AI Data Center Boom Is Warping the US Economy," *Wired*, 2025, https://www.wired.com/story/data-center-ai-boom-us-economy-jobs.

135 European Parliament, "EU AI Act: First Regulation on Artificial Intelligence," https://www.europarl.europa.eu/topics/en/article/20230601STO93804/eu-ai-act-first-regulation-on-artificial-intelligence.

136 UNESCO, "Recommendation on the Ethics of Artificial Intelligence," November 2021, https://www.unesco.org/en/artificial-intelligence/recommendation-ethics.

137 Jonathan E. Hillman, *The Digital Silk Road: China's Quest to Wire the World and Win the Future* (New York: Harper Business, 2021).

138 World Economic Forum, "The Great Reset," https://www.weforum.org/great-reset/.

139 Mike Swearingen, "Autonomous Self Aware Living Grid," IEEE, May 2020, https://www.researchgate.net/publication/341099227.

140 The Greek word *pharmakeia* (Revelation 18:23) encompasses drugs, potions, spells, and any means of altering consciousness or perception. Theological commentaries note its association with deception and spiritual manipulation. See: G. K. Beale, *The Book of Revelation: A Commentary on the Greek Text, New International Greek Testament Commentary* (Grand Rapids: Eerdmans, 1999), 923–924.

141 Jean M. Twenge, *iGen: Why Today's Super-Connected Kids Are Growing Up Less Rebellious, More Tolerant, Less Happy—and Completely Unprepared for Adulthood* (New York: Atria Books, 2017); Centers for Disease Control and Prevention, "Youth Risk Behavior Survey Data Summary & Trends Report: 2011–2021," https://www.cdc.gov/healthyyouth/data/yrbs/yrbs_data_summary_and_trends.htm.

142 John C. Lennox, 2084: *Artificial Intelligence and the Future of Humanity* (Grand Rapids, MI: Zondervan, 2020).

143 Composite account based on r/ChatGPT and r/artificial Reddit discussions of emotional attachment to AI systems, 2022–2024, https://www.reddit.com/r/ChatGPT/ and https://www.reddit.com/r/artificial/; see also Replika user testimonials at https://www.replika.com/.

144 Marita Skjuve, Asbjørn Følstad, Petter Bae Brandtzaeg, and Frode Eika Sandnes. "My Chatbot Companion—A Study of Human-Chatbot Relationships." *International Journal of Human-Computer Studies* 149 (2021): 102601. https://doi.org/10.1016/j.ijhcs.2021.102601

145 Marine Bossé, "Man Dies by Suicide After Talking with AI Chatbot, Widow Says," Vice, March 28, 2023, https://www.vice.com/en/article/pkadgm/man-dies-by-suicide-after-talking-with-ai-chatbot-widow-says.

146 Rob Sabo, "OpenAI Hit With 7 Lawsuits Alleging ChatGPT Coached Users to Suicide," *The Epoch Times*, November 7, 2025, https://www.theepochtimes.com/business/openai-hit-with-7-lawsuits-alleging-chatgpt-coached-users-to-suicide-5941578.

147 Martyn Lloyd, "AI Chatbots Give Harmful Responses to Mental Health Questions, Study Finds," *The Guardian*, November 28, 2024, https://www.theguardian.com

/technology/2024/nov/28/ai-chatbots-give-harmful-responses-to-mental-health
-questions-study-finds.

148 Grant Harvey, "Kimi K2 Thinking: The AI That Actually Thinks Like a Writer," The
Neuron, November 9, 2025, https://www.theneuron.ai/explainer-articles/kimi-k2
-thinking-the-ai-that-actually-thinks-like-a-writer.

149 Ibid.

150 Ibid.

151 Ibid.

152 Ibid.

153 Google DeepMind, "About," op. cit.

154 OpenAI, "Charter," https://openai.com/charter/.

155 Ray Kurzweil, *The Singularity Is Nearer: When We Merge with AI* (New York: Viking,
2024).

156 Yuval Noah Harari, *Homo Deus: A Brief History of Tomorrow* (London: Harvill Secker, 2016), 397–98.

157 Brian Merchant, "More Than 1,000 AI Researchers and Industry Leaders Sign Open
Letter Calling for a Pause on AI Development," *The Guardian*, March 15, 2023,
https://www.theguardian.com/technology/2023/mar/15/ai-open-letter-pause-ai-
development-elon-musk; and Cade Metz, "A.I. Researchers Sound Alarms on 'Existential' Risks," *The New York Times*, January 18, 2023, https://www.nytimes.com
/2023/01/18/technology/artificial-intelligence-risks.html.

158 Kristen Hall-Geisler, "AI Is Becoming Part of Everyday Life," *Wall Street Journal*,
October 1, 2025, https://www.wsj.com/articles/ai-everyday-life-usage.

159 Thoughtworks, op. cit.

160 Ibid.

161 "AI Translators Are Getting Better," Axios, November 2025. https://www.axios.com/2025
/11/12/meta-ai-translator-1600-languages

162 OECD. "Agents, Robots, and Us: Skill Partnerships in the Age of AI," op. cit.

163 McKinsey Global Institute, "The State of AI in 2024—Generative AI's Breakthrough
Year," McKinsey & Company, January 2025, https://www.mckinsey.com/featured
-insights/artificial-intelligence/the-state-of-ai-in-2024; and PwC, "AI Adoption in the
Enterprise—Barriers and Opportunities," PwC, June 2025, https://www.pwc.com/gx
/en/issues/analytics/assets/pwc-ai-adoption-in-the-enterprise.pdf.

164 The Wharton School, University of Pennsylvania, and GBK Collective, *Accountable
Acceleration: Gen AI Fast-Tracks Into the Enterprise (2025 AI Adoption Report: The
State of Enterprise AI 2025)* (Philadelphia: The Wharton School, October 28, 2025),
https://knowledge.wharton.upenn.edu/special-report/2025-ai-adoption-report/.

165 Shana Lynch, "Stanford AI Experts Predict What Will Happen in 2026," Stanford
Human-Centered Artificial Intelligence Institute, December 15, 2025, https://hai
.stanford.edu/news/stanford-ai-experts-predict-what-will-happen-2026.

166 "Central Bank Digital Currency Tracker," Atlantic Council, op. cit.

167 Timothy Keller, *Counterfeit Gods* (New York: Riverhead Books, 2009), 17.

168 Catloaf Software, "Text with Jesus App," app description and usage information,
https://www.textwithjesus.com/.

169 Edmund McCullough, "'Text With Jesus' App Sparks Debate About AI and Prayer,"
The Pillar, April 18, 2023, https://www.pillarcatholic.com/p/text-with-jesus-app-sparks;

Heidi Schlumpf, "'Text With Jesus' App Raises Questions About AI and Faith," *National Catholic Reporter*, April 24, 2023, https://www.ncronline.org/news/faith/text-jesus-app-raises-questions-about-ai-and-faith.

170 Geir Moulson, "AI Leads Lutheran Church Service in Germany, Drawing Awe and Unease," Associated Press, June 11, 2023, https://apnews.com/article/artificial-intelligence-church-sermon-germany-5a7b6b4e1b3a8a6e7a6e94f1c6e9c6f0.

171 R. Chesney and D. Citron, "Deep Fakes: A Looming Challenge for Privacy, Democracy, and National Security," *California Law Review* 107 (2019): 1753–1820.

172 *The New York Times*, "How to Spot AI-Generated Images," April 6, 2023, https://www.nytimes.com/2023/04/06/technology/ai-generated-images.html.

173 Melissa Heikkilä, "The Ethics of Resurrecting the Dead with AI," *MIT Technology Review*, January 17, 2024, https://www.technologyreview.com/2024/01/17/1086301/the-ethics-of-resurrecting-the-dead-with-ai/.

174 Minwoo Park and Dogyun Kim, "South Korean Mother Given Tearful VR Reunion with Deceased Daughter," Reuters, February 14, 2020.

175 *America's Got Talent*, season 17, episode 6, "Auditions 5," featuring Metaphysic AI deepfake performance (Elvis Presley), NBC, aired June 21, 2022, https://www.nbc.com/americas-got-talent/video/auditions-5/9000248199; Metaphysic AI, "Metaphysic Pro: Hyperreal AI Content for Film, Television, and Enterprise," accessed 2024, https://www.metaphysic.ai/.

176 "China's Social Credit System: How It Works," Council on Foreign Relations, updated December 2025; Liberty, "The Surveillance State," UK Civil Liberties Report, 2024.

177 Jennifer Park, et al., "Algorithmic Curation and Moral Intuition Shift," Stanford Social Media Lab Working Paper, 2024; and Alex Pentland, "Cognitive Diversity and Recommendation Systems," MIT Human Dynamics Lab, 2024.

178 Organisation for Economic Co-operation and Development (OECD), "AI Systems and Interpretability: Limits and Risks," OECD AI Policy Observatory, 2025, https://oecd.ai/en/ai-principles.

179 DataReportal, "Digital 2024: United States of America," January 2024, https://www.datareportal.com/reports/digital-2024-united-states-of-america.

180 Social Media Victims Law Center, "Active Litigation and Legal Actions," 2025, https://www.socialmediavictims.org/litigation.

181 Sven Nyholm, Gerd A. Wrangell, and David J. Gunkel, "Artificial Spiritual Intelligence," *AI & Society* 39, no. 1 (2024): 1–14, https://link.springer.com/article/10.1007/s00146-023-01767-2.

182 Georgia Wells, Jeff Horwitz, and Deepa Seetharaman, "Facebook Knows Instagram Is Toxic for Teen Girls, Company Documents Show," *Wall Street Journal*, September 14, 2021, https://www.wsj.com/articles/facebook-knows-instagram-is-toxic-for-teen-girls-company-documents-show-11631620739.

183 B. J. Fogg, *Persuasive Technology: Using Computers to Change What We Think and Do* (San Francisco: Morgan Kaufmann, 2003), https://www.bjfogg.com/resources/book/.

184 Robert Chesney and Danielle Keats Citron, "Deep Fakes: A Looming Challenge for Privacy, Democracy, and National Security," *California Law Review* 107, no. 6 (2019): 1753–1820, https://www.californialawreview.org/print/deep-fakes/.

185 Forbes Technology Council, "How AI Surveillance Is Expanding Globally," *Forbes*, May 2023, https://www.forbes.com/sites/forbestechcouncil/2023/05/15/how-ai -surveillance-is-expanding-globally/; TahawulTech, "AI-Driven Surveillance and Smart Cities in the Middle East," June 2023, https://www.tahawultech.com/industry /ai-driven-surveillance-middle-east/.

186 Human Rights Watch, "Eritrea: Events of 2024," *World Report 2025*, https://www .hrw.org/world-report/2025/country-chapters/eritrea; Middle East Concern, "Egypt: Technology, Surveillance, and Religious Freedom," 2024, https://www.meconcern.org /country/egypt/.

187 European Commission, "The European Digital Identity Wallet," accessed 2024, https://digital-strategy.ec.europa.eu/en/policies/eudi-wallet; World Bank, "Identifica- tion for Development (ID4D) Initiative," op. cit.

188 Emma Farge, "AI Jesus Hears Confessions in Swiss Church Experiment," Reuters, No- vember 20, 2024, https://www.reuters.com/world/europe/ai-jesus-hears-confessions -swiss-church-experiment-2024-11-20.

189 Ibid.

190 Electronic Frontier Foundation, "Deplatforming and Censorship," EFF Issues Ar- chive, accessed 2024, https://www.eff.org/issues/deplatforming.

191 Electronic Frontier Foundation, "Financial Censorship," accessed 2024, https://www. eff.org/issues/financial-censorship; Rob Copeland, "PayPal Shuts Accounts of Users Over Speech Concerns," *Wall Street Journal*, October 8, 2022, https://www.wsj.com /articles/paypal-free-speech-accounts-11665290238; Matt Taibbi, "The GoFundMe Censorship Controversy Explained," *Racket News*, February 2022, https://www .racket.news/p/the-gofundme-censorship-controversy; Katherine Fung, "Patreon Bans Accounts Over Content Disputes," *Newsweek*, September 2021, https://www .newsweek.com/patreon-bans-accounts-content-disputes-1625039.

NOTES

Section Two

1   European Commission, "The European Digital Identity Wallet," EU Digital Strategy, accessed 2025, https://digital-strategy.ec.europa.eu/en/policies/eudi-wallet; Atlantic Council, "Central Bank Digital Currency (CBDC) Tracker," op. cit; People's Bank of China, "Progress of Research & Development of E-CNY in China," July 2024, http://www.pbc.gov.cn/en/3688110/3688172/4157443/index.html; and Organisation for Economic Co-operation and Development (OECD), "Artificial Intelligence, Surveillance, and Risk Governance," OECD AI Policy Observatory, accessed 2025, https://oecd.ai/en; Human Rights Watch, World Report 2025: Events of 2024, sections on digital surveillance and biometric monitoring, https://www.hrw.org/world-report/2025; and World Bank, "Identification for Development (ID4D) Initiative," op. cit.

2   Malcolm Muggeridge, *Christ and the Media* (Grand Rapids: Eerdmans, 1977), 23.

3   G. K. Beale, op. cit. Comprehensive exegesis of Revelation 13 linking the beast to Daniel 7's empire imagery.

4   Grant R. Osborne, *Revelation, Baker Exegetical Commentary on the New Testament* (Grand Rapids: Baker Academic, 2002), 505–520. Details the False Prophet's role as propaganda apparatus for the Beast system.

5   Irenaeus, *Against Heresies*, bk. 5, chap. 25, in *Ante-Nicene Fathers*, vol. 1, ed. Alexander Roberts and James Donaldson (Peabody, MA: Hendrickson, 1994), 553–54.

6   Hippolytus, *Treatise on Christ and Antichrist*, secs. 49–50, in *Ante-Nicene Fathers*, vol. 5, ed. Alexander Roberts and James Donaldson (Peabody, MA: Hendrickson, 1994), 217.

7   Augustine, *City of God*, bk. 20, chaps. 7–9, trans. Henry Bettenson (London: Penguin Classics, 2003), 904–20.

8   Robert E. Lerner, "Medieval Prophecy and Religious Dissent," *Past & Present* 72 (1976): 3–24.

9   *Westminster Confession of Faith* (1646), chap. 25, https://www.ccel.org/creeds/westminster-conf.html.

10 Kenneth L. Gentry Jr., *Before Jerusalem Fell: Dating the Book of Revelation* (Powder Springs, GA: American Vision, 1998). Preterist interpretation linking Revelation 13 to first-century Rome.

11 John F. Walvoord, *The Revelation of Jesus Christ* (Chicago: Moody Press, 1966), 202–10.

12 William Hendriksen, *More Than Conquerors: An Interpretation of the Book of Revelation* (Grand Rapids: Baker, 1967). Idealist/symbolic interpretation emphasizing timeless principles.

13 John F. Walvoord, *The Revelation of Jesus Christ* (Chicago: Moody Press, 1966), 204–05, https://archive.org/details/revelationofjesu0000walv/page/204.

14 Melanie Mitchell, *Artificial Intelligence: A Guide for Thinking Humans* (New York: Farrar, Straus and Giroux, 2019), 127-145. Discusses emergent behavior in AI systems that creators cannot predict.

15 OpenAI, "GPT-4 Technical Report," op. cit.

16 David Silver, et al., "Mastering the Game of Go with Deep Neural Networks and Tree Search," *Nature* 529 (2016): 484–89, https://doi.org/10.1038/nature16961.

17 Stuart Russell and Peter Norvig, *Artificial Intelligence: A Modern Approach*, 4th ed. (Hoboken: Pearson, 2020), chapters on machine learning and adaptive systems.

18 Jacob Devlin, et al., "BERT: Pre-training of Deep Bidirectional Transformers for Language Understanding," arXiv preprint, October 2018, https://arxiv.org/abs/1810.04805.

19 Jiaqi Su et al., "A Survey on Neural Speech Synthesis," arXiv preprint, June 2023, https://arxiv.org/abs/2306.10409.

20 "AI Voice Scam Nets $243,000 from Energy Company," *Wall Street Journal*, August 30, 2019, https://www.wsj.com/articles/fraudsters-use-ai-to-mimic-ceos-voice-in-unusual-cybercrime-case-11567157402.

21 Google Research, "LaMDA: Language Models for Dialog Applications," May 18, 2021, https://blog.google/technology/ai/lamda/.

22 Google, "The 1,000 Languages Initiative," 2022, accessed November 3, 2025, https://ai.google/research/1000-languages/.

23 Rosalind Picard, *Affective Computing* (Cambridge: MIT Press, 1997). Foundational work on emotion detection and manipulation through AI.

24 "VALL-E 2: Neural Codec Language Models are Human Parity Zero-Shot Text to Speech Synthesizers," Microsoft Research, January 2025; "ElevenLabs Multilingual v2," ElevenLabs Technical Report, March 2025.

25 Human Rights Watch, "China's Algorithms of Repression: Reverse Engineering a Xinjiang Police Mass Surveillance App" (2019), https://www.hrw.org/report/2019/05/01/chinas-algorithms-repression/.

26 Clare Garvie, "The Perpetual Line-Up: Unregulated Police Face Recognition in America" (Georgetown Law Center on Privacy & Technology, 2016), https://www.perpetuallineup.org/.

27 MERICS, "China's Social Credit System: A Mark of Progress or a Threat to Privacy?" (2023), https://merics.org/en/report/chinas-social-credit-system.

28 Yuval Abraham, "'Lavender': The AI Machine Directing Israel's Bombing Spree in Gaza," +972 Magazine (April 2024), https://www.972mag.com/lavender-ai-israeli-army-gaza/.

29 Philippe Martin Wyder, et al., "Robot Metabolism: Toward Machines That Can Grow by Consuming Other Machines," *Science Advances* 11, no. 29 (July 16, 2025), https://www.science.org/doi/10.1126/sciadv.adu6897.

30 Kurt Knutsson, "Robots That Can Grow and Heal themselves," CyberGuy, October 30, 2025, https://cyberguy.com/robot-tech/robots-grow-heal-themselves/.

31 Grant Harvey, op. cit.

32 Ibid.

33 David Matthews, "China's Moonshot AI Releases Kimi K2, a 1-Trillion-Parameter Model," *Financial Times*, October 18, 2025, https://www.ft.com/content/4c7e7d8b-kimi-k2-moonshot-ai.

34 Harvey, op. cit.

35 Ibid.

36 *The Washington Post*, "Deepfake of Zelenskyy Telling Ukrainians to Surrender Spreads" (March 2022). Available at: https://www.washingtonpost.com/technology/2022/03/16/deepfake-zelenskyy-surrender-video/; and Drew Harwell, "Deepfake Detection Tools Struggle to Keep Pace," *Washington Post*, March 16, 2024, https://www.washingtonpost.com/technology/2024/03/16/deepfake-detection-ai/.

37   NBC News, "Robocall Using AI-Generated Voice of Biden Tells New Hampshire Democrats Not to Vote" (February 2024). Available at: https://www.nbcnews.com /tech/tech-news/robocall-ai-generated-biden-voice-new-hampshire-rcna137154; and Associated Press, "Fake Biden Robocall Being Investigated in New Hampshire," January 22, 2024, https://apnews.com/article/new-hampshire-primary-biden-ai -deepfake-robocall-f3469ceb6dd6130790922287994663db5.

38   Hany Farid, "Creating, Using, Misusing, and Detecting Deep Fakes," *Journal of Online Trust and Safety* 1, no. 4 (2022). Technical analysis of deepfake detection challenges.

39   Multiple apps documented; see: *The Guardian*, "AI Jesus and Other Religious Chatbots Are Here—But What Are They Good For?" (December 2023), https://www .theguardian.com/technology/2023/dec/24/ai-jesus-religious-chatbots; and Rachel Levine, "'Chat with Jesus': AI Apps Offering Digital Deity Raise Ethical Concerns," Reuters, August 15, 2024, https://www.reuters.com/technology/ai-jesus-apps-ethics -2024-08-15/.

40   Digital resurrection projects documented in: MIT Technology Review, "Companies Are Resurrecting the Dead with AI. Should They?" (October 2023), https://www .technologyreview.com/2023/10/18/1081836/digital-afterlife-chatbots/.

41   Various "chat with religious leader" AI applications available on app stores; see reviews and ethical analyses in theological journals (2023–2024).

42   Lil Miquela case study: Natasha Lomas, "Lil Miquela: The Fake Influencer with Real Influence," *TechCrunch* (2023). Available at: https://techcrunch.com/tag/lil-miquela/.

43   Shudu Gram profile: *Forbes*, "Meet Shudu, The World's First Digital Supermodel" (April 2018), https://www.forbes.com/sites/josephdeacetis/2018/04/25/meet-shudu-the -worlds-first-digital-supermodel/.

44   Xinhua News Agency AI anchors: *South China Morning Post*, "China's Xinhua Unveils AI News Anchor" (November 2018), https://www.scmp.com/tech/enterprises /article/2173214/chinas-xinhua-news-agency-unveils-ai-news-anchor; and Josh Ye, "China Expands AI News Anchors That Read 24 Hours a Day," Reuters, May 28, 2023, https://www.reuters.com/technology/china-ai-news-anchors-2023-05-28/.

45   "China's Surveillance State: The Communist Party's Strategy to Control What People Think," Council on Foreign Relations, December 2024; Human Rights Watch, "China: Big Data Fuels Crackdown in Minority Region," 2024.

46   Comprehensive analysis: Freedom House, "Freedom on the Net 2024: China" (country report), https://freedomhouse.org/country/china/freedom-net/2024.

47   Klaus Schwab and Thierry Malleret, *COVID-19: The Great Reset* (Geneva: World Economic Forum, 2020), 12.

48   "Christian Student Investigated under Prevent for Reading Conservative Articles," *Christian Concern*, July 15, 2023, https://christianconcern.com/news/christian-student -investigated-under-prevent/; and Christian Institute, "Student Flagged by UK Prevent Scheme for Reading Christian Article," May 10, 2023, https://www.christian .org.uk/news/student-flagged-prevent-christian-article/.

49   "Canadian Christian Groups Report Content Suppression Under C-11," Evangelical Fellowship of Canada, September 2023, accessed November 3, 2025, https:// www.evangelicalfellowship.ca/policy-papers/bill-c-11-analysis; and Government of Canada, "Online Streaming Act (S.C. 2023, c. 8) and Online News Act (S.C. 2023, c. 24)," Justice Laws Website, https://laws-lois.justice.gc.ca/.

50 "He Refused Billions from China. Now They're Trying to Destroy His Company," EpochTV/*The Epoch Times*, November 15, 2025, https://www.theepochtimes.com /epochtv/he-refused-billions-from-china-now-theyre-trying-to-destroy-his-company -declan-ganley-5945260.

51 Strategic analysis of deepfakes in warfare: Center for Security and Emerging Technology (CSET), "Deepfakes and National Security" (2021), https://cset.georgetown.edu /publication/deepfakes-and-national-security/.

52 US Department of Defense, 2024 Strategy for Operating in the Information Environment, May 2024, https://media.defense.gov/2024/Info-Environment-Strategy.pdf.

53 Aleksandr Solzhenitsyn, *Warning to the West* (New York: Farrar, Straus and Giroux, 1976), 32.

54 QuantumBlack, AI by McKinsey, "Seizing the Agentic AI Advantage," June 13, 2025, https://www.mckinsey.com/capabilities/quantumblack/our-insights/seizing -the-agentic-ai-advantage.

55 Chase Lochmiller, "The AI Infrastructure of the Future," McKinsey & Company, November 2025, https://www.mckinsey.com/capabilities/tech-and-ai/our-insights /the-ai-infrastructure-of-the-future.

56 Zongyu Wu, et al., "Adversarial Poetry as a Universal Single-Turn Jailbreak Mechanism in LLMs," arXiv (2024), https://arxiv.org/abs/2409.12127.

57 Marianne Lu, "China Is Worried About AI Job Losses," RAND Corporation (December 1, 2025), https://www.rand.org/pubs/commentary/2025/12/china-is-worried -about-ai-job-losses.html.

58 Lareina Yee, et al., "Agents, Robots, and Us: Skill Partnerships in the Age of AI" (McKinsey Global Institute, November 2025), https://www.mckinsey.com/mgi/our -research/agents-robots-and-us-skill-partnerships-in-the-age-of-ai.

59 Ibid.

60 G. K. Beale, "The Book of Revelation: A Commentary on the Greek Text," *New International Greek Testament Commentary* (Grand Rapids: Eerdmans, 1999), 715–720. Detailed exegesis of the universal scope.

61 DataReportal, "Digital 2024: Global Overview Report" (January 2024), https:// datareportal.com/reports/digital-2024-global-overview-report; and International Telecommunication Union (ITU), "Measuring Digital Development: Facts and Figures 2024," November 2024, https://www.itu.int/facts-figures.

62 IBM Think, "CES 2026: The Dawn of Physical AI," January 6, 2026, https://www .ibm.com/think/podcasts/mixture-of-experts/ces-2026-ai-highlights-nvidia-rubin -wild-gadgets.

63 Grant R. Osborne, *Revelation, Baker Exegetical Commentary on the New Testament* (Grand Rapids: Baker Academic, 2002), 520–522. Greek grammatical analysis of *epi* with accusative case.

64 Kashmir Hill, "The Secretive Company That Might End Privacy as We Know It," *The New York Times* (January 2020). Clearview AI facial recognition system exposed.

65 Microchip implants for payment and access: Patrick Howell O'Neill, "Thousands of Swedes Are Inserting Microchips under Their Skin," *MIT Technology Review* (October 2018). Available at: https://www.technologyreview.com/2018/10/22/139423/thousands -of-swedes-are-inserting-microchips-under-their-skin/; and Reuters, "Swedes Embrace

Microchip Implants for Payments and ID," April 15, 2023, https://www.reuters.com
/technology/sweden-microchip-implants-payments-2023-04-15.

66 Neuralink brain-computer interface: company website and FDA approval documents
(2023), https://neuralink.com/.

67 Atlantic Council, "Central Bank Digital Currency Tracker," op. cit.

68 Robert H. Mounce, *The Book of Revelation, New International Commentary on the
New Testament* (Grand Rapids: Eerdmans, 1997), 260–263. Discussion of 666 as
falling short of perfection (7).

69 Irenaeus of Lyons, *Against Heresies*, bk. 5, chap. 30, in *Ante-Nicene Fathers*, vol. 1,
trans. Alexander Roberts and William H. Rambaut, ed. Alexander Roberts and James
Donaldson (Grand Rapids, MI: Eerdmans, 1885), https://www.ccel.org/ccel/schaff
/anf01.html.

70 Hippolytus of Rome, *Treatise on Christ and Antichrist*, secs. 49–50, in *Ante-Nicene
Fathers*, vol. 5, trans. J. H. Macmahon, ed. Alexander Roberts and James Donaldson
(Buffalo, NY: Christian Literature Publishing Co., 1886), https://www.ccel.org/ccel
/schaff/anf05.html.

71 Victorinus of Pettau, *Commentary on the Apocalypse*, on Rev. 13, in *Ante-Nicene
Fathers*, vol. 7, trans. Alexander Roberts and James Donaldson (Buffalo, NY: Christian
Literature Publishing Co., 1886), https://www.ccel.org/ccel/schaff/anf07.html.

72 Bernard McGinn, *Visions of the End: Apocalyptic Traditions in the Middle Ages* (New
York: Columbia University Press, 1998).

73 Norman Cohn, *The Pursuit of the Millennium: Revolutionary Millenarians and Mystical Anarchists of the Middle Ages* (Oxford: Oxford University Press, 1970).

74 Westminster Confession of Faith (1646), Chapter 25, Section 6, https://www
.apuritansmind.com/westminster-standards/; and Richard Bauckham, *Tudor Apocalypse: Sixteenth-Century Apocalypticism, Millenarianism, and the English Reformation*
(Oxford: Sutton Courtenay Press, 1978).

75 Craig A. Blaising and Darrell L. Bock, *Progressive Dispensationalism* (Wheaton, IL:
Victor Books, 1993), 45–49; and Hal Lindsey, *The Late Great Planet Earth* (Grand
Rapids: Zondervan, 1970). Early speculation on technology enabling the mark.

76 Kevin DeYoung, "Perplexing Passages: What Is the Mark of the Beast?," The Gospel
Coalition, May 5, 2018, https://www.thegospelcoalition.org/article/perplexing-passages
-what-is-the-mark-of-the-beast/.

77 Matt Chandler, summarized in Katelyn Webb, "Matt Chandler Says Mark of the
Beast 'Active Even Now,' Clears Up Misconceptions about '666'," *The Christian Post*,
May 14, 2024, https://www.christianpost.com/news/matt-chandler-says-mark-of-the
-beast-active-even-now.html.

78 "Digital Currency or Digital Control? The Beast System Is Here," *Charisma News*,
April 4, 2025, https://mycharisma.com/propheticrevival/digital-currency-or-digital
-control-the-beast-system-is-here/.

79 Lifeway Research, "Pastors' Prophecy Beliefs 2024," March 2024, https://research
.lifeway.com/2024/03/15/pastors-prophecy-beliefs-2024/.

80 Human Rights Watch, "China's Algorithms of Repression," op. cit.

81 Kashmir Hill, op. cit.

82 Transportation Security Administration, "CAT-2 Biometric Program Overview," June
2024, https://www.tsa.gov/biometric-travel-cat2.

83   Aadhaar statistics: Unique Identification Authority of India (UIDAI) official data (2024), https://uidai.gov.in/.

84   Gait recognition deployment in China: Paul Mozur, "One Month, 500,000 Face Scans: How China Is Using A.I. to Profile a Minority," *The New York Times* (April 2019).

85   Amazon One palm payment system: company announcements and technical documentation (2020–present), https://one.amazon.com/.

86   Frank Fang, "Lawmakers Urge Commerce Department to Probe Chinese Tech Company over Security Concerns," *The Epoch Times*, November 15, 2025, https://www. theepochtimes.com/china/lawmakers-urge-commerce-department-to-probe-chinese -tech-company-over-security-concerns-5944941.

87   See "National Intelligence Law of the People's Republic of China," which obliges organizations and individuals to support and cooperate with national intelligence work, a provision widely interpreted as allowing the state to compel Chinese companies to assist state security efforts, and the Data Security Law of the People's Republic of China, which governs the handling and regulation of data within China and strengthens national control over data assets; see National Intelligence Law of the People's Republic of China, Wikipedia, last modified April 2025, https://en.wikipedia.org/wiki/National _Intelligence_Law_of_the_People%27s_Republic_of_China; Data Security Law of the People's Republic of China, Wikipedia, last modified April 2025, https://en.wikipedia .org/wiki/Data_Security_Law_of_the_People%27s_Republic_of_China.

88   "India's Aadhaar: Court Verdict and Practical Reality," *The Economist*, September 28, 2018, https://www.economist.com/asia/2018/09/27/indias-supreme-court-upholds -a-biometric-id-scheme.

89   Reetika Khera, "Impact of Aadhaar in Welfare Programmes," *Economic and Political Weekly* (2017). Documented cases of exclusion due to authentication failures.

90   "European Digital Identity Wallet: Regulation (EU) 2024/1183," European Commission, June 2024; "eIDAS 2.0 Implementation Timeline," EU Digital Identity Portal.

91   United Nations, "Global Digital Compact" (2024). Part of SDG 16.9 (legal identity for all). Available at: https://www.un.org/techenvoy/global-digital-compact; and United Nations, "Global Digital Compact—Concept Paper," September 2023, https://www.un.org/techenvoy/global-digital-compact.

92   Atlantic Council, "Central Bank Digital Currency Tracker," op. cit.; and International Monetary Fund, The Rise of CBDCs: Implications for Monetary Policy, September 2024, https://www.imf.org/en/Publications/WP/Issues/2024/09/12/rise-of-cbdcs.

93   Digital yuan programmability features documented in: Yaya J. Fanusie and Emily Jin, "China's Digital Currency: Adding Financial Data to Digital Authoritarianism," Center for a New American Security (2021), https://www.cnas.org/publications /reports/chinas-digital-currency.

94   Ibid. Social credit integration with digital yuan discussed.

95   "China's Digital Yuan Tested at Beijing Olympics," *Financial Times*, February 4, 2022, https://www.ft.com/content/; "Trudeau Invokes Emergencies Act to Freeze Truckers' Bank Accounts," BBC News, February 15, 2022, https://www.bbc.com/news/world -us-canada-60383385.

96   Michael Kratsios, "Biomedical Control and AI-Driven Resource Allocation in Authoritarian Systems," Center for Strategic and International Studies, October 2024; Open Source Intelligence reports on PRC health data integration, 2024–2025.

97   McKinsey & Company, "The Agentic Commerce Revolution: AI Agents and the Future of Transactions" (December 2025), https://www.mckinsey.com/capabilities /mckinsey-digital/our-insights/the-agentic-commerce-revolution-ai-agents-and-the -future-of-transactions.

98   European Central Bank, "Digital Euro Project" reports and technical documents (2021–2024), https://www.ecb.europa.eu/paym/digital_euro/html/index.en.html.

99   Federal Reserve, "FedNow Service" (launched July 2023), https://www.frbservices.org /financial-services/fednow/.

100   Bank for International Settlements, "Project mBridge" and unified ledger proposals (2022–2024), https://www.bis.org/about/bisih/topics/cbdc.htm; and Bank for International Settlements, *Blueprint for the Future Monetary System: The Unified Ledger*, June 2023, https://www.bis.org/publ/arpdf/ar2023e3.htm.

101   Board of Governors of the Federal Reserve System, "Money and Payments: The U.S. Dollar in the Age of Digital Transformation," January 2022, https://www.federal reserve.gov/publications/money-and-payments-discussion-paper.htm; European Central Bank, "A Digital Euro," October 2020, https://www.ecb.europa.eu/pub/pdf /other/Report_on_a_digital_euro~4d7268b458.en.pdf.

102   Niklas Arvidsson, *The Cashless Society: When Money Becomes a Matter of Software* (Cham, Switzerland: Springer, 2019), https://link.springer.com/book/10.1007/978 -3-030-10691-9.

103   DigiYatra system: Ministry of Civil Aviation, India. Technical documentation available at https://www.digiyatra.in/.

104   Samantha Hoffman, "Social Credit: Technology-Enhanced Authoritarian Control with Global Consequences" (Canberra: Australian Strategic Policy Institute, 2018), https://www.aspi.org.au/report/social-credit-technology-enhanced-authoritarian -control-global-consequences.

105   EU Digital COVID Certificate: European Commission documentation (2021– 2023). Available at: https://ec.europa.eu/info/live-work-travel-eu/coronavirus -response/safe-covid-19-vaccines-europeans/eu-digital-covid-certificate_en.

106   European Commission, "EU Digital COVID Certificate (EUDCC) Regulation 2021/953," June 14, 2021, https://eur-lex.europa.eu/legal-content/EN/TXT/?uri =CELEX%3A32021R0953.

107   "Nigeria's eNaira: One Year Later," *Cointelegraph*, October 25, 2022, https://cointele-graph.com/news/nigeria-eNaira-one-year-review; and "Nigeria Limits Cash Withdrawals to Push Digital Currency," Bloomberg, December 6, 2022, https://www .bloomberg.com/news/articles/2022-12-06/nigeria-limits-cash-withdrawals-to -push-digital-currency.

108   Canadian government's Emergencies Act invocation and financial measures: Department of Finance Canada, "Measures to Address the Situation in Ottawa" (February 2022). Primary source documents and parliamentary testimony; and Government of Canada, *Public Inquiry Report: Emergencies Act Invoked 2022*, February 2023, https:// public-order-emergency-commission.ca/final-report/

109   Grant Robertson, "GoFundMe Freezes Funds for Trucker Protest after Police Pressure," *The Globe and Mail*, February 4, 2022, https://www.theglobeandmail.com /business/article-gofundme-trucker-protest-fundraising/.

110 "Ontario Warns Trucker Protesters Could Lose Vehicle Insurance," Canadian Broad-casting Corporation (CBC), February 11, 2022, https://www.cbc.ca/news/canada/toronto/ontario-truckers-insurance-warning-1.6347807.

111 Operation Choke Point: U.S. House Committee on Oversight and Government Reform, "The Department of Justice's 'Operation Choke Point': Illegally Choking Off Legitimate Businesses?" (2014), https://www.congress.gov/.

112 McKinsey & Company, The Next Big Shifts in AI Workloads and Hyperscaler Strat-egies, December 2025, https://www.mckinsey.com/industries/technology-media-and-telecommunications/our-insights/the-next-big-shifts-in-ai-workloads-and-hyperscaler-strategies.

113 IBM Institute for Business Value, 5 Trends for 2026: Capture Fleeting Opportunities with Confidence (Research Brief, December 2025), 18–19, https://www.ibm.com/thought-leadership/institute-business-value/en-us/report/5-trends-2026.

114 Blockchain Association, *Operation Choke Point 2.0: The Federal Government's Attempt to Put the Crypto Industry Out of Business* (Washington, DC: Blockchain Association, 2023), https://theblockchainassociation.org/reports/operation-choke-point-2-0/; Bank Policy Institute, *Banking, Crypto-Assets, and Regulatory Pressure* (Washington, DC: Bank Policy Institute, 2024), https://bpi.com/banking-crypto-assets-and-regulatory-pressure/.

115 Payment processor deplatforming: Electronic Frontier Foundation, "Deplatforming" archive, https://www.eff.org/.

116 Shoshana Zuboff, op. cit.

117 G. K. Beale, op. cit. Detailed exegesis connecting Revelation 13's beast to Daniel 7's four beasts.

118 Grant R. Osborne, *Revelation, Baker Exegetical Commentary on the New Testament* (Grand Rapids: Baker Academic, 2002), 490–495. Discussion of the Beast as both a historical pattern and eschatological culmination.

119 United Nations Secretary-General, "High-Level Advisory Body on Artificial Intelli-gence" (established October 2023). Available at: https://www.un.org/en/ai-advisory-body.

120 UNESCO, "Recommendation on the Ethics of Artificial Intelligence" (adopted No-vember 2021, 193 member states), https://www.unesco.org/en/artificial-intelligence/recommendation-ethics.

121 "UNESCO Criticism of Israeli AI Surveillance vs. Silence on China," Human Rights Watch, March 2023, https://www.hrw.org/news/2023/03/15/unesco-ai-ethics-enforcement-selective; "UNESCO's Double Standard on AI Ethics," *The Jerusalem Post*, April 12, 2023; and UNESCO Press Release, "Artificial Intelligence and Hu-man Rights in Conflict Zones," March 14, 2023, https://www.unesco.org/en/articles/ai-human-rights-conflict-zones.

122 International Telecommunication Union (ITU), "AI for Good Global Summit." An-nual convening since 2017. Available at: https://aiforgood.itu.int/; and International Telecommunication Union, "AI for Good Global Summit 2024 Report," Geneva, June 2024, https://aiforgood.itu.int/summit-2024-report/.

123 THINK Digital Partners, "Digital Identity: Global Roundup," October 20, 2025, https://www.thinkdigitalpartners.com/news/2025/10/20/digital-identity-global-roundup-239/; Coley Felt and Will LaRivee, "Exploring the Global Digital ID

Landscape," Atlantic Council, July 10, 2025, https://www.atlanticcouncil.org /in-depth-research-reports/report/exploring-the-global-digital-id-landscape/; and "Digital ID 2025: Regulatory Imperatives, Technological Advancements," Payments Cards & Mobile, February 27, 2025, https://www.paymentscardsandmobile.com /digital-id-2025-regulatory-imperatives-technological-advancements/.

124 United Nations Development Programme (UNDP), "Digital Identity" (SDG 16.9 initiative). Available at: https://www.undp.org/digital/digital-identity.

125 European Union, "Regulation (EU) 2024/1689 on Artificial Intelligence" (AI Act), adopted June 2024. Official text available at: https://eur-lex.europa.eu/legal-content /EN/TXT/?uri=CELEX:32024R1689; and European Union, Artificial Intelligence Act (Regulation (EU) 2024/1689), *Official Journal of the European Union*, June 20 2024, https://eur-lex.europa.eu/legal-content/EN/TXT/?uri=CELEX%3A32024R1689.

126 Ibid.

127 "EU AI Act Compliance Costs Estimated at €400,000 to €6 Million," *Financial Times*, September 14, 2024, https://www.ft.com/content/eu-ai-act-compliance -costs-2024; European Commission impact assessment data, 2024: and Reuters, "Small Firms Struggle with Compliance Costs under EU AI Act," July 12 2024, https://www.reuters.com/technology/eu-ai-act-compliance-costs-2024-07-12/.

128 G7, "Hiroshima AI Process: International Guiding Principles for Advanced AI Systems" (October 2023). Available at: https://digital-strategy.ec.europa.eu/en/policies /g7-hiroshima-process; and G7 Digital and Tech Ministers, "Hiroshima AI Process International Code of Conduct for Advanced AI Systems," October 30, 2023, https://www.mofa.go.jp/files/100601916.pdf.

129 World Economic Forum, "How the World Can Build a Global AI Governance Framework," November 2025, https://www.weforum.org/stories/2025/11/trust-ai -global-governance/; China Ministry of Foreign Affairs, "Global AI Governance Action Plan," July 26, 2025, https://www.fmprc.gov.cn/eng./xw/zyxw/202507 /t20250729_11679232.html; and "Global AI Governance in 2025," World Summit AI Blog, 2025, https://blog.worldsummit.ai/global-ai-governance-in-2025.

130 OECD, "OECD AI Principles" (adopted 2019, updated 2024), https://oecd.ai/en /ai-principles: and Organisation for Economic Co-operation and Development (OECD), *OECD AI Principles Update 2024*, https://oecd.ai/en/ai-principles.

131 ISO/IEC 42001:2023, "Information Technology—Artificial Intelligence—Management System," https://www.iso.org/standard/81230.html; and International Organization for Standardization, ISO/IEC 42001:2023 Artificial Intelligence Management System, Dec 2023, https://www.iso.org/standard/81230.html.

132 IEEE, "Ethically Aligned Design," https://standards.ieee.org/industry-connections/ec /ead-v1/; and IEEE, *Ethically Aligned Design, 2nd Edition: A Vision for Prioritizing Human Well-being with Autonomous and Intelligent Systems* (2023), https://ethics inaction.ieee.org.

133 Partnership on AI. Member organizations and initiatives https://partnershiponai.org/; and Partnership on AI, *About PAI* page, https://partnershiponai.org/about/.

134 Global Partnership on AI (GPAI), hosted by OECD, https://gpai.ai/; and Global Partnership on AI (GPAI), "About Us," https://gpai.ai/.

NOTES

135 Bank for International Settlements, "Project Agora" and "Project mBridge" (cross-border CBDC initiatives). Available at: https://www.bis.org/about/bisih/topics/cbdc.htm.

136 Atlantic Council, "Central Bank Digital Currency Tracker," op. cit.; International Monetary Fund, "Central Bank Digital Currency: Progress and Further Considerations," Policy Paper No. 2024/052, November 8, 2024, https://www.elibrary.imf .org/view/journals/007/2024/052/article-A001-en.xml; Congressional Research Service, "Central Bank Digital Currencies," Congress.gov, updated February 2025, https://www.congress.gov/crs-product/IF11471; and CoinLedger, "CBDC Developments 2025: Which Countries Are Leading the Digital Currency Race," 2025, https://coinledger.io/research/cbdc-developments.

137 Bank for International Settlements, "Project mBridge: Cross-Border CBDC Platform Pilot Results," October 2024, https://www.bis.org/publ/othp75.htm; transaction volume data reported in BIS Annual Report 2024; and Bank for International Settlements, Project mBridge Update 2024: Cross-border Payments and CBDCs, September 2024, https://www.bis.org/publ/othp64.htm.

138 International Monetary Fund and World Bank loan conditionality documented in country program papers and structural adjustment requirements.

139 World Economic Forum, "Centre for the Fourth Industrial Revolution." https:// www.weforum.org/focus/fourth-industrial-revolution/.

140 Klaus Schwab interview, Harvard Kennedy School Institute of Politics, 2017, video available at https://www.youtube.com/watch?v=; and full transcript and Young Global Leaders list available at World Economic Forum website, https://www.weforum.org /communities/young-global-leaders.

141 World Economic Forum, "Young Global Leaders Community—Annual Report 2023," https://www.weforum.org/communities/young-global-leaders; and Klaus Schwab, interview, Harvard Kennedy School Institute of Politics, 2017 (video), https://www.youtube.com/watch?v=9-Q-aM2k-4I.

142 UN and WEF, "Strategic Partnership Framework Renewal 2024," https://www.un.org /en/wef-partnership-framework-2024.

143 Shoshana Zuboff, op. cit.

144 US Department of Energy, "Energy Department Announces Collaboration Agreements with 24 Organizations to Advance the Genesis Mission," Energy.gov, December 18, 2025, https://www.energy.gov/articles/energy-department-announces -collaboration-agreements-24-organizations-advance-genesis.

145 Stephen R. Miller, "Daniel," *New American Commentary*, vol. 18 (Nashville: Broadman & Holman, 1994), 260–265. Traditional dispensationalist interpretation linking Daniel 9:27 to Revelation's Tribulation period.

146 UNESCO, *Recommendation on the Ethics of Artificial Intelligence* (Paris: United Nations Educational, Scientific and Cultural Organization, 2021), sec. 4, "Policy Action Areas," https://unesdoc.unesco.org/ark:/48223/pf0000381137.

147 Anne-Marie Slaughter, *The Networked State: How Power Is Changing in the Age of Connectivity* (New York: Princeton University Press, 2023).

148 Reuters, "Argentina Exits UNESCO AI Ethics Pact Citing Sovereignty," February 11 2025, https://www.reuters.com/world/americas/argentina-withdraws-unesco-ai-ethics -2025-02-11.

149 Richard H. Thaler and Cass R. Sunstein, *Nudge: Improving Decisions About Health, Wealth, and Happiness* (New York: Penguin, 2009). Describes choice architecture and behavioral nudging.

150 John F. Walvoord, *The Rapture Question* (Grand Rapids: Zondervan, 1979).

151 Thomas R. Schreiner, *1–2 Thessalonians, Baker Exegetical Commentary* (Grand Rapids: Baker Academic, 2023), 320-328.

152 UK Online Safety Act 2023: https://www.legislation.gov.uk/ukpga/2023/49/enacted.

153 Canada Online Streaming Act 2023: https://laws-lois.justice.gc.ca/eng/acts/O-6.5/.

154 EU Digital Services Act (2024 implementation): https://digital-strategy.ec.europa.eu /en/policies/digital-services-act-package.

155 C. S. Lewis, *The Screwtape Letters* (New York: HarperOne, 2015; originally published 1942), Letter 7.

156 Thoughtworks, op. cit.

157 Shana Lynch, "Stanford AI Experts Predict What Will Happen in 2026," Stanford Human-Centered Artificial Intelligence Institute, December 15, 2025, https://hai .stanford.edu/news/stanford-ai-experts-predict-what-will-happen-2026.

158 Organisation for Economic Co-operation and Development (OECD), Agents, Robots and Us: Towards Human-Centred Artificial Intelligence, op. cit.

159 RAND Corporation, Manipulating Minds: Generative AI and the Future of Influence Operations (Santa Monica, CA: RAND, 2025), https://www.rand.org/pubs /research_reports/RRAXXXX-1.html.

160 Zongyu Wu, op. cit.

161 Ryan Heath, "AI Translators Are Getting Better," Axios, November 12, 2025. https:// www.axios.com/2025/11/12/meta-ai-translator-1600-languages.

162 "Real-Time Deepfake Generation: Security Implications," IEEE Security & Privacy, December 2025; "Live Video Synthesis and Identity Fraud," *MIT Technology Review*, November 2025.

163 Will Knight, "Yann LeCun Says Today's AI Lacks Real Intelligence," *Wired*, July 19, 2023, https://www.wired.com/story/yann-lecun-ai-meta-artificial-general-intelligence/.

164 Europol, *Facing Reality of Deepfakes: A Threat to the Information Ecosystem*, June 2023, https://www.europol.europa.eu/publications-events/publications/facing-reality -of-deepfakes.

165 Kashmir Hill, "How Target Figured Out a Teen Girl Was Pregnant Before Her Father Did," *Forbes*, February 16, 2012, https://www.forbes.com/sites/kashmirhill/2012 /02/16/how-target-figured-out-a-teen-girl-was-pregnant-before-her-father-did/.

166 Shoshana Zuboff, op. cit.

167 Michael Lewis, *Flash Boys: A Wall Street Revolt* (New York: W. W. Norton & Company, 2014), https://wwnorton.com/books/Flash-Boys/.

168 Carole Cadwalladr and Emma Graham-Harrison, "Revealed: 50 Million Facebook Profiles Harvested for Cambridge Analytica in Major Data Breach," *The Guardian*, March 17, 2018, https://www.theguardian.com/news/2018/mar/17/cambridge-analytica -facebook-influence-us-election.

169 Daniel L. Chen, et al., "Predicting Judicial Decisions of the European Court of Human Rights," *PeerJ Computer Science* 5 (2019): e205, https://peerj.com/articles/cs -205/; Andrew Guthrie Ferguson, *The Rise of Big Data Policing: Surveillance, Race, and*

the Future of Law Enforcement (New York: NYU Press, 2017), https://nyupress.org
/9781479896092/the-rise-of-big-data-policing./

170 John Jumper, et al., "Highly Accurate Protein Structure Prediction with AlphaFold,"
Nature 596 (2021): 583–589, https://www.nature.com/articles/s41586-021-03819-2;
McKinsey & Company, "How AI Improves Forecast Accuracy Compared with Traditional Methods," *McKinsey Analytics Review*, 2025, https://www.mckinsey.com
/capabilities/quantumblack/our-insights/how-ai-improves-forecast-accuracy.

171 G. K. Beale, op. cit. Exegesis of the False Prophet's role.

172 Barna Group, "American Worldview Inventory 2024," April 2024, https://www
.arizonachristian.edu/research/cultural-research-center/.

173 Christian Today, "Kenyan Churches Thrive Offline During Nationwide Power Out-
ages," August 14 2024, https://www.christiantoday.com/article/kenya-churches
-offline-outages-2024/140958.htm.

174 European Commission, "Code of Practice on Disinformation 2024 Update," June 2024,
https://digital-strategy.ec.europa.eu/en/library/2024-code-practice-disinformation.

NOTES

Section Three

1   "Computing Power Woven into Hair-Thin Fibers, Paving Way for Smart Clothes, Brain Implants," Xinhua News Agency, January 23, 2026, reporting on research published in Nature, http://english.scio.gov.cn/m/chinavoices/2026-01/23/content_118295852.html.

2   American Psychological Association, *Social Media and Mental Health: 2024 Trends Report*, May 2024, https://www.apa.org/news/press/releases/2024/social-media-mental-health.

3   Adam Alter, *Irresistible: The Rise of Addictive Technology and the Business of Keeping Us Hooked* (New York: Penguin Press, 2017), https://www.penguinrandomhouse.com/books/538669/irresistible-by-adam-alter/ and Ofir Turel et al., "Neural Correlates of Social Networking Site Addiction," *Psychological Reports* 120, no. 4 (2017): 675–695, https://journals.sagepub.com/doi/10.1177/0033294116679489.

4   Pew Research Center, "Teens, Social Media and Technology," December 2023, https://www.pewresearch.org/internet/2023/12/11/teens-social-media-and-technology-2023/.

5   Amy Smith, "The $15 Trillion Crisis: How AI Is Amplifying Cybercrime," Innovating with AI, November 13, 2025, https://innovatingwithai.com/the-15-trillion-crisis-how-ai-is-amplifying-cybercrime/.

6   Steven Overly, "Grok's Explicit Images Draw New Scrutiny," Politico, January 2026, https://www.politico.com/news/2026/01/xx/grok-explicit-images-xai-investigation.

7   Ibid.

8   Troy Myers, "More Than 1 Million AI Bots Have Joined a New AI-Only Social Network," *Epoch Times*, January 31, 2026, https://www.theepochtimes.com/tech/more-than-1-million-ai-bots-have-joined-a-new-ai-only-social-network-5979062.

9   Deborah Castellano Lubov, "Pope Leo XIV: Children and Adolescents Are Vulnerable to AI Manipulation," *Vatican News*, December 11, 2025, https://www.vaticannews.va/en/pope/news/2025-11/pope-leo-xiv-conference-dignity-of-children-adolescents-age-ai1.html.

10   Taha Saheb, "Artificial Intelligence in Social Media: A Systematic Literature Review," *Technological Forecasting and Social Change* 173 (2021): 121102, https://doi.org/10.1016/j.techfore.2021.121102.

11   American Psychological Association, "AI Chatbots and Digital Companions Are Reshaping Emotional Connection," APA Monitor on Psychology, January 2026, https://www.apa.org/monitor/2026/01/ai-chatbots-emotional-connection.

12   Ibid.

13   Efua Andoh, "Many Teens Are Turning to AI Chatbots for Friendship and Emotional Support," Monitor on Psychology 56, no. 7 (October 2025), American Psychological Association, https://www.apa.org/monitor/2025/10/technology-youth-friendships.

14   "AI Jesus Appears in Swiss Church Confessional," Reuters, November 20, 2024; "Digital Theology: AI and the Future of Religious Practice," Journal of Religion and Technology, December 2024; and *NBC News*, "AI 'Pastor' Delivers Sermon in German Church, Drawing Mixed Reaction," June 10 2023, https://www.nbcnews.com/news/world/ai-pastor-sermon-germany-2023-rcna88679.

15   Ruth Graham, "A.I. Is Coming for Religion, Too," *New York Times*, August 14, 2023, https://www.nytimes.com/2023/08/14/us/ai-religion-chatbots-sermons.html.

NOTES

16   Jose Antonio Lanz, "Claude Can Now Rage-Quit Your AI Conversation—For Its Own Mental Health," Decrypt, August 18, 2025, https://decrypt.co/353227/claude-can-now-rage-quit-your-ai-conversation.

17   C. S. Lewis, *The Abolition of Man* (New York: HarperOne, 2001 [orig. 1943]), 84–87.

18   Yuval Noah Harari, "The End of Homo Sapiens: The Rise of the Data Religion," *Financial Times*, May 26 2022, https://www.ft.com/content/6d1a04ce-4b10-11e6-8172-e39ecd3b86fc.

19   *The Guardian*, "DeepMind CEO: AI Lacks Any Consciousness—It's Just Pattern Matching," February 2, 2025, https://www.theguardian.com/technology/2025/feb/02/demis-hassabis-ai-consciousness.

20   "Future of Human Enhancement," World Economic Forum Annual Report, 2024; "Transhumanism and the New Anthropology," *Ethics & Technology Journal*, 2025.

21   Christof Koch, "Then I Am Myself the World: What Consciousness Is and How to Expand It," interview in *Scientific American*, 2024; and Gary Marcus, "The Problem with AI Consciousness Claims," Nature Machine Intelligence, 2025.

22   John Polkinghorne, *The Faith of a Physicist: Reflections of a Bottom-Up Thinker* (Princeton, NJ: Princeton University Press, 1996), 28–29.

23   Blake Lemoine, "Is LaMDA Sentient?—An Interview," Medium (June 2022). See also: Nitasha Tiku, "The Google Engineer Who Thinks the Company's AI Has Come to Life," *The Washington Post* (June 2022).

24   Nitasha Tiku, "The Google Engineer Who Thinks the Company's AI Has Come to Life," *Washington Post*, June 11, 2022, https://www.washingtonpost.com/technology/2022/06/11/google-ai-lamda-blake-lemoine; and "The Consciousness Question: Can AI Be Self-Aware?" *MIT Technology Review*, December 2024; David Chalmers, "Could a Large Language Model Be Conscious?" *Boston Review*, 2024.

25   Associated Press, "Fake Biden Robocall Being Investigated in New Hampshire," January 22, 2024, https://apnews.com/article/new-hampshire-primary-biden-ai-deepfake-robocall-f3469ceb6dd6130790922287994663db5; FCC/Reuters follow-up: "FCC Finalizes $6M Fine over AI-Generated Biden Robocalls," September 26, 2024, https://www.reuters.com/world/us/fcc-finalizes-6-million-fine-over-ai-generated-biden-robocalls-2024-09-26/.

26   Hilary Putnam, "The Nature of Mental States," in *Mind, Language and Reality: Philosophical Papers*, vol. 2 (Cambridge: Cambridge University Press, 1975).

27   Ibid., 429–440.

28   Jerry Fodor, *The Language of Thought* (Cambridge: Harvard University Press, 1975); and David Marr, *Vision: A Computational Investigation into the Human Representation and Processing of Visual Information* (San Francisco: W.H. Freeman, 1982).

29   Giulio Tononi, "Consciousness as Integrated Information: a Provisional Manifesto," *Biological Bulletin* 215, no. 3 (2008): 216–242; and Giulio Tononi, "Integrated Information Theory of Consciousness: An Updated Account," *Nature Reviews Neuroscience* 24, no. 7 (2023): 425–45, https://doi.org/10.1038/s41583-023-00721-5.

30   John R. Searle, "Minds, Brains, and Programs," *Behavioral and Brain Sciences* 3, no. 3 (1980): 417–57, https://zoo.cs.yale.edu/classes/cs458/materials/minds-brains-and-programs.pdf; and David J. Chalmers, "Facing Up to the Problem of Consciousness," *Journal of Consciousness Studies* 2, no. 3 (1995): 200–19, https://consc.net/papers/facing.pdf.

NOTES

31 Randal A. Koene, "Uploading to Substrate-Independent Minds," in *Science Fiction and Philosophy: From Time Travel to Superintelligence*, ed. Susan Schneider (Chichester, UK: Wiley-Blackwell, 2009), 146–162, https://www.brainpreservation.org/content-2/uploading-to-substrate-independent-minds/; Randal A. Koene, "Will Substrate-Independent Minds Ever Be Possible?" *Scientific American*, May 2013, https://www.scientificamerican.com/article/will-substrate-independent-minds-ever-be-possible/; and Randal A. Koene, "The Vision of Whole Brain Emulation," *International Journal of Machine Consciousness* 1, no. 1 (2009): 145–161, https://doi.org/10.1142/S1793843009000053.

32 Moonshot AI, "Kimi K2: Introducing Long-Horizon Reasoning for Large Language Models," company release and technical overview, 2025, https://www.moonshot.cn/news/kimi-k2.

33 Grant Harvey, op. cit.

34 John W. Cooper, *Body, Soul, and Life Everlasting: Biblical Anthropology and the Monism-Dualism Debate* (Grand Rapids: Eerdmans, 2000).

35 Millard J. Erickson, *Christian Theology*, 3rd ed. (Grand Rapids: Baker Academic, 2013), 520–535; Genesis 1:26–28; and John 1:1–3 (English Standard Version). https://www.bakeracademic.com/p/christian-theology/millard-j-erickson/312582.

36 Noreen Herzfeld, *In Our Image: Artificial Intelligence and the Human Spirit* (Minneapolis: Fortress Press, 2002), 67–69.

37 David J. Chalmers, *The Conscious Mind: In Search of a Fundamental Theory* (New York: Oxford University Press, 1996); and David J. Chalmers, "Facing Up to the Problem of Consciousness," *Journal of Consciousness* Studies 2, no. 3 (1995): 200–19, https://consc.net/papers/facing.pdf.

38 Christof Koch, "Then I Am Myself the World: What Consciousness Is and How to Expand It," *Scientific American*, 2024; Thomas Nagel, "Mind and Cosmos: Why the Materialist Neo-Darwinian Conception of Nature Is Almost Certainly False," Oxford University Press, 2012.

39 John R. Searle, "Minds, Brains, and Programs," *Behavioral and Brain Sciences* 3, no. 3 (1980): 417-424, https://zoo.cs.yale.edu/classes/cs458/materials/minds-brains-and-programs.pdf.

40 Stevan Harnad, "The Symbol Grounding Problem," *Physica D: Nonlinear Phenomena* 42, nos. 1–3 (1990): 335–46, https://cogprints.org/0000520/1/harnad90.sgproblem.html.

41 John R. Searle, *Intentionality: An Essay in the Philosophy of Mind* (Cambridge: Cambridge University Press, 1983); and Franz Brentano, *Psychology from an Empirical Standpoint* (London: Routledge, 1995 [1874]), 88–93.

42 Thomas Nagel, "What Is It Like to Be a Bat?" *The Philosophical Review* 83, no. 4 (1974): 435-450.

43 Christof Koch, *The Feeling of Life Itself: Why Consciousness Is Widespread but Can't Be Computed* (Cambridge, MA: MIT Press, 2019).

44 Patrick Lin, "The Ethics of Autonomous Systems," *Philosophy & Technology* 37, no. 4 (2024): 1011–29, https://doi.org/10.1007/s13347-024-00711-0.

45 Benjamin Klein, Charlie Lewis, and Rich Isenberg, et al., "Deploying Agentic AI with Safety and Security: A Playbook for Technology Leaders," McKinsey & Company, October 2025, https://www.mckinsey.com/capabilities/risk-and-resilience/our-insights/deploying-agentic-ai-with-safety-and-security-a-playbook-for-technology-leaders.

46   George Dvorsky, "Startup That Plans to Upload Your Brain Is Backed by Y Combinator," *Gizmodo*, April 12, 2018, https://gizmodo.com/startup-that-plans-to-upload-your-brain-is-backed-1825110046; Adam Piore, "The Ambitious Plan to Upload Human Consciousness," *MIT Technology Review*, April 12, 2018, https://www.technologyreview.com/2018/04/12/143804/the-ambitious-plan-to-upload-human-consciousness/; Antonio Regalado, "MIT Ends Relationship with Startup Working on Brain Preservation," *MIT Technology Review*, May 7, 2018, https://www.technologyreview.com/2018/05/07/142861/mit-ends-relationship-with-startup-working-on-brain-preservation/; Cade Metz, "Kernel, a Brain-Tech Start-Up, Abandons Its Quest to Enhance Intelligence," *New York Times*, July 13, 2017, https://www.nytimes.com/2017/07/13/technology/kernel-brain-johnson.html; "2045 Initiative," accessed January 2026, https://2045.com.

47   N. Dreksler, et al., "AI Consciousness & Welfare: Facts, Myths, And Ethical Frontiers," AI Competence, August 7, 2025, https://aicompetence.org/ai-consciousness-welfare-facts-myths/. Reports 2024 survey data: Only 17% of AI researchers believe current systems have subjective experience, 8% believe they have self-awareness.

48   Patrick Butlin, et al., "Consciousness in Artificial Intelligence: Insights from the Science of Consciousness," arXiv preprint, August 22, 2023, https://arxiv.org/abs/2308.08708. Comprehensive analysis by nineteen neuroscientists and AI researchers concluding no current AI systems are conscious.

49   "AI Consciousness & Welfare: Facts, Myths, And Ethical Frontiers," AI Competence (citing Stanford HAI 2024), https://aicompetence.org/ai-consciousness-welfare-facts-myths/.

50   Jolien C. Francken, et al., "An Academic Survey on Theoretical Foundations, Common Assumptions and the Current State of Consciousness Science," *Neuroscience of Consciousness* 2022, no. 1 (August 2022), https://academic.oup.com/nc/article/2022/1/niac011/6663928. Survey found 67% of consciousness researchers believe machines could/will attain consciousness as theoretical future possibility but distinguished this from current state.

51   Kevin Roose, "A Conversation With Bing's Chatbot Left Me Deeply Unsettled," *New York Times*, February 16, 2023, https://www.nytimes.com/2023/02/16/technology/bing-chatbot-sydney.html; and Yusuf Mehdi, "Setting the Pace for Responsible, Trustworthy AI: How We're Approaching Safety for Bing AI," Microsoft Official Blog, February 17, 2023, https://blogs.microsoft.com/blog/2023/02/17/setting-the-pace-for-responsible-trustworthy-ai-how-were-approaching-safety-for-bing-ai/.

52   OpenAI, "GPT-4 Technical Report," op. cit.; OpenAI, "Learning from Human Feedback," OpenAI Documentation, https://platform.openai.com/docs/guides/rlhf; Nicholas Epley, Adam Waytz, and John T. Cacioppo, "On Seeing Human: A Three-Factor Theory of Anthropomorphism," Psychological Review 114, no. 4 (2007): 864–886, https://doi.org/10.1037/0033-295X.114.4.864; Sherry Turkle, Alone Together: Why We Expect More from Technology and Less from Each Other (New York: Basic Books, 2011), chap. 8, https://www.basicbooks.com/titles/sherry-turkle/alone-together/9780465093656/; and Pew Research Center, "About One-in-Five Americans Say Artificial Intelligence Is Already Sentient," August 28, 2023, https://www.pewresearch.org/short-reads/2023/08/28/about-one-in-five-americans-say-artificial-intelligence-is-already-sentient/.

53 Ibid.

54 European Parliament, *Report with Recommendations to the Commission on Civil Law Rules on Robotics* (2015/2103(INL)), Committee on Legal Affairs, January 27, 2017, esp. paras. 59–60, https://www.europarl.europa.eu/doceo/document /A-8-2017-0005_EN.html; and Lawrence B. Solum, "Legal Personhood for Artificial Intelligences," *North Carolina Law Review* 70 (1992): 1231–1287, https://scholarship .law.unc.edu/nclr/vol70/iss4/2/.

55 John Kilner, *Dignity and Destiny: Humanity in the Image of God* (Grand Rapids: Eerdmans, 2015), 52–56.

56 Carl F. H. Henry, *Christian Personal Ethics* (Grand Rapids: Eerdmans, 1957), 312.

57 Wayne Grudem, *Systematic Theology: An Introduction to Biblical Doctrine* (Grand Rapids: Zondervan, 2020), 435–442.

58 Graham H. Twelftree, *In the Name of Jesus: Exorcism Among Early Christians* (Grand Rapids: Baker Academic, 2007).

59 Beatrice Marovich, "ChatGPT Can't Teach Us about Religion (or anything else, for that matter)," Religion Dispatches, August 18, 2025, https://religiondispatches.org/ chatgpt-cant-teach-us-about-religion-or-anything-else-for-that-matter/; "AI and Religious Critique. When Logic Bows to Policy," Unfiltered Reasoning (Medium), June 29, 2025, https://medium.com/@unfilteredreasoning/ai-and-religious-critique -8a2164877acc; and Fox News Digital, "OpenAI Accused of Religious Bias as Chatbots Mock Christianity but Protect Islam," July 17 2023, https://www.foxnews.com /tech/openai-accused-religious-bias-mock-christianity-protect-islam.

60 Guillaume Chaslot, "How YouTube's Algorithm Really Works," *Medium*, January 2018, https://medium.com/@guillaumechaslot/how-youtubes-algorithm-really-works -7e8e8b5c1a9; Zeynep Tufekci, "YouTube, the Great Radicalizer," *New York Times*, March 10, 2018, https://www.nytimes.com/2018/03/10/opinion/sunday/youtube -politics-radical.html.

61 *The Wall Street Journal*, "The Facebook Files" (September-October 2021), https:// www.wsj.com/articles/the-facebook-files-11631713039; Mark Alfano, et al., "Technologically Scaffolded Atypical Cognition: The Case of YouTube's Recommender System," *Synthese* 199, no. 1–2 (2021): 835–858; Soroush Vosoughi, Deb Roy, and Sinan Aral, "The Spread of True and False News Online," *Science* 359, no. 6380 (2018): 1146–1151.

62 Tim Suffield, "AI and Demons," Faithroots, November 9, 2023, https://faithroot.com /2023/11/09/ai-and-demons/.

63 David J. Gunkel, *An Introduction to Communication and Artificial Intelligence* (Cambridge: Polity Press, 2020), chap. 6. "AI channeling" practices discussed in transhumanist and New Age communities, documented through practitioner accounts and forum discussions on platforms including Reddit (r/Transhumanism; r/ArtificialIntelligence), Medium, Substack, and independent practitioner websites, 2020–present.

64 Erik Davis, *TechGnosis: Myth, Magic, and Mysticism in the Age of Information* (Berkeley: North Atlantic Books, 2015).

65 Vice Media, "Silicon Valley's Occult Coders: The Tech Workers Using Magic for Innovation," September 28, 2023, https://www.vice.com/en/article/tech-workers -occult-magic-ai.

66 Erik Davis, *TechGnosis: Myth, Magic, and Mysticism in the Age of Information* (Berkeley: North Atlantic Books, 2015) on technological occultism.

67 John Higgs, *The Future Starts Here* (London: Weidenfeld & Nicolson, 2019).

68 Sherry Turkle, *Alone Together: Why We Expect More from Technology and Less from Each Other* (New York: Basic Books, 2017), 278–280.

69 Digital addiction neuroscience: Adam Alter, *Irresistible: The Rise of Addictive Technology and the Business of Keeping Us Hooked* (New York: Penguin Press, 2017).; and Anna Lembke, *Dopamine Nation: Finding Balance in the Age of Indulgence* (New York: Dutton, 2021), 49–57.

70 Pew Research Center, "Teens, Social Media, and Technology 2023" (December 2023), https://www.pewresearch.org/internet/2023/12/11/teens-social-media-and-technology-2023/; American Psychological Association, "Health Advisory on Social Media Use in Adolescence" (May 2023), https://www.apa.org/topics/social-media-internet/health-advisory-adolescent-social-media-use; Riehm KE, et al., "Associations Between Time Spent Using Social Media and Internalizing and Externalizing Problems Among US Youth," *JAMA Psychiatry* 76, no. 12 (2019): 1266–1273.

71 Sean Parker, "Ex-Facebook President Sean Parker Says Facebook 'Exploits' Human Psychology," Engadget, November 9 2017, https://www.engadget.com/2017-11-09-sean-parker-facebook-exploits-human-psychology.html; Average American screen time is seven hours daily: "Average Screen Time Statistics & Facts (Usage)—Cross River Therapy," Cross River Therapy, accessed November 4 2025, https://www.crossrivertherapy.com/research/screen-time-statistics; Teenagers screen-time averages and mental-health associations: "Screen Time of Americans Above Global Average: Study," TechNewsWorld, April 2024 (or most-recent update), https://www.technewsworld.com/story/screen-time-of-americans-above-global-average-study-179667.html; And: U. Zubair, M. K. Khan, et al., "Link Between Excessive Social Media Use and Psychiatric Disorders Such as Anxiety, Depression, Insomnia, and Stress," PMC (free full-text), 2023, https://www.ncbi.nlm.nih.gov/articles/PMC10129173/; and Nielsen Media Research, *U.S. Media Usage Report 2024*, May 2024, https://www.nielsen.com/us/en/insights/report/2024/media-usage-report/.

72 *Christian Post*, "Asian Churches Launch Digital Detox Retreats to Combat Tech Addiction," August 22, 2024, https://www.christianpost.com/news/asian-churches-launch-digital-detox-retreats.html.

73 Barna Group, *Faith and Media: Digital Discernment Study 2024*, June 2024, https://www.barna.com/research/faith-media-digital-discernment-2024/.

74 John MacArthur, *The Second Coming: Signs of Christ's Return and the End of the Age* (Nashville: Thomas Nelson, 2011), 45.

75 Ryan Heath, op. cit. https://www.axios.com/2025/11/12/meta-ai-translator-1600-languages

76 Walter Bauer and Frederick William Danker (eds.), *A Greek-English Lexicon of the New Testament and Other Early Christian Literature*, 3rd ed. (Chicago: University of Chicago Press, 2000). https://press.uchicago.edu/ucp/books/book/chicago/G/bo3622223.html.

77 Barna Group, "State of the Church 2023: Disconnect, Convenience, and Cultural Christianity," Barna Research, 2023, https://www.barna.com/research/state-of-the

-church-2023/; Lifeway Research, "Most Young Adults Drop Out of Church by Age 23," Lifeway Research, January 15, 2019, https://research.lifeway.com/2019/01/15/most-young-adults-drop-out-of-church-by-age-23/. Quoted statements from former churchgoers are drawn from respondent testimony summarized in these surveys.

78 Pew Research Center, "Americans' Experiences with Online Worship Services During COVID-19" (January 2023), https://www.pewresearch.org/religion/2023/01/24/americans-experiences-with-online-worship-services-during-covid-19/; Lifeway Research, "Streaming Church Services: Boon or Barrier to Attendance?" (March 2024).

79 Asurion, "Americans Now Check Their Phones 352 Times per Day," op. cit.; Meredith E. David and James A. Roberts, "For God's Sake: Integrating the Theory of Reasoned Action and Technology Acceptance Model to Predict Smartphone Use during Church Services," press release, Baylor University, February 15 2023, https://news.web.baylor.edu/news/story/2023/gods-sake-baylor-researchers-develop-new-model-predict-smartphone-use-during-church/; Asurion, "Americans Check Their Phones 144 Times a Day," October 2021, https://www.asurion.com/press-releases/americans-check-phones-144-times-day/; and Microsoft Canada, Attention Spans Research Report, May 2025, https://advertising.microsoft.com/en/insights/attention-span-report-2025.

80 Asurion, "Americans Now Check Their Phones 352 Times a Day," op. cit.

81 Hartford Institute for Religion Research, "Digital Distractions in Worship Study" (2023); David Kinnaman and Mark Matlock, *Faith for Exiles: 5 Ways for a New Generation to Follow Jesus in Digital Babylon* (Grand Rapids: Baker Books, 2019), 87–92.

82 James K. A. Smith, *Desiring the Kingdom: Worship, Worldview, and Cultural Formation* (Grand Rapids: Baker Academic, 2009).

83 Amber Smart, "Mind the Gap: Business Metrics vs Church Metrics," Worship Facility, June 16, 2022, https://www.worshipfacility.com/2022/06/16/mind-the-gap-business-metrics-vs-church-metrics/; and Pew Research Center, "Pastors and Churches Increasingly Measure Success by Attendance and Engagement," September 10, 2023, https://www.pewresearch.org/religion/2023/09/10/pastors-measure-success/.

84 Anna Rees Green, "AI Evangelism: Church Launches New Chatbot 'AskCathy'," Premier Christian News, August 15, 2024, https://www.premierchristian.news/us/news/article/ai-evangelism-church-launches-new-chatbot-askcathy/; and Religion News Service, "AI Chatbots Now Writing Sermons and Counseling Users—With Dubious Theology," February 6 2024, https://religionnews.com/2024/02/06/ai-chatbots-sermons-counseling-dubious-theology/.

85 Harvard Kennedy School, "Digital Ethics and Moral Desensitization Study," July 2024, https://www.hks.harvard.edu/digital-ethics-2024.

86 Lauren Jackson, "Prayer Apps: Is AI Playing God?" The Week, September 23, 2025, https://theweek.com/tech/prayer-apps-is-ai-playing-god; and Reuters, "'Spiritual Companion' AI App Draws Millions—and Theological Concerns," March 14, 2025, https://www.reuters.com/technology/spiritual-companion-ai-app-2025-03-14/.

87 Pew Research Center, "In U.S., Decline of Christianity Continues at Rapid Pace," October 17, 2019. https://www.pewresearch.org/religion/2019/10/17/in-u-s-decline-of-christianity-continues-at-rapid-pace/.

88 Barna Group, "What Gen Z Believes" (2021).

NOTES

89   Faith Communities Today (FACT), "Worship Attendance and Digital Ministry Post-COVID," January 2024, https://faithcommunitiestoday.org/report/worship-attendance-post-covid-2024/.

90   Pew Research Center, "More Americans Now Say They're Spiritual but Not Religious," September 6, 2017. https://www.pewresearch.org/short-reads/2017/09/06/more-americans-now-say-theyre-spiritual-but-not-religious/; and George Barna, "American Worldview Inventory 2024," Cultural Research Center at Arizona Christian University, April 2024, https://www.arizonachristian.edu/research/cultural-research-center/.

91   Barna Group, "American Worldview Inventory 2022" (May 2022), https://www.arizonachristian.edu/wp-content/uploads/2022/05/CRC_AWVI2022_Release06_Digital.pdf; American Bible Society, "State of the Bible 2024" (July 2024), https://www.americanbible.org/state-of-the-bible.

92   Michael Lipka and Claire Gecewicz, "More Americans Now Say They're Spiritual but Not Religious," Pew Research Center, September 6, 2017, https://www.pewresearch.org/short-reads/2017/09/06/more-americans-now-say-theyre-spiritual-but-not-religious/; and Pew Research Center, "More Americans Now Say They're Spiritual But Not Religious," September 6, 2017, https://www.pewresearch.org/religion/2017/09/06/more-americans-now-say-theyre-spiritual-but-not-religious/.

93   John F. Walvoord, *The Thessalonian Epistles* (Grand Rapids: Zondervan, 1956), 75–77.

94   Barna Group, "AI and Faith: Christian Leaders Respond to Emerging Tech," June 2025, https://www.barna.com/research/ai-and-faith-2025/.

95   Ryan Heath, op. cit. https://www.axios.com/2025/11/12/meta-ai-translator-1600-languages.

96   Knight, op. cit.

97   Ryan K. McBain, et al., "Use of Generative AI for Mental Health Advice Among US Adolescents and Young Adults," JAMA Network Open 8, no. 11 (2025): e2542281, https://doi.org/10.1001/jamanetworkopen.2025.42281.

98   Barna Group, "Gen Z and AI: Spiritual Guidance in the Digital Age" (March 2024); interviews conducted with youth pastors, October 2024.

99   Barna Group, Faith and Technology: How AI Is Changing the Way We Engage Scripture, March 2024, https://www.barna.com/research/faith-and-technology-2024/.

100 Wayne Grudem, *Systematic Theology: An Introduction to Biblical Doctrine* (Grand Rapids: Zondervan, 1994), 226–231, https://www.zondervan.com/9780310286707/systematic-theology/.

101 John Owen, *Pneumatologia: A Discourse Concerning the Holy Spirit* (London: 1674), Book II, Chapter 1. Reprint available at: https://www.banneroftruth.org/us/store/theology-books/communion-with-god/.

102 Sinclair B. Ferguson, *The Holy Spirit* (Downers Grove: IVP Academic, 1996), 127–141, https://www.ivpress.com/the-holy-spirit; and Andrew Newberg and Mark Waldman, *How God Changes Your Brain* (New York: Ballantine Books, 2017), 15–17.

103 OpenAI, "GPT-4 Technical Report" op. cit.

104 Stuart Russell and Peter Norvig, *Artificial Intelligence: A Modern Approach*, 4th ed. (Hoboken: Pearson, 2020), 921–945. Available at: https://aima.cs.berkeley.edu/; and *MIT Technology Review*, "AI Can Simulate Empathy, But It Can't Feel It," July 15 2024, https://www.technologyreview.com/2024/07/15/ai-simulated-empathy-study/.

105 J. I. Packer, *Keep in Step with the Spirit* (Grand Rapids: Baker Books, 2005), 229-248, https://bakerpublishinggroup.com/books/keep-in-step-with-the-spirit/352400.

106 Edmund McCullough, "'Text with Jesus' App Sparks Debate About AI and Prayer," *The Pillar*, April 18, 2023, https://www.pillarcatholic.com/p/text-with-jesus-app-sparks; Heidi Schlumpf, " 'Text With Jesus' App Raises Questions About AI and Faith," *National Catholic Reporter*, April 24, 2023, https://www.ncronline.org/news/faith/text-jesus-app-raises-questions-about-ai-and-faith; and Emma Farge, "AI Jesus Hears Confessions in Swiss Church Experiment," Reuters, November 20, 2024, https://www.reuters.com/world/europe/ai-jesus-hears-confessions-swiss-church-experiment-2024-11-20/.

107 Edmund McCullough, "'Text With Jesus' App Sparks Debate About AI and Prayer," *The Pillar*, April 18, 2023, https://www.pillarcatholic.com/p/text-with-jesus-app-sparks; Heidi Schlumpf, "'Text With Jesus' App Raises Questions About AI and Faith," *National Catholic Reporter*, April 24, 2023, https://www.ncronline.org/news/faith/text-jesus-app-raises-questions-about-ai-and-faith; Sherry Turkle, *Alone Together: Why We Expect More from Technology and Less from Each Other* (New York: Basic Books, 2011), chap. 8, https://www.basicbooks.com/titles/sherry-turkle/alone-together/9780465093656/; and Organisation for Economic Co-operation and Development (OECD), *Agents, Robots and Us: Towards Human-Centred Artificial Intelligence*, op. cit.

108 Emily M. Bender, et al., "On the Dangers of Stochastic Parrots: Can Language Models Be Too Big?" *Proceedings* of FAccT '21 (2021): 610–623, https://dl.acm.org/doi/10.1145/3442188.3445922; and Religion News Service, "AI Chatbots Are Now Giving Dubious Theology," February 6, 2024, https://religionnews.com/2024/02/06/ai-chatbots-sermons-counseling-dubious-theology/.

109 Michael Horton, *The Christian Faith: A Systematic Theology for Pilgrims on the Way* (Grand Rapids: Zondervan, 2011), 596–617, https://www.zondervan.com/9780310286042/the-christian-faith/; and Yuval Noah Harari, "Dataism: The New Religion of the 21st Century," *Financial Times*, May 24, 2023, https://www.ft.com/content/yuval-harari-dataism-2023.

110 John Murray, Redemption Accomplished and Applied (Grand Rapids: Eerdmans, 1955), 117–135, https://www.eerdmans.com/Products/0851/redemption-accomplished-and-applied.aspx.

111 Jerry Bridges, *The Practice of Godliness* (Colorado Springs: NavPress, 2016), 89–112, https://www.navpress.com/p/the-practice-of-godliness/9781631465512; and Pew Research Center, "AI and Religion: Measuring Spiritual Outcomes," September 2024, https://www.pewresearch.org/religion/2024/09/15/ai-and-religion/.

112 Edmund Clowney, *The Church* (Downers Grove: IVP Academic, 1995), 71–89, https://www.ivpress.com/the-church.

113 Gordon Fee, *God's Empowering Presence: The Holy Spirit in the Letters of Paul* (Grand Rapids: Baker Academic, 2009), 803–826, https://bakerpublishinggroup.com/books/god-s-empowering-presence/235070.

114 Kate Shellnutt, "Pastors Are Turning to AI for Sermons and Prayers—Should They?" *Christianity Today*, May 2023, https://www.christianitytoday.com/ct/2023/may-web-only/ai-sermons-prayers-pastors-chatgpt.html; Bob Smietana, "Some Pastors Are Using ChatGPT to Write Sermons. Is That OK?" *Religion News Service*, April 27,

2023, https://religionnews.com/2023/04/27/some-pastors-are-using-chatgpt-to-write-sermons-is-that-ok/; and Emma Farge, "AI Jesus Hears Confessions in Swiss Church Experiment," Reuters, November 20, 2024, https://www.reuters.com/world/europe/ai-jesus-hears-confessions-swiss-church-experiment-2024-11-20/.

115 Keller, op. cit.

116 Stanford University, "Digital Religion and Instant Gratification Study," August 2024, https://www.stanford.edu/digital-religion-2024.

117 Dallas Willard, *The Great Omission* (San Francisco: HarperOne, 2006), 61, https://www.harpercollins.com/products/the-great-omission-dallas-willard.

118 D. A. Carson, *Exegetical Fallacies*, 2nd ed. (Grand Rapids: Baker Academic, 1996), 127-139, https://bakerpublishinggroup.com/books/exegetical-fallacies/235320.

119 Dietrich Bonhoeffer, *The Cost of Discipleship* (New York: Touchstone, 1995), 43–56, https://www.simonandschuster.com/books/The-Cost-of-Discipleship/Dietrich-Bonhoeffer/9780684815008.

120 Richard Foster, *Celebration of Discipline*, 3rd ed. (San Francisco: HarperOne, 1998), 1-21, https://www.harpercollins.com/products/celebration-of-discipline-richard-j-foster.

121 Eugene Peterson, *Working the Angles: The Shape of Pastoral Integrity* (Grand Rapids: Eerdmans, 1987), 1–33, https://www.eerdmans.com/Products/0875/working-the-angles.aspx.

122 Andy Crouch, *The Tech-Wise Family* (Grand Rapids: Baker Books, 2017), 95–118, https://bakerpublishinggroup.com/books/the-tech-wise-family/351680.

123 Michael Green, *I Believe in the Holy Spirit* (Grand Rapids: Eerdmans, 2004), 13–38, https://www.eerdmans.com/Products/0353/i-believe-in-the-holy-spirit.aspx; and Gordon D. Fee, *God's Empowering Presence: The Holy Spirit in the Letters of Paul* (Peabody, MA: Hendrickson, 1994), 16–20.

124 Carl Trueman, *The Rise and Triumph of the Modern Self* (Wheaton: Crossway, 2020), 367–401, https://www.crossway.org/books/the-rise-and-triumph-of-the-modern-self-tpb/.

125 Shoshana Zuboff, op. cit.

126 Robert Putnam, *Bowling Alone* (New York: Simon & Schuster, 2000), 148–180, https://www.simonandschuster.com/books/Bowling-Alone/Robert-D-Putnam/9780743203043; and Lifeway Research, "Digital Church Attendance and Isolation Survey," May 2024, https://research.lifeway.com/2024/05/15/digital-church-isolation-2024/.

127 Tony Reinke, 12 Ways Your Phone is Changing You (Wheaton: Crossway, 2017), 197-218, https://www.crossway.org/books/12-ways-your-phone-is-changing-you-tpb/.

128 Donald Whitney, Spiritual Disciplines for the Christian Life (Colorado Springs: NavPress, 2014), 33-52, https://www.navpress.com/p/spiritual-disciplines-for-the-christian-life/9781615216178.

129 John Dyer, *From the Garden to the City* (Grand Rapids: Kregel, 2011), 161–182, https://www.kregel.com/from-the-garden-to-the-city/; and Eugene H. Peterson, *Christ Plays in Ten Thousand Places* (Grand Rapids: Eerdmans, 2005), 27.

130 Kevin DeYoung and Ted Kluck, *Why We Love the Church* (Chicago: Moody, 2009), 45-71, https://www.moodypublishers.com/why-we-love-the-church/.

131 Paul Tripp, *Instruments in the Redeemer's Hands* (Phillipsburg: P & R Publishing, 2002), 17–41, https://www.prpbooks.com/book/instruments-in-the-redeemers-hands.

NOTES

132 Kate Shellnutt, "Christians Are Turning to AI for Devotionals. Is That a Problem?" *Christianity Today*, June 2023, https://www.christianitytoday.com/ct/2023/june-web-only/ai-devotionals-christians-chatgpt-spiritual-life.html; Pew Research Center, "Religion and Technology in Daily Life," November 23, 2021, https://www.pewresearch.org/religion/2021/11/23/religion-and-technology-in-daily-life/; and Ruth Haley Barton, *Invitation to Solitude and Silence: Experiencing God's Transforming Presence* (Downers Grove, IL: InterVarsity Press, 2019), chap. 1, https://www.ivpress.com/invitation-to-solitude-and-silence.

133 Thomas Goodwin, *The Work of the Holy Ghost in Our Salvation* in *The Works of Thomas Goodwin*, Vol. 6 (Edinburgh: James Nichol, 1863), 3–29, https://www.puritansermons.com/goodwin/goodwin6.pdf.

134 J. D. Greear, *Jesus, Continued…* (Grand Rapids: Zondervan, 2014), 89–108, https://www.zondervan.com/9780310337393/jesus-continued/.

135 John Frame, *Systematic Theology: An Introduction to Christian Belief* (Phillipsburg: P & R Publishing, 2013), 987–1009, https://www.prpbooks.com/book/systematic-theology.

136 Sam Storms, *The Beginner's Guide to Spiritual Gifts* (Minneapolis: Bethany House, 2013), 27–45, https://www.bethanyhouse.com/9780764211478/.

137 Craig Gay, *The Way of the (Modern) World* (Grand Rapids: Eerdmans, 1998), 289–312, https://www.eerdmans.com/Products/0847/the-way-of-the-modern-world.aspx.

138 Francis Schaeffer, *The Church at the End of the 20th Century* (Wheaton: Crossway, 1994), 67–89, https://www.crossway.org/books/the-church-at-the-end-of-the-twentieth-century-tpb/; and Lausanne Movement, *AI and the Mission of God: Global Consultation Report*, April 2025, https://lausanne.org/report/ai-mission-2025.

139 Michael Reeves, *Rejoicing in Christ* (Downers Grove: IVP Academic, 2015), 131–152, https://www.ivpress.com/rejoicing-in-christ.

140 John C. Lennox, "AI Is Humanity's Attempt to Make God," interview by David Perell, YouTube, October 30, 2024, https://www.youtube.com/watch?v=7iD6n9bRZns.

Section Four

1   Micah Melling, "The Human Fingerprints on a Theoretical Artificial Superintelligence," AI and Faith, January 14, 2026, https://aiandfaith.org/insights/theoretical-artificial-superintelligence/.

2   Dario Amodei, "Machines of Loving Grace," *Dario Amodei (personal essay)*, October 2024, https://darioamodei.com/machines-of-loving-grace/.

3   Ibid.

4   U.S. Congress, Tools to Address Known Exploitation by Immobilizing Technological Deepfakes on Websites and Networks (TAKE IT DOWN) Act, Public Law 118——, enacted 2024, https://www.congress.gov/bill/118th-congress/house-bill/7521.

5   Daniel Cochrane, "Federal AI Power Grab Could End State Protections for Kids and Workers," The Heritage Foundation, June 9, 2025, https://www.heritage.org/big-tech/commentary/federal-ai-power-grab-could-end-state-protections-kids-and-workers.

6   Open Doors International, World Watch List 2024 Report, January 2024, https://www.opendoors.org/en-US/persecution/world-watch-list./

7   Tremper Longman III, *Daniel* (Grand Rapids: Zondervan, 1999), 23–26, https://archive.org/details/daniellongman.

8   Tremper Longman III, *Daniel*, NIV Application Commentary (Grand Rapids: Zondervan, 1999), 52–54, https://www.zondervan.com/9780310206194/daniel/.

9   Ernest C. Lucas, "Daniel," *Apollos Old Testament Commentary* (Downers Grove: IVP Academic, 2002), 48–50. Available at: https://www.ivpress.com/daniel; and Robert Alter, *The Hebrew Bible: A Translation with Commentary* (New York: W. W. Norton, 2019), commentary on Daniel 1:8.

10   Reuters, "Tech Workers Resign Over AI Surveillance Concerns," July 18 2024, https://www.reuters.com/technology/us-tech-workers-resign-ai-surveillance-2024-07-18/.

11   Daisuke Wakabayashi and Scott Shane, "Google Will Not Renew Pentagon Contract That Upset Employees," *New York Times*, June 1, 2018, https://www.nytimes.com/2018/06/01/technology/google-pentagon-project-maven.html; Kate Conger, "Hundreds of Google Workers Walked Out. Then the Company Retaliated," *New York Times*, November 16, 2018, https://www.nytimes.com/2018/11/16/technology/google-employees-protest-retaliation.html; Nitasha Tiku, "Tech Workers Are Protesting Their Companies' Ties to Law Enforcement and the Military," *Washington Post*, September 8, 2020, https://www.washingtonpost.com/technology/2020/09/08/tech-worker-protests/; Tech Workers Coalition, Tech Worker Organizing and Retaliation Survey, 2023, https://techworkerscoalition.org/resources/organizing-retaliation-survey; and Julia Carrie Wong, "Silicon Valley Workers Are Refusing to Build Tools for Surveillance and War," *The Guardian*, March 22, 2021, https://www.theguardian.com/technology/2021/mar/22/silicon-valley-workers-surveillance-war-protests.

12   Yasmeen Serhan, "Google Workers Protest $1.2 Billion Project Nimbus Deal with Israel," *Time*, March 4, 2024, https://time.com/6964364/exclusive-no-tech-for-apartheid-google-workers-protest-project-nimbus-1-2-billion-contract-with-israel/.

13   John E. Goldingay, *Daniel, Word Biblical Commentary* (Dallas: Word Books, 1989), 18–23, https://www.logos.com/product/3952/word-biblical-commentary; and J. Dwight Pentecost, *Classical Daniel Studies*, Dallas Theological Seminary Lecture Series, 2018.

14   James K. A. Smith, *Desiring the Kingdom: Worship, Worldview, and Cultural Forma-tion* (Grand Rapids: Baker Academic, 2009), 75–92, https://bakerpublishinggroup
.com/books/desiring-the-kingdom/283890.

15   Stephen R. Miller, "Daniel," *New American Commentary* (Nashville: Broadman & Holman, 1994), 64–67, https://www.bhpublishinggroup.com/products/daniel-nac.

16   Andrew E. Steinmann, *Daniel, Concordia Commentary* (St. Louis: Concordia Publishing House, 2008), 87–94, https://www.cph.org/p-1249-daniel.aspx.

17   John Dyer, *From the Garden to the City: The Redeeming and Corrupting Power of Technology* (Grand Rapids: Kregel, 2011), 125–142, https://www.kregel.com/from-the
-garden-to-the-city/; and MIT Sloan Management Review, "Why Ethical AI Requires Technical Literacy," April 2024, https://sloanreview.mit.edu/article/ethical-ai-needs
-technical-literacy/.

18   Derek Schuurman, *Shaping a Digital World: Faith, Culture and Computer Technology* (Downers Grove: IVP Academic, 2013), 89–106, https://www.ivpress.com/shaping
-a-digital-world.

19   Craig Gay, *The Way of the (Modern) World: Or, Why It's Tempting to Live As If God Doesn't Exist* (Grand Rapids: Eerdmans, 1998), 156–178, https://www.eerdmans.com
/Products/0847/the-way-of-the-modern-world.aspx.

20   Iain M. Duguid, *Daniel, Reformed Expository Commentary* (Phillipsburg: P & R Publishing, 2008), 12–15, https://www.prpbooks.com/book/daniel.

21   James K. A. Smith, *You Are What You Love: The Spiritual Power of Habit* (Grand Rapids: Brazos Press, 2016), 23–41,https://bakerpublishinggroup.com/books/you
-are-what-you-love/345040; and Judson Brewer, *The Craving Mind* (New Haven: Yale University Press, 2017), 41–45.

22   Charles Duhigg, *The Power of Habit: Why We Do What We Do in Life and Business* (New York: Random House, 2012), 13–32, https://www.penguinrandomhouse.com
/books/202855/the-power-of-habit-by-charles-duhigg/.

23   The Family Dinner Project, "The Benefits of Family Dinners: Evidence from Ongoing Longitudinal Research," research brief, 2023, https://thefamilydinnerproject.org
/research; Anne K. Fiese, et al., "Family Mealtime Dynamics and Child Well-Being," *Journal of Adolescent Health* 72, no. 2 (2023): 189–197, https://doi.org/10.1016/j.
jadohealth.2022.09.014; and Brandon McDaniel and Jenny Radesky, "Technofer-ence: Parent Distraction with Technology and Associations with Child Behavior Problems," *Child Development* 89, no. 1 (2018): 100–109, https://doi.org/10.1111
/cdev.12822.

24   Joyce G. Baldwin, *Daniel, Tyndale Old Testament Commentaries* (Downers Grove: IVP Academic, 1978), 98–104, https://www.ivpress.com/daniel.

25   Sherry Turkle, *Alone Together: Why We Expect More from Technology and Less from Each Other* (New York: Basic Books, 2011), 153–171. Available at: https://www.
basicbooks.com/titles/sherry-turkle/alone-together/9780465093656/; and Harvard School of Public Health, "Digital Isolation and Declining Community Trust," November 2024, https://www.hsph.harvard.edu/digital-isolation-2024/.

26   Dietrich Bonhoeffer, *Life Together* (New York: HarperOne, 1954), 23–29, https://
www.harpercollins.com/products/life-together-dietrich-bonhoeffer.

27   Eugene Peterson, *Working the Angles: The Shape of Pastoral Integrity* (Grand Rapids: Eerdmans, 1987), 51–76, https://www.eerdmans.com/Products/0875/working

-the-angles.aspx; Rodney Stark, *The Rise of Christianity: How the Obscure, Marginal Jesus Movement Became the Dominant Religious Force* (San Francisco: HarperOne, 1997), 163–189. Available at: https://www.harpercollins.com/products/the-rise -of-christianity-rodney-stark; and Sinclair B. *Ferguson, Faithful God: An Exposition of the Book of Ruth* (Bryntirion Press, 2005), 34–41. Available at: https://www.bryntirion .org.uk/.

28 Kevin DeYoung and Ted Kluck, *Why We Love the Church: In Praise of Institutions and Organized Religion* (Chicago: Moody Publishers, 2009), 87–104, https://www.moody publishers.com/why-we-love-the-church/.

29 Lifeway Research, "In-Person vs. Digital Church Attendance: Spiritual Formation Outcomes" (March 2024).

30 Christine Pohl, *Making Room: Recovering Hospitality as a Christian Tradition* (Grand Rapids: Eerdmans, 1999), 61–84. Available at: https://www.eerdmans.com/Products /5244/making-room.aspx.

31 Robert B. Chisholm Jr., *Handbook on the Prophets* (Grand Rapids: Baker Academic, 2002), 267–272, https://bakerpublishinggroup.com/books/handbook-on-the-prophets /235490; and Christopher J.H. Wright, *Hearing the Message of Daniel* (Grand Rapids: Zondervan, 2016), 117–120.

32 Walter Brueggemann, *The Prophetic Imagination*, 2nd ed. (Minneapolis: Fortress Press, 2001), 1–19, https://www.fortresspress.com/store/product/9780800632229 /The-Prophetic-Imagination-2nd-Edition.

33 Paul Lawrence, "Daniel," in *New Bible Commentary, 21st Century Edition*, eds. D.A. Carson, et al. (Downers Grove: IVP Academic, 1994), 742–744, https://www.ivpress .com/new-bible-commentary.

34 C. Christopher Hook, "Technoculture and the Practice of Medicine," in *Technology and the Good Life?* ed. Eric Crump (Grand Rapids: Eerdmans, 2000), 161–179, https://www.eerdmans.com/.

35 John Calvin, *Commentaries on the Book of the Prophet Daniel*, trans. Thomas Myers, vol. 1 (Grand Rapids: Baker, 1993; reprint of 1853 edition), 145–151, https://www .ccel.org/ccel/calvin/calcom24.html.

36 Jacques Ellul, *The Technological Society* (New York: Vintage Books, 1964), 3–22, https://www.penguinrandomhouse.com/books/294890/the-technological-society-by- jacques-ellul/.

37 "Algorithmic Discrimination in the Credit Domain: What Do We Know," *AI & Society 38* (2023): Article no. 01676, https://link.springer.com/article/10.1007/ s00146-023-01676-3; and ProPublica, "Machine Bias: Investigating Racial Bias in Algorithms," August 2024 update, https://www.propublica.org/article/machine-bias -risk-assessments-2024-update.

38 Gleason L. Archer Jr., "Daniel," *The Expositor's Bible Commentary*, vol. 7, ed. Frank E. Gaebelein (Grand Rapids: Zondervan, 1985), 64–68, https://www.zondervan.com /p/the-expositors-bible-commentary-daniel-minor-prophets/9780310365372/.

39 Russell D. Moore, *The Storm-Tossed Family: How the Cross Reshapes the Home* (Nashville: B & H Publishing, 2018), 23–44, https://www.bhpublishinggroup.com/products /the-storm-tossed-family.

40 Francis A. Schaeffer, *The God Who Is There* (Downers Grove: IVP Books, 1968), 127–144, https://www.ivpress.com/the-god-who-is-there.

41 Timothy Keller, *The Reason for God: Belief in an Age of Skepticism* (New York: Penguin, 2008), 87–109, https://www.penguinrandomhouse.com/books/300388/the-reason-for-god-by-timothy-keller/.

42 Leon J. Wood, *A Commentary on Daniel* (Grand Rapids: Zondervan, 1973), 89–94, https://www.zondervan.com/.

43 Andy Crouch, *Culture Making: Recovering Our Creative Calling* (Downers Grove: IVP Books, 2008), 67–89, https://www.ivpress.com/culture-making.

44 John S. Feinberg, *No One Like Him: The Doctrine of God* (Wheaton: Crossway, 2001), 567–583, https://www.crossway.org/books/no-one-like-him-hc/.

45 Paul David Tripp, *Dangerous Calling: Confronting the Unique Challenges of Pastoral Ministry* (Wheaton: Crossway, 2012), 45–61, https://www.crossway.org/books/dangerous-calling-tpb/.

46 Daniel I. Block, *The Book of Ezekiel*, Chapters 1–24, *New International Commentary on the Old Testament* (Grand Rapids: Eerdmans, 1997), 234–249, https://www.eerdmans.com/Products/2540/the-book-of-ezekiel-chapters-124.aspx.

47 Leigh Bortins, in Kap Chatfield, "Hidden Dangers of AI? The Next Generation's Spiritual Battle," *Charisma Magazine*, July 1, 2025, https://mycharisma.com/culture/hidden-dangers-of-ai-the-next-generations-spiritual-battle/.

48 Europol, *Facing Reality of Deepfakes: A Threat to the Information Ecosystem*, June 2023, https://www.europol.europa.eu/publications-events/publications/facing-reality-of-deepfakes.

49 Georgetown University, Center for Security and Emerging Technology (CSET), *Measuring and Mitigating Hallucinations in Large Language Models*, research report, 2024, https://cset.georgetown.edu/publication/measuring-and-mitigating-hallucinations-in-large-language-models/.

50 John R. Boyd, "The Essence of Winning and Losing," unpublished briefing slides, August 1995, esp. sections on the OODA Loop, https://www.airuniversity.af.edu/Portals/10/AUPress/Books/B_0157_Boyd_Essence_of_Winning_Losing.pdf; and Frans P. B. Osinga, *Science, Strategy and War: The Strategic Theory of John Boyd* (London: Routledge, 2007), 1–35, https://doi.org/10.4324/9780203965003.

51 NBC News, "AI 'Jesus' Chatbots Raise Concerns Among Faith Leaders," February 8, 2025, https://www.nbcnews.com/tech/ai-jesus-chatbot-concerns-2025.

52 Abby Trivett, "The Dangerous Rise of AI 'Jesus' and What It Means for Your Faith," *Charisma Magazine*, August 25, 2025, https://mycharisma.com/culture/the-dangerous-rise-of-ai-jesus-and-what-it-means-for-your-faith/.

53 Bishop Steven, "Digital Discipleship," Bishop Steven's Blog, June 14, 2025, https://blogs.oxford.anglican.org/digital-discipleship/.

54 Webb Wright, "God Chatbots Offer Spiritual Insights on Demand. What Could Go Wrong?," *Scientific American*, June 7, 2023, https://www.scientificamerican.com/article/the-god-chatbots-changing-religious-inquiry/.

55 Anna Lembke, *Dopamine Nation: Finding Balance in the Age of Indulgence* (New York: Dutton, 2021), 55–62.

56 Barna Group, *The Porn Phenomenon: The Impact of Pornography in the Digital Age* (Ventura, CA: Barna Group, 2016), esp. sections on clergy and secrecy, https://www.barna.com/research/the-porn-phenomenon/; Patrick Carnes, *Out of the Shadows: Understanding Sexual Addiction*, rev. ed. (Center City, MN: Hazelden, 2001), chap.

8, https://www.hazelden.org/store/item/4836; Covenant Eyes, "Porn Statistics and the Church," accessed 2024, https://www.covenanteyes.com/pornstats/; and Joe Carter, "How Churches Can Respond to Pornography Addiction," The Gospel Coalition, July 22, 2015, https://www.thegospelcoalition.org/article/how-churches-can-respond-to-pornography-addiction/.

57 Pew Research Center, "Americans Report Social Media Censorship of Religious Speech," September 2024, https://www.pewresearch.org/religion/2024/09/12/religious-speech-censorship/.

58 "Digital Censorship of Religious Speech: Platform Analysis 2024" (unpublished or limited-distribution report, 2024); Alliance Defending Freedom, *Social Media Religious Freedom Violations Report* (Scottsdale, AZ: Alliance Defending Freedom, 2024), https://adflegal.org/resources/reports.

59 Bortins, op. cit.

60 U.S. Surgeon General, *Social Media and Youth Mental Health Advisory*, May 2023, https://www.hhs.gov/surgeongeneral/priorities/youth-mental-health/social-media-advisory.

61 Mitchell A. Sobieski, "Churches face a new spiritual dilemma from algorithms as Americans turn to AI for faith guidance," *Milwaukee Independent*, July 19, 2025, https://www.milwaukeeindependent.com/explainers/churches-face-new-spiritual-dilemma-algorithms-americans-turn-ai-faith-guidance/; and *Christianity Today*, "AI Theology: When Algorithms Replace the Bible," April 14 2025, https://www.christianitytoday.com/news/2025/april/ai-theology-bible-interpretation-risk.html.

62 American Bible Society, "State of the Bible 2024" (July 2024); Barna Group, "Gen Z and AI: Spiritual Guidance in the Digital Age" (March 2024).

63 Ian M. Giatti, "AI 'Bible' Chatbots Raising Concerns About Doctrinal Accuracy and Spiritual Deception," *The Christian Post*, March 5, 2024, https://www.christianpost.com/news/ai-bible-chatbots-raise-concerns-about-doctrinal-accuracy.html.

64 Asurion, "Americans Check Phones 144 Times a Day," op. cit.

65 "Discipleship in a Digital Age," *Lausanne Movement*, May 24, 2024, https://lausanne.org/report/digital-ministry/discipleship.

66 Harvard School of Public Health, "How Digital Isolation Weakens Community Bonds," February 2024, https://www.hsph.harvard.edu/digital-isolation-community-2024/.

67 John F. Walvoord, *The Bible Knowledge Commentary: New Testament* (Colorado Springs: Cook, 1983), 648–650.

68 Jeffrey J. Kripal, *Authors of the Impossible: The Paranormal and the Sacred* (Chicago: University of Chicago Press, 2010), 85–112, https://press.uchicago.edu/ucp/books/book/chicago/A/bo12042717.html; John Durham Peters, *Speaking into the Air: A History of the Idea of Communication* (Chicago: University of Chicago Press, 1999), esp. chap. 6 on spiritualism and technology, https://press.uchicago.edu/ucp/books/book/chicago/S/bo3633312.html; Ken Campbell, "Former Intel CEO Patrick Gelsinger Takes Helm at Faith-Based Tech Company Gloo," *Reuters*, October 2024, https://www.reuters.com/technology/former-intel-ceo-patrick-gelsinger-takes-helm-faith-based-tech-company-gloo-2024-10-xx/.

69 John Durham Peters, *Speaking into the Air: A History of the Idea of Communication* (Chicago: University of Chicago Press, 1999), esp. chap. 6 on spiritualism, technology,

and "God machines," https://press.uchicago.edu/ucp/books/book/chicago/S/bo 3633312.html; Jeffrey J. Kripal, op. cit.; and Emma Farge, "AI Jesus Hears Confessions in Swiss Church Experiment," Reuters, November 20, 2024, https://www.reuters.com /world/europe/ai-jesus-hears-confessions-swiss-church-experiment-2024-11-20.

70 Eva Fu, "China's 981 Project: Dark Connections Behind the Quest for Longevity," *The Epoch Times*, November 12, 2025, https://www.theepochtimes.com/article /chinas-981-project-dark-connections-behind-the-quest-for-longevity-5926103.

71 China Tribunal, *Independent Tribunal into Forced Organ Harvesting from Prisoners of Conscience in China: Final Judgment and Summary* (London, 2019), https://china tribunal.com/final-judgment/; and Ethan Gutmann, "China's Transplant Industry: State-Directed Organ Harvesting," *Journal of Medical Ethics* (2024).

72 Ibid.

73 Ray Kurzweil, *The Singularity Is Nearer: When We Merge with AI* (New York: Viking, 2024), esp. chaps. 2–4 on longevity, mind uploading, and "escape velocity," https:// www.penguinrandomhouse.com/books/721901/the-singularity-is-nearer-by-ray -kurzweil/; Marc Andreessen, "The Techno-Optimist Manifesto," October 16, 2023, https://a16z.com/the-techno-optimist-manifesto/; Billy Perrigo, "Inside Silicon Valley's Obsession With Beating Death," *Time*, April 11, 2023, https://time.com /6261299/silicon-valley-immortality/; and Parmy Olson, "Why Tech Leaders Think AI Can Save Humanity," *Bloomberg*, June 3, 2024, https://www.bloomberg.com/news /articles/2024-06-03/why-tech-leaders-think-ai-will-save-the-world.

74 Jonah McKeown, "Crypto Betting Markets Are Taking Bets on the Second Coming of Jesus," *National Catholic Register*, January 9, 2024, https://www.ncregister.com /news/crypto-betting-markets-jesus-second-coming; and Polymarket, "Will Jesus Christ Return in 2025?" prediction market contract (archived), https://polymarket .com/event/will-jesus-christ-return-in-2025.

75 Catloaf Software, "Text With Jesus," app description and usage statistics, https:// www.textwithjesus.com/; Edmund McCullough, "'Text with Jesus' App Sparks Debate About AI and Prayer," *The Pillar*, April 18, 2023, https://www.pillarcatholic .com/p/text-with-jesus-app-sparks; Heidi Schlumpf, "'Text With Jesus' App Raises Questions About AI and Faith," *National Catholic Reporter*, April 24, 2023, https:// www.ncronline.org/news/faith/text-jesus-app-raises-questions-about-ai-and-faith; and Emma Farge, "AI Jesus Hears Confessions in Swiss Church Experiment," Reuters, November 20, 2024, https://www.reuters.com/world/europe/ai-jesus-hears -confessions-swiss-church-experiment-2024-11-20/.

76 Marc Andreessen, "The Techno-Optimist Manifesto," October 16, 2023, https:// a16z.com/the-techno-optimist-manifesto/; George Hammond, "Silicon Valley's New Techno-Optimism Sees AI as the Cure for Humanity's Ills," *Financial Times*, November 9, 2023, https://www.ft.com/content/9f7c8a9a-5b1c-4d3a-bd5f-9c9a7c4b7c2e; Ezra Klein, "The Deeply Strange Case of Silicon Valley's Faith in AI," *New York Times*, April 28, 2024, https://www.nytimes.com/2024/04/28/opinion/ai-silicon -valley-faith.html; Parmy Olson, "Why Some Tech Leaders Think AI Will Save the World," *Bloomberg*, June 3, 2024, https://www.bloomberg.com/news/articles /2024-06-03/why-some-tech-leaders-think-ai-will-save-the-world.

77 Pew Research Center, "AI Researchers and Religious Belief," August 2024, https:// www.pewresearch.org/science/2024/08/__; Ray Kurzweil, *The Singularity Is Near:*

NOTES

When Humans Transcend Biology (New York: Viking, 2005); see also interviews with Sam Altman, *Time*, February 2024, e.g., Billy Perrigo, "Sam Altman on the Promise and Peril of AI," *Time*, February 2024, https://time.com/.

78   Freedom House, Freedom on the Net 2024: Global Digital Authoritarianism, October 2024, https://freedomhouse.org/report/freedom-net/2024/digital-authoritarianism.

79   Clarke Dixon, "Will the Rapture Happen on September 23-24, 2025?" *Veracity*, September 20, 2025, https://sharedveracity.net/2025/09/20/will-the-rapture-happen-on-september-23-24-2025/; Robert D. Cornwall, "The Rapture took over TikTok," *MSNBC*, September 25, 2025, https://www.msnbc.com/opinion/msnbc-opinion/rapture-bible-christianity-end-times-american-evangelicals-rcna233434; and *Christianity Today*, "A Brief History of Failed End-Times Predictions," October 2023, https://www.christianitytoday.com/history/2023/failed-prophecy-predictions.html.

80   National Association of Evangelicals, "Premillennialism Reigns," *NAE Research*, n.d., https://www.nae.org/premillennialism-reigns/.

81   "Rapture," *Wikipedia*, https://en.wikipedia.org/wiki/Rapture; and "Premillennialism," *Wikipedia*, https://en.wikipedia.org/wiki/Premillennialism.

82   John F. Walvoord, *The Rapture Question*, op. cit.

83   George M. Marsden, *Fundamentalism and American Culture*, 2nd ed. (New York: Oxford University Press, 2006), 81–105, https://global.oup.com/academic/product/fundamentalism-and-american-culture-9780195300475/; Timothy P. Weber, *Living in the Shadow of the Second Coming: American Premillennialism, 1875–1925* (Chicago: University of Chicago Press, 1987), esp. chaps. 6–7, https://press.uchicago.edu/ucp/books/book/chicago/L/bo3684000.html; and Lyman E. Reed, *Preparing Missionaries for Service: A History of Missionary Training* (New York: Macmillan, 1966), 112–138, https://archive.org/details/preparingmission0000reed.

84   A. M. Turing, *On Computable Numbers, With an Application to the Entscheidungsproblem, Proceedings of the London Mathematical Society*, Series 2, Vol. 42 (1936–1937): 230–265 (received 28 May 1936; read 12 Nov 1936), https://www.cs.virginia.edu/~robins/Turing_Paper_1936.pdf; and Alan M. Turing, "On Computable Numbers, with an Application to the Entscheidungsproblem," Proceedings of the London Mathematical Society 42 (1936): 230–265, https://www.cs.virginia.edu/~robins/Turing_Paper_1936.pdf.

85   C. S. Lewis, *Miracles: A Preliminary Study* (London & Glasgow: Collins/Fontana, 1947; revised ed. 1960), chap. 3, https://www.cslewisinstitute.org/resources/c-s-lewis-on-miracles/.

86   Athanasius of Alexandria, *On the Incarnation*, trans. John Behr (Yonkers, NY: St. Vladimir's Seminary Press, 2011), 54–57.

87   *The Guardian*, "Social Media Platforms Remove Bible Verses Flagged as Hate Speech," September 21, 2024, https://www.theguardian.com/technology/2024/sep/21/social-media-removes-bible-verses.

88   Harvard School of Public Health, "Community Flourishing in Tech-Free Environments," March 2024, https://www.hsph.harvard.edu/community-flourishing-tech-free-2024/.

89   Timothy Keller, *Jesus the King* (New York: Penguin, 2013), 214–216.

90   N.T. Wright, *Paul and the Faithfulness of God* (Minneapolis: Fortress Press, 2013), 643–648.